24.95

HT
123.5
.S6
D69
1990

New Men,
New Cities,
New South

D0012853

*The Fred W. Morrison Series
in Southern Studies*

New Men, New Cities, New South

ATLANTA,

NASHVILLE,

CHARLESTON,

MOBILE,

1860–1910

Don H. Doyle

The University of
North Carolina Press
Chapel Hill and London

The publication of this work was made possible in part through a grant from the
Division of Research Programs of the National Endowment for the Humanities, an
independent federal agency whose mission is to award grants to support education,
scholarship, media programming, libraries, and museums, in order to bring the results
of cultural activities to a broad, general public.

The paper in this book meets the guidelines for permanence
and durability of the Committee on Production Guidelines
for Book Longevity of the Council on Library Resources.

Printed in the United States of America

94   93   92   91   5   4   3   2

Library of Congress Cataloging-in-Publication Data

Doyle, Don Harrison, 1946–
     New men, new cities, new South : Atlanta, Nashville, Charleston, Mobile,
1860–1910 / by Don H. Doyle.
          p.   cm. — (The Fred W. Morrison series in Southern studies)
     Bibliography: p.
     Includes index.
     ISBN 0-8078-1883-6 (alk. paper). — ISBN 0-8078-4270-2 (pbk. : alk. paper)
     1. Cities and towns—Southern States—History. 2. Southern States—Social
conditions. I. Title. II. Series.
HT123.5.S6D69   1990
307.76′0975—dc20   89-34924
                                                                CIP

This one's for Kelly

Contents

Tables

Figures

Illustrations

Preface

*The present social tendencies of the South
are the social tendencies of the cities,
and it is here that we must study the
trend of Southern life and thought
at the present time.*
—Gustavus W. Dyer, 1909

This book is about the cities of the post–Civil War South, the business leaders who helped create them, and their role in shaping the new order that followed war, emancipation, and Reconstruction. Until recently most historians of the South have focused on the agrarian sources of southern distinctiveness: the plantation, slavery, and the planter elite. This book turns from the rural South to the development of towns and cities and from the masters, slaves, and plain folk who farmed the soil to the entrepreneurs who built the factories, banks, railroads, and cities that were central forces in the making of the modern South.

The rise of cities, merchants, and industrialists in the New South is standard fare in American history textbooks, but surprisingly little research supports the broad generalizations that now summarize the region in this era. Contemporary observers of the New South marked the ascendant merchant and industrialist class as the major source of change within the region. Henry Grady, the most eloquent spokesman for the New South movement, celebrated the emergence of the South's new men and the cities and factories they built: "[They] won fame and fortune by no accident of inheritance . . . but by patient, earnest, heroic work." A Richmond editor noted approvingly: "[W]e find a new race of rich people have been gradually springing up among us, who owe their wealth to successful trade and especially to manufacturers. . . . [They] are taking the leading place not only in our political and financial affairs, but are pressing to the front for social recognition." With less enthusiasm, Mark Twain commented on this new breed as "brisk men, energetic of movement and speech: the dollar their god, how to get it their religion."[1]

C. Vann Woodward, the preeminent historian of the New South, made the ascendance of an urban entrepreneurial class a central theme of his majestic survey of the region, *Origins of the New South*. It was "essentially new, strikingly resembling the same class in Midwestern and Northern cities." By Woodward's account, the planter regime was severely crippled, if not destroyed, in the aftermath of defeat. Though the plantation survived "a revolution in land titles" as the major mode of agricultural production, it was a sorry descendant of its antebellum forerunner. The path was clear for an aggressive throng of merchants, industrialists, and entrepreneurs of every stripe, men who were, for the most part, indigenous to the South but eager to remake the region in the image of northern industrial society. Woodward described the rapid if flawed triumph of the rising commercial and industrial interests in shaping the postwar South and compared it with earlier events in England: "The 'victory of the middle classes' and 'the passing of power from the hands of landowners to manufacturers and merchants,' which required two generations in England, were substantially achieved in a much shorter period in the South."[2]

Woodward's interpretation of the New South has often been cast as a revisionist challenge to Wilbur J. Cash and others who had stressed the unswerving continuity of the South's social order and values, even through the bloody crisis of the 1860s.[3] Among historians, Woodward's revisionist views soon gained currency, but they were in many respects consonant with earlier observations of the New South. With none of the subtlety and critical scrutiny Woodward brought to his subject, contemporary propagandists like Grady, as well as more detached spectators of the New South, had buoyantly heralded the progressive course of southern economic development, sectional reconcilia- tion, and racial harmony, and they applauded those who led the way as "new men" who had risen from outside the old planter aristocracy and brought forth a new vision for their region.[4] Where Grady and other New South spokesmen sometimes strained to demonstrate consistencies between the Old and New South, Woodward also pointed to the "divided mind" of the New South, even as he stressed the ascendance of a "New Order." If contemporaries were cheerfully optimistic about the New South's material and social progress, Woodward emphasized the limitations inherent in a colonial economy im- posed from outside the region and the debilitating effects of class and racial strife that came from within.

Woodward's view of the tumultuous change and conflict that attended the New South era soon became the unchallenged orthodoxy, and it prevailed as such until the 1970s, when some historians began to rediscover various strains of continuity and social unity in southern history. Most of those who have challenged Woodward's view of the postwar South have taken the debate to the cotton fields, not the city streets. Some discount Woodward's claim for a postwar upheaval in land ownership to argue for a persistent, powerful planter class that was able to maintain control of land and labor and to subordinate rival merchant and industrial interests. The planters, these scholars argue, continued to dominate the South and remained a class opposed to bourgeois principles, notably those involving free labor. Furthermore, the planter class, determined to maintain its hegemony within the region, confronted insurgent commercial and industrial interests by using the power of the state to thwart intrusive merchants and by deliberately arresting technological innovation and economic development that would undermine the plantation system. An alternative theory argues that the planters directed an industrial revolution "from above," with factories taking the form of industrial plantations and with labor subject to paternalistic control. Whatever its stance, the planter class, in this view, took the South down a road fundamentally different from that taken by bourgeois industrial society outside the South.[5]

In reviewing some of these more extreme challenges to the older orthodoxy, economic historian Harold Woodman advised a moderate approach by looking at the South as an "evolving bourgeois society" that was moving from a social system based on slavery toward one organized around free market relations. But few have followed Woodman's sensible cue by turning to the towns and cities of the South, which are, by definition, the wellsprings of any bourgeois society.[6] If the plantation was the world the slaveholders made, the urban centers of the New South formed the world made by the merchants, manufacturers, and financiers. In turn, the cities were the nerve centers of a changing economy and culture that penetrated the rural hinterland and remade the South in the decades following the Civil War.

The growing interest in urban history during the past two decades migrated south tardily, but with some promise of correcting a perennial oversight. Studies by several historians quickly established the unappreciated significance of the urban South and demonstrated its fruitfulness as a perspective on the region. But surprisingly little of this work has dealt with the New South era and less still with the urban businessmen who loomed so large in this period.[7]

This book demonstrates that the urban business class played a prominent role in shaping this definitive era of the modern South, though I stress how uneven and varied its impact was in different types of cities. It is not necessary to deny the influence of a persistent and even powerful planter class, at least within the plantation regions of the Deep South, in order to make the case for the significance of a rising business class. Whatever remained of the planters' power in the New South era, it did not seem to impede the growth of towns and cities and the ascendance of their business and industrial leaders. Nor is it necessary to insist that the South became dominated in this period by a new urban bourgeoisie, or to exaggerate the progress claimed by the New South's promoters. There were, of course, limitations to the New South agenda inherent in the region's late start in economic development, the persistence of the plantation economy, the powerful reaction from the Populists, and, more generally, the burdens of defeat, poverty, and racism that continued to act as drags on southern progress. But for all these problems, the business class that first took solid form in the cities of the New South during this period, for better or worse, shaped the world in which most southerners live today.

Understanding the origins of this business class in the New South requires close study of concrete local settings and the individual business leaders operating within them. The whole concept of social class, particularly when applied to nations and regions, is an abstraction imposed upon complex historical reality as a way of understanding social structure and change. I use the term "business class" to avoid the more amorphous expression "middle class," which does not properly identify the greater wealth and social status my subjects claimed.[8] I also prefer to avoid the equally imprecise and loaded term "bourgeoisie." When speaking of "business leaders" or "business elites," I am referring to the wealthier and more prominent members of the business community—the merchants, manufacturers, and financiers—and their allies in the press, politics, law, and other professions who supported the business community. In a formal collective biography I have included a sample of these business leaders selected, in most instances, from the lists of directors and officers of the major banks, railroads, corporations, and commercial associations. I have adopted E. Digby Baltzell's distinction between a business elite, defined by its position and power within the economy, and an overlapping "upper class," a constellation of families defined by their social status and their associations with one another.[9]

People who share similar occupations, economic interests, or levels of wealth do not automatically become a class or act in harmony, a point labor historians have frequently noted. Perhaps even more than wage-earning workers, business people were divided by competitive forces inherent in the marketplace. I argue that a business class took form in the cities of the New South as its leaders created a set of formal organizations that served their common interests, fostered a social affinity among themselves, and helped them form a common view of the goals they wanted to pursue for their cities, their region, and themselves. It is by studying the sum of individual business leaders, their backgrounds and careers, the clubs and neighborhoods they formed, and the vision they advanced for their cities and region that the idea of a business class becomes more than an abstraction.

My research was intended to probe the nature of the South's new order at its strongest and weakest points, and in places between. I chose four cities to capture the diversity of the region and to reveal the different responses businessmen took in the face of the challenges and opportunities the postbellum South presented. A choice of other cities might have resulted in slightly different conclusions or points of emphasis, but there is no reason to think these four cities together produce a distorted view of the urban South. All four were about the same size at some point in the half century under study. But their paths of growth differed markedly, and so did their responses to the possibilities and challenges of the New South.

Two interior railroad centers displayed the most vibrant commercial and industrial energy of the region. Atlanta embodied the raw young power of the New South and was, to all appearances, unimpeded by the dead hand of the past. A city that grew out of the scrubby hills of upland Georgia on the sheer strength of the railroad, Atlanta spawned a vigorous cohort of entrepreneurs whose boldness and concerted effort gained strength from the city's phenomenal growth. Though an older and more socially defined city, Nashville, Tennessee, was one of the most aggressive centers of economic development and social change in the postwar South. It, too, bred an assertive cadre of business leaders who pushed their city forward and made it a close rival to Atlanta as pacesetter for the New South.

The older seaports, which had served the plantation economy with eminent success, now were confronted by the burden of the past as they adjusted uneasily to the new day. Charleston, South Carolina, seemed content to languish in the backwaters of the New South. The old city had ambitious and successful individual entrepreneurs, but efforts at community enterprise failed repeatedly after the war. Many in Charleston seemed bent on preserving the remnants of the Old South and were slow to adapt to the "new order of things." Capital and entrepreneurial talent drifted away from Charleston, and as ambitious men left, or in many instances remained outside the social elite, conservative ways became more firmly entrenched and efforts at community enterprise suffered repeated and demoralizing failures. Mobile, Alabama, a rich antebellum cotton port, suffered the same discouraging stagnation that afflicted its Atlantic counterpart, Charleston. The Gulf City retreated into a pleasure-loving way of life that expressed a sublime indifference to the sober earnestness of the New South. Both of these old seaports experienced modest economic revivals beginning in the late 1890s. Though initially stimulated by forces coming from beyond their realms, particularly the federal harbor improvements and military installations that came with America's ascendance as an imperial power, these stirrings in the local economy helped galvanize the ambitious younger element in the business community of each city and pull them into the main currents of the New South.

I began this study with an interest in explaining the contrasting patterns of growth among these cities by looking to the social and cultural context of entrepreneurial behavior within each setting. As the work evolved, I became more interested in the coalescence of an urban business class and the city-building process as interactive forces. The problem is more complex than a simple causal relationship between entrepreneurial drive and urban growth. Charleston and Mobile did not stagnate solely because their business leaders failed to define and carry out an effective strategy of development, nor simply because those leaders were "old fogies" who rejected modern definitions of progress and the ideals of the New South. That was certainly part of the story, I remain convinced. The nineteenth-century American mania for individual self-striving and community boosterism were not universally accepted values, and where they were embraced not every person and community were equally skilled in pursuing them. But the lack of economic opportunities, conditioned by larger forces beyond their control, also limited the options in cities like Charleston and Mobile. In that context the motivation for energetic, cooperative effort among business leaders was weak.

Conversely, the staggering growth of Atlanta was not due purely to the much-lauded enterprise of its energetic boosters. Its location, railroads, and the shifting patterns of trade and industry in the New South favored the kind of dynamic economic growth that would have silenced even the most pessimistic croaker. Still, it was undeniably the human enterprise of Atlantans and their well-developed organizational skills that allowed the city to capitalize on the opportunities presented by geography and regional economic shifts. Community enterprise and urban growth stimulated one another, just as urban stagnation encouraged timidity and lethargy.

The four cities selected for this study offered an abundance of material, and it proved unwieldy to give balanced treatment to each. In places one city is pulled forward to explore themes that may have been common to all four cities, to some degree, but were more pronounced—or were supported by richer historical documentation—in the featured city. Thus, Atlanta offered the best example of successful community enterprise, as presented in chapter 6, while Charleston provided the clearest case of its frustration, as chapter 7 reveals. Nashville offered a good picture of public policies affecting black education and health, as explored in chapter 10, while Charleston dramatized the persistence of more traditional forms of white paternalism that are examined in chapter 11.

The title of this book is meant to evoke the rhetorical flourish of New South boosterism, and in doing so it surely oversimplifies the story told within. The focus of this book is necessarily on the men who dominated the city-building process, although it also explores the key role of women in defining the urban upper class. The exuberance of the title may also suggest a glossier view of the subject than I intended. No objective assessment of the New South can ignore its failures in economic development and social reform, particularly in the realm of race relations. But among the supreme achievements of the New South were the creation of a broad urban foundation of towns and cities and, upon that, the formation of an urban business class whose agenda for economic development and social change, for all its unfulfilled promises, did much to shape the formative years of the modern South.

Acknowledgments

This book has incurred many debts to people and institutions who have helped along the way. The Vanderbilt University Research Council played an instrumental role from the beginning, when it provided research and travel expenses, to the end, when it granted me a University Fellowship to help support a year's leave to write the book and then came through with vital funds for the illustrations. Thanks especially to deans Ernest Campbell and Russell Hamilton, who presided over the Research Council when I received support. The American Philosophical Society provided a small grant for research expenses early in the project. The American Council of Learned Societies gave me a grant-in-aid to defray travel expenses and, later, a research fellowship that supported a year on leave to do research. I spent the academic year 1982–83 as a fellow of the Charles Warren Center for the Study of American History at Harvard University, and I am grateful to Steve Thernstrom, Pat Denault, and all my colleagues there for making that year pleasant and productive. The most precious resource any historian requires is time; for allowing me generous amounts of it during three research leaves, I owe special thanks to Dean Jacque Voegeli of the College of Arts and Science at Vanderbilt.

Over the course of many years and many miles of travel while working on this book, I have appreciated the aid of a multitude of librarians, archivists, and local history experts. In Nashville, Mary Glenn Hearne and her able staff at the Nashville Room of the Ben West Public Library were indispensable. The friendly people at the Tennessee State Library and Archives were always helpful and cooperative. The Atlanta Historical Society provided a pleasant place to work during several visits; thanks especially to Eugene Craig, who helped me on my initial visit and showed me Atlanta from downtown to black side. No book dealing with Atlanta could be completed without drawing upon the remarkable knowledge of Franklin Garrett of the Atlanta Historical Society, who saved me from numerous errors by reading a draft of the chapters on his city. The Georgia Department of Archives and History and the Atlanta Public Library were also helpful. In South Carolina, I spent many pleasant days during several trips to the South Caroliniana Library at the University of South Carolina where Allen Stokes and his staff opened their treasures on Charleston's history. In Charleston, David Moltke-Hansen guided me by day through the rich collections of the South Carolina Historical Society and by evening through his city's less serious diversions. David read a draft of the Charleston chapters, challenged several of my arguments, and saved me from numerous embarrassing errors while graciously making clear his disagreements with portions of my interpretation of Charleston. The staffs of the Charleston Library Society and the College of Charleston Library also provided much help to me in my labors. In Mobile, the Local History and Genealogy branch of the Mobile Public Library was of immeasurable aid to me. Caldwell Delaney of the Museum of the City of Mobile was a savvy guide to his city's past and a very helpful critic whose reading of my Mobile chapters rescued me from several mistakes. Michael Thomason of the University of South Alabama's photographic archives was a great help to me. Thanks also to the staff of the Alabama Department of Archives and History in Montgomery.

One of the genuine pleasures of working on a book like this has been collaborating with numerous colleagues near and far who have lent their knowledge and time on my behalf. I found in Mike Russell a rich resource on Atlanta's history and a reliable critic. He read the manuscript in its early and late incarnations, saving me from many errors. Not least, he offered camaraderie during periodic Appalachian trout-fishing expeditions when we spent many hours discussing our mutual interest in the urban South. David Goldfield read the final manuscript and offered a number of helpful suggestions for strengthening the book, as he had in response to earlier presentations of my research. Vernon Burton also reviewed the completed manuscript and helped me improve the final product. I relied on several experts to read portions of the manuscript and, in addition to David Moltke-Hansen, Franklin Garrett, and Caldwell Delaney, whom I have already mentioned, I wish to express my thanks to Walter Edgar for reading the chapters on Charleston and Mobile and to Jimmie Franklin and George Fredrickson for help with the chapters on race relations. David Carlton has proved a tough but helpful critic and reliable resource on all manner of subjects in southern history, and I am grateful to him. Randy Shifflett offered timely advice and moral support over the Bitnet wires. None of my readers can be held responsible for the errors that remain or the advice not taken. Special thanks go to Lew Bateman for his able handling of this book, and its author, at every stage. And thanks to Pam Upton for her skillful and tactful editing of the manuscript.

I came to realize at some point in my career as a historian that one of the most compelling reasons we write books is to dedicate them to the people we love. No one was more interested in seeing me complete this book than my youngest daughter, Kelly Doyle, who knew her turn in the family hierarchy was coming due. Kelly grew from a little girl into a bright and beautiful young woman during the years I was working on this book, and she became a southerner. While her own interest in "new men," which has grown in scope and intensity during the past few years, is a bit different from what I had in mind here, she will understand how the past this book explores has shaped the future for her and for the South.

—Nashville, April 1989

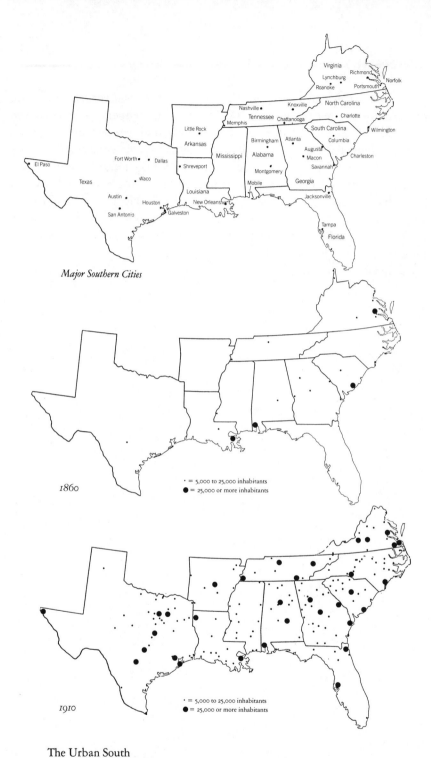

Major Southern Cities

• = 5,000 to 25,000 inhabitants
● = 25,000 or more inhabitants

1860

• = 5,000 to 25,000 inhabitants
● = 25,000 or more inhabitants

1910

The Urban South

Sources: Charles O. Paullin, *Atlas of the Historical Geography of the United States* (Baltimore, Md., 1932); U.S. Census Bureau, *Statistical Atlas of the United States* (Washington, D.C., 1914).

New Men,
New Cities,
New South

The Urbanization of Dixie

1

We have sown towns and cities in the place of theories, and put business above politics.
—*Henry Grady, 1886*

A steamboat chugged down the Mississippi River sometime in the 1850s. On deck a passenger from New York, visiting the South for the first time, paced nervously. He peered with great curiosity at the river banks lined with trees which, knowing southerners aboard realized, hid from view many a "princely plantation" surrounded by vast cotton fields. The apparent desolation, in the mind of this northern visitor, was only more evidence of the "curse of slavery." Perplexed by the unfamiliar landscape, he finally blurted out to his southern shipmates: "Where's your towns?"[1]

Where indeed were the towns of the South? In all of Mississippi and Louisiana—the richest of the plantation states—the 1850 census reported only three places in each state with a population of even 2,500. The entire eleven states of what would become the Confederate South had only thirty-four such places. Ten years later, in the wake of substantial railroad and industrial development, the South claimed only fifty-one of the nation's nearly four hundred urban places.[2] Beginning in colonial times, critics of the South saw the absence of towns as one of the most striking distinctions of the region. They invariably blamed slavery and the plantation system and argued that the lack of urban development was both cause and symptom of a region incapable of economic and social progress.[3] Even in largely rural societies, towns and cities had always been the centers of economic, government, religious, and educational activities, not in the North alone, but in all of Western civilization as it had been known in England and Europe for centuries.[4] What made the South so different?

Antebellum Shackles

Slavery and the plantation *did* limit urban development, as the Yankee visitor and other critics of slavery so often claimed. But quite apart from the special character of its economy and society, the historical timing of the South's urbanization also did much to shape patterns of growth long after slavery ended. The process of urban development had been retarded in the South, and the region suffered persistent disadvantages simply because it grew in the shadow of more advanced regions.

The patterns of regional urbanization are illustrated in figure 1.1, which shows the percentage of the population living in urban places (2,500 or more people) for the South and other sections over a period of nearly two hundred years.[5] All sections of the nation had fewer than 10 percent of their populations living in urban places until the 1820s, when the Northeast began its takeoff. Historical estimates from the period predating the official censuses indicate that even then, urban growth barely kept up with that of the general population, with the towns and cities claiming a share of the population that fluctuated between 5 and 10 percent. As each section of the nation passed the 10 percent threshold, a sustained process of rapid urban development ensued, and the slope of the trend line turned markedly upward in each case. In the Northeast (New England and the Mid-Atlantic states) this occurred after 1820, when the transportation revolution brought by new turnpikes, canals, steam-

Figure 1.1 Urban Population, by Region, 1790–1980

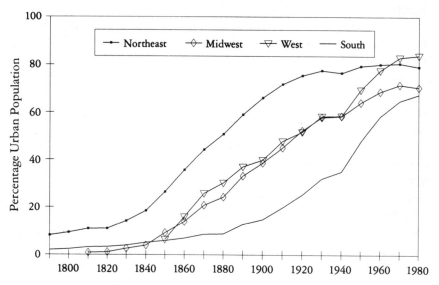

Source: U.S. Census Bureau, *1980 Census of Population,* vol. 1, *Characteristics of the Population,* chap. A, "Number of Inhabitants," pt. 1 (Washington, D.C., 1983), table 13.
Note: The South is defined as the eleven Confederate states. An urban place is defined as having a population over 2,500.

boats, and railroads opened the western interior and set off a heated rivalry among New York, Philadelphia, Boston, and Baltimore for commercial empire in the West. Largely as a result of this expansion of northeastern markets, the Midwest shot above the urban threshold in the 1850s. Even though the far West was sparsely settled, its population was concentrated in towns and cities from the beginning, and thus it saw a process of sustained urbanization from the outset.[6]

The pattern of southern urban development reveals two major trends. One is that the South lagged far behind other sections and did not break through the 10 percent threshold until the 1880s. As measured by the level of urbanization, it continued to trail behind other regions by four to five decades until the 1940s. If the persistent lag in southern urban development is the most obvious feature revealed in figure 1.1, though, it is no less significant that the growth line is virtually parallel to that of other regions, particularly after 1880. The period from 1880 to 1940 appears as a crucial intermediate stage in southern development. It was during this period that the percentage of the South's population living in urban places climbed from less than 9 percent to 35 percent (a mark the Northeast had passed just before the Civil War).

Then, after 1940, with the stimulus of World War II and the shift of new economic development away from the old northeastern urban core and toward the towns and cities of what came to be known as the "Sunbelt," the South experienced another sharp upward turn in its urban growth. As urbanization leveled off in the Northeast and Midwest, a pattern of convergence became evident by the 1960s. The South arrived late, but—as measured by urbanization at least—it was moving along a path similar to the one other sections had taken before it.[7]

To explain why the urban South lagged behind the rest of the nation originally but then took off strongly after 1880, one must examine the basic nature of the region's economy and social structure. Simply put, the Old South did not have a large urban population because it did not *need* a large one. Plantation agriculture, and the cotton crop in particular, required only minimal urban development. Before the Civil War, the urban South consisted of only a small number of cities with a low share of the population; this weakly integrated scattering of cities often had stronger links to cities outside the region than to one another. Southern urban development was mostly limited to seaports and a few river ports, typically located on the periphery of the plantation districts, which they served as entrepôts, or gathering and shipping depots for raw staples such as cotton, rice, tobacco, and sugar. The ports were usually linked to river systems and, by the 1850s, to a growing number of railroads. These transportation lines penetrated the agricultural hinterland and bound the plantations to the coastal cities, but they rarely generated interior urban development or linked towns and cities to one another in an urban system. They operated less as components of an integrated network than as independent conveyor belts serving each port.

Most of these southern cities were exporting the same staples, so there was no obvious need for them to trade with one another. Geographer Allan Pred's study of Charleston's exports from 1840 to 1860, for example, shows that between 50 and 80 percent of the cotton shipped out of Charleston went to New York, and the remainder went to other northeastern ports. Even a food product like rice, which was a regional specialty of Charleston's hinterland and might have provided trade linkages to other southern cities, went primarily to New York and the Northeast, New Orleans being the only southern city to receive any large shipments of rice directly from Charleston. Nor did Charleston import significant amounts of the products shipped from other southern cities. New Orleans's exports of sugar, molasses, and meat, for example, went overwhelmingly to northeastern ports, with only a minuscule direct trade to Charleston. Furthermore, the failure of Charleston, along with most southern cities, to develop a solid manufacturing base meant that there was no final market within the region for cotton and other raw products.[8] Even though manufacturing did take hold in a few places such as Richmond, Pred shows that there was virtually no trade between Richmond and Charleston in the 1850s.

Nor did the major entrepôts of the South generate urban development in their hinterlands or trading areas in the interior. Again using Charleston as an example, except for two small feeder ports, Georgetown and Beaufort, the area surrounding this city was an urban desert interrupted only by four small river settlements on the fall line and, further upstate, by five small Piedmont villages. Columbia, the state capital, was the only place in South Carolina besides Charleston with more than 2,500 population in 1860. Charleston was what geographers call a "primate city," serving a dispersed rural population with few links to other urban places within the state or region. To be sure, Charleston was part of a national urban system with strong ties to New York and other northeastern ports. But it was, as Pred explains, "more a 'colonial' outlier of the northeast regional city-system than a member of a southern regional city-system."[9]

Charleston's role is illustrative of the urban South—particularly the plantation region—before the Civil War. By 1860 the South's largest city, New Orleans, with nearly 169,000 people, served a Mississippi Valley hinterland that extended northward far into the Midwest. The next nine largest cities in the South ranged in size from Charleston (a little over 40,000) to Alexandria, Virginia (under 13,000). All of these were either seaports serving the surrounding plantation areas (Norfolk, Charleston, Savannah, Mobile) or river ports in the upper South (Richmond, Alexandria, and Petersburg in Virginia, Memphis and Nashville in Tennessee). Behind the coastal ports on the Atlantic and Gulf were a thin string of "second line" cities, usually positioned at or near the fall line of rivers that penetrated the interior.[10]

Overall, the urban South before the Civil War was a hierarchy consisting of a few medium-sized sea and river ports on top, a narrow base of small towns on bottom, and few urban centers in between. This pattern of urban development—a primate port city with a scattering of small settlements in the hinterland—was typical of economically undeveloped regions, especially those devoted to plantation agriculture and staple exports.[11]

In the South's case, the cotton culture and the modes of business surrounding it further inhibited urban development in the antebellum era. Cotton required virtually no mechanical aid during the growing season and only limited processing after harvest. Ginning and compressing cotton into bales were usually done at or near the plantation. From there the cotton was shipped by wagon, river, or sea to a coastal entrepôt for export to the Northeast or England, usually by way of New York. Because cotton was a nonperishable crop, there was little pressing need for rapid transportation or storage facilities that might have fostered more urban services in the way that grain elevators or slaughterhouses so often provided the bases for midwestern town development.[12]

Whatever urban services *were* required of cotton tended to concentrate in the hands of the factor who stood at the gate between plantation and marketplace. His mode of business reinforced the pattern of retarded antebellum urban development. Factors, who served a dispersed population of planters in the hinterland, generally located in the major entrepôt cities. The planter shipped his crop to the factor, who arranged for its storage, transportation, and sale. The factor charged a sales commission, typically 2.5 percent, and extracted fees for the other services, taking altogether between 6 and 10 percent of the proceeds.[13] In the other direction, he often acted as a commission merchant who purchased for the planter provisions such as seed, guano, tools, food, clothing, and other supplies that were needed on the plantation, again all for a percentage of the cost. The same factor might absorb other business services, acting as banker extending credit to planters, as accountant keeping track of purchases and sales, and in countless other ways serving as the intermediary between the plantation and the world market.

The factorage system adversely affected southern urban development by concentrating urban services within a few peripheral ports. Had these factoring services been dispersed within the interior (as they increasingly were after 1865) they might have become nodes for town development on the lower end of the urban hierarchy. As it worked, the factor stayed in the large coastal and river cities where waterborne transportation, credit, and trading facilities were all close at hand. His customers, the planters, also came to the city to make purchases, bypassing local merchants in the hinterland. Furthermore, in many of these cotton ports the factors typically were itinerant agents of firms based in New York and other northeastern cities. The presence of these "foreign" agents assured that both profit and business talent would benefit cities outside the region.[14]

The plantation system stunted urban development in another way because it depended on black slave labor, which by 1860 constituted one-third of the South's population. Slaves, of course, were not free to move in response to the opportunities cities offered. Nor, as a rule, were they free to act as consumers in the marketplace in ways that might have stimulated mercantile activity and town growth.

Slavery did exist in the cities of the South and, in a strictly economic sense, it was both profitable and adaptable to skilled industrial labor as well as to domestic and unskilled labor in the cities. But slaveowners frequently accommodated the demands of the urban labor market by allowing slaves to hire out on their own and even to live away from their masters. These practices offered incentives for the slaves and profit for their owners, but they undermined the social control essential to slavery. The city environment allowed slaves to mix with free blacks and with whites, often on an equal—and therefore dangerous— basis. The fear of urban slave revolts may have been exaggerated, but it reflected a genuine concern over the corrosive effects of city life on slavery. By 1860 the urban slave population, particularly its young males, had been significantly reduced. If rising prices offered for plantation slaves pulled them back to the country, the dangers of urban slavery also pushed them from the cities.[15]

Urban slaves were replaced in most cities of the South by newly arrived Irish and German immigrants. But the prospect of competing with slaves or even cheap free-black labor kept most foreign immigrants away from the South. In 1860 the South claimed less than 10 percent of America's foreign-born population. There were other reasons for foreigners to avoid the South, but the prevalence of slave labor reduced the flow of migration that, in other regions, fed into the cities.

Whatever obstacles the plantations and slavery presented to urbanization, most of the South's population lived outside these institutions. In 1860 about three-fourths of all white families owned no slaves, and half of those who did own slaves had four or fewer.[16] The bulk of the white population outside the cities were yeoman farmers who worked their own land with little extra help, or they were small farmers who owned one or two slaves. In the Midwest these small family farms became the foundation for a thriving urban system. They produced grain and livestock that required towns to process, store, and ship these products to distant markets. But the antebellum South operated within what historian Morton Rothstein has described as a "dual economy." One sector raised staple crops for a world market, while the other raised food and livestock for their families and experienced very little market contact. In practice many southern planters and farmers kept a foot in each sector, as with the small subsistence farmer who raised cotton on the side for cash or the planter who grew food crops for his slaves.[17] Most of the South's white population, in any case, operated largely outside the market economy and were confined to local barter. Most did not require towns and cities to process, transport, or market the products of their labor, or to supply them with basic provisions or luxuries.

The plantation and slavery were also, of course, the foundations for the South's most powerful social class. Historian Eugene Genovese has argued that the planters deliberately stymied—or, when necessary, sponsored and con-trolled—urban and industrial developments within the region. Cities and factories, they feared, would provide foundations for rival social classes: an urban bourgeoisie and an urban working class. Each would be hostile to the planter regime and a threat to its hegemony, Genovese argues. The town, by the planters' design, remained subservient to the country.[18]

Other historians have shown that planters were heavily involved in the South's industrial and railroad ventures, often in partnership with urban industrialists and city boosters. Southern economic development was neces-sary, the urban promoters argued, in order to assure genuine independence from the North. There was, in other words, a basis for class alliance and not just bourgeois subservience to the planters.[19]

Whether or not the planters as a class effectively supported or thwarted the aspirations of urban and industrial promoters may be a moot question. The overwhelming weight of the South's resources in labor and capital was commit-ted to a profitable and proven mode of plantation agriculture and slave labor. The predominance of the plantation economy and the large, self-sufficient sector of the population combined to limit the need for anything more than a rudimentary system of peripheral sea and river ports. The town was subser-vient to the country by the sheer force of population, capital, and resources, to say nothing of the power of the plantation ideal. If the planters were not the enemies of a frustrated bourgeoisie, they did not need to be, for the antebellum South's economic arrangements precluded the rise of a sizable and powerful urban business class.

Emancipating the Urban South

The obstacles to southern urban development were dislodged by the upheaval that reshaped the South in the 1860s and 1870s. The war itself, quite apart from the fact that the South lost, opened the region to change by mobilizing wartime entrepreneurs, stimulating industry, and uprooting millions of farmers. But it was the defeat in 1865, with all its consequences, that forced a new order upon the South.

Defeat, above all, meant the sudden emancipation of slaves and their entry into the market economy. Some freedmen left for nearby cities, others migrated to richer farm land in the Gulf states. Their hopes for a new start with "forty acres and a mule" were dashed by the failure of Reconstruction, and only a small percentage worked their way into independent land ownership. Most rural blacks became tenant farmers, usually sharing the crop with the landlord as rent for the use of land and perhaps the use of tools and farm animals. More than slaves, if less than fully free, these sharecroppers nonetheless gained some measure of control over their lives and exercised their freedom in migration and as participants in the marketplace.[20]

As former slaves entered a market economy, the white yeomanry also began to leave the self-sufficient life most had known in antebellum times. Lured at first by high prices offered for cotton, a growing number of them sacrificed the "safety first" strategy that concentrated on raising food for the family and began to commit all their resources to raising cotton. Increasingly they entered tenant farming, purchasing fertilizers to increase yields, borrowing money if necessary, and pledging a share of next year's crop against what they owed. The plight of the southern farmer, white and black, was a depressing cycle of overproduction and, consequently, declining cotton prices, a cycle locked in by the rigidities of sharecropping, crop liens, and indebtedness. It was a guarantee for rural poverty throughout much of the South. That poverty became at once a limitation and a stimulus to southern urban growth.

Had southern agriculture become more diversified and mechanized earlier, the urban South surely would have grown more vigorously than it did. Such agricultural development, as in the Midwest, would have created demands for urban services and pushed unneeded farm labor off the land. The breakup of the plantations into tenant farms and the entry of formerly self-sufficient farmers into the market economy did stimulate urbanization to some degree, however. There were now far more actors in the marketplace, and the decline of self-sufficiency demanded more urban services as country people turned increasingly to store-bought food, clothing, furniture, hardware, and other goods.

The reorganization of southern agriculture also contributed to the decline of the factorage system and the end of the port cities' monopoly on trade with the plantations. The decentralization of cotton buying was aided by a vast expansion of railroad mileage throughout the South. From less than 10,000 miles of track in 1860, much of which was destroyed during the war, the South's railroad mileage grew rapidly, nearly doubling in the 1880s alone and reaching 60,000 miles of railroad by 1900.[21]

Accompanying the expansion in total mileage was the integration of numerous short and disconnected lines into more extensive systems under the control of a few large corporations. By the late 1880s these railroads had adopted the northern standard gauge, allowing traffic to flow easily across systems and regions. Now, as Charleston and Mobile and other cotton ports discovered painfully, crops could move overland to northeastern markets instead of through the ports.

At the same time, cotton and other crops no longer had to pass through the hands of the factor or be nicked by his expensive commissions. A new breed of merchant invaded the southern interior, buying cotton directly from the farmers and sending it on to the Northeast by rail or ship. The expansion of the telegraph system followed the rail lines and gave every small city direct access to information on prices in distant markets. The railroad's introduction of through bills of lading allowed easy passage to market with little interruption at transshipment points.

Banks began to open in interior cities to serve the new centers of the cotton market. Cotton compresses and cottonseed mills also gravitated to these market centers. Furnishing merchants spread throughout the hinterland to sell supplies to a new clientele of farmers engaged in commercial agriculture. Some large landlords set up their own plantation stores in competition with these new merchants. In either case, the day of the factor was over. These mercantile and financial services formed the nuclei for hundreds of new crossroads towns. They constituted a broad and solid base upon which larger towns and cities would build in the postwar era.[22]

Industrialization also emerged as a force shaping the urban South after the war. Measured simply by the number of manufacturing establishments, there was an explosion of industrial activity after 1880. The number of firms had risen from less than 21,000 in 1860 to almost 30,000 by 1880, then shot up to nearly 69,000 over the next two decades.[23] The major thrust of New South industrialization occurred in textiles, tobacco, and iron and steel, much of it concentrated in a new urban and industrial belt stretching from the mineral district surrounding Birmingham up through the Carolina Piedmont. The manufacture of lumber, fertilizer, and a few other products found a place in the old seaports of the Deep South, but this did not offset the tilt of New South economic changes toward the younger towns and cities of the interior.

The Civil War and Reconstruction had emancipated the urban South. The results were most apparent in a sustained increase both in the percentage of the South's population living in urban places and in the number of urban places. With only 8.7 percent of the region's population living in urban places in 1880 urbanization had barely progressed since 1860, when the figure had stood at 6.9 percent (see fig. 1.1). Then, in the 1880s, the urban population jumped over four percentage points, to 12.8 percent, bursting through the threshold that earlier had signaled the onset of rapid and sustained urbanization in other regions. The urban South gained another two, then five, percentage points in the 1890s and 1900s to claim almost one-fifth of the region's population by 1910.[24]

The significance of 1880 as a turning point in the urbanization of Dixie is more clearly illustrated by the index of relative urbanization, derived by dividing the South's share of the nation's *urban* population by its share of the *total* population (fig. 1.2). A region with 30 percent of the U.S. urban population and 30 percent of the total population would have an index of one; a value of less than one indicates an underdeveloped urban sector relative to the rest of the nation. The decline of the southern index between 1820 and 1880 is explained largely by the dynamic burst of urbanization that took place outside the South during a period of slow urban growth within the region (see fig. 1.1). After 1880, while the non-South continued its rapid pace of urban growth, the South turned the corner and began a sustained upward trend as its share of the nation's urban population came more into line with its share of the general population.

Figure 1.2 Index of Relative Urbanization, by Region, 1790–1980

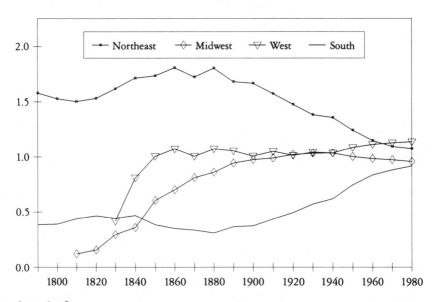

Source: See figure 1.1.
Note: The index of relative urbanization is derived by dividing a region's share of the national urban population by its share of the total population.

The South's urban development was also manifest in a surge in the growth of new towns. The number of urban places in the eleven southern states increased from 51 in 1860 to 103 by 1880. This was actually a drop in the region's share of national urban places, from 13 to 11 percent. By 1910 the number of southern towns and cities had jumped to 396, almost eight times the 1860 figure and a gain in the national share of urban places to almost 18 percent (see fig. 1.3). The boom in urban growth was especially notable among places with populations under 10,000, which nearly quadrupled in number during the three decades following 1880. These were the crossroads hamlets grown into small towns with the expansion of the railroad and the proliferation of new market centers.

The rise of the urban South in this period is all the more impressive because it was generated almost entirely by internal regional migration. The impact of foreign migration, which was a major source of urban growth in the North and West, remained negligible within Dixie after the Civil War. Outside the South, over one-quarter of the members of the 1880 urban population were born in a foreign country, and many more were the American-born children of immi-

Figure 1.3 Proliferation of Urban Places in the South, 1790–1980

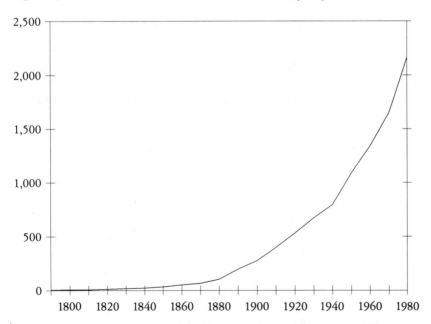

Source: U.S. Census Bureau, *1980 Census of Population,* vol. 1, *Characteristics of the Population,* chap. A, "Number of Inhabitants," pt. 2 (Washington, D.C., 1982), table 1 [in individual volumes for the eleven Confederate states].

Table 1.1 Composition of Southern Urban Population, by Race and Nativity,
1880 and 1910

	Percentage of Urban Population		Percentage of Each Group in Urban Places	
	1880	1910	1880	1910
Native whites	50.7	61.7	7.6	19.5
Foreign-born	10.0	4.7	43.2	47.5
Blacks	39.3	33.6	8.1	18.8
Total	100	100	8.5	19.8

Source: Derived from Hope T. Eldridge and Dorothy S. Thomas, *Population Redistribution and Economic Growth, United States, 1870–1950,* vol. 3, *Demographic Analysis and Interrelations* (Philadelphia, 1964), 198, 204, 207.
Note: Data applies to the eleven Confederate states.

grants. But within the South's urban population at that time, only 10 percent were foreign-born. Despite an enormous tide of European immigration to the United States, and despite strenuous efforts by promoters of the New South to channel that tide southward, the foreign-born share of the urban South's population had dropped to 4.7 percent by 1910 (see table 1.1).[25]

The failure to draw foreign immigrants afflicted cities large and small, seaports as well as interior centers. Few cities had a foreign-born population larger than 6 percent in 1910. Several small Texas cities (including Galveston with 17 percent, San Antonio with 18, and El Paso with 37) far exceeded the average due only to their sizable Mexican population. Even in New Orleans, a major international port, only slightly more than 8 percent of the people were foreign-born. Certainly there were large numbers of *second*-generation immigrants, particularly among the Irish and German communities of the older southern cities. But the dearth of fresh European immigrants was felt across the urban South in the late nineteenth century.

At the same time, the slowly accelerating cityward migration of blacks channeled a growing stream from the rural areas of the South to cities outside the region, where race relations and economic opportunities seemed more promising. Nationally, the percentage of blacks living in urban places nearly doubled, from 14.3 percent in 1880 to 27.3 percent in 1910. Within the South, black urbanization was only slightly less impressive, rising from 8.1 to 18.8 percent of the black population.[26]

But the black presence in the urban South failed to keep up with the overall pace of urbanization. Blacks' share of the city population, following a strong rise immediately after emancipation, dropped from over 39 percent in 1880 to about 34 percent in 1910. This was due in part to the devastating mortality blacks experienced in the cities, where poverty, filth, and poor health care drove death rates up to more than twice those of whites. If blacks functioned as the southern equivalent of European immigrants in the urban North, they did not always follow similar paths to the city. In the North, as geographer David Ward has shown, foreign immigrants concentrated in the largest cities and in several heavily industrial small cities. They fed into what were economically the most vigorous centers of the nation.[27] Blacks in the South tended to concentrate in the smaller cities, frequently in the least vital centers of economic growth. The populations of the old seaports Charleston and Savannah, along with that of Montgomery, were over 50 percent black in 1910. Two rising industrial centers, Chattanooga and Birmingham, drew about 40 percent of their people from the black population, but most other cities with above-average concentrations of blacks were small cities in the plantation districts. New Orleans, only 27 percent black, was well below the 34 percent average in 1910. It is clear that Atlanta, Nashville, Memphis, and Richmond all grew on the strength of their black populations, but each had about average concentrations of blacks in 1910.

The foreigners' tendency to avoid the urban South, and the blacks' limited additions to it, meant that the leading contributors to the growth of southern cities were native-born whites, whose share of the urban South's population grew from 50.7 percent in 1880 to 61.7 percent by 1910.[28] This increase, too, was a product of migration, because southern cities did not normally generate natural increases; indeed, before World War I deaths usually exceeded births even within the healthier white population. White migration to the cities came almost entirely from within the region, for the net flow of intersectional migration, among both blacks and whites, was away from the South.[29] The urbanization of Dixie, in short, was fed by the growing migration of a rural, predominantly white population, whose relatively high fertility continued to supply urban migrants, and whose bleak economic circumstances pushed them off the farms and into the cities.

The urban magnets that pulled the rural migrants from the hinterland were stronger in some cities than in others. The most striking feature of southern urban development in the decades following the 1880 takeoff was the unevenness of growth from one city to the next. This was particularly noticeable toward the top of the urban hierarchy, where the leading cities of the antebellum period were displaced by younger upstarts that rose from nowhere to the top of a new urban scale.

The cities that had prospered as entrepôts for the plantation slavery economy generally grew slowly or stagnated in the wake of the new currents of change that flowed through the post–Civil War South. Young railroad and industrial centers in the interior now had their day in the sun. The new order was more than just a reshuffling of city rankings; it reflected the integration of southern cities into a regional urban complex and the more complete integration of the urban South into the national system of cities that formed around an elaborate railroad network and new centers of trade and industry. The urban South was becoming less a scattering of disparate peripheral entrepôts for the plantation economy, linked independently to northern metropolises, and more an interconnected regional network of towns and cities that varied in both function and size.[30]

The shifts in population growth and rank among the leading southern cities of 1860, 1880, and 1910 are summarized in tables 1.2 and 1.3. Although the decades of the Civil War and Reconstruction witnessed some shifting in city ranks, a more volatile shakeup in the urban South occurred after 1880. Cities that had been ranked in that year lost an average of 2.4 places by 1910. The rapid ascendance of Birmingham, an upstart town of 3,000 in 1880, and the continued surges of Atlanta and Memphis pushed Richmond and Nashville lower on the scale. More striking was the sudden appearance of the Texas cities that sprang up with the expansion of the western rail system. Sliding downhill just as rapidly as the newcomers climbed upward were older seaports like Charleston (–10), Mobile (–7), Galveston (–14), and Wilmington, North Carolina (–19), along with some of the older river cities that lost out in the new competition. Smaller cities like Petersburg, Vicksburg, Columbus, and Alexandria dropped out of the rankings altogether. The ascendant cities were, with few exceptions, unranked (that is, had populations under 10,000) or nonexistent in 1860, and most were interior cities that depended on railroads, not rivers or sea lanes, for transportation.

City-building Enterprise

Railroads and markets penetrating the hinterland, people migrating from farm to city, new towns popping up, cities rising and falling within the urban hierarchy—these were the signs of the urban revolution that transformed most developed regions of the world in the nineteenth century. Too often social scientists explain this process as an automatic response to irresistible economic forces and geographic conditions—forces to which humans *react* rather than ones that they *direct*. The statistics of city populations and ranks appear, in this light, to be merely the sum of human actors who come on stage in one-dimensional roles as rational beings responding to economic stimuli in order to maximize gain and reduce risk. Motives are assumed to be universally shared, unchanging over time, uncomplicated by noneconomic concerns, and unerring in their aim.

Table 1.2 Growth of Southern Cities with Populations over 25,000, 1860–1910

	Population			Percentage Gain		
	1910	1880	1860	1880–1910	1860–1880	1860–1910
New Orleans, La.	339,075	216,090	168,675	57%	28%	101%
Atlanta, Ga.	154,839	37,409	9,554	314	292	1,521
Birmingham, Ala.	132,685	3,086		4,200		
Memphis, Tenn.	131,105	33,592	22,623	290	48	480
Richmond, Va.	127,628	63,600	37,910	101	68	237
Nashville, Tenn.	110,364	43,350	16,988	155	155	550
San Antonio, Tex.	96,614	20,550	8,235	370	150	1,073
Dallas, Tex.	92,104	10,358		789		
Houston, Tex.	78,800	16,513	4,845	377	241	1,526
Ft. Worth, Tex.	73,312	6,663		1,000		
Norfolk, Va.	67,452	21,966	14,620	207	50	361
Savannah, Ga.	65,064	30,709	22,292	112	38	192
Charleston, S.C.	58,833	49,984	40,522	18	23	45
Jacksonville, Fla.	57,699	7,650	2,118	654	261	2,624
Mobile, Ala.	51,521	29,132	29,258	77	0	76
Little Rock, Ark.	45,941	13,138	3,727	250	253	1,133
Chattanooga, Tenn.	44,604	12,892	2,545	246	407	1,653
Augusta, Ga.	41,040	21,891	12,493	87	75	229
Macon, Ga.	40,665	12,749	8,247	219	55	393
El Paso, Tex.	39,279	736	428	5,237	72	9,077
Montgomery, Ala.	38,136	16,713	8,843	128	89	331
Tampa, Fla.	37,782	720		5,148		
Galveston, Tex.	36,981	22,248	7,307	66	204	406
Knoxville, Tenn.	36,346	9,693	5,379	275	80	576
Roanoke, Va.	34,874	669		5,113		
Charlotte, N.C.	34,014	7,094	2,265	379	213	1,402
Portsmouth, Va.	33,190	11,390	9,496	191	20	250
Austin, Tex.	29,860	11,013	3,494	171	215	755
Lynchburg, Va.	29,494	15,959	6,853	85	133	330
Shreveport, La.	28,015	8,009	2,190	250	266	1,179
Waco, Tex.	26,425	7,295		262		
Columbia, S.C.	26,319	10,036	8,052	162	25	227
Wilmington, N.C.	25,748	17,350	9,552	48	82	170
Average gain, all cities				819	131	1,022
Average gain, ranked 1860 cities				123	54	252

Sources: U.S. Census Bureau, *Statistics of the United States . . . in 1860,* book 4 (Washington, D.C., 1866), xviii–xix; idem, *Compendium of the Tenth Census,* pt. 1 (Washington, D.C., 1883), table 24; idem, *Thirteenth Census of the United States . . . Abstract* (Washington, D.C., 1913), table 27.

Table 1.3 Rank Shifts of Southern Cities with Populations over 25,000, 1860–1910

	Rank by Size			Rank Change		
	1910	1880	1860	1880–1910	1860–1880	1860–1910
New Orleans, La.	1	1	1	0	0	0
Atlanta, Ga.	2	5		3		
Birmingham, Ala.	3					
Memphis, Tenn.	4	6	5	2	−1	1
Richmond, Va.	5	2	3	−3	1	−2
Nashville, Tenn.	6	4	8	−2	4	2
San Antonio, Tex.	7	13		6		
Dallas, Tex.	8	25		17		
Houston, Tex.	9	16		7		
Ft. Worth, Tex.	10					
Norfolk, Va.	11	10	9	−1	−1	−2
Savannah, Ga.	12	7	6	−5	−1	−6
Charleston, S.C.	13	3	2	−10	−1	−11
Jacksonville, Fla.	14					
Mobile, Ala.	15	8	4	−7	−4	−11
Little Rock, Ark.	16	19		3		
Chattanooga, Tenn.	17	20		3		
Augusta, Ga.	18	11	11	−7	0	−7
Macon, Ga.	19	21		2		
El Paso, Tex.	20					
Montgomery, Ala.	21	15		−6		
Tampa, Fla.	22					
Galveston, Tex.	23	9		−14		
Knoxville, Tenn.	24					
Roanoke, Va.	25					
Charlotte, N.C.	26					
Portsmouth, Va.	27	23		−4		
Austin, Tex.	28	24		−4		
Lynchburg, Va.	29	17		−12		
Shreveport, La.	30					
Waco, Tex.	31					
Columbia, S.C.	32	27		−5		
Wilmington, N.C.	33	14		−19		
Average rank change, all cities				−2.4	−0.3	−4.0
Average rank change, ranked 1860 cities				−3.7	−0.3	−4.0

Sources: See table 1.2.

On another level, economists and geographers frequently portray cities simply as large, impersonal growth machines that respond reflexively to opportunities for economic expansion and to the dictates of geographic advantage. In their view all cities react alike, according to what are assumed to be the universal and unchanging goals of maximizing opportunities for community growth. The rise or decline of one city is seen as the result of systematic relations among cities that determine the location and hierarchy of urban places.[31]

Underlying this rather mechanistic view of urbanization is an assumption that the entrepreneurial skills and experience involved in building cities and the motivations behind them do not vary significantly from one community to the next. Social science studies usually treat innovations affecting urban growth as inevitable events, rational responses to economic stimuli in the environment and not the product of special genius.[32] Finally, the role of politics and government at the local, state, and federal level is often slighted in theories that view cities as passive components of large urban systems.

This approach obscures too much of the dynamic human force behind the city-building process. City building, particularly in nineteenth-century America, was a grand capitalist enterprise. It was arguably the largest one in America, even if it was not usually a formally organized business. At the head of each local enterprise were the leading businessmen, who may be likened to the major stockholders and board of directors. Not only did their individual businesses hinge on the success of their cities, their investments in local real estate rose or fell with their city's fortunes. They enlisted the aid of local and state governments, whose leaders often came from their own ranks, and engaged newspaper editors as propagandists, but the main energy and much of the capital that fueled the city-building process flowed from the business elite.[33]

City boosters often exaggerated their power to effect growth because they understood their community's development as a manifestation of human will. This was not mere delusion. Behind the growth and decline of cities were thousands—indeed millions—of human decisions, and these must be understood as choices rather than as automatic responses to clearly perceived opportunities. On one level, migrants from the countryside and abroad chose to come to the city, and others chose to leave it. More fundamental than these choices were decisions made by businessmen and government leaders that affected the economic drawing power and amenities their cities offered to migrants. Railroads, banks, factories, hotels, industrial expositions, and sewer systems did not just spring up; they were the products of local planning, promotion, investment, and government legislation. Many projects failed, often to the detriment of the community. Others were carried out, but to no avail.

Whatever limitations the larger urban system imposed on their communities, most business and civic leaders in the nineteenth century saw the job of city building as their responsibility. They thrived on the blissful optimism that—with enough public-spirited good will, a flood of booster propaganda, and some bold entrepreneurship—a few earnest citizens could boom almost any town into a bustling metropolis. They tended to see their communities' prospects in the same light that Horatio Alger viewed his heroes. Hard work, virtue, and a bit of honest luck would surely be rewarded in an open race for success. The rare Chicagos and Atlantas were like the Vanderbilts and Rockefellers. They provided the full realization of the dreams and aspirations that would remain only a fantasy for most.

Not everyone shared the same dream. While most towns and cities produced a business elite dedicated to the tireless promotion of their city's growth and improvement, America's urban history reveals that not all cities were equally driven. It is one of the conceits of present-day Americans to assume that people everywhere, at all times, have tried (or would prefer, if free to choose) to orient their behavior toward maximizing material gain. The same assumption operates on the community level, where small towns and slow growth are seen as signs of failure measured against a normative yardstick that equates growth and progress with improvement.

It is more historically accurate to examine what modern capitalist culture now considers rational economic behavior on the individual and community level, as a set of rules that had to be learned and sometimes imposed against what were often stubborn habits and values. Historians have explored the resistance to industrial capitalism among workers in the United States, but they generally assume that all businessmen embraced the ethos of capitalism with blind enthusiasm.[34] As labor historians have taught us, the pursuit of individual mobility frequently came at the expense of family security, filial loyalty, or ethnic distinctiveness, a price some were not willing to pay.[35] Similarly, urban growth and the economic changes that fueled it were disruptive of community tradition and social status. The "croakers" and "old fogies," who were so often excoriated in the booster press, were those who resisted—usually passively, sometimes aggressively—the definitions of progress that were ascendant in the age of industrial capitalism.

The underlying justification for urban boosterism was the nineteenth-century conception of history as a beneficial progression directed by enlightened leaders. But that concept was not universally accepted in nineteenth-century America. Southerners, especially, had reason to see history in less sanguine terms. They could easily view history as the agent of defeat, economic deprivation, and—on more than one level—loss of mastery. The advocates of the New South worked relentlessly to instill an optimistic vision of regional progress and to fit that vision to a delicate interpretation of the South's past. In their view, the ideas and men who led the South to secession were honorable but mistaken. The war, from their perspective, had the unintended benefit of purging the South of slavery and destroying enormous obstacles to economic and social progress.

The very persistence and zeal of the New South propaganda effort tells us that not everyone in the audience shared the faith. Indeed, it was out of this struggle to achieve some degree of community and regional coherence that the New South creed—and the business class that promoted it—took form. To talk of a city's enterprise or indifference is a convenient shorthand, but misleading in that it presumes community consensus. City boosting was largely the domain of the business and civic elite, those with a deep economic stake in the future of the city and those with the power to affect that future. The elite's goals may not have been in accord with the interests of lesser players, who were at times capable of obstruction, whether by voting against a bond issue, striking against their employers, or otherwise not cooperating with the city fathers. Furthermore, members of the business elite were not always united. Though they shared a common status as wealthy and influential members of the community, that was no guarantee of class solidarity. American capitalism in the nineteenth century accentuated individual competition, which was, if anything, *more* pronounced among businessmen than among workers. Aside from competition among individual rivals, factional divisions between sectors of the local economy often placed wholesalers, retailers, financiers, and manufacturers at odds. The constant exhortations for unity that emanated from the booster press, and the equally vociferous denunciations of the "croakers" and "old fogies" who offered unwelcome criticism, are reminders that a unified leadership was hard-won, fragile, and never to be taken for granted.

It was largely by the process of city building that local business leaders became a class, a social entity bound by a similar view of the world, by common interests, and by associations and instruments of power that could advance those interests. That social coalescence took place upon a platform constructed above the competitive and often divisive currents of the marketplace. Its planks were the chambers of commerce and boards of trade, along with the more purely social devices of downtown lunch clubs and suburban country clubs that were put in place among the upper ranks of urban society in the late nineteenth century. Upon such platforms, erected by the score in a rapidly expanding urban society, a powerful business class formed, a class imbued with shared values that welded self-seeking individualism to ideals of community progress.

The struggle for business-class unity in support of the city-building enterprise centered on the need for a common strategy of urban promotion. Behind the often flamboyant prose of the booster press was the serious business of working out a feasible plan for developing the local economy.[36] That effort took place within a competitive environment, as rival cities contested for trade, industry, investors, and entrepreneurial talent. To attract and hold a growing population, cities had to offer profitable economic opportunities, certainly, but urban amenities—from schools and hospitals to pure water and sewer services—were no less essential. All of these things required concerted effort in the public and private sector, and the business elite usually pointed the way.

The entrepreneurial skill, both individual and collective, that drove the city-building process varied from place to place and over time. The origin of individual entrepreneurial talent may be as complicated as any personality trait, but, given an array of temperament and skill from pioneering innovators to obstinate drones, it is usually the community at large that decides which type of person will play the more dominant role at a given time.[37] It is the community that confers honor on the successful businessman, and not simply in material rewards or power but in the "psychic income" that comes with membership in prestigious clubs and boards and other less tangible awards of public honor and social status.[38]

Despite the nineteenth-century conceit that it was men who built the cities, it is more historically realistic to see the relationship between entrepreneurship and urban growth as interactive. Rising cities with expanding opportunities naturally attracted and fostered aggressive entrepreneurs, and, of course, a robust local economy greatly increased chances for individual aggrandizement. To the extent that the links between individual and community success are obvious in this favorable economic climate, urban entrepreneurs in fast-growing cities would be more inclined to lend their energies and risk their resources in collective enterprises. An expanding cadre of newly rich families encouraged a class structure open to new entrants or perhaps challenged an exclusive, old-monied class where one was already entrenched. Prosperity fostered a positive view of the growth and innovation that brought it about, and this confidence, in turn, encouraged more aggressive enterprise, proving the rule that nothing succeeds like success.

Stagnant cities, on the other hand, offered scarce economic opportunities and less support (particularly in the form of venture capital) to the ambitious entrepreneur. Talent, youth, and investment funds all leached away from such environments. In a declining economy, risk and innovation may be necessary to reverse the trend, but they are less likely to appear precisely because circumstances do not warrant the confidence that such ventures require.

These very conditions assured that economic leadership in a failing city would tend to fall to conservative, timid, generally older people, who accentuated the cumulative disadvantages of economic stagnation by discouraging innovative efforts to arrest the decline. Furthermore, the laggards in the race for urban ascendance were more likely to cultivate a veneration for tradition as something to be preferred over crass material progress, thereby repudiating the standard by which they were measured as failures. Thus the slow growth and small size of a community were often praised as virtues demonstrating solidity, community, and evidence of its citizens' appreciation of the finer qualities of life.

The cyclical and interactive relationship between entrepreneurship and urban growth was complicated by change over time. In the nineteenth century, the economic climate of opportunity shifted rapidly with changes in transportation technology and business organization. A city whose entrepreneurial talent was perfectly matched to one historical stage of development could easily find its leaders unable to respond to new conditions, due in part to their entrenched habits and outdated views of the world. Less established cities just entering the race, or younger entrepreneurs in any setting, might be more flexible in molding their strategy for economic growth to the new conditions.

It was out of the struggles to meet the challenges before them that people of wealth and influence forged a business class that came to champion their own visions of the New South. In the four cities examined in this book, the new order of things that came with the war, emancipation, and Reconstruction opened a multitude of opportunities to some business leaders while confronting others with unprecedented hardships. Local responses to these conditions varied according to the objective conditions presented by nature and circumstances, but also with differences in the climate of enterprise within which businessmen sought their main chance. Among the forces shaping the local response to the challenge of the New South, as the next two chapters will demonstrate, few were more formative than the history each city carried with it from the old order.

The New Order of Things

*The people of the South learned in the tremendous energy
they put forth in war . . . that they had a dormant and
inherent energy, and a capacity for industry and commerce
of which they had never dreamed before.*
—Nashville American, 1878

{Atlanta} is . . . a city of the new regime, erected on the
ruins of the old.
—Thomas H. Martin, 1898

Fought to defend the old order of slavery and plantation agriculture, the Civil War gave an unprecedented importance to the South's cities as centers for economic and social mobilization. Grasping the strategic importance of the Confederacy's cities, the invading Union armies targeted them for attack, siege, blockade, and, in several cases, massive destruction. When the smoke cleared, each city had to adjust to what contemporaries referred to as "the new order of things."

For some, war and defeat brought demoralizing losses from which it would take a generation or more to recover. Others seemed to thrive on the crisis and on the new opportunities that opened after the war. Charleston, South Carolina, and Mobile, Alabama, were two of the former kind. In Nashville, Tennessee, and Atlanta, Georgia, the subjects of this chapter, the latter spirit led a powerful postwar resurgence. Understanding the new order of things demands some knowledge of these cities under the old order. The story in this chapter and the next begins when each of these cities fell to the invading Union armies, then looks at the paths they all followed to secession, their experiences during the war, and their economic adjustments to the new order that came with defeat, emancipation, and Reconstruction.

The Fall of Confederate Nashville

Nashville was the first major Confederate city to fall to the Union. It was occupied by military forces longer than any other American city during or since the Civil War. During World War II, military officials studied the Union occupation of Nashville for lessons that might be applied to Europe.[1] Nashville's experience of early defeat and prolonged occupation did much to shape its response to the postwar South. The city surrendered without a shot and with no armed resistance by the civilians who remained. Thousands of them stood in dumbstruck silence on the banks of the Cumberland River as boatloads of soldiers in blue disembarked. A Union army band tried to excite patriotic spirit by playing rousing versions of "The Star Spangled Banner" and "Yankee Doodle." But the brassy music echoed against silent crowds. The soldiers formed a line and marched into the city, through the public square and up the hill to the capitol. There General William Nelson declared the city under formal military control and raised the flag of the United States.[2] A Chicago merchant who arrived with the invading army described the Nashville crowds standing "like statuary and as silent and as sad. . . . The scene was like that of a funeral—a military funeral." The spectacle placed on open exhibit the "humiliation of Southern pride."[3]

The fall of Nashville was a major blow to the Confederacy, as debilitating to the South's morale as it was to its strategic control of the Tennessee heartland, for it opened the Deep South to invasion. For the Union, on the other hand, Nashville was a grand prize. From its founding as a crude frontier outpost in 1780, it had grown into a prosperous little city of nearly 17,000 people by 1860. It perched on limestone hills overlooking the Cumberland River, which connected it northward to the Ohio River. It was surrounded by the fertile Nashville Basin. Carpeted with bluegrass, the basin produced a rich supply of livestock, grain, cotton, and tobacco. Though there were many large plantations surrounding Nashville, Middle Tennessee included a mixed population of yeomen and small slaveholders.[4] Nashville served as the market center for dozens of small settlements that took hold amid the relatively diversified agriculture of the area. Its hinterland extended beyond the Highland Rim surrounding the basin to take in much of southern Kentucky and northern Alabama, stretching west to the Tennessee River and east into the Cumberland Mountains.

The city occupied a key position on the Cumberland River. Since the arrival of the first steamboat in 1818, Nashville had grown into a leading river port. Flowing down to Nashville from the Upper Cumberland Mountains of Tennessee and Kentucky, the Cumberland River passed through rugged and sparsely settled terrain that had not yet been penetrated by the railroads. Dangerous shoals and seasonal low water hampered navigation, but Nashville's upriver trade amounted to a virtual monopoly in the Upper Cumberlands. Downriver from Nashville the Cumberland was easily navigable year-round, and it passed through rich tobacco, grain, and livestock lands en route to the north through Kentucky, intersecting with the Ohio River above Paducah.

Nashville's real transportation advantages were man-made. Five railroads entered the city by 1861, fanning out to small towns and cities in the surrounding hinterland. The Louisville and Nashville Railroad (L&N), though not completed until 1859, was to become the city's dominant railroad. At the time of the war it was the only major road to straddle the Union and the Confederacy, and it was a vital supply route for the Union invasion. From the L&N, to the Nashville and Chattanooga, and along the Western and Atlantic to Atlanta, Nashville's rail lines defined the path of invasion into the heart of the Confederacy.[5]

Nashville was also the key to controlling major Confederate sources of iron and gunpowder. West of the city, beyond the Highland Rim, lay the "Great Western Iron Belt," a vast iron-producing region dotted with furnaces and foundries. Along the Cumberland were important gunpowder mills that had supplied the Confederate army in the first Battle of Bull Run. Much of the iron flowed into Nashville, where before the war several factories were engaged in the manufacture of plows, stoves, and machinery. After Tennessee's secession, these factories churned out cannon, sabers, rifles, pistols, munitions, and other military supplies.[6]

Despite Nashville's strategic importance to the Confederacy, it remained unfortified and vulnerable. Fort Donelson, located downriver near the Kentucky border, was the bulwark of defense for Confederate Nashville. Kentucky's ties to the South, Confederates hoped, would make it a buffer against the Union invasion. But early in 1862 the Union forces under General Don Carlos Buell swept deep into Kentucky, and in the western part of the state General U. S. Grant led his troops across the Ohio River and launched an amphibious invasion up the Tennessee and Cumberland river valleys. On February 15, 1862, after three days of fighting, Grant received the famous "unconditional surrender" he demanded of the Confederate commanders of Fort Donelson. When the news reached Nashville the next day, the Confederates, recognizing the futility of defending such a poorly fortified city, prepared to withdraw, leaving the citizens to take their chances with the Union occupation or flee south behind Confederate lines.

Having been deluded earlier by rumors of a Confederate victory at Fort Donelson, Nashville citizens now awaited in a panic the arrival of federal troops ten days later. "An earthquake could not have shocked the city more," one contemporary observed.[7] Throngs of citizens and soldiers swarmed through the streets, panicked at once by false rumors of imminent invasion by bloodthirsty Yankees and by equally false rumors of a ferocious Confederate defense of the city. Thousands packed the railroad station and, once the cars were filled, grabbed onto the sides and climbed on top as the trains pulled out. Others fled wildly by wagon, horse, and foot. Some of the Confederate food supplies were given out to the public, and these disbursements drew riotous swarms of people, some hauling away meat, others clamoring for more. Colonel Nathan Bedford Forrest, having narrowly escaped Fort Donelson with his cavalry regiment, had to establish order by sword and pistol. At one point the mayor ordered a fire hose turned on an unruly crowd.[8]

Determined to destroy as many of Nashville's strategic advantages as possible before retreating, the Confederates shipped munitions, machinery, and food supplies south and destroyed what they could not carry. Soldiers dismantled ordnance factories, burned the armory, destroyed gunboats, set ablaze the suspension bridge across the Cumberland and cut it down, and then tried to burn down the only railroad bridge across the river to the North. Nashville businessmen protested this last act of destruction with the argument that the bridges had no military importance, exposing either a weak grasp of the strategic significance of Nashville's fall or a savvy understanding of what the federal invasion could mean to local business prospects, particularly the vital commercial artery to the North.[9] At night the sky was aglow from the burning bridges and armory, and from campfires across the city. The final Confederate retreat on February 23 meant that the city would be spared any further destruction, but what would the arrival of Union troops mean to the city's future?

Nashvillians stood between two armies, and their political loyalties now had to accommodate practical considerations. Many eminent secessionists abandoned the city and fled south, but most people stayed to wait out what they hoped would be a short occupation before the Union moved on or the Confederates reseized the city by force. On February 25 Mayor Richard B. Cheatham crossed the river to meet an advance guard of Union soldiers. He returned to anxious citizens with the promise that the invaders would protect their rights and property—including slaves. The passive reception of the troops two days later, with the army's patriotic music echoing amid the silent crowds, revealed more pragmatic resignation than resistance.

The permanence of the occupation was not clear until the end of 1862. The Confederates threatened several times to recapture Nashville and continued to harass Union troops and disrupt rail lines outside the city. At the end of 1862 the Union position in Nashville was ensured at the Battle of Stones River south of the city, following which the Confederate Army of Tennessee retreated south. By this time Nashville was protected by a string of massive fortifications, breastworks, trenches, and rifle pits that stretched nearly twenty miles around the city's southern and western perimeter, meeting the river at both ends. It was considered the most thoroughly fortified city in America outside of Washington. No Confederate army dared challenge the Union's hold on Nashville until the end of 1864, when the reckless General John Bell Hood led a disastrous siege of the city.[10]

The war and occupation brought hardship to Nashville, but most of it was transitory. Andrew Johnson, appointed by Lincoln as the military governor of Tennessee, ruled the city with a harsh hand, imprisoning Confederate sympathizers with abandon, dismissing the city council and replacing it with loyal pro-Union men, and allowing the army to impress property and labor at will. Johnson was driven by political expediency and prejudice. He was convinced that Confederate treason must be ruthlessly purged from Tennessee. He also brought to Nashville an East Tennessean's disdain for the "aristocratic" wealth and privilege the capital city harbored. Certain that the Confederates would try to retake Nashville, he was instrumental in transforming the city into a huge, fortified garrison. Capitol Hill became Fort Andrew Johnson. Army troops and impressed slaves cut down trees, erected breastworks of cotton bales and cedar stockades and placed artillery around the stately structure that had been the pride of Nashville. Years later the capitol grounds remained "in a rough, dilapidated condition, very much as the army had left them."[11] Around the city the construction of fortifications destroyed farms, stripped the hills of trees, and displaced more than two hundred homes, creating a stark, denuded military camp in a city once renowned for its lush pastoral setting. Inside the city, the army tore up brick streets for tent foundations, and wagons and caissons cut deep ruts into the muddy thoroughfares. Thousands of soldiers camped throughout the city, and they freely requisitioned trees and fences for firewood to warm the night.[12]

The occupying army also converted buildings and homes into hospitals for the wounded Union soldiers who were brought into Nashville by the thousands during the war. Many were victims of venereal disease, which flourished among the prostitutes who had flocked to the garrison city for their own brand of war profiteering. At one point, the mayor rounded up 150 ladies of the night and sent them out of Nashville on a steamboat, but no other city would have them, and they returned.[13] Along with the female camp followers was a rougher sort of criminal. "The city is filled with thugs, robbers, highwaymen, and assassins. Murder stalks throughout the city almost every night," one inhabitant reported.[14] Runaway slaves also poured into this Union sanctuary, lured by the ambiguous promise of emancipation. The army regarded them as contraband of war; white Nashvillians regarded them as a grave threat to social order. The army put the slaves to work on the fortifications and settled them in makeshift contraband camps. By 1865 nearly 11,000 blacks lived in Nashville, up from 4,000 in 1860.[15]

Taking into account the soldiers, military contractors, camp followers, and runaway slaves, Nashville's population nearly doubled during the war. Jerry-built shantytowns cropped up beside the fortifications, rats swarmed through the city, smallpox and other diseases spread quickly amidst the poor sanitary conditions, and there were continual eruptions of violence, often stimulated by an intoxicating flow of whiskey through the myriad saloons and tippling houses that sprang up to meet the demands of a city at war.[16] The occupation had rapidly dissolved the social order of this quiet city.

Profits of War

The occupation of Nashville also meant that business was subordinated to the needs of the military. Civilians suffered chronic shortages of food and clothing and exorbitant prices for rare items like coffee and sugar. Trains and steamboats were in short supply, and shipments of consumer goods for Nashville citizens took second priority to the military's needs. The war also caused turmoil in the rural hinterland of Nashville; farm production and trade diminished drastically.

But the conflict also brought windfall profits to military contractors and provided benefits that carried over into the postwar era. Local businessmen, joined by interloping entrepreneurs, found opportunities to turn the occupation to advantage. Nashville's role as a regional distribution center was dramatized by the Union's decision to make the city its major western depot for food, supplies, and ordnance. New government warehouses went up near the railway stations to supplement the existing storage facilities that were bulging with supplies brought into Nashville and from there distributed to the troops in the field. "Nashville presents a very business-like appearance now," one Union officer wrote late in 1863. "The streets are daily crowded with citizens and soldiers. The markets are full, business houses well stored with goods, trains running day and night."[17] The Quartermaster Corps in Nashville estimated that $50 to $60 million worth of goods stood in Nashville's warehouses by the end of the war.[18]

Notwithstanding some destruction and adversity, the railroads serving Nashville flourished during the emergency. The federal government quickly assisted in rebuilding the L&N and did what it could to defend the road against Confederate raids. It also requisitioned additional locomotives and freight cars for use in supplying Nashville. Despite constant complaints from L&N officials about financial hardships, the company's profits soared during the war, and it emerged from the crisis in a preeminent position among southern railroads, poised to expand and become the dominant force in the vast territory between the Ohio River and the Gulf of Mexico. From a small railroad with fewer than 300 miles of track after the war, the L&N grew into a giant regional system with 3,000 miles by 1900. It was a story that could not have been told were it not for the profits of war.[19]

Of all major southern cities, Nashville emerged from the war with fewer physical and political scars and with advantages gained in the war that pre-

The state capitol in Nashville during the federal occupation. (National Archives)

pared it for a formidable role in the new order of things. There was no serious physical damage to the city, except for the aesthetic blight of the stripped landscape, torn up with trenches and fortifications. Nor was the economy significantly disrupted by blockade or destruction. The surrounding agricultural hinterland had been severely disturbed, but there was little permanent damage, and Nashville's wartime role, on balance, enhanced its power as a regional distribution center.

Nor did Nashville suffer the demoralized sense of defeat that struck the business and civic leaders of other southern cities after 1865. Confederate Nashville met defeat early in 1862, and by the war's end the city had been through more than three years of what can only be called collaboration with the

Union war effort. Local historical tradition makes much of the overwhelming pro-Confederate sympathies of Nashvillians, and there is no denying the point. But most of the evidence for such leanings comes from the first year of occupation, when Union control was uncertain and Governor Johnson was suppressing "treason" with imprisonment and loyalty oaths. His heavy-handed methods probably alienated many moderates who would have been disposed to support the Union. Nevertheless, imprisoning clergymen, prominent politicians, and other citizens was an effective way of discouraging pro-Confederate sentiment in Nashville.[20]

After the fortifications were in place, and after the Confederate retreat from Stones River, rebel allies were less conspicuous in Nashville, particularly amid the swarm of locals and newcomers who were involved in supplying the invading army. Initially the treatment of northern soldiers was almost like that accorded a foreign conqueror. Women tended to be the bravest in their display of resistance, probably trusting masculine chivalry to protect them even among Yankees in blue. They shunned, jeered, and even spat upon Union soldiers and officers whom they passed in the streets.[21] Most Nashville men simply remained aloof and refused to openly cooperate with the occupying army. Naturally, they did not wish to appear as turncoats should the Confederates retake the city.

As the threat of a Confederate assault waned after 1862, so too did resistance to the Union presence in Nashville. Many of the city's women warmed to the men in blue in ways that carried the meaning of collaboration to its fullest. At least thirteen Union officers and dozens of enlisted men took Nashville brides during the war. All the officers, and many of the men, stayed on in the city, not as social pariahs but as prominent, respected citizens. It became an article of local pride that the conquerors of Nashville themselves became the conquered.[22]

Whig Legacy

Nashville's adjustment to the new order was also eased by a strong political tradition rooted in the old Whig party, continued in the Unionist movement of the 1850s and in wartime collaboration. It was a tradition that flowed easily into the spirit of sectional reconciliation and New South economic development after the war. From the same soil that had nurtured Democratic heroes Andrew Jackson and James K. Polk, Nashville's local politics had produced a strong Whig element dedicated to internal improvements, economic progress, and—above all—the Union. Though the Whigs disappeared as a party in the early 1850s, Whig leaders and ideas continued to have a powerful voice in state and local affairs. It was the old Whigs in Nashville who had opposed secession and rallied behind their native son, John Bell, and his Constitutional Union party in the presidential election of 1860. Nashville voters for Breckinridge, the southern Democrats' candidate, were outnumbered about two to one, with Bell winning a decisive majority.[23]

Only upon Lincoln's call to arms following Fort Sumter did Bell and the Unionists throw in with the secessionists in the Democratic party. But the disaster that followed was vindication for this Whig-Unionist element. They saw the war as the product of fanatical politicians and a desperate ploy to preserve the archaic institution of slavery. Defeat, in their view, was a disguised blessing that destroyed slavery and liberated the South from the backward economic and social system that oppressed it.

Now the way was clear to fulfill the old Whig vision, to transform the South "from a funeral wilderness into a city-dotted, flower-blooming Eden."[24] This path would be paved by northern capital, by an open emulation of northern virtues, and by a willingness to bury past sectional animosities and put economic progress above political dogma. Arthur St. Clair Colyar spoke forcefully for this Nashville element in 1871, when he prophesied that the end of "sectional hates, would sell our surplus lands, open our coal mines, develop our iron and copper, give business to our railroads, build up our cities and towns, and make us a great manufacturing State."[25]

The efforts of postwar Nashville civic leaders to welcome northern capital for industry were never so successful—or so subversive to the old order—as in the campaigns to attract northern funds for new educational institutions. Fisk University, founded in 1866 by the abolitionists of the American Missionary Society and named after the head of the Freedmen's Bureau in Nashville, was dedicated to the education of former slaves. Roger Williams College, founded in 1864, Central Tennessee College, founded in 1866, and Meharry Medical College, founded in 1876 and named after its midwestern benefactors, were all dedicated to the education of the freedman and were all dependent in varying degrees on northern philanthropy. Vanderbilt University, founded in 1873 by the Southern Methodists, bore the name of the New York railroad tycoon who had enlarged his fortune during the late war and now bequeathed a small portion of it to foster sectional reconciliation. Later, George Peabody College for Teachers, named after the Massachusetts philanthropist, became part of the constellation of colleges in this self-proclaimed "Athens of the South." The educational complex built on antebellum precedents, but it was more an outgrowth of Nashville's recent collaborative role during the war. All of these northern-sponsored institutions, busily producing teachers, clergy, businessmen, and politicians, were extensions of the northern campaign, now joined by southern reformers, to reconstruct the mind of the South. This was the Nashville in which J. T. Trowbridge, visiting from the North in 1866, "could feel the influence of Northern ideas and enterprise pulsating through it." "It is a nostril," he went further, "through which the State has long breathed the Northern air of free institutions."[26]

If the war was comparatively kind to Nashville, neither did Reconstruction leave deep and lasting scars on the city's rather conciliatory face. True, William G. Brownlow, elected governor in 1866, brought from East Tennessee the same vindictive hatred of Nashville that his predecessor, Andrew Johnson, had harbored. Earlier, during the occupation, Brownlow had offered spectacular public displays of his enthusiasm for the Union troops that marched through Nashville's streets. Pro-Confederate Nashvillians loathed the man and on one occasion made him presents of used bandages from smallpox victims.[27]

It was Brownlow who engineered the election of Augustus E. Alden, a former Union officer and fellow Republican, to the office of mayor in 1867 and 1868—before Confederate veterans could vote in city elections. Alden and his "ring" tried to build Republican strength in Nashville by expanding public schools and other services to the newly enfranchised blacks. Tax revenues did not keep up with expenditures, and there was widespread suspicion of graft and corruption. In the spring of 1869, the city's largest property holders—led by many of the old Whig-Unionist element—staged a taxpayers' revolt, threw the city into receivership, ousted Alden and his ring, and in the next election placed their own men in office.[28] The same year Brownlow left Nashville for a senate seat in Washington, D.C. By 1870 Tennessee had a new constitution that enfranchised all Confederate veterans and brought an end to Reconstruction in the state. Republican power remained surprisingly strong in Nashville until the 1890s, however, and business-class Conservative Democrats had to fight hard at every election—and then rarely with success at the mayoral level.[29] But the era of uncontested "carpetbag" rule was a brief intrusion on Nashville's eager adjustment to the new order of things.

The Fall of Atlanta

Atlanta felt what Sherman called the "hard hand of war" with greater fury than any other southern city—perhaps more than any American city ever. If there was a single point at which the official northern war policy became an assault against the southern people instead of a military action against the Confederate armies, it was at Atlanta in 1864. Sherman's army drove south hard from Chattanooga, meeting tough resistance from Confederate troops under General Joseph Johnston from May into early July, when the Confederates fell back across the Chattahoochee River to the outskirts of Atlanta. General John Bell Hood then took over command from Johnston and, in a series of offensive assaults, threw thousands of Confederate troops at the Union line, which, notwithstanding, continued to close around the city, finally cutting off all rail lines to the outside. The siege of Atlanta continued for forty-two days, a slow ordeal of starving an army and a city, a task hastened by Sherman's strategy of constantly shelling Atlanta's interior as well as its military fortifications. "War is cruelty, and you cannot refine it," Sherman wrote, defending his Atlanta policy, "and those who brought war into our country deserve all the curses and maledictions a people can pour out."[30] Hood finally abandoned Atlanta on the first day of September, after ordering the massive destruction of its railroad cars, locomotives, and depots, along with dozens of carloads of ammunition, a large rolling mill, and all other property that might prove useful to the invaders.

The next day Sherman entered the city, with smoke and flames still rising from the ruins. He saw civilians scurrying for protection and a few openly welcoming the men in blue who filled the streets. Sherman has been criticized for becoming obsessed with the capture of Atlanta and failing to take his opportunity to destroy Hood's Army of Tennessee, which now marched to its tragic appointment at Franklin and Nashville. But Atlanta had become a vital organ of a society—not just an army—at war. After the fall of Nashville, Atlanta became a major Confederate center for the manufacture and distribution of war matériel and supplies. In Sherman's eyes, Atlanta was strategically important to capture, but it was also culpable for the suffering of the armed troops and deserved to be punished. It was this mix of tough-minded military strategy and cold-hearted vindictiveness that informed Sherman's decision to command all civilians to evacuate. The city would then be destroyed before Union troops turned south to begin their devastating march to the sea. The purpose, as Sherman explained with ruthless clarity, was to "make old and young, rich and poor, feel the hard hand of war as well as the organizing armies." "Now that war comes home," he addressed the conquered people of Atlanta, "you feel very different—you deprecate its horrors, but did not feel them when you sent car-loads of soldiers and ammunition and molded shells and shot, to carry war into Kentucky and Tennessee."[31]

By mid-November Sherman's army left Atlanta and completed the job that the artillery shells and Hood's retreating troops had begun earlier. The systematic torching of an estimated four to five thousand buildings left only about four hundred structures untouched. The rest of the city was nothing but charred ruins. This was the event by which Atlanta's whole future history would be defined. The fires that scourged the fallen Confederate city of Atlanta allowed it, as local histories invariably repeat, to rise "Phoenix-like from the ashes," a city reborn, a city that would transcend defeat and lead the New South to ultimate victory.

Antebellum Atlanta

Atlanta's pre-Sherman history extended back less than three decades, and it was a logical prelude to what emerged from the ashes left by Sherman's men. Founded in 1837 as the southeastern "terminus" (its first unofficial name) of the new Western and Atlantic Railroad from Chattanooga, the city was, above all, the man-made product of the railroad age. Located at the southern edge of the Appalachian Mountains between the watersheds flowing to the Atlantic and the Gulf, it commanded a site that, in the day of the railroad, became a logical gateway for the freight passing between the South and the Northeast or the West.

The Western and Atlantic was to be the first part in a great highway of trade linking the West and South. Terminus was a small cluster of rude frame homes and railroad structures in 1843 when citizens renamed it "Marthasville" (a politic tribute to the daughter of former Georgia governor Wilson Lumpkin). At the same time, they received from the state legislature a charter of incorporation. Within two years the Georgia Railroad was completed from Augusta, followed in 1846 by the Macon and Western Railroad, which, in turn, connected with the Central of Georgia from Macon to Savannah, the closest Atlantic port.[32]

By this time Marthasville was a rugged little railroad town with sawmills, stores, banks, several newspapers, and a population that would exceed 2,500 by the next census. In 1847 the citizens applied for a new city charter under the name "Atlanta," invented by local promoters to suggest its role as gateway to the Atlantic.[33] During the 1850s, Atlanta percolated with new enterprises, as the expanding railroad network made the city a central transfer point in the Southeast.

New roads strengthened the city's role as the gateway of the South. The Memphis and Charleston connected with the Western and Atlantic via the Nashville and Chattanooga, opening a second route to the sea. The Atlanta and West Point fed into Atlanta from the Georgia and Alabama cotton belts. With the railroad trade soaring, the population of Atlanta nearly quadrupled by 1860, when it stood at over 9,500.

Before the Civil War, Atlanta's growth was mostly the product of outside interests located in rival Georgia cities. They built railroads for their own aggrandizement, railroads that happened to meet in Atlanta as a geographically convenient site. Atlanta had yet to develop an indigenous corps of entrepreneurs with the numbers, organization, and wealth to effectively advance their own interests and challenge the presumptions of rivals.[34] During the 1850s, those conditions began to change as Atlanta's small but zealous cadre of promoters concentrated on checking railroad policies that favored rivals and on launching home-owned railroads.[35] Among these early city builders were a surprising number of northern-bred men who had migrated south with the 1850s railroad boom and who came to form the entrepreneurial core of the young city.[36] Among the most prominent were Jonathan Norcross of Maine, a general-store and sawmill operator, who was behind nearly every public enterprise in the city; Edward E. Rawson of Vermont, a dry-goods merchant; Richard Peters of Pennsylvania, a railroad man; William Markham of Connecticut, an industrialist; Lemuel P. Grant of Maine, another railroad promoter; Sidney Root of Massachusetts, a dry-goods wholesaler; and Joseph Winship, also from Massachusetts, an iron foundry owner.[37]

Atlanta, even before the Civil War, came to be regarded as a northern enclave on foreign soil, and much of the famous "Atlanta spirit" has been routinely attributed to this infusion of Yankee enterprise. But Atlanta's population at large was overwhelmingly southern in origin, and even its leading businessmen were, in the main, from native soil. They came from Georgia, Virginia, South Carolina, and Tennessee for the most part. Though slaveowners and their slaves established a presence in Atlanta by 1860, the bulk of the population in this upcountry railroad town was from the white yeomanry and small-town middle class of Georgia and adjacent states.[38] "The planter with his semi-feudal ideas and mode of life had little to do with laying the foundation" of Atlanta, one local historian explained. Atlanta, even before the war, was a city for young men on the make.[39]

War, Destruction, Resurgence

The Civil War offered Atlanta a windfall opportunity to enlarge its role as a transportation hub and manufacturing center. But many Atlanta businessmen had been reluctant to join the secession movement. In the election of 1860 a plurality in Atlanta supported the Unionist John Bell. Samuel Richards, an English-born merchant, dismissed the local secessionists as "professional men and young squirts who have little or nothing to lose."[40] But as Georgia, and Atlanta, committed to secession after the events at Fort Sumter, both non-southerners and natives of Unionist sympathies became suspect and took their sentiments underground.

Like all Confederate cities, Atlanta suffered severe economic dislocations during the war. The flow of trade through the Gate City slowed drastically with the Union invasion of the South, which cut off food supplies from the west, while the blockade restricted Atlanta's gate to the sea. Local farmers and herdsmen avoided Atlanta markets for fear of losing produce to the Confederate's ruthless exercise of impressment. Inflation undermined Confederate money, prices on scarce supplies soared, and a terrifying bread riot erupted in 1863.⁴¹

Although Atlanta's wartime commerce foundered, the war gave new life to manufacturing. Confederates reestablished in Atlanta the arsenal they had been forced to abandon in Nashville, and its work force of over 5,400 was soon turning out ammunition and other war matériel.⁴² The Atlanta Quartermaster Depot manufactured boots and uniforms and employed over 3,000 hands. Private enterprise also joined the Confederate war effort. New ventures soon were engaged in manufacturing cannon, pistols, swords, and other articles of war. Atlanta took second place only to Richmond as the manufacturing and supply center of the Confederacy.⁴³

Atlanta's wartime population swelled to nearly 22,000, more than twice its 1860 level, mostly due to the influx of civilians working in the ordnance plants. When Sherman invaded northern Georgia, many began to evacuate Atlanta, but there were still about 12,000 people in the city when northern troops entered.⁴⁴

When the Union Army left, Atlanta presented "a scene of charred and desolate ruins, and the decaying carcasses of animals."⁴⁵ Citizens began returning immediately after Sherman's departure to survey the damage and to commence the mythic struggle to rebuild the ruined city. By July 1865 Samuel Richards, in refuge in New York, heard from his brother and business partner, who described the hectic scene in Atlanta: "Almost as busy a crowd fill its ruined streets as in the days of its greenest prosperity." Richards hurried home, amazed to find that "busy life is resuming its sway over its desolate streets and any number of stores of all kinds are springing up as if by magic in every part of the burnt district."⁴⁶

This was more than an expression of Richard's local pride. A parade of northern and foreign reporters witnessed Atlanta's amazing resurgence. Sidney Andrews, a northern visitor who arrived later in 1865, described the frenetic energy of the city with glee. "From all this ruin and devastation a new city is springing up with marvelous rapidity. The narrow and irregular and numerous streets are alive from morning till night . . . with a never-ending throng of pushing and crowding and scrambling and eager and excited and enterprising men, all bent on building and trading and swift fortune-making."⁴⁷ Whitelaw Reid, another northern witness to renascent Atlanta, commented that "the city was adapting itself, with remarkable rapidity, to the new order of things." "What is more remarkable," he noted, "the men who were bringing a city out of this desert of shattered brick . . . were not Yankees, but pure Southerners." "The people," Reid concluded, "were infected with the

Atlanta's Peachtree Street, looking north from tracks, 1866. (Atlanta Historical Society)

mania of city building."[48] Another visitor, John R. Dennett, was struck by Atlanta's willingness to "indulge in glowing anticipation of the future prosperity and growth of their town," even while "the middle of the city is a great open space of irregular shape, a wilderness of mud, with a confused jumble of railroad sheds."[49]

"It is marvelous how quickly towns are rebuilt in America," an English visitor to Atlanta enthused. "It is almost still more surprising . . . where the money comes from in a ruined country."[50] By the early 1870s, Robert Somers described Atlanta as "rising up a grander, fairer, and more ambitious town than before." Still in the throes of "architectural chaos," the city was a hodgepodge of charred ruins, shanties, and gleaming new brick structures. At its center, Atlanta was "gathering in thick and hot haste about the railways," which cut the city in two, with no bridges or underpasses to circumvent the trains that constantly blocked city streets. A new train station was under construction, Somers noted, "but, like everything else in Atlanta, it is unfinished."[51]

Atlanta invited comparison with northern cities and, in its robust eagerness for progress, came to be seen as a southern exception rather than an indigenous spearhead for a New South. "Chicago in her busiest days could scarcely show such a sight as clamors for observation here," Sidney Andrews exulted.[52] "These people were taking lessons from Chicago," Whitelaw Reid concurred.

"Excepting that the map and climate tell me I am in the heart of Dixie," another incredulous midwestern visitor wrote home in 1875, "I would believe this to be a bustling, thriving, growing city of the North or West."[53] "There is little that is distinctly Southern in Atlanta," Edward King wrote in 1874, "it is eminently modern and unromantic."[54]

Atlanta's receptivity to northern influence was part of the image its promoters deliberately encouraged after the war. The perception of Atlanta as a Yankee outpost, a legacy of the city's antebellum reputation, took on new importance now. Northern capital was thought to be essential to rebuilding the city's economy, and northern creditors and investors needed reassurance of loyalty and sectional reconciliation. How else can one explain the remarkable Atlanta campaign in 1867 to raise funds for a memorial to President Lincoln? Or the obsequious public display of acquiescence when Federal troops reentered the city under orders of the Reconstruction Act in March 1867? Or, more remarkable still, the cordial reception offered to Atlanta's returning conqueror, General William T. Sherman, in 1879?[55] Reconciliation to defeat was one thing; here was a city that embraced its conquerors with unabashed enthusiasm.

Reconstructed Atlanta

Atlanta faced Reconstruction with a divided mind. As a group, the leading businessmen favored immediate reconciliation and cooperation with the Congressional Reconstruction acts. When General John Pope was installed as military governor over Georgia, Alabama, and Florida, local business and civic leaders greeted him with lavish entertainment and laudatory toasts. In local politics, Radical Reconstruction brought the Republican party into contention, largely on the strength of Atlanta's rapidly growing black population. Republicans won seats in the city council and challenged Democrats at each election, but they never took full control of the city. By 1871 state legislation allowing citywide elections diluted Republican voting strength and virtually ended any threat to Democratic hegemony.[56] As in Nashville, Reconstruction was a short episode in local politics that left few permanent scars. In contrast to Nashville, however, Atlanta's post-Reconstruction local politics, particularly at the mayoral level, witnessed the dominance of Conservative Democrats who generally were drawn from the business class.[57]

On the state level, Radical Republicans gained more decisive power, but only for one truncated term. Under Governor Rufus Bullock, who came to power in 1868, Georgia suffered numerous incidents of corruption, but Atlanta was often the better for them. During the constitutional convention of 1868, for example, Republicans added an amendment to remove the state capital from Milledgeville, where it had been since 1807. Atlanta boosters smoothed the path by offering the state free use of buildings at the city's expense and a large plot of land for a new capitol. Atlanta's Republican newspaper ridiculed "swampy, mosquito-infested" Milledgeville and applauded the "capital set of fellows" in the state convention and city council who engineered the move.[58] Atlantans approved the new constitution, as did the state, and the Georgia legislature was installed in temporary quarters, first in the city hall and then in the new opera house being built by Hannibal I. Kimball and his brother. As Georgia's capital, Atlanta enjoyed the material benefits of new buildings and having legislators and lobbyists visit the city, along with increased political clout.

Kimball, a northerner who had arrived in Atlanta in 1867, was one of the key allies of the Bullock regime. He later sold the opera house to the state at tremendous profit, managed to extract endorsements for huge railroad bond issues from the legislature, and used his influence to finance construction of the Kimball House, the most lavish hotel in the entire South. Rising six stories into the Atlanta skyline, the Kimball House was a symbol of the Gate City's aspirations and of the freewheeling days of Reconstruction that brought Atlanta as much boodle as it did corruption.

When the Republican regime collapsed in 1871, Kimball's fortunes fell apart as well. He and Governor Bullock fled the state to escape the wrath of Democrats. But Kimball returned to his adopted city in 1874 to a warm welcome, complete with a "vindication banquet" at the Kimball House, where businessmen toasted him as a leader of the new Atlanta.[59] Nothing served as better proof of Atlanta's determination to, as Henry Grady put it, "put business above politics."

These signs of deference to northern men and their politics were not inspired solely by the presence of northerners in Atlanta. Nor were all the Atlantans madly dashing about the streets certain to be "nervous Yankees." These were a new breed of southerner, one that had perhaps been quietly nurtured in the region's antebellum towns and was now in boisterous display in the boomtown environment of Atlanta. Census figures showed that the city's population was over 90 percent southern-born in 1880, as it had been in 1860, and most of the remaining tenth was from border states or foreign countries.[60] Northerners were more prevalent among the wealthy business leadership of the city, to be sure, but even among this element they constituted a declining minority of between 10 and 15 percent after the war. Taking into account the foreign-born, about two-thirds to three-fourths of Atlanta's most prominent businessmen were sons of the South.[61] It was they, as much as the northern invaders, who reconstructed Atlanta.

Foundations of Growth

Atlanta and Nashville were ideally situated to take advantage of the great shifts in the economic structure of the South after the war. The foundations of growth in each city were fundamentally commercial, with finance and manufacturing playing important supporting roles. It was the railroads that made both cities major trading centers of the New South. Atlanta's unnavigable Chattahoochee River rendered the city entirely dependent on the railroad. The Cumberland River continued to serve Nashville's trade in certain lines, but in the day of the railroad it was less important as a commercial artery than as a pretext for the L&N to allow lower freight rates to Nashville because of alleged waterborne competition.[62] Nashville, or Rock City as it was now styled, served as the commercial emporium to trade between the Midwest and the Gulf States of the South and built a solid, diversified base of manufacturing and finance as well. Atlanta's position at the southern end of the Appalachian barrier made it the Gate City for trade moving between most of the Deep South and the Northeast and, in competition with Nashville, between the West and the Southeast.

Local entrepreneurs and capitalists contributed to the expansion of each city's railroad network, but in both settings transportation came to be dominated by huge railroad corporations controlled by outside interests. Nashville was served by no less than five separate railways before the Civil War. By 1880 all had come under the control of the L&N. The valiant struggle by Nashville's Jere Baxter to establish the Tennessee Central as an independent road beginning in the 1890s met with, at best, limited success.[63]

Atlanta's railway network, composed of four carriers in 1860, soon fell under the control of the Richmond and West Point Terminal Company, a holding company for the Richmond and Danville system. When this company collapsed in 1893, the Southern Railway system was formed and took over as the dominant force in Atlanta rail transport. As in Nashville, a locally controlled, independent railroad became an obsessive but repeatedly frustrated goal among Atlanta boosters. The complaints from Atlanta and Nashville against the abuses by the "octopus" continued from the 1870s into the early twentieth century, when progressive-era reforms brought state and federal government regulations to bear.

Actually, both cities benefited enormously as regional shipping centers. The L&N gave preferential rates on freight moving to and from Nashville, so that it became the only important distribution and gathering center for the entire territory below the Ohio River and above the Tennessee River west of the Appalachians.[64] The reshipping privileges on grain coming from the Midwest,

Atlanta's Whitehall Street, looking south from Alabama Street, 1882. (Atlanta Historical Society)

which were conferred on Nashville by the L&N, made it the major milling and distribution center for wheat and corn flour—the "Minneapolis of the South."

Nor, on balance, did Atlanta suffer at the hands of the railroads. In 1879 southern railway operators, in an effort to regulate rates, designated Atlanta as the key basing point upon which freight rates from the North and West to all parts of the South were to be geared. This system acknowledged and reinforced Atlanta's role as a central distribution center in the South.[65] Reviewing the city's long-standing grievance against the railroads, one Atlanta businessman noted with unintended humor that "more than forty-five years [later] . . . the question [of "unjust" freight rates] is still a live issue, notwithstanding the city has grown fifteen hundred percent in population."[66]

If railroads controlled by outside interests were the principal commercial arteries of Nashville and Atlanta, it was local wholesale merchants who quickened the flow of trade along those arteries. After the Civil War, merchants in most major lines of trade no longer went to New York or Philadelphia for annual or biennial buying trips. Wholesale merchants or jobbers were now located in large and medium-sized cities throughout the interior, and railroad centers like Nashville and Atlanta became natural centers for their offices and warehouses.

Whitehall Street, same view, 1903. (Atlanta Historical Society)

Not content to wait for retailers and other jobbers to come to them, the wholesalers of Atlanta and Nashville sent out armies of drummers, traveling sales agents who dealt directly with retail store owners in the small towns and rural crossroads that were scattered throughout a far-flung commercial realm. The wholesaler and his traveling salesmen competed with their counterparts from rival firms and cities for control of the hinterland and fought to expand the limits of their trading area. On this level, railroad freight rates were just one factor affecting trade, to which wholesalers and their drummers added an innovative array of enticing discounts, credit terms, and samples to lure customers. The drummer, with his suitcase full of samples, his flashy suit, whiskers, derby hat, and his fast-talking sales patter, was the advance guard of the metropolitan economy that reached out to the surrounding small towns and deep into the rural frontiers of a distant trading empire.[67]

The aggressive tactics of Atlanta's and Nashville's wholesale merchants and their legions of hard-driving drummers were the source of frequent comments, often tinged with a tone of jealous envy in the newspapers of rival cities. "The energy and skill of the merchants of Atlanta have pushed their trade beyond the utmost limits looked for by the most sanguine," one partial observer boasted in 1881. "The drummers of Atlanta, by the hundred, are sent out

Atlanta under construction, Marietta and Broad streets, 1901. (Atlanta Historical Society)

annually, travel regularly over all the country between Richmond and Key West and between Charleston and the Mississippi river [*sic*], and certain specialties are carried even beyond this territory."[68]

By 1898 Atlanta's wholesale trading area was said to extend halfway to Baltimore and Cincinnati to the north and from the southeast coast to the Mississippi River to the south. More conservative estimates described the sphere within a two-hundred mile radius as Atlanta's domain.[69] Nashville's jobbers dominated most of Tennessee and northern Alabama within the boundaries of the Tennessee River, and much of southern Kentucky. In some specialized lines, such as whiskey, tobacco, or coffee, wholesalers could extend farther; in others they were more restricted.

Reliable information on the trading area and the volume and value of trade were not systematically reported in either city. Occasional estimates, usually issued by the local chamber of commerce, give some idea of the diversity of commercial activity in each city. Table 2.1 shows the wholesale trade in various products in the early 1880s. Because of the erratic way in which commercial data were gathered, these figures should not be used for anything more than

Table 2.1 Wholesale Trade, Atlanta and Nashville, ca. 1882–1885 (in thousands of dollars)

	Atlanta	Nashville
Agricultural implements	200	1,500
Books, stationery	1,500	750
Boots and shoes	400	1,500
Clothing	1,250	1,750
Coal	2,500	600
Corn		2,100
Cotton	7,650	6,000
Drugs	1,500	2,000
Dry goods	9,500	6,000
Flour		2,800
Furniture	800	750
Groceries	16,000	11,000
Guano	9,000	
Hardware	2,350	2,000
Hats, millinery		675
Hay		250
Hides		250
Horses, mules	1,100	
Leather		250
Liquor	4,500	3,000
Livestock	1,500	1,750
Lumber	1,500	2,000
Musical instruments	2,000	
Notions	350	1,600
Oats		300
Paper		400
Printing	800	
Produce		1,750
Provisions		1,500
Queensware		350
Saddlery and harnesses		350
Saddlery hardware		350
Salt		200
Stoves, tinware		1,500
Straw goods	250	
Tobacco, cigars	1,560	3,550
Wagons, carriages	1,000	
Wheat		2,500
Wool		150
Miscellaneous	1,000	4,000
Total	68,210	65,425

Source: I. W. Avery, *Atlanta, the Leader in Trade, Population, Wealth, and Manufacturers in Georgia* (Atlanta, Ga., 1885), 17; *Manufacturing and Mercantile Resources of Nashville, Tennessee* (Nashville, Tenn., 1882), 30–31.

rough comparisons. It is striking, nonetheless, how similar the commercial economies of Atlanta and Nashville appear to have been in the 1880s.

The role of wholesale groceries as the leading commercial line in the 1880s is itself testimony to the rise of the urban South and to the decline of subsistence agriculture in the rural South. The earlier southern grocery trade, such as it was, had been routed primarily through Baltimore and New Orleans. Railroads made it possible to ship groceries and other perishable goods quickly and directly to central distribution points in the interior.[70] By the early 1880s, Atlanta had twenty-eight wholesale grocery houses, and Nashville had fifteen.[71] Warehouses on Atlanta's Alabama Street and along Nashville's Market Street bulged with food products that were either imported, usually from the west, or from surrounding farms that now had an expanding urban market to serve.

A growing volume of food products was processed locally: flour, cornmeal, meat, candy, coffee, Coca-Cola, beer, whiskey. Tobacco, dry goods, clothing, boots and shoes, furniture, books, hardware, and several other lines featured in the Atlanta and Nashville trade give further proof of the growing southern market for basic consumer goods.

The major southern exports passing through these cities were cotton and lumber. Nashville's cotton trade was restricted to what was produced in Middle Tennessee and northern Alabama, an amount that declined rapidly after the war as farmers shifted to raising grain, mixed crops, and livestock. By 1885 Nashville's annual cotton receipts had dwindled to less than 42,000 bales, about half of what they had been just five years earlier. Hardwood lumber, locally processed from timber rafted down the Cumberland River, was a growing trade that had a considerable impact on local wood-product manufacturing as well.[72]

The growth of Atlanta's cotton trade became a major force in the city's commercial prosperity. The volume of bales shipped out of Atlanta rose from about 17,000 bales in 1867 to almost 76,000 in 1876 and to 120,000 ten years later. After railroad gauges were standardized in 1886, Atlanta's cotton trade soared to 270,000 bales by 1890.[73] The leading force behind the Atlanta cotton trade was Samuel M. Inman. He began with his father "in a small way" immediately after the war and rapidly built the largest cotton brokerage firm in the country. With branches in Houston, Bremen, and New York, where Samuel's brother, railroad financier John Inman, was a partner in Inman, Swann, and Company, the Inman empire did a vast business that one year captured a record 600,000 bales. When Samuel Inman retired in 1897, he had firmly established Atlanta as one of the preeminent cotton centers of the South.[74]

Money from the commercial activities in both cities fed into the banks and other financial institutions that came to form another solid block in the

Nashville's Cumberland River waterfront, 1880s. (Tennessee State Library and Archives)

economic foundations of Atlanta and Nashville. Nashville's superiority as a
banking center was manifest in 1880, when it claimed over 50 percent more
capital stock invested in its banks and three to four times the deposits and
resources of Atlanta banks.[75] It was not until the depression of the 1890s, when
Nashville suffered massive bank failures, that Atlanta pulled well ahead. Eight
of Nashville's thirteen banking institutions went into liquidation, and a few of
the others closed their doors. Large depositors withdrew their money, and

business confidence plummeted, with broadly depressing effects.[76] Nashville began to recover by 1897, but Atlanta had glided through the depression with no visible scars and stood well ahead of Nashville by 1900. Though its banks were each more poorly capitalized, their deposits and total resources easily exceeded those of Nashville. Following a warmly contested competition between the two cities to host the Federal Reserve bank of the sixth district in 1914, Atlanta's triumph assured its claim as the financial metropolis of the Southeast.[77]

The insurance companies of New York and other northern cities continued to dominate the South after the war, as they had in antebellum times. Atlanta nonetheless gained financial strength as the regional headquarters for numerous fire, life, and casualty insurance companies of northern origin that invaded the South after the war. They were joined by local entrepreneurs, who began the Life Insurance Company of Georgia in 1891. It sold low-cost industrial insurance to blacks, one of the few niches in the market that northern companies had ignored. Soon Atlanta became the leading southern insurance center and claimed to be third in the nation behind New York and Chicago.[78]

Nashville, too, attracted several northern insurance firms that set up state and regional headquarters in what had long been the financial capital of Tennessee. Though most insurance companies continued to operate out of northern cities, local entrepreneurs in Nashville, as in Atlanta, developed their own companies after 1900; two companies, National Life and Accident and Life and Casualty, prospered on sales of industrial insurance to blacks.[79]

The expansion of commerce and finance were essential to the city-building enterprise, but most local boosters regarded manufacturing as the highest aspiration, a goal to which the others ought to be subservient. Instead of nicking a small commission from the flow of raw materials out of, and finished goods into, the South, "home manufacturing" promised generous profits from the value added to regional products. The newspapers of both Atlanta and Nashville never tired of pointing out the special attractions of industrial development. Editorials cheered each new enterprise that was launched and urged new measures to inspire others. "What Atlanta needs is manufactories, shops, mills, forges, looms, factories," Henry Grady's *Atlanta Constitution* exhorted in 1888 while calling citizens to a mass rally for industry. "Atlanta ought to be the great manufacturing city of the South. She is going to be. We are going to make her so."[80] Atlanta's boldest displays of industrial spirit came in a series of extravagant expositions in 1881, 1887, and 1895, which drew national attention to the city's aggressive pursuit of the New South.

Nashville's boosters were no less enthusiastic about industry and no less impatient with the "old fogy" element that withheld its capital from Rock City. Described by visitors in 1888 as an "essentially conservative" banking center of

Table 2.2 Occupational Distributions, Atlanta and Nashville, 1880

	Atlanta			Nashville		
	Male	Female	All	Male	Female	All
Agriculture	3%	0%	2%	1%	0%	1%
Manufacturing	29	17	25	33	16	28
Trade, transportation	35	1	23	36	2	25
Professional, personal service	34	81	50	30	82	46
Total	101	99	100	100	100	100
N =	(11,118)	(5,960)	(17,078)	(11,591)	(5,147)	(16,738)

Source: U.S. Census Bureau, *Tenth Census of the United States, 1880,* vol. 1, *Population* (Washington, D.C., 1883), table 37.
Note: Totals do not always equal 100 percent due to rounding.

old families and old money, Nashville was "considerably shaken up" by the industrial enterprise of young men during the 1880s.[81] Nashville staged its own industrial expositions, beginning in a small way with a series of local fairs in the 1870s and topped by the 1897 Tennessee Centennial Exposition.

Both cities remained diversified commercial gathering and distribution centers with financial, administrative, and manufacturing functions serving important auxiliary roles in the local economy. As tables 2.2 and 2.3 show, the occupational distribution of both cities remained quite stable between 1880 and 1900, with manufacturing, as broadly defined in the census, employing

Table 2.3 Occupational Distributions, Atlanta and Nashville, 1900

	Atlanta			Nashville		
	Males	Females	All	Males	Females	All
Agriculture	1%	0%	1%	1%	0%	1%
Domestic and personal service	21	71	39	24	69	38
Manufacturing	28	18	24	29	19	26
Professional	7	4	6	5	5	5
Trade	43	7	30	41	7	30
Total	100	100	100	100	100	100
N =	(25,871)	(14,929)	(40,800)	(24,784)	(11,430)	(36,214)

Source: U.S. Census Bureau, *Twelfth Census of the United States, 1900, Population,* pt. 2 (Washington, D.C., 1902), table 94.

Table 2.4 Manufacturing Statistics, Atlanta and Nashville, 1880 and 1900

	Atlanta		Nashville	
	1880	1900	1880	1900
Number of manufacturing establishments	196	390	268	489
Capital invested (millions)	$2.5	$16.0	$3.9	$13.2
Capital invested per establishment (thousands)	$12.6	$41.0	$14.5	$27.0
Employees (thousands)	3.7	9.4	4.8	8.4
Employees per establishment	14.0	24.0	14.0	17.0
Value of product (millions)	$4.9	$16.7	$8.6	$18.5

Source: U.S. Census Bureau, *Twelfth Census of the United States, 1900, Manufacturers,* pt. 2 (Washington, D.C., 1902), table 2.

about one-quarter of the work force in both cities over that period. Industrial employment was expanding at a rate comparable to the general growth of the urban work force in each case, but little more.

But, as table 2.4 indicates, manufacturing pursuits were, by other measures, becoming a more important part of each local economy, particularly in Atlanta. The number of manufacturing establishments in each city nearly doubled within two decades. More impressive was the substantial increase in capital invested and the value of manufactured products. Though Nashville spawned more separate enterprises, Atlanta industrialists concentrated their investments in fewer but larger establishments.

Nevertheless, there was a remarkable similarity in the industrial profile of each city. Both exploited the availability of regional or imported raw materials, and both emphasized basic consumer products. In Nashville the leading industries in 1900 (by value of product) were flour and grist mills, lumber mills, printing and publishing, and foundries and machine shops, with dozens of smaller enterprises turning out clothing, confectionery, wood products, and leather goods. In Atlanta the major industries were lumber mills, foundries and machine shops, printing, and patent medicines, along with smaller lines in clothing, food products, and furniture.[82] Though Atlanta and Nashville launched successful textile mills with great public fanfare, they never played a major role in the industrial development of either city.

It was upon these economic foundations that the populations of Nashville and Atlanta grew in the decades following the Civil War. Nashville's advantageous start in the aftermath of a war that destroyed much of Atlanta helped it hold its lead in population until the depression of the 1890s. To the west, rival

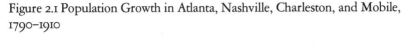

Figure 2.1 Population Growth in Atlanta, Nashville, Charleston, and Mobile, 1790–1910

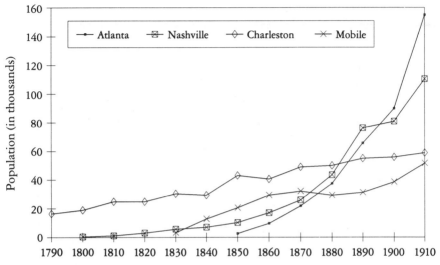

Source: U.S. Census Bureau, *1980 Census of the Population,* vol. 1, *Characteristics of the Population,* chap. A, "Number of Inhabitants" (Washington, D.C., 1983), historical population figures in separate state volumes.

Memphis was laid low by a grisly series of yellow fever epidemics during the 1870s, which killed off large portions of the population and scared away many more. To the south, Birmingham did not emerge as an industrial center until the 1880s, and although it stole much of Nashville's industrial thunder, Birmingham posed little challenge to the Tennessee city's merchants and bankers.

As figure 2.1 illustrates, Atlanta came out of the war years showing a more rapid rate of growth. From "the home of half-starved and half-wild dogs" that Sherman left behind, Atlanta quickly regained its prewar population and then rapidly surpassed it, reaching nearly 22,000 by 1870.[83] But after 1870 its growth only kept pace with that of Nashville, which—despite its rather staid, quiet image, in contrast to the boisterous "Atlanta spirit"—set the pace for the Gate City. The depression of the 1890s hit Nashville banks with extraordinary force and left the Rock City behind its more resilient rivals. The 1900 census showed that Atlanta and Memphis had both passed Nashville in population, as would Birmingham in 1910. Nashville's economy picked up after 1897, and a major annexation in 1905 helped the city's showing in the next census. But Nashville would never regain the preeminent position in the urban South that it had enjoyed in the immediate postwar years. Atlanta had triumphed as the new interior metropolis of the Southeast, both as a commercial and financial center and as the quintessential symbol of the New South.

Out of a war that brought prolonged occupation to Nashville and massive destruction to Atlanta, each city had found the men and resources to adapt quickly to the opportunities the crisis offered and to the new order of things that defeat brought. The expanding rail system pumped commercial blood through each city, stimulating a diversified local economy and rapid population growth. The winds of history were in the favor of the entrepreneurs of each city, and they responded with exceptional vigor to the chances presented by the new order.

3 | *Ebb Tide*

Seldom with a deeper ruin of the old has there been a more hopeless chaos out of which to construct a new order of things than Charleston presented in those days.
—*Robert Somers, 1870*

"New men" will soon be the order of the day, in Mobile and in many another center of Southern aristocracy.
—*Whitelaw Reid, 1866*

The tide of the postwar South, which buoyed the economy of Atlanta and Nashville, moved against many of the seaports that had flourished under the old order. Charleston, South Carolina, an eastern seaboard city founded two centuries earlier, and Mobile, Alabama, a thriving Gulf port that had served some of the richest plantation country in the Old South, languished in the backwaters of the New South.

War, emancipation, and Reconstruction brought economic chaos and political subjugation that left lasting marks on each city. As the new order emerged in the commercial realm, merchants who for years had grown fat from the profits of a virtually captive clientele now found themselves facing unfamiliar competition. Small general-store merchants in interior crossroads towns, along with hordes of drummers from the larger railroad centers who invaded the southern hinterland, were now stealing business that by custom had always belonged to the seaports. The railroad, which earlier had supplemented the river systems that fed trade into the ports, now siphoned away cotton and other goods into a growing stream of overland trade.

In what seemed an almost helpless response to the political and economic forces that reshaped their world, Charleston and Mobile sank into a prolonged season of demoralizing stagnation. Where private enterprise failed to overcome the obstacles to economic revival, local and state governments offered little aid. In the face of massive debts incurred both before and after the war, the public sector entered a phase of severe retrenchment precisely when aid might have made a crucial difference. It was not until the end of the nineteenth century that new opportunities surfaced. Change was provoked by external forces that came with the Spanish-American War, federal harbor improvements, and new ventures by outside capitalists. Only then did a new generation of business leaders emerge to exploit the belated benefits of the postwar order.

The Siege of Charleston

Charleston held out against Union forces until February 18, 1865, in one of the longest sieges of the war. Union troops finally entered the city without resistance, for the Confederates had evacuated the previous night. Before leaving, Confederate soldiers piled cotton bales and bushels of rice in the public squares and set them afire rather than leave them to the invaders. They blew up a large cannon on the Battery, sending huge fragments into nearby mansions. They also blasted the munitions magazine on Sullivan's Island north of the city, blew up gunboats, and torched bridges. Fires erupted across the city during what one observer described as a night of "horror and chaos," with the flames "casting an eerie glow over the entire city."[1] Early that morning an enormous cache of gunpowder stored near the Northeastern Railway station exploded, apparently by accident, killing at least 150 of the city's poor who were pillaging food supplies left by retreating Confederates.

Protected by a constellation of forts and swampy environs, Charleston had proved impregnable to federal assault. Fort Sumter, where the war had begun four years earlier, stood battered but unconquered at the mouth of the harbor, a symbol of Charleston's, and the Confederacy's, will. Its defenders had survived a series of three massive bombardments from Union guns, and even when the walls of the fort were reduced to a smoking heap of rubble, the men of Sumter never surrendered. Failing to take the fort, the federals threatened to bombard the city itself. Confederate General P. G. T. Beauregard responded with indignation (much as Hood had denounced Sherman at Atlanta): "[Y]ou now resort to the novel measure of turning your guns against the old men, the women and children, and the hospitals of a sleeping city, an act of inexcusable barbarity."[2]

The Union's blunt answer came in a ferocious barrage of shells lobbed into the city from batteries placed in the swamps four miles away, a bombardment that began late in August 1863 and continued until the Confederate evacuation nearly eighteen months later. Using the proud steeples of St. Michael's and St. Phillip's churches to sight the guns, the Union cannoneers lobbed hundreds of shells into the stronghold of the Confederacy. By the end there was hardly a building in the southern part of the city that was not at least partially damaged by the shelling, and many that had suffered direct hits were totally destroyed. The citizens of Charleston withdrew north of Calhoun Street, out of range of most of the shells, leaving the heart of the city a ghost town (except for Union prisoners who were brought to the Battery in hopes of discouraging the bombardment).[3] Added to the war damage was an enormous, blackened scar that cut diagonally across the city, the result of a great fire in December 1861, a disaster blamed alternately on careless slaves and anti-Confederate arsonists. It was a measure of Charleston's sacrifice during the war years that the "burnt district" remained a vast wasteland for the next two decades.

The capture of Charleston had been a major objective of the Union forces ever since the surrender of Fort Sumter in April 1861. It was important both symbolically and strategically. Charleston, the "cradle of secession," led South Carolina out of the Union, and South Carolina led the South. It was here that the war had begun, and Charleston had come to embody all the haughty arrogance that northerners identified with the South. Federal troops had planned the siege of Charleston from early in the war, when they invaded the sea islands around Port Royal and Beaufort, south of the city. At war's end, as Sherman prepared to march into South Carolina from Savannah, General Halleck wrote from Washington: "Should you capture Charleston, I hope that by some accident the place may be destroyed, and if a little salt be sown upon its site it may prevent the growth of future crops of nullification and secession." Sherman responded ominously, "I will bear in mind your hint as to Charleston and don't think salt will be necessary."[4]

Sherman's army never got to Charleston, but the motive of revenge had long guided the Union's strategy against the city. There were important strategic objectives at stake as well. Charleston was the premier port of the south Atlantic coast. Despite the Union blockade, Charleston's well-protected harbor was filled with ships exporting cotton and naval stores, usually to neutral ports in the West Indies, where English boats met them. They returned with war matériel and vital supplies. Charleston became "the Confederate nerve center" for the blockade runners, boasting ten ships for every one active in all the other southern ports.[5]

For many Charleston merchants, the war opened new possibilities for the city to triumph in its long and frustrating quest to regain commercial preeminence. Although it was the fourth-largest city in the nation before 1800, Charleston's growth slowed just as other eastern seaports began aggressive expansion. While New York, Philadelphia, Boston, and Baltimore carved out vast commercial empires in the West and expanded their trade abroad, Charleston's commerce and population stagnated, and the city slid to twentieth place by 1860, though it remained second to New Orleans within the South. At times Charleston's business leaders worked valiantly to reverse the trend. They sought to enlarge the city's hinterland with bold railroad ventures, and to expand maritime commerce by building a home-owned merchant marine fleet, improving the harbor, and trading directly with European ports. But they remained exclusively committed to Charleston's role as an entrepôt to a plantation economy, and as the soil of South Carolina grew less fertile, so did Charleston's fortunes.[6]

Since its founding in 1670, Charleston had grown by the strength of its expanding hinterland of rice and, later, cotton plantations. Its commercial empire was virtually unchallenged above Savannah, below Wilmington, North Carolina, and throughout the interior of South Carolina. That empire rested on the city's well-protected harbor and a system of navigable rivers that penetrated the South Carolina interior. The city was located on a narrow peninsula between two of those rivers, the Ashley and the Cooper, which, according to local conceit, met at Charleston to "form the Atlantic Ocean."

Charleston was the economic and cultural capital to a wealthy plantation society. At its wharves, jutting confidently into the Cooper River, rice and cotton from the sea islands and low country were gathered for export. Upcountry plantations and farms also poured their bounty of cotton toward the "City by the Sea." Many wealthy planters made Charleston their home, either year round or during the summer season when the swampy environment of the low country was rife with malaria, or "country fever." Surrounded by salt water, Charleston was regarded—against all evidence in the mortality statistics—as a healthy refuge.[7]

For the planters and their families, Charleston was also a pleasure resort, a retreat from work designed for their enjoyment. The city offered a busy fare of horse races, fancy balls, theater, music, and lavish parties. These came to form a well-established social season for the city's upper crust. Charleston's debutantes of 1861 "were greatly chagrined" when the St. Cecilia Society and Jockey Club allowed the war to interfere with the social season.[8] Even during the war, Charleston's ladies managed to uphold some of the old standards with parties at Fort Sumter between bombardments and balls in honor of General Beauregard and other Confederate officials.[9]

The planters' resort was also the vital center of their business lives. The planters depended on a corps of factors, bankers, and merchants to sell their rice and cotton and to supply the plantations with food, clothing, and supplies of all kinds. Unlike other southern ports, whose factors were typically itinerant agents from New York or other "foreign" cities, Charleston's factors, by the 1850s at least, were, in the majority, native Carolinians, many of them former planters or relatives of the great planter families in the city's hinterland. Earlier in the nineteenth century, northern, English, Scots, and Jewish merchants had dominated much of Charleston's trade, but beginning about 1840 an indigenous crowd of merchants reclaimed their place in Charleston's mercantile community. It was the city's antebellum stagnation as much as the assertiveness of Carolina merchants that opened the field to them before the war.[10]

The efforts of Charleston's antebellum mercantile community to develop railroads and effect harbor improvements often conflicted with the interests of planters, particularly when Charleston solicited state support. But the city enjoyed enough political power in South Carolina to ensure critical support for its projects. Commercial interests also prevailed upon the city government to support internal improvements, saddling local taxpayers with enormous debts for projects designed to revive Charleston's commercial vitality.[11]

It was in part the failure of that revival that colored the political attitudes of Charleston merchants as they faced the secession crisis. Whereas business interests in other southern cities tended to shun secessionist sentiment as disruptive, Charleston Unionists were becoming a rare and quiet breed by the 1850s. In Charleston the range of debate was narrowed to a question of whether South Carolina should lead the South by seceding first, or wait and secede in cooperation with other states. Many of the city's business leaders favored the cooperationist view, which ultimately lost out to the radical secessionists, but there was no strong voice for Unionism among them.[12] Had South Carolina not seceded, according to local lore, Charleston would have seceded from the state, and had Charleston hesitated, those "South of Broad"—the rich enclave of Charleston's wealthy merchant and planter families below Broad Street— would have seceded from the city.[13]

Many of Charleston's commercial leaders welcomed independence from the North, in part because they dreamed it would allow Charleston to regain its stature as the "natural emporium" of the South.[14] The fortunes of war seemed at first to favor Charleston in its pursuit of that dream. New Orleans was captured early in 1862, and among other southern ports only Mobile, Savannah, and Wilmington shared Charleston's preeminent role in running the Union blockade. Blockade running was a dangerous and highly lucrative business. Established shipping firms like John Fraser and Company, the leading blockade runner in the Confederacy, were joined by newcomers eager to express Confederate patriotism at a profit. Many, like William Bee, George and William Trenholm, and George W. Williams, came out of the war with tremendous fortunes.[15] The war opened to Charleston businessmen unprecedented opportunities to exercise their capacity for enterprise independent of northern interests.

But as the Union blockade tightened, and as the Confederate interior was invaded, the flow of trade through Charleston slowed, prices skyrocketed, and shortages of meat, salt, cloth, shoes, and other basic necessities became acute.[16] Charleston's blockade-running merchants, who saw themselves as Confederate patriots operating at great personal risk, were now vilified by consumers furious at what they considered outrageous prices.[17]

City of Desolation

The fall of Charleston dashed whatever was left of earlier hopes for the city's commercial revival within an independent Confederate nation. Reporter

The ruins at Charleston, seen from the Circular Church, 1865. (National Archives)

Sidney Andrews, arriving in September 1865, saw "a city of ruins, of desola-tion, of vacant houses, of widowed women, of rotting wharves, of deserted warehouses, of weed-wild gardens, of miles of grass-grown streets, of acres of pitiful and voiceful barrenness." The physical damage was compounded by the demoralization of the city's white population, leaving "enough of woe and want and ruin and ravage to satisfy the most insatiate heart." "We never again can have the Charleston of the decade previous to the war," Andrews added confidently, because "the beauty and pride of the city are as dead as the glories of Athens."[18]

Charleston became a required stop for northern visitors reporting on the devastated postwar South. All described the ravaged condition of the city, and at least one noted the "picturesque" quality of the ruins, as though recalling the dead civilizations of Athens or Rome. One of the more astute observers from the North, Whitelaw Reid, came to the "City of Desolation" in 1866 to describe the mansions engulfed by vines, streets torn up, and gun emplace-ments blocking the view of "many an aristocratic window." But he noted,

Charleston's Battery, ca. 1865. (National Archives)

almost with disappointment, that the "extent of the damage by the bombard-ment has . . . been generally overrated at the North."[19]

One visitor, entering the city immediately after its fall, wrote: "The wharves looked as if they had been deserted for half a century—broken down, dilapi-dated, grass and moss peeping up between the pavements. . . . No imagination can conceive of the utter wrecks, the universal ruin, the stupendous desola-tion."[20] Carl Schurz, the Republican senator, also came to inspect the ruins in 1866. He saw the same overgrown wharves, cows grazing in the streets, turkey buzzards perching atop roofs as though brooding over a dead city, the burned district "looking like a vast graveyard of broken walls and tall blackened chimneys for monuments."[21]

The physical damage was more tangible but hardly more commented upon than the demoralized spirit of Charleston's once-proud citizens. With a mix-ture of charity and contempt, visitors also remarked on the humbled "aristoc-racy" that once ruled this proud city. "Here centered the fashion and aristocracy of South Carolina, before the war," Trowbridge wrote in 1866, "where the rich cotton and rice planters . . . came to lounge away the summer season . . . but, since those recent days of its pride and prosperity, it has been woefully battered and desolated. . . . The proud city lies humbled in its ashes, too poor to rise again without the helping hand of Northern capital."[22] An English visitor sensed the same deflated spirit: "The tone in Charleston seems to be one of despair and indifference; the young men were bent on going to seek their fortunes elsewhere, the elders having ceased to take interest in the future."[23]

Seven years after the fall of Charleston, the malaise still hung over the city. "The birth-place of the great rebellion still slumbered in the deep sluggard languor of Southern cities on a winter morning," Stephen Powers wrote in 1872. He found the burned district still in ruins and the economy in disarray, a product, he thought, of native demoralization and northern venality:

> Charleston was a city, first, of idle ragged negroes . . . ; of small dealers, la-
> borers, and German artisans, starving on the rebel custom [business] . . . of
> widows and children of planters, keeping respectable boarding-houses, or
> pining in hopeless and unspeakable penury . . . of young men loafing in the
> saloons, and living on the profits of their mother's boarding houses . . . of
> Jews and Massachusetts merchants, doing well on the semi-loyal and negro
> custom . . . of utterly worthless and accursed political adventurers from the
> North, Bureau leeches, and promiscuous knaves, all fattening on the humilia-
> tion of the South and the credulity of the Freedman.[24]

Coming to Charleston with different perspectives, many visitors witnessed the same melancholy scene of demoralized helplessness. Long after the initial shock of defeat—even after the turn of the century, by some accounts—Charleston seemed to face the postwar order with a despair unrelieved by the optimism that invigorated cities like Nashville and Atlanta.[25] Francis W. Dawson, the editor of the *Charleston News and Courier,* certainly matched Henry Grady in his enthusiasm for economic progress. He was relentless in his efforts to move Charleston into the New South, but his efforts were matched by his frustrations. Charlestonians were too passive, he concluded; they "were not mixed up enough."[26]

The reasons for Charleston's reluctant response to the new order were many. For one, Charleston's civic leaders had been, with rare exceptions, heartily committed to "throw[ing] off northern rule," whatever their views on exactly when to secede. In 1860–61 Charleston drew upon a tradition of resistance to federal intervention that dated back to the nullification contro-versy of 1832. In Charleston, during the events leading to secession, there was little ground for moderates to stand upon and speak for compromise and the Union, unlike the comparatively broad political spectrum found in Atlanta and

Nashville. The aging James L. Petigru, an ardent Whig, was virtually alone in his strenuous opposition to secession. (South Carolina, he lamented, was "too small to be a republic and too large to be an insane asylum.") Charleston businessmen urged a deliberate, sober response to the crisis that Lincoln's election presented, but they shared a strong Charleston commitment to secession as the only answer in the end.[27]

For these men, the Confederate disaster of 1865 meant defeat of their principles, their interests, their way of life. It was certainly not to be taken, as it could be among the Whig-Unionist element in Nashville and Atlanta, as vindication of their moderate views. Whereas the moderates might, without insurmountable hypocrisy, revive themes of intersectional harmony and invite a southward flow of northern capital and talent, Charlestonians found that behavior loathsome. "The idea that Charleston might possibly become a 'Yankee City' seemed revolting to the old South Carolina pride," Carl Schurz noted. One "venerable" and impoverished "patrician" admitted to him that outside capital was essential to Charleston's revival, "but, he added, South Carolina could not appeal to the North for financial aid without humiliating herself."[28]

Emancipation and Reconstruction

The damage Charleston suffered to its buildings and its economy seemed insignificant next to the destruction of slavery. Unlike Nashville or Atlanta, Charleston was the capital of a slave society—a social system and a culture, as well as a system of labor, that rested on black servitude. Over one-third of the city's 1860 population was slave, and in the surrounding plantation districts, 80 to 90 percent of the population was made up of black slaves. Much more than in Nashville or Atlanta, the white people of Charleston saw themselves fighting to defend the essential foundation of white civilization.

Leading the first Union troops to enter Charleston was a black Union soldier who rode a mule up Meeting Street, carrying a banner emblazoned "Liberty." Black soldiers with the famous Massachusetts Fifty-fourth Regiment, survivors of the bloody assault on Fort Wagener outside Charleston, marched behind him singing "John Brown's Body," the abolitionist anthem. Some soldiers split off and entered the homes of Charleston's white families, shouting to the slaves that they were now free to leave and urging them to do so if they wanted to escape slavery. Many slaves left their masters forever and went off to join what became a spontaneous celebration of freedom in the streets of Charleston.[29] Later the former slaves formed a huge procession and marched through the streets of the city, celebrating the death of slavery with a mock slave auction on a wagon bed and behind it a coffin marked "Slavery Is Dead." In no area was the new order of things more revolutionary than in the radically altered relations between the races.[30]

For most white Charlestonians, Reconstruction was a punishing ordeal that left deep marks. The enfranchisement of freedmen empowered what became a black majority, or nearly so, in the city and a strong majority in the state.[31] Following passage of the new state constitution in 1868, Charleston's mayor and city council were removed from office, and a Republican regime of white and black politicians took over city government. For more than a decade, the political control of the city remained in the hands of either a faction-ridden and racially fragmented Republican coalition, or a fusion of Republicans and Democrats, which left the former in control. Their regime was as frustrating to the aspirations of Charleston's black population as it was to business leaders who watched the city's debt soar and credit plummet, while services and property values deteriorated, race relations became violent, and the city floundered.[32] Not until 1879, when Conservative Democrat William A. Courtenay declared victory in the election for mayor, did Charleston win back the confidence of the business community at home and begin to establish sound credit abroad. But power, once regained by the Conservatives, was used to strictly limit the expenses, and therefore the role, of local government. City services—water, sewers, streets, and schools—all suffered deplorable neglect. Likewise, internal improvements of the harbor, waterfront, and railroad terminal facilities, which might have stimulated the lagging commercial life of Charleston, went by the boards as the city entered a prolonged period of severe retrenchment.[33]

Reconstruction ended at the state level with the election of Governor Wade Hampton in 1876, but its ill effects on Charleston's fortunes had lasting influence. The city's antebellum dominance in South Carolina affairs was dashed by political gerrymandering, upcountry resentment of the Charleston "aristocracy," and white fears of the low country's black majority. After the war, the Charleston delegation in the state legislature saw its traditional leadership role diminish, and no one from Charleston was elected governor until 1938.[34] After Reconstruction upcountry resentment of Charleston and the low country remained a powerful political force. Populist governor "Pitchfork" Ben Tillman channeled sectional and class jealousies against the City by the Sea into a powerful political movement. Charleston's beleaguered political status in South Carolina stood in striking contrast to the growing clout of Atlanta and Nashville in their states.

Charleston and South Carolina also suffered unusually heavy battle casualties. From a white male population of 146,000, South Carolina sent 75,000 men to the field, and another 10,000 served in local militia as part of the home defense. In all, some 40,000 South Carolina men were killed or disabled, a rate of loss far greater than that suffered by other states in the Confederacy, in which the average was about 10 percent killed.[35] Out of a white population of less than 27,000, only a fraction of which was eligible for service, Charleston alone supplied between 5,000 and 6,000 men, who made up twenty-three infantry, eleven artillery, and eight cavalry companies. Though there is no reliable estimate of the numbers killed and maimed, many of the Charleston companies lost 30 percent of their members. "They were the very flower of this old city, her young hope as fair renown. . . . Charleston was in mourning from First Manassas to Bentonville—at every board a vacant chair!"[36] Charleston's sacrifice in war produced something like a lost generation, a persistent dearth of men who had come of age in the 1850s and 1860s. The absence of those killed and disabled in war robbed the city and its hinterland of men whose youth and wartime experience might have infused Charleston with new energy and leadership. In a more vigorous city, migration from the country and from abroad would have quickly filled in any gaps in the population left by the war. But in Charleston, the sluggish economy offered little opportunity for young men of ambition. Many left for Columbia and the upcountry cotton-mill towns, or they went to Atlanta, Birmingham, Florida, Tennessee, and other more thriving centers of the New South. The "very flower of the youth of Charleston," Robert G. Rhett lamented, joined an exodus from the home of their ancestors. "Most of them won enviable places for themselves in the communities in which they settled. . . . Their departure drained the city of much of its vitality."[37]

Even after the turn of the century, novelist Owen Wister described Charleston as a community shattered by war, a city of "lavender and pressed-rose memories," a "beautiful, sad place" filled with "deeply veiled ladies . . . hushed in their perpetual mourning."[38] Henry James, during a brief visit in 1905, saw Charleston as "a city of gardens and absolutely of no men—or of so few that, save for the general sweetness, the War might still have been raging and all the manhood at the front." This emasculated, "feminized" city offered for James an "eloquent antithesis" to the "ancient order" that was "masculine, fierce and mustachioed." Now he found it "a sort of sick lioness who has so visibly parted with her teeth and claws that we may patronizingly walk all round her."[39]

The Fall of Mobile

Mobile, Alabama, was the last of the major Confederate cities to fall to the Union forces, and of the four considered here, it was, with Nashville, the least damaged by war. Located on the mouth of the Mobile River, at the northern edge of a bay that extends thirty miles inland from the Gulf, Mobile was so well protected and fortified that General Joseph Johnston claimed it was the best-defended city in the Confederacy. When Admiral Farragut won the Battle of Mobile Bay for the Union in August 1864, he ended the city's role as the major Gulf port for blockade running. But the harbor mines and the city's inner defensive line of fortifications, armed by boys and old men, continued to guard Mobile from invasion. A small force of Confederate soldiers at Spanish Fort, east of the city, was able to repulse an enemy more than eight times its size. Then, on April 9, 1865—after twelve days of siege, and on the same day that Lee surrendered his army in Virginia—Fort Blakeley, east of the city, fell under heavy federal attack. It was the last real battle of the war. Three days later, on April 12, the Confederates evacuated.[40]

"A heavy calm has fallen upon the city," Laura Roberts Pillans recorded in her diary. On April 12, Mayor R. H. Slough and a group of citizens, under a flag of truce, went out Old Shell Road to meet the approaching troops and surrender the city. When the Yankee soldiers marched into Mobile, most citizens remained indoors, but some welcomed the conquerors. "The Yankees after being received with loud hurrah by assembled traitors," Mrs. Pillans observed, "hoisted the hated evil banner of tyranny over the 'Battle House' [Hotel] and then marched quietly to the Suburbs."[41]

With the Confederacy defeated and the war over, one might have expected a more conciliatory, resigned tone in occupied Mobile, especially as it had suffered no physical damage (save for the prized magnolias on the Shell Road that the Confederates had felled to fortify the city). But the federals were accorded the same insolent treatment as alien enemies they had received in cities that fell earlier and more violently. Mobile's men were circumspect, for the most part, but the women were demonstrative in their disdain. They refused to talk to the soldiers and walked down the center of the road rather than pass beneath the Union flag, which the federals displayed on every public building.[42] "How long the fair rebs will hold out is yet to be learned," mused one Mobile man in mid-May; "if they are equal to those of New Orleans it will be a long siege."[43] Clergymen, too, defied the federal authority. Bishop Wilmer, a "staunch southerner," refused to instruct his Episcopalian ministers to conduct a prayer for President Lincoln after he was shot. The federal forces responded by closing all Episcopal churches in Mobile for several months.[44]

Throughout the war, Mobile—true to its traditions as a pleasure-loving city—had been a center of gaiety, alive with festive dances, parties, and sporting events. As late as the winter of 1865, a Mobile woman recorded in her diary: "Mobile is gayer than ever; it seems as if people have become reckless. . . . [N]ot a night passes but some large ball or party is given."[45] "Now it wore the aspects of the grave," with blinds drawn, streets deserted. "The place could not have donned a gloomier appearance if a plague had engulfed it," one historian remarked. Union soldiers tried to kindle patriotism with band music and military reviews, but Mobile's women shunned these affairs, and they ostracized any who accorded the Yankees the slightest hospitality.[46]

Antebellum Mobile

The mood in Mobile seemed to be more that of melancholy resignation to defeat than of proud defiance toward the conquerors. It was as though Mobilians understood that the war had brought an end to whatever hopes they had of a return to the robust prosperity the city had enjoyed earlier in the century, a time that took on the luster of a golden age as the century wore on.

Originally settled by the French, Mobile dated back to 1702. The British had nominal control of the city from 1763 to 1780, but Mobile remained an exotic mix of French, Spanish, and African cultures. The Spanish gained a foothold in Mobile in 1780, ruling until 1813, when the American expedition under General James Wilkinson wrested control for an expanding young United States. Mobile continued to bear a cosmopolitan, Latin imprint long after the Americans took over. A British visitor in 1861, struck by the architecture as well as by the people, remarked that it was "the most foreign-looking city I have yet seen in the States." "After dinner," he wrote, "we walked through the city which abounds in oyster saloons, drinking houses, lager-bier and wine shops, and gambling and dancing places. The market was . . . crowded with negroes, mulattos, quadroons, and mestizos of all sorts, Spanish, Italian, and French, speaking their own tongues, or a quaint lingua Franca, and dressed in very striking and pretty costumes."[47]

It was as an American city that Mobile emerged as a major Gulf Coast port. After the War of 1812, the rich soil of the Black Belt north of the city attracted a large migration of planters, particularly from the worn-out soil of South Carolina and other eastern states. Though it grew in the shadow of New Orleans, just 133 miles to the west, Mobile enjoyed a natural dominance over a hinterland tied to the city by a vast river system that penetrated the rich cotton-growing region known as the Black Belt. As the Black Belt filled with plantations and slaves, a rich flow of cotton coursed through Mobile. The Mobile River was formed by the confluence of the Tombigbee, which extended north through the western portion of the Black Belt into Mississippi, and the Alabama River, which meandered through the center of the Black Belt by way of Montgomery and Selma. From over 100,000 bales of cotton exported from Mobile in 1830, the volume soared to over 500,000 bales by the 1850s and hit a record high of 843,000 in 1860.[48] Mobile was, by then, second only to New Orleans as an exporter of cotton and third among all U.S. ports, behind New York and New Orleans, in value of exports. Cotton, as one Mobilian put it, was "the circulating blood that gives life to the city."[49] The bales were gathered on bluffs above the rivers and sent flying down long, covered chutes to the steamboats and barges that brought the cotton to Mobile, where it was loaded onto larger ships for the ocean voyage to the North.

The economic life of Mobile revolved around cotton and the plantations that grew it. During the fall, the wharves bulged with cotton bales, and the harbor filled with tall-masted ships. Factors, bankers, insurance agents, shippers, and longshoremen all hustled to serve King Cotton. In the spring, and throughout the year to a lesser extent, the factors, acting as commission merchants, supplied the planters with provisions for the slaves and materials for the operation of the plantation. During much of the "dull season" between planting and harvest, people fled the unbearable heat of Mobile, leaving it a summertime ghost town. In winter Mobile played the same role as Charleston, as a festive resort for planters who came to town to escape the isolation and tedium of rural life. The rhythm of urban life was set by the tempo of the plantation.

There was virtually no other enterprise in Mobile worthy of mention except for lumber, which constituted only about 1 percent of the value of exports. Those employed in manufacturing constituted a little over 2 percent of the population in 1860.[50] During the late 1840s and the 1850s, some businessmen, disturbed by Mobile's slow growth and by the growing shadow of New Orleans, promoted new enterprises in wood-product manufacturing, cotton textiles, coal mining in northern Alabama, lumber mills, shipbuilding, and new railroads. But most money and energy remained committed to cotton, the least risky path to prosperity.

Mobile's inability to diversify was often blamed on the dominance of northern men and money in the city. Far more than Charleston, Mobile's cotton trade was in the hands of New York and other "foreign" firms.[51] New York agents flocked to Mobile in the 1820s, establishing an early advantage that was difficult for natives to overcome. The city also suffered by its proximity to the giant entrepôt of the Mississippi, New Orleans. Mobile came to play the role of feeder port, shipping an estimated 35 to 50 percent of its cotton exports to the Crescent City and relying on it for supplies of western foodstuffs and imports from the North and Europe.[52] Struggling to control trade within the powerful orbit of New Orleans, a city of 175,000, Mobile, with only 29,000 people in 1860, seemed doomed to play a subservient role in the Gulf. But this was a destiny that Mobile's advocates tried valiantly to avoid.

Those who favored Mobile's industrial development and economic diversification linked their cause to southern independence, as well as to rivalry with New Orleans. A complaint in 1847 articulated themes that were to recur constantly in Mobile's view of the world as the war approached.

Our whole commerce except a small fraction is in the hands of Northern men, . . . ⅞ of our Bank Stock is owned by Northern men. . . . Half our real-estate is owned by non residents, of the same section. Our wholesale and retail business—everything in short worth mentioning is in the hands of men who invest their profits at the North. . . . [This has] deprived us of a mercantile class. . . . Financially we are more enslaved than our negroes.[53]

The most aggressive enterprises to come out of antebellum Mobile were the railroads. They were designed to enlarge the commercial hinterland beyond the rivers and counter the city's destiny as "a mere suburb and outpost of New Orleans."[54] The Mobile and Ohio Railroad, chartered in 1848, was to connect with the Ohio River almost five hundred miles to the North, in effect cutting off the river route from the Ohio Valley to the Gulf at New Orleans. Mobile promoters led the campaign to extract state and federal grants and to issue a special city tax, all in support of the new road. Mobile's magnificent rail link to the North was finally completed in 1861, just as the war obliterated any promise on the railroad's part to invigorate the city's economy.[55]

Mobile taxpayers in 1853 also supported construction of the Mobile and Girard Railroad eastward to Columbus, Georgia. Fed by fears of rivalry from Montgomery and Pensacola, the Florida port to the east, Mobile eagerly issued city bonds, bought stocks, and levied special taxes to build the road. Construction began at Columbus and failed to get anywhere near its destination before the people of Mobile rallied behind another eastern line, the Mobile and Great Northern Railroad.

Like Charleston, Mobile's commitment to railroads relied heavily on local and state government grants, rather than on private investment. As a consequence, Mobile entered the Civil War era deeply in debt to railroads that had added little, if any, prosperity to the city.[56]

Mobile at War

As the secession crisis approached, Mobile's stance, by Alabama standards at least, was tempered. Stephen Douglas, the National Democratic candidate, received the largest vote in 1860, followed by John Bell, the Unionist, who was said to be favored by the cotton factors and others in the business community who depended on trade with the North and were frequently of northern origin.[57] Mobile's commitment to southern nationalism was compromised, too, by the presence of large numbers of foreign-born residents, who constituted nearly one-quarter of the population in 1860. Throughout the war, foreigners avoided Confederate conscription and otherwise limited their commitment to the cause.[58]

With secession accomplished, the city's merchants made the most of what appeared to be a new opportunity for Mobile's commercial independence and expansion. When New Orleans fell to the Union invasion early in 1862, Mobile's importance as the major outlet for cotton from the Gulf states suddenly increased. During the war, Alabama supplied more cotton than any other southern state. Most of the ships that cut through the Union blockade around Mobile sailed to Havana, a neutral harbor, where British ships brought war materials and civilian supplies in exchange for the cotton. The Confederate government regulated all cotton exports, purchasing the crop at Mobile, selling it abroad, and channeling the profits into the Confederate treasury. Private wartime entrepreneurs operating in Mobile profited more from carrying exported cotton than from importing scarce and high-priced goods. Speculators bought up whatever scarce supplies of calico cloth, dresses, and shoes were brought in and took them into the Black Belt for sale at high profits.[59] Resentment against "alien" speculators who kept "half the city hungry" echoed the antebellum animosity toward "foreign" merchants. In some instances this feeling was aimed at Mobile's German Jewish merchants, who were reported to have enriched themselves at blockade running. After the war they and others took over palatial mansions on Government Street and became a vital force in the local economy.[60]

The sleek, fast ships made in England for the Confederate trade became the standard vessel for Mobile shippers. "Blockade running goes on very regularly at Mobile," one British observer recorded in May 1863. "[T]he steamers nearly always succeed, but the schooners are generally captured." Though Mobile's own shipbuilders had contributed to the scant Confederate fleet that guarded the harbor, by August 1864 there were only three small gunboats and a new ironclad to meet Admiral Farragut's fleet of four ironclads and fourteen other warships. Once the outer perimeter of forts was overtaken, Farragut was able to seal off the harbor and end most of the blockade running. Mobile's war-born hopes of commercial aggrandizement were now defeated. The economy suffered slow strangulation until the city fell in April 1865.[61]

The Genius of Destruction

"Every day I realize more vividly the fact that business here is utterly ruined for a long time to come," wrote James Williams to his wife after Mobile's capture. "[T]hose who were rich are poor now as myself . . . we must emigrate."[62] Mobile was loaded with cotton at war's end, but federal authorities confiscated "abandoned" bales and required the loyalty oath of all who wished to engage in trade.

What was doom to Mobile's whites was an occasion of jubilation for the freed slaves. Blacks swarmed into the liberated city from Black Belt planta-

Mobile following the explosion of the ordnance depot, May 1865. (Mrs. Carter C. Smith Collection, University of South Alabama Photographic Archives)

tions, taking up residence in makeshift shantytowns and celebrating their freedom with abandon. "Almost the entire negro population of South Alabama and a large portion of Mississippi is looking to Mobile as the *Ultima Thule* of its hopes," wrote one Mobilian in October 1865.[63] By the end of the 1860s, according the inexact measure of the 1870 census, the black population in Mobile had grown 66 percent, to nearly 14,000; the white population, at the same time, declined 13 percent, to just over 18,000.[64]

Some of these migrant blacks were hired in May 1865 by federal authorities to load powder and ammunition that had been abandoned by the Confederates and later had been brought to the main ordnance depot, located on Commerce Street in the center of Mobile's warehouse district. In the midst of this activity, something happened to set off an enormous explosion. Federal authorities suspected a Confederate booby trap—other such devices had been set by the retreating armies. White Mobilians blamed careless black laborers. None of the workers survived to defend themselves, and the latter interpretation prevailed. "The air was filled with brick and debris of every kind, flying in every direction," one witness recalled.[65] Two more explosions followed the initial blast. The smoke, according to newspaper accounts, rose from the explosion like "a writhing giant—gaunt and grim, poised in mid air. . . .

[B]ursting shells, flying timbers, bales of cotton, horses, men, women, and children co-mingled and mangled into one immense mass."[66]

The explosions blew away at least five solid blocks in the heart of the city, and a strong wind drove the fire through another five blocks, sweeping it down to the wharves, where several ships ignited. Deaths were estimated at two to three hundred and property damage at $.7 million. The federal government refused to award any compensation, and Mobile, which had survived the war in immaculate physical condition, now saw the commercial heart of the city turned into a twenty-block mass of rubble and ashes.[67] "It would seem as if the genius of Destruction was determined to strike a final blow at the city," a northern visitor mused.[68]

There was other physical damage owing to the war, of course. The harbor was still littered with the wrecks of warships, pilings, and torpedoes, and after years of neglect the channel was badly silted up. The Mobile and Ohio Railroad had been torn up, rails twisted, bridges burned, and its Mobile shops ravaged by fire.[69]

Whitelaw Reid saw Mobile in the torpor of postwar shock and depression in June 1865. He described a large military review designed to honor Chief Justice Salmon P. Chase, with whom Reid was traveling. "The Mobile men gathered about the corners, or sullenly contemplated the pageant. . . . One needed indeed to be sanguine, as he watched the scene, and especially as he studied the bearing of the inhabitants, not to think of Warsaw." White Mobilians were withdrawn but seething with anger toward the conquerors, and especially toward the black soldiers. "One had to mingle with them to find how sore they were at the degradation of being guarded by these runaway slaves of theirs," Reid wrote. "To be conquered by the Yankees was humiliating, but to have their own negroes armed and set over them they felt to be cruel and wanton insult," he added. "Their combination of rage and helplessness," he noted, "would have been ludicrous, but for its dark suggestions of the future."[70]

Mobilians were anxious to restore coercive control over blacks and return to the antebellum status quo in all ways possible. But, Reid observed, "that anybody wanted 'acceptance of the new order of things' to have wider significance, I failed to discover." Too many whites, he thought, "were listlessly awaiting events, and talking of selling their houses or lands to get bread," instead of getting on with rebuilding their city. Reid witnessed the ruins of the old order in Mobile with a mixture of condemnation and optimism: "The fresh tide of Northern enterprise will soon sweep rudely enough against these broken remnants of the *ancien regime,* and wash them under. The 'old families' seem, in many cases, exhausted of force and energy. They had enough originally to gain position; they have not enough left now to retain it; and it waits the grasping hand of the coming parvenues [*sic*]. 'New men' will soon be the order of the day, in Mobile and in many another center of Southern aristocracy."[71]

Four years later, the depressed appearance of the city struck a British visitor, who spared no feelings: "[T]he place has a wretched out-at-elbows appearance." He found Mobilians amusing themselves with frequent cockfights, a "tenth-rate theatre and a public gaming-hell [*sic*] in the main street. . . . Mobile struck me as being one of the dismallest, dirtiest, and most depressed towns I had ever seen. The stores are mean, and the streets ill-lighted and filthily dirty."[72]

The Ordeal of Reconstruction

In Mobile, as in Charleston, Reconstruction was a prolonged, traumatic experience for whites. The influx of blacks into Mobile raised their share of the population to 43 percent by 1870, providing a significant base for Republican power. Old Whigs and Democrats struggled to find common cause in a Conservative Democrat coalition but were unable to form a successful alliance until after the Constitution of 1868 enfranchised blacks and the Radical regime had gained full power. Though on the state level the Conservatives recaptured power permanently in 1874, in Mobile the Radicals continued to influence local affairs until 1879.[73]

Political reconstruction in Mobile intensified the new strains in race relations already present from the flood of black migrants, whose sudden elevation in status stirred resentment in whites quite apart from any political power blacks might exercise. In May 1867 these tensions erupted at a political rally at which Pennsylvania Republican William "Pig Iron" Kelly addressed an audience of four thousand, mostly blacks, who crowded into the center of Mobile. Whites heckled Kelly, police moved in to control them, a pistol went off, and a heavily armed mob started firing randomly, mostly into the air. The crowd broke into a panic, running through the streets. Random violence broke out between the races. In the end one white and one black were killed and twenty were wounded.[74]

Using the riot as a pretext, federal military officials suspended the city government, threw out its officials, and, in effect, imposed martial law in Mobile. General John Pope, commander of the Third Military District, declared all of Mobile's government offices vacant and promptly filled them with hand-picked loyal Republicans. The appointed mayor, Gustavus Horton, filled the police force and several city offices with blacks, provoking cries of severe humiliation from whites.[75]

During the Radical regime, Mobile, and Alabama at large, took on a multitude of new public projects, from schools to railroads. Taxes rose, new bonds were issued, and the total debt at the state and local level soared to $53 million. When the depression of 1873 came, the fiscal integrity of Mobile was in serious jeopardy.[76] The "redemption" of Mobile required the financial ruin of its government.

Mobile's debt alone grew to over $5 million, mostly from bond issues in support of the several railroad projects launched during the Radical era. In addition, the Radical city officials, after a long controversy with wharf owners, took over the wharves as city property in 1870 at a cost of $360,000, also financed by city bonds.[77] Thus, one more link in Mobile's commercial infrastructure fell into the public sector. As the long-term debt mounted with each new bond issue, current expenditures far exceeded tax receipts, which dwindled with the decline in real property values and with the inability—or, in many cases, the refusal—of Mobilians to pay their taxes. The Republican-sponsored railroads and schools were all needed, but most of these projects were sullied by corruption and, in any case, proved too much of a burden for a city in economic distress.

By 1875, in the midst of depression, the city's finances broke down completely when the interest due to bond holders could not be met. The creditors took their case to federal court and sued, forcing Mobile officials to confront bankruptcy. Early in 1879, following a prolonged legal contest, the city of Mobile, in effect, declared bankruptcy, surrendered its charter, and allowed the state to appoint a commission of three receivers to settle the debt with creditors. At the same time, the legislature created a new entity, the Port of Mobile, which would elect new commissioners to an eight-man board and run a "simple, economical and efficient form of local government."[78] The act redrew the city's boundaries, excluding some thinly settled suburban neighborhoods. Under the new regime city expenditures were slashed by more than half and taxing power was severely restricted.

The debate surrounding this drastic remedy to Mobile's debt crisis revealed an ulterior motive, which was to rid city politics of the last remnants of the Radical regime. The Conservative Democrats had regained power with the election of Alphonse Hurtel to a term as mayor from 1875 to 1877. But Radicals managed to blame the debt crisis on the Democrats and helped elect a fusion candidate, George Duffee, to a term beginning in 1878.[79] When Duffee and his followers opposed the plan to restructure Mobile, a plan championed by the business and professional leaders of Mobile, the conservative press turned the movement for debt settlement into a campaign against Radical Reconstruction. The Democratic legislature approved the bills and established the Port of Mobile, whose officials were elected by March 1879. If Reconstruction had overburdened a weakened city economy, however, Redemption also came at a

Figure 3.1 Cotton Trade in Charleston and Mobile, 1865–1910

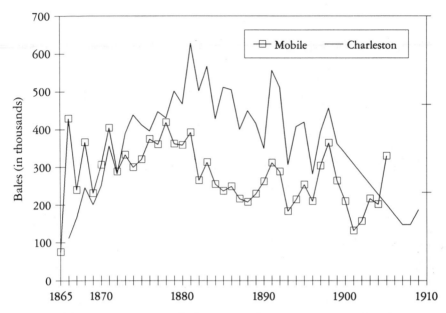

Sources: Mobile Register, Sept. 1, 1905; *Charleston News and Courier,* Sept. 11, 1899; City of Charleston, *Yearbook, 1909.*

price. Mobile now entered the New South era under a cloud of unpaid debt and a charter that guaranteed a weak city government unable to provide public services that would be desperately needed and more affordable in the years ahead.[80]

Charleston in the Backwater

Whatever damage the war and Reconstruction may have inflicted, the venerable seaports of Charleston and Mobile might have shrugged it off with aplomb had the new economic conditions of the postwar South not affected them so cruelly. Much more than Atlanta or Nashville, whose economic foundations were more diverse, these cities were appendages of the plantation economy. They lived or died by the flow of cotton, the "blood of your veins," as one Mobilian told it.[81]

Figure 3.1 shows the volatility of that blood supply for Charleston and Mobile in the decades following the war. In both cities the recovery of the cotton trade was slow and discouraging compared with the rich antebellum trade, which had comprised twice the annual number of bales handled during

Mobile's cotton warehouse district, ca. 1894. (University of South Alabama Photographic Archives)

the 1870s. Nevertheless, until about 1880 the trend was up, prices were strong, and the cotton crop across the South was increasing. During the 1880s and 1890s, though, both Charleston and Mobile suffered losses in the cotton trade, losses that were compounded by a sudden drop in prices. The reversal in the early 1880s only accelerated an earlier downward trend in the share of the total cotton crop that came to each city. The cotton market was, by this time, decentralizing, moving away from the ports and toward interior towns where new merchants, banks, and compresses were emerging to serve cotton farmers. Railroads, with their expanded and integrated networks, also had invaded the Carolina upcountry and the Alabama Black Belt, siphoning away cotton that once had flowed to the ports.

The railroads serving the ports failed to overcome the shifts in the cotton trade. In South Carolina, the Richmond and Danville system, and later the Southern Railway, dominated the railroad corridor from Atlanta through the Piedmont to Richmond, Norfolk, and points north, cutting through the hinterland that had been the unchallenged domain of the City by the Sea. The railroads set rates that encouraged shipment on their lines northward instead of east to the sea via Charleston.[82] These shifts in trade were reinforced by the

Workers drying cotton, Charleston, 1879. (Library of Congress)

growing sectional animosity toward Charleston and the low country that "Pitchfork" Ben Tillman so adroitly exploited.

Charleston's effort to rebuild and enlarge its own rail service was fraught with difficulties. The Savannah and Charleston Railroad, completed just before the war at great expense, was almost completely destroyed by Union forces during the war. Insolvent and deeply in debt to the state of South Carolina, it did not reinstate through traffic to Savannah until 1870, and then it had to rely on a rented road into the Georgia port. At the Charleston end, there were no funds to rebuild the bridge across the Ashley River, so passengers and freight had to enter the city by boat, a sore reminder of Charleston's isolation from the territory it once dominated. Edward King, an uncomfortable traveler, remarked that the only good thing about the road was the scenery. George A. Neuffer, a disgruntled employee of the company, blasted its "old fogy" management in an 1870 prizewinning essay on Charleston's economic ills. The company, Neuffer said, was riddled with cronies and relatives, so that "a man of merit and capacity had no chance." By 1874 the road went into receivership and was sold in 1880 to railroad magnate Henry B. Plant, who renamed it the Charleston and Savannah.[83]

The railroad served what had been some of the richest rice and sea-island cotton plantations in the low country. But after the war this area, along with much of Charleston's hinterland, experienced a drastic decline. In the sea islands surrounding Port Royal, federal troops had confiscated plantation lands for taxes and then distributed them to the former slaves. The new proprietors resorted largely to subsistence agriculture, thereby depriving Charleston of an important source of trade. The plantations that survived intact were, after several years of neglect, often overgrown, financially encumbered, and unable to resume operations without cheap credit and a stable labor supply. Once the mainstay of the low country economy, rice culture proved unadaptable to sharecropping and free labor, and it went into slow decline, hastened by competition from new rice-growing regions.[84]

Further inland, on a westward route to the Piedmont, the venerable South Carolina Railroad—"Old Reliable"—had been a symbol of Charleston's bold enterprise in the 1820s. It was the pioneering road to Hamburg on the Savannah River near Augusta, which was to be the first link in a grand western road to Cincinnati. This was Senator Robert Y. Hayne's magnificent—and perpetually unfulfilled—dream. After Sherman's march across South Carolina, the road lay in ruins, facing staggering losses of over $5 million from the war and a huge burden of debt. The company failed to revive and finally went into receivership in 1878. This "child of Charleston capital" passed into the hands of New York financiers in 1881. No road was more important for Charleston's overland commerce, but it remained a poorly equipped line with limited service to a declining agricultural region.[85]

Charleston commercial leaders also tried to revive the Blue Ridge Railroad, a trans-Appalachian route designed in the 1850s to fulfill the city's undying dream of a road to the West. Built largely at state expense, the Blue Ridge managed, with prodding from Charleston interests, to garner new state funds in the late 1860s. But then the project became ensnarled in Reconstruction politics, and the company was sold in 1871. It was revived briefly in 1876, but the line was never completed through the mountains before it was abandoned.[86]

The Northeastern, the third railroad serving Charleston, provided a line northward to Florence and the Peedee River section north of Charleston. Built in the 1850s with the investment of city funds, this road, along with the Cheraw and Darlington, also fell under the control of northern financiers in the 1870s.[87] Across the board, Charleston's railroad facilities and service slid to deplorable levels by the 1890s. The shabby passenger terminals belonging to each road were symbolic of the neglect Charleston endured, and repeated calls for a new union station became just one more symptom of despair.

The city also suffered from its own stubborn traditions. Since the 1830s, locomotives had been prohibited from entering the city, part of the general restrictions against steam engines that were intended as fire safety measures but also served as an obstacle to manufacturing. As a result, railroad terminal facilities were located on what was then the northern perimeter of the city, several blocks from the wharves. Freight had to be hauled by dray and reloaded at the waterfront, a costly expression of Charleston's resistance to the age of steam. In an era of growing competition and narrowing margins of profit on the cotton trade, Charleston's refusal to complete this vital link between rail and sea amounted to willful self-destruction. During the 1890s a terminal company owned jointly by the railroads assumed a long-term lease on much of the city's waterfront property. The company built a belt-line railroad along the waterfront, but Charleston businessmen complained of high rates and continued to rely on the horse-drawn drays.[88]

During the 1890s all of Charleston's railroads came under the control of large systems controlled by outside interests. The Northeastern Railroad and the adjacent Cheraw and Darlington became part of the Atlantic Coast Line system in 1898. The following year, the South Carolina road was absorbed into the Southern Railway system. Earlier the Charleston and Savannah had been taken over by the Plant system, and in 1902 the entire Plant system was merged into the Atlantic Coast Line.[89] All were north-south systems whose interests were in moving freight up and down their lines, not in making Charleston a viable terminal for east-west trade. Their freight rates favored ports north of Cape Hatteras, and their neglect of Charleston's terminal facilities guaranteed the city's commercial stagnation.[90]

While its rail connections to the interior crumbled, Charleston's lanes to the sea suffered as well. The harbor remained strewn with wreckage and fortifications for years after the war. More serious, the shipping channel was silting up to water levels of twelve feet in places. A chronic problem since antebellum times, the depth of the channel became critical in the age of deep-draft steamers. After the war, Charleston's business leaders began a long and often frustrating campaign to extract federal funds for deepening the harbor through a program of dredging and construction of large stone jetties that would funnel the outgoing tide and scour the channel deeper. Charleston, the cradle of secession, was thus at the mercy of political powers in Washington. The allotments came in parcels, sometimes uselessly small, and it was not until the 1890s that the jetties were complete. The harbor now could accept ships with twenty-three-foot drafts and was soon deepened to thirty feet. Federal intervention, in the end, emancipated Charleston's maritime commerce.[91]

As though fire, war, political hostility, and transportation problems were not enough to stymie Charleston, nature struck a blow as destructive as any dealt by Union cannon or by Governor Tillman. In 1885 the city's waterfront was torn apart by a furious hurricane, leaving $1.5 million in losses. The following year a severe earthquake shook the city into a state of ruin that was all too reminiscent of the scenes of 1865. Across the peninsula, buildings were cracked or altogether reduced to rubble. Estimates of $5 million in damages were considered conservative. During the prolonged aftershocks, thousands of citizens abandoned their homes to mass in a huge camp on the Citadel green. There, black preachers proclaimed that the day of judgment had come, and to many Charlestonians that was no exaggeration. The earthquake seemed to summarize Charleston's victimization by forces beyond local control. The charity that came pouring in from the North and Europe after the quake expressed sympathy toward a city—once so arrogant—now humbled and defenseless.[92]

Mobile at Low Tide

Mobile confronted many of the same obstacles as Charleston in adjusting to the new order. It was wholly dependent on the plantation economy, which was in the throes of adjusting to free labor conditions. Moreover, Mobile and its once unchallenged river system now faced stiff competition from new merchants in the interior and from railroads invading the Black Belt from the north to meet the river headwaters at Montgomery and Selma.[93]

The railroads serving Mobile seemed only to benefit rivals. The Mobile and Ohio (M&O) had been ravaged during the war and limped along with poorly maintained roads and equipment before it fell into receivership in 1874. Though it remained under local control, the M&O was the target of constant criticism in Mobile. Its rigid rules and high rates were accused of stifling the trade with planters, ruining Mobile's grocery trade with the interior, and diverting cotton to Memphis. After the war a new road between New Orleans and Mobile met with fierce opposition in Mobile, where merchants denounced

Mobile, the Gulf City, drawn by J. O. Davidson (from *Harper's Weekly,* 1884; courtesy of University of South Alabama Photographic Archives)

it as a suicidal venture that would guarantee subservience to the neighboring metropolis. The city threw up numerous legal obstacles to the road, but this link was completed in 1870. As predicted, it came to operate as a siphon, diverting trade to the neighboring colossus.[94]

But Mobile's strategy for survival also took an aggressive posture that made liberal use of the public sector to launch a counteroffensive against economic decline. Citizens applauded the Mobile and Alabama Grand Trunk, a proposed new railroad that would enter the northern Alabama mineral district. It would turn Mobile into a major coal port and, its promoters argued, at last put an end to the city's exclusive dependence on the cotton trade. After years of delay following the line's incorporation in 1866, construction began in 1870, funded by $.8 million in state and private funds and a $1.5 million bond issued by the city of Mobile. Less than 60 of the 270 projected miles in the line had been completed before the panic of 1873 struck. The company defaulted on its payment in 1874, and the project was suspended. Five years later, the city collapsed in bankruptcy from the burden of this and other debts.[95]

The Mobile and Montgomery, a consolidation of two roads that had been launched in antebellum times, also received state support in 1870 and was completed in 1872. But it remained a financially weak railroad that was little more than a "decrepit sliver of rust" before the Louisville and Nashville (L&N) took it over in 1881. In extending its domain to the Gulf, the L&N was following a strategy that fell hard on Mobile. It developed a road to Pensacola, a rival port to the east. Then, in order to avoid competition from the M&O at Mobile, the L&N took over the Mobile-New Orleans road and began routing cotton through Mobile to its giant rival on the west. Mobile had become a way station for traffic to New Orleans, just as earlier critics of the road had predicted.[96]

Another railroad project, the Mobile and Northwestern, was launched with much fanfare in 1871 and was projected to cross the Mississippi River at Helena, Arkansas, en route to Little Rock. Again, the city boldly put up $150,000 in bonds, and the states of Mississippi and Alabama joined in support. But the road was not yet completed when it failed in 1886.[97]

These railroad projects all stemmed from the premise that Mobile could no longer depend on the natural advantages its river system afforded and must compete with New Orleans and other rivals by extending railroads into a new hinterland. That these projects became identified, for the most part, with the era of Radical rule discredited this strategy and, with it, the whole idea that Mobile could decide its destiny.

Mobile's maritime commerce also met serious obstacles that remained unsolved until the 1890s. At the end of the war, the harbor's main channel, which had been cleared to ten feet in the 1850s, after years of neglect and warfare had silted up to only five and one-half feet at the Choctaw Pass. Large ships had to dock at Dauphin Island outside the bay and have their freight lightered (transported by small "lighter" boats) up to Mobile's wharves, thirty miles away. The added costs and hazards meant that, in competition with railroads or with New Orleans and Pensacola, Mobile was doomed as a seaport. County bond funds went some way toward removing war wreckage in the harbor beginning in 1869, but no permanent harbor improvements were carried out. County funding ceased in 1873 in the face of a massive debt incurred during the Reconstruction era.

Throughout most of the postwar era, Mobile stood in line with every other ocean and river port in America for federal river and harbor appropriations, all subject to political influence. A series of federal projects did deepen Mobile's shipping channel, first to thirteen feet and eventually to twenty-seven feet. Few rebel cities, save Charleston, owed more to federal favors; by 1915 a total of $7.4 million had been expended on Mobile's harbor.[98]

Mobile also pressed Congress for river improvement projects to construct locks, dams, and channels on the Tombigbee-Alabama system that would enable her to extend navigation up the Warrior River to the Alabama mineral district. Her merchants and politicians led the campaign to stage conventions and rally support for federal expenditures to improve Alabama's rivers. The result was a liberal flow of funds from Washington, D.C., and a system of newly channeled and dammed rivers that kept Mobile alive in the age of the railroad.[99]

Finance and Industry

The troubles afflicting commerce and transportation were reflected also in the financial weakness of Charleston and Mobile after the war. Charleston's role as a banking center for South Carolina was shattered in 1865. In 1860 Charleston banks had controlled about $13 million of the state's $15 million in banking capital. By the end of the war, Charleston could claim no more than $.4 million, and that was money from New York invested in two recently chartered national banks. The rest was in worthless Confederate money. By 1872 Charleston's aggregate banking capital had climbed slowly to $2.9 million in seven banks; in addition, four savings banks had assets of $1.2 million.[100] But even these modest gains were set back during the depression following 1873, and the capital invested in Charleston's banks dropped back to a little over $2 million in 1880. Over the next two decades, this declined further to $1.6 million, though deposits and total resources climbed slowly. Charleston's near monopoly on banking services in South Carolina was at an end, in any case, as new banks cropped up in the interior to serve the now-decentralized cotton market. At the same time, an immeasurable amount of Charleston investment capital drained out of the city, to upcountry cotton-mill towns or to the rising cities of the interior.[101]

The panic of 1873 dealt Mobile's weakened economy a sharp and lasting blow. The city's banking capital, small before the war, had slowly rebuilt to $1.8 million in three banks by 1870, with another $.2 million in several new insurance companies. By 1875 banking capital barely exceeded $1.75 million, and by 1880 it had declined further, to a little over $1 million. While most of the South recovered from the panic by the late 1870s, Mobile sank deeper into what came to be known locally as the "seven years' depression," beginning in 1878. The final blow came in 1884 with the collapse of the Bank of Mobile. By the turn of the century the capital invested in Mobile's banks had slipped to $.8 million.[102]

As the fortunes of these old seaports ebbed in the postwar South, each tried to develop new enterprises to offset losses in cotton and other commercial lines. Charleston's salvation in this period was the discovery of phosphates, the main ingredient for modern fertilizers, which came into high demand with the expansion of cotton production. It seemed fitting that this "ancient city" would find in the remains of prehistoric beasts, which lay beneath the plantation lands and the rivers, the fuel for a minor economic boom in the New South era.

Table 3.1 Manufacturing Statistics, Charleston and Mobile, 1880 and 1900

	Charleston		Mobile	
	1880	1900	1880	1900
Number of manufacturing establishments	194	364	91	222
Capital invested (millions)	$1.7	$12.5	$.5	$3.3
Capital invested per establishment (thousands)	$8.9	$34.3	$5.8	$14.8
Employees (thousands)	2.1	5.0	.7	2.8
Employees per establishment	11.0	13.8	7.7	12.7
Value of product (millions)	$2.7	$9.6	$1.3	$4.5

Source: U.S. Census Bureau, *Twelfth Census of the United States, 1900, Manufacturers*, pt. 2 (Washington, D.C. 1902), table 2.

Failing initially to draw local investors into phosphate mining, the scientists who discovered the phosphates invited Philadelphia capitalists in to pioneer the industry. Most of the area's planters took their profits as passive rentiers, allowing others to mine and manufacture the phosphates. Several Charleston entrepreneurs and capitalists, by contrast, actively entered into phosphate mining and fertilizer manufacturing. Robert Adger's Coosaw Mining Company, capitalized and managed entirely by Charlestonians, was the leading river-mining operation and a source of enormous profit to its stockholders. Discoveries of richer deposits in Florida and Middle Tennessee in the 1890s, among other factors, brought an abrupt end to phosphate mining in South Carolina, but Charleston remained a leading center for the manufacture of fertilizers. The Virginia-Carolina Company, the southern wing of the fertilizer trust, bought out the Charleston companies in 1902, releasing a surge of fresh capital into the local economy. Fertilizer manufacturing remained a major force in the industrial complex that began to form on the Charleston Neck.[103]

Table 3.1 indicates a substantial expansion in Charleston's manufacturing enterprises between 1880 and 1900, particularly when measured by the capital invested and the value of product. Most of these firms were engaged in a diversity of small-scale handicraft manufacturing, but fertilizers, lumber, naval stores, and paper manufacturing were all produced by large factories that came to absorb a growing number of Charleston workers. The occupational distributions depicted in tables 3.2 and 3.3 show only minor shifts in the allocation of Charleston's work force. With 25 percent of her workers engaged in manufacturing, as broadly defined by the census at this time, Charleston was in line with Atlanta and Nashville.

Table 3.2 Occupational Distributions, Charleston and Mobile, 1870

	Charleston	Mobile
	1870	1870
Agriculture	2%	1%
Manufacturing	26	17
Trade, transportation	19	24
Professional, personal service	53	58
Total	100	100
N =	(18,705)	(12,186)

Source: U.S. Census Bureau, *A Compendium of the Ninth Census* (Washington, D.C., 1872), table 66.

Mobile did not develop as strong a manufacturing sector as Charleston, but it did manage to diversify its economy in the postwar years. The leading enterprise outside the cotton trade was the lumber and timber industry. Albert C. Danner, one of postwar Mobile's "new men," pioneered in lumber manufacturing and in the export of lumber and coal. Others followed his example in exporting lumber and timber to the north and to the West Indies. Mobile also took the lead in the fruit-importing business after opening the banana trade with Central America in the 1890s. United Fruit later designated Mobile as its primary port and became a major source of employment on Mobile's water-

Table 3.3 Occupational Distributions, Charleston and Mobile, 1900

	Charleston			Mobile		
	Male	Female	All	Male	Female	All
Agriculture	2%	4%	3%	3%	0%	2%
Domestic and Personal service	29	66	43	29	80	46
Manufacturing	29	19	25	25	10	20
Professional	4	5	4	4	4	4
Trade, transportation	36	6	25	39	5	28
Total	100	100	100	100	99	100
N =	(15,578)	(9,250)	(24,828)	(11,893)	(5,948)	(17,841)

Source: U.S. Census Bureau, *Twelfth Census of the United States, 1900, Population,* pt. 2 (Washington, D.C., 1902), table 94.

A view of Mobile, 1891. (University of South Alabama Photographic Archives)

Mobile's Government Street, looking west, 1895. (T. E. Armistead/Museum of the City of Mobile Collection, University of South Alabama Photographic Archives)

front. With the fruit trade, Mobile's imports began for the first time to grow in relation to its exports.[104]

By the end of the nineteenth century, both Charleston and Mobile were surrounded by extensive truck-farming operations, which took advantage of the long growing season to produce fresh vegetables that were shipped by sea or rail to northern cities. Mobile also developed a thriving oyster business that supplied a national market with one of its most abundant products.

Though none of these new enterprises alone broke the pattern of stagnation that followed the war, by the turn of the century both of these seaports experienced modest economic revivals. Federal aid to harbors and rivers and, in Charleston, the arrival of a large Navy shipyard, had a major impact on lagging maritime commerce. The Spanish-American War and the expansion of a new American empire also gave new life to these strategic points on the Atlantic and Gulf coasts. More favorable railroad policies and new terminal facilities at the same time reduced some of the disadvantages the old ports had suffered in overland commerce. An influx of new investment capital from outside private sources also enlivened the two cities. The introduction of new urban services, particularly a reliable and sanitary water supply, was another important prerequisite for growth in Charleston and Mobile. No less impor-

Mobile's lumber industry, ca. 1913. (Erik Overbey/Mobile Public Library Collection, University of South Alabama Photographic Archives)

tant was the ascendance of a fresh generation of business and civic leaders who emerged beginning in the late 1890s. They were generally younger men who brought new energy and organizational skills to meet the opportunities that now opened in each city.

The patterns of population growth in Charleston and Mobile (see fig. 2.1 above) provide a good measure of the ebb and flow of local economic fortunes. Charleston's halting growth was a symptom of chronic decay in its economic foundations, evident since the early part of the nineteenth century. From a city of more than forty thousand inhabitants before the war—second only to New Orleans within the Confederacy—Charleston managed to gain only another ten thousand by 1880 and dropped down one place in the rankings, yielding to Richmond. During the next thirty years, the city gained population even more slowly and slid ten notches in the South's urban hierarchy. The revival that began in the late 1890s did little to lift Charleston's rather flat growth line. Much of the economic development that came with the Navy yard and new

Mobile's banana import industry. (Erik Overbey/Mobile Public Library Collection, University of South Alabama Photographic Archives)

industrial activities brought new population to the Neck, which was not included in the city of Charleston's boundaries.[105]

Mobile's pattern of growth was more erratic. From a city of over 29,000, ranked fourth among southern cities in 1860, Mobile actually had 126 fewer residents in 1880 and had slipped to eighth place. Some population loss resulted from boundary constrictions in 1879, but even discounting the suburban areas, Mobile's population declined in the 1870s.[106] The city's growth picked up again after 1885 and showed a strong upward trend in the revival that followed the depression of the 1890s. Even so, by 1910 Mobile's population was still under 52,000, and the city had dropped another seven places among southern cities, leaving it ranked fifteenth.

Mobile and Charleston each faced the New South defeated and demoralized. Emancipation and Reconstruction traumatized the economic, social, and political systems that had so long served the cities' merchants and planters. The same forces that allowed Atlanta and Nashville to gain strength from a reorganized South worked consistently against these old seaports. The new railroad system favored the interior cities because they provided more direct trade routes to and from the Northeast and Midwest. Cotton factors watched their trade wither in competition with the new country merchants and cotton brokers who invaded the interior. The youth, talent, capital, and publicity that favored rising cities like Atlanta and Nashville shunned the declining seaports, adding to the difficulties of reversing the decline and challenging the old customs that were out of step with the New South. It would take, as Whitelaw Reid had predicted in Mobile, the "grasping hand" of "new men" to turn the tide in these old seaports.

4   *New Men*

*This is a new era. Its necessities and opportunities call for
new men, young men with a future, not dead men with a
miasmatic smell of dead issues clinging to their garments.*
—Nashville Banner, *1872*

*Atlanta is full of these self-made men. They enrich her
blood, quicken her pulse and give her vitality. . . . They
have won fame and fortune by no accident of inheritance. . . . They have sunk the corner-stones of the only
aristocracy that Americans should know. . . .*
—Henry Grady, *1880*

The new order of things that followed the war and Reconstruction magnified
the role of an urban business class within the South. To be sure, this class had
antecedents in the antebellum towns and cities. But its incarnation in the New
South era was far more imposing in scale, in geographic breadth, and in
ideological vigor. The New South movement that gathered full power in the
1880s was the product of this ascendant business class of merchants, financiers,
and industrialists and their allies, particularly those in the press. Through this
program, business leaders proposed an agenda for economic development and
social uplift that cast them in preeminent roles as architects of the new order.[1]
As such they held up their factories and railroads, their cities, and, above all,
their own lives as models for the South to emulate.

For all the peculiar features of southern history, the formation of its business
class can be told in the familiar American parable of country boys who rose to
become merchant princes. The urbanization of Dixie was the result of thousands of young people's decision to leave the countryside in a calculated risk to
seek their main chance in the cities, to pursue new jobs and new urban ways of
living. Though most began and finished their lives as wage-earning laborers,
many others entered a broad middle class of merchants, financiers, manufacturers, and professionals. From this element, a few emerged to build great
fortunes and take their places as leaders of business and civic affairs within
their cities. "We find a new race of rich people have been gradually springing
up among us, who owe their wealth to successful trade and especially to
manufactures," a Richmond editor observed in 1876. They "are taking the
leading place not only in our political and financial affairs, but are pressing to
the front for social recognition."[2]

It was these men of the ascendant business class who led in building the
cities of the New South. In turn, the rising cities molded the southern business

class that took form in the late nineteenth century. To understand the social origins and nature of that business class—and the communities in which they formed—requires exploring many small stories of individual lives in order to illuminate the larger social forces of which they were part.

The recruitment of a city's business leaders was the product both of impersonal market forces that rewarded successful entrepreneurs with wealth, and of a social selection that appointed them to prestigious positions of authority as officers and board members of the community's leading economic institutions. Granted that men of wealth could wield enormous power outside the board rooms as individuals, but it was the formal designation of leadership through election to offices and boards that signaled the conferral of status and power by the community, or at least by peers in the business elite. So it is these officers and directors of the major financial institutions, corporations, and commercial associations, selected from the city directories for 1880, that here provide a select sample of the urban business class.[3] Their lives offer points of view into the nature of both the southern business class and the communities in which its members arose.

Natives and Newcomers

It was commonplace in New South rhetoric to speak of the movement's leaders as young men who had come of age since the war. The sectional crisis, so it was said, had been of their fathers' making, the result of political fanaticism inherent in the old order. The innocent sons, free of Old South sectional dogma, were now building a New South on wholly different principles.[4] Its proponents celebrated a class of "new men" who came of age after the war with a fresh vision of economic and social progress for their region. They were young, enterprising, self-made men, cut from different cloth than the "old regulation" southern planter. "Everywhere trade and manufacturing is almost entirely in the hands of men who are sprung from the non-planter class, and . . . the professions seem to be going the same way," one enthusiastic witness to the rising middle class exclaimed.[5] Atlanta's leaders, the *Atlanta Constitution* claimed in 1887, "never knew the Old South, and they care not a button what has been said for and against her." The "wonderful growth of Atlanta," the *Constitution* reported in 1890, is due to its "push and pluck and enterprise," and to "the young men in the lead."[6] "There is nothing of the Old South about it," Alexander McClure said of Atlanta,

> and all the traditions of the old-time South, which are made poetical to
> dignify effete pride and logical poverty, have no place in the men of the
> present in the young and thriving Gate City. There must be old regulation
> Southerners in this region, but they have either died untimely in despair, or

they have drifted into the current and moved on with the world around them. The young men are not the dawdling, pale-faced, soft-handed effeminates which were so often visible in the nurslings of the slave. They have keen, expressive eyes; their faces are bronzed; their hands are often the tell-tales of labor; their step is elastic and their habits are energetic.[7]

In fact, remarkably few of Atlanta and Nashville's leading men in 1880 had come of age since the Civil War. The average birth date of these new men was 1827 in Atlanta and 1826 in Nashville, making them a mature fifty-three and fifty-four years of age at the opening of the 1880s (see table 4.1). As the decade moved on, more young men were recruited into the Atlanta elite, but they joined rather than replaced the 1880 group. Only a few had not passed their mid-teens before the Civil War was over. So most of these leading men of 1880 were not innocent of the sectional animosity that had torn the nation apart. It was their generation's war, not their fathers'.[8]

But not many of Atlanta's and Nashville's leading men actually fought in the war, and their sympathies, though usually described as being "pro-southern," were compromised by strong pro-Union sentiments and publicly expressed doubts about the wisdom of secession. Only twelve among Atlanta's elite and nine among Nashville's could be identified as having served in the Confederate army; another two in Atlanta and one in Nashville served on the Union side. While the biographical accounts of many noncombatants testified to their Confederate loyalties, just as many were silent on the issue, reporting only that they had continued in business during the war, or fled to New York City in a few cases. Many (26 percent in Atlanta and 31 percent in Nashville) were over forty when the war broke out and may have considered themselves too old to serve in uniform. Even among those whose sympathies were clearly aligned with the Confederacy, their biographies often alluded to their early opposition to secession, usually stemming from their Whig-Unionist persuasion. It was only after Fort Sumter and Lincoln's call to arms that these men took their stand.

Table 4.1 Ages of Business Elites, 1880

	Atlanta	Nashville	Charleston	Mobile
Average age	53	54	57	52
Standard deviation	11.06	13.23	10.20	12.28
Percentage over 60	26	34	37	36
Percentage under 40	10	20	5	18
N =	(42)	(35)	(59)	(55)

Sources: City directories and miscellaneous biographical sources. See sources for the collective biographies in chapters 3 and 4.

Note: The standard deviation is defined as the average variance from the mean.

A surprisingly large number had arrived in Atlanta and Nashville before the war broke out. Among all the men included in the initial pool of business leaders in 1880, about 57 percent in Nashville and 26 percent in Atlanta were listed in city directories in 1860. Among the more select business elite, biographical details on the date of their arrival in their city frequently contradicted my own rough estimate of their arrival date, based on city directories. Over 70 percent of Nashville's 1880 economic elite had roots in antebellum Nashville. Even in Atlanta, where everything was said to have sprung anew from the ashes of Sherman's army, 38 percent of the 1880 elite had arrived before 1861. Nashville's business elite in 1880 had an average of thirty-one years of experience in the city. In Atlanta, a younger city with a recent population boom, the elite of 1880 had been in the city an average of fifteen years. Many were new men on the rise, but not all were new to their city.

In Atlanta it was the newcomers, those who had arrived since 1865, who had ascended with their fast-growing city to occupy a larger share of the economic elite. Such men, the *Constitution* wrote in 1877, were "representative of the later and better Atlanta—the solid, respectable, prosperous, rich Atlanta, that succeeded the . . . chaotic, reckless city that was built upon the ashes that were sprinkled from the torches of Sherman's bummers."[9] Nonetheless, both cities contained a seasoned corps of business leaders who were well established in their cities before the war.

Whatever their age or length of residence, the economic leaders of both cities were men who, with few exceptions, had been born in modest circumstances in the rural South, had migrated into the cities in their youth, and had built their own fortunes there. They were indeed new men in the sense that they had climbed into positions of wealth and power in their own lifetimes. Several of the life sketches below illustrate this theme better than statistics can summarize.

The elites of both cities had their origins outside the local community (see table 4.2). It may not be surprising that none of Atlanta's 1880 leaders had been born in the city. The city was still too young in 1880 to have spawned a native business elite. "It is a known fact," an admiring Nashville editor said of Atlanta, "that the successful and live progressive men of a community as a rule are not natives of the place but comparative new comers [*sic*]."[10] But even in the older settlement of Nashville, only about one in eight of these leaders were natives of the city. On the other hand, only a minority in each city came from outside the South. Both cities included in their economic elite some who were born in foreign countries, most often Ireland, Germany, or England. In Atlanta these foreign-born claimed 12 percent, and in Nashville 17 percent, of the elite, a substantial presence given the small proportion of foreigners in the general population of each city (7 percent in Nashville and 4 percent in Atlanta in 1880).[11]

Table 4.2 Birthplace of 1880 Business Elites

	Atlanta	Nashville	Charleston	Mobile
City	0%	11%	57%	14%
State	33	45	10	16
South	31	22	10	30
North	24	6	0	21
Foreign country	12	17	24	19
Total	100	101	101	100
N =	(42)	(36)	(42)	(43)

Sources: See table 4.1.

Note: Totals do not always equal 100 percent due to rounding. Those elites whose birthplaces are unknown have been omitted.

Northern-born migrants also found a prominent place in these cities. Nashville's business elite included only two northerners in 1880, surely an underrepresentation of the many who lived and prospered in the city. In Atlanta, though, nearly one in four members of the elite hailed from the North, most of them from New England.[12] This was a strong showing from a group that represented a much smaller fraction of the general population in 1880. It was this "infusion of Yankee blood" that was so often credited as the source of Atlanta's extraordinary enterprise. Many came to Atlanta with specialized skills, in railroad management and engineering, for example, while others imported more general entrepreneurial knowledge and talent not readily available in the surrounding hinterland. But it was as models of enterprise, rather than as sole suppliers of entrepreneurial energy, that Yankees had their impact. Atlanta's business leaders included enough indigenous southern entrepreneurs to indicate that the city was not solely reliant on immigrant talents.

The Yankee presence in Atlanta was no less important for what it revealed of the cordial reception extended to outsiders, a result of the city's self-conscious campaign to eradicate any vestige of sectionalism in its midst by warmly welcoming northern people, and especially northern money. This was precisely what Henry Grady alluded to when he said the New South had learned to place business above politics. The effort to appease and eradicate sectional animosity was a major theme of the New South movement, and Atlanta provided a practical demonstration of its benefits. Grady's *Atlanta Constitution* made its editorial columns a welcome mat for Yankees. "Strangers no longer fear that they will encounter unpleasant prejudices," the editor wrote in 1887. "Sectional and political feeling is not likely to make itself heard when people are busy stuffing their pockets with dollars."[13]

The main source of leadership for both these cities came neither from the North nor from abroad, but from within the South. Nearly two out of three Atlanta business elites in 1880 had been born in the South. More than three in four of Nashville's were from native soil. Their biographical sketches and obituaries reveal that most of these men had migrated to the cities from farms and small towns within the trading region of each city: Middle Tennessee and southern Kentucky for Nashville, northern Georgia and East Tennessee for Atlanta. They came from rural areas and small towns, often on the new rail lines that penetrated the hinterland and pulled southern rural people, along with their farm products, into the cities.

"Who Built Atlanta?" the headlines of an 1887 article asked. "Georgia Crackers and Not Northern Men Did It," was the defiant answer. Editor Henry Grady wanted to dispel the notion, so often invoked to explain Atlanta, that "the North has a monopoly of enterprise and energy, [and] the wonderful progress made by the South is ascribed to the importation of these qualities." "From every community and country cross-roads in Georgia came the men who made Atlanta, as veins in the human body lead back to the human heart. Of all cities, this is preeminently the home of the 'crackers'—built by his energy and dominated by his ideas." The leading men in all lines of business, Grady showed, were southern and Georgia-born, or had been in Atlanta for thirty years or more. "Atlanta was built by southern energy and southern money and southern brains and pluck. . . . A city of the 'crackers,' by the 'crackers,' and for the 'crackers.' "[14]

Nashville, in more subdued fashion, also pointed to its rural hinterland as an important source of business leadership. An 1891 article on the upper Cumberland region, for example, listed several prominent citizens who had begun life in the hills, part of "a large number of men who have attained great prominence in Nashville's commercial and financial circles."[15] Like humble birth, coming to the city from the near or distant rural hinterland, or even from outside the region, was acclaimed in both Atlanta and Nashville as a proud mark among those who saw the city as a stairway of opportunity for the ambitious. In both settings, this celebration of migrant upstarts demonstrated that descendants of established local families had no inherited advantages—the city was open to talent.

Self-made Men

Few of the New South urban leaders were sons of the slaveholding planter elite who commanded so much of the wealth and power in the Old South. Atlanta's John D. Cunningham, Joel Hurt, Samuel Inman, and Robert F. Maddox were alone in describing their fathers as "wealthy" or "enterprising" planters. Most of the others referred to their fathers as farmers, often with no hint as to how prosperous they were or whether they had owned slaves. Frequently the biographical accounts made it clear that these men were the sons of "small farmers" of "limited means," or owners of "a poor farm." With few exceptions, the men who led the New South in Atlanta and Nashville were not transplanted from the planter class that had held sway in the Old South.

Though the majority came from agrarian backgrounds, roughly a third of the southern-born 1880 elite in Atlanta and Nashville were descended from the small antebellum middle class of merchants, lawyers, physicians, school-teachers, and clergy. They grew up in or near country towns, typically small outposts in the hinterlands of Atlanta and Nashville.

Whatever position and wealth the fathers may have claimed in the southern social order, the biographical sketches of these urban business leaders demonstrate a recurring theme of childhood poverty, often following a sudden decline in family fortunes due to financial panic, war, or emancipation. More frequent still was the incidence of a father's early death, which left the boy—often the first-born son—to begin the "struggle of life" prematurely. Others left home while still in their middle teens to make their way in the city or in a surrounding town that served as a stepping-stone to the city.

Their biographical sketches probably exaggerated the hardships of youth and the struggle for social advancement. That device was typical in the self-congratulatory, often highly sentimental life stories of American men of wealth in the nineteenth century. It helped justify wealth as the fruit of virtue, hard work, and suffering. If these accounts stretched the point a bit, however, in doing so they revealed the great admiration in which these men and their peers held the "self-made men" of the nineteenth century, men who owed little to the privileges of birth and everything to their own hard-won achievements.

Henry Grady's lengthy tribute to the "sturdy genius" of Atlanta's "self-made men, whose grit has made them" was typical. It included a series of Horatio Alger–like sketches that traced the city's wealthy merchants in their rise from poverty. C. W. Hunnicutt, a wealthy merchant who "came to Atlanta in yellow copperas breeches, barefooted and topped with a wool hat." Ben Crane, a "foot-sore" Confederate veteran, "was so poor that he could not buy a new coat, but wore his old confederate [*sic*] grey" and camped with his partners outside Atlanta, where they would later build a fortune. Similar anecdotes were told of the Kiser brothers, ("poor boys with little education"), Anthony Murphy (a "sagacious capitalist" who "started life as a penniless boy"), E. P. Chamberlin (a "penniless boy from New York"), Frank Rice (who began as a newsboy in Atlanta), and several others who, by 1880, stood among "the self-made men of Atlanta, exemplars to their fellows."[16]

These ideals were elaborated in contemporary accounts of carefully calculated upward mobility, linked always to such personal virtues as industry, thrift, and temperance. The biographical sketch of Nashville railroad and banking tycoon Edmund W. "King" Cole, published in the back of the city's 1890 history, traced Cole's ancestry to Giles County, Tennessee, where he was born in 1827. "His father died when he was three months old, leaving his mother with six sons and three daughters and extremely limited means." Young Cole worked on his widowed mother's farm until he was eighteen and then set off for Nashville in 1845. "Without any acquaintances in the city, he had to rely on his own resources." He began, as most aspiring businessmen in the nineteenth century did, as a clerk. His work soon attracted other offers with higher salaries. "By close application to business and the interests of his employers he advanced rapidly in position and salary . . . all the time utilizing every spare hour in educating himself for the important and responsible positions he was destined to fill in life."[17]

Atlanta's William A. Moore told a similar story of youthful suffering and humility as a prelude to his rise to fortune. Born in Kingston in eastern Tennessee in 1819, "while yet a boy Mr. Moore was left an orphan and he, with the aid of his brother, was compelled to support the younger children. This was the severe school in which he was taught frugality, patience and perseverance and developed the noble traits of manhood." At age sixteen, he "accepted a humble position" and began his upward climb.[18]

Even the biographical accounts of those children of privileged families, whose path to wealth and position was more assured, played down the advantages and often emphasized early setbacks. Thus Atlanta's Joel Hurt, son of an Alabama planter, at age fifteen saw the family's fortune in slaves and Confederate bonds "swept away" in 1865. "By these reverses young Hurt was confronted at this early period in life by a condition of affairs which made it necessary for him to earn the means to continue his education. But he was self-reliant, and determined."[19]

We need not accept all of the sentimental rhetoric employed by these Victorian writers to embellish the life stories of prominent citizens in order to grasp the moral code these accounts were intended to illustrate. These biographies linked success to personal virtue and explained virtue as coming from an arduous struggle against adversity in youth, as well from pious influences in childhood. The frequent references to fatherless youths who entered the "race of life" alone and "friendless" underscore the central lessons: one's place in the social rankings of Atlanta or Nashville was truly "self-made," and the men at the top were morally worthy of their positions. The social hierarchy was thereby justified as the logical expression of diverse talent and industry. In the end, these life stories were intended not only to pay homage to individual virtues, but also to celebrate the willingness of Atlanta and Nashville to reward men of ambition and talent, regardless of their backgrounds.

Atlanta's publicists seemed aware of the contrast their city presented when compared to the South's old order. An 1879 editorial tweaked jealous merchants in rival cities who resented the pushy Atlanta drummers invading their areas. "We may not have any better merchants than other cities, but they are live, energetic men. They have no long line of ancestry with coat-of-arms to keep up. . . . They live to drive their business." The editor went on to describe the Atlanta work ethic and, at the same time, ridicule the sloth and arrogance of counterparts in other cities:

> Many of our leading merchants come to their daily labors at 7 A.M. They continue it all day with a short intermission at noon for dinner and sometimes after dark they are at their business. Of course these men can sell goods cheaper than merchants who come to their business at 10 A.M. in a fine carriage, smoking an elegant Havana cigar; who lounge around their counting-room . . . just as if they held a lucrative office by appointment for life, and did not have to depend on their customers for their trade; who go home about four in the evening in the same carriage, and spend the balance of the day at dinner, where they entertain a fashionable visitor on the fat of the land and a full description of the age of their city, and the pure blood of their ancestors; spiced, as it always is, with "d——n Atlanta"; "turn a dollar loose on Whitehall street and every man is after it." "The d——d fellows . . . don't know how to dress genteelly"—"never wear glove, sir." "They are crackers, sir, crackers—Georgia crackers."[20]

As exemplars of individual morality and of the openness of the new order, the economic elite were held up as models for the entire community. Accordingly, the language of their biographies and obituaries often lapsed into the style of "advice to young men." The local press staged interviews with rich men, who offered homely platitudes on how to get ahead, while the reporters lost no chance to join their adulation of individual success to a celebration of the community's favorable climate of opportunity. Newspapers proudly advertised the wealth of the newly rich with lists of the leading property holders and probing articles on the cities' richest families. Typically, Atlanta was more brazen in boasting of its nouveaux riches and more crass in publicizing their wealth. An 1889 article, entitled "With Our Millionairs [*sic*]: Atlantans Who Have Grown Rich since the War," offered a local version of the national listings that appeared toward the end of the Gilded Age as a means of identifying the new plutocracy.[21] It included a list of thirty-five men ranked by estimated wealth, with comments on how they had built their fortunes. "Almost one by one—from poverty to plenty—from cottages up to mansions—from weary struggling into tranquil competence." "These fortunes," the article continued, "have been scraped out of the postbellum poverty and ashes." "Read and Heed Young Man, If You Want to Succeed," was the headline of a two-part article in the *Constitution* that drew together the advice of Atlanta's wealthy men "who from barefoot boys, have become merchant princes."[22]

Even in the more sedate atmosphere of Nashville, the press delighted in listing the names and property values of the rich. Reporters applauded the grand new homes the parvenus were building to display their wealth and, in the process, advertise the riches their city offered.[23] In both cities, the celebration of the self-made men who had risen to positions of great wealth and influence expressed a more general conviction that this was truly a New South, under construction by new men.

Pious Stewards

In their religious affiliations and beliefs, the business elite often exhibited a spiritual complement to the strains of self-improvement and social uplift that ran through so many of their personal biographies and their programs for regional progress. If the rich men of Atlanta and Nashville were lionized for their worldly successes, they were no less praised for their character and religious piety. In most of their biographical accounts, it seemed that personal virtue, more than business skill, was interpreted as the key to success. Only a few kept their distance from organized religion or at least made no mention of their religious affiliations.[24]

Among those in Atlanta and Nashville whose religion was identifiable, the overwhelming majority were Methodists, followed by Presbyterians. Baptists and other Protestant sects claimed the rest, along with a sprinkling of Irish Catholics. In both cities, German-Jewish merchants played an important role in the merchant community, but their growing economic power translated into appointments on prominent boards of directors in only a few instances by 1880.[25] In Nashville over half (55 percent) of businessmen with identifiable religions were Methodists, while in Atlanta the figure was 29 percent. Presbyterians accounted for 21 and 29 percent, respectively. In both cities, certain Methodist and Presbyterian churches, in particular, became strongly identified with the wealthy urban elite that was emerging in the postwar era. In Nashville the most prominent upper-class churches were McKendree Methodist and First Presbyterian, with Christ Church Episcopal and First Baptist playing important supporting roles. As the elite dispersed from the city center beginning in the 1880s, these downtown Nashville churches found suburban rivals in West End Methodist and Moore Memorial Presbyterian. In Atlanta the First

Methodist, First Presbyterian, Central Presbyterian, First Baptist, and St. Luke's Episcopal churches all served wealthy neighborhoods near the city center.

In both cities, the Methodists especially played an important role in defining social values and promoting an agenda for moral reform, philanthropy, and educational uplift—a program to be supported and carried out by wealthy men and, more often, their wives. Nashville's Southern Methodist Publishing House, with its widely circulated *Gospel Advocate,* helped make the city a center of Methodist ideas and leadership throughout the region. A measure of the Methodist presence in each city is indicated by the founding of two important Methodist universities. Vanderbilt University, which began in Nashville in the early 1870s, was the joint product of Methodist piety and northern plutocracy.[26] It soon became the beneficiary of the New South fortunes within Nashville and became closely associated with the city's upper-class families. After Vanderbilt severed its ties with the church in 1914, Emory University was established in Atlanta, where it continued as a monument to the alliance between Methodist educational aspirations, New South wealth, and northern philanthropy.

Though rooted in the rural South and closely identified with circuit-riding preachers, revivalism, and conservative social values, the Methodists adapted skillfully to the urban environment and to New South ideals. By the mid-1870s, one historian observed, the Southern Methodist church was "becoming a church of the rising middle class, reflecting the mores of this segment of the population."[27] Perhaps nothing gave better evidence of this trend than a book put out by the Southern Methodist Publishing House in Nashville in 1885, entitled *The Law of Success,* by Nashville educator and author William Speer. In a text drawn from the lives of "twelve hundred successful men . . . all self-made," Speer proffered advice for getting ahead in the world by rules that were said to be "in harmony with all moral obligations." Readers were treated to tips on "selecting a wife with a view to making [one's] life a success," teachings on "the commercial value of the Ten Commandments and a righteous life," and the advice that "even social calls and visiting the club-room may prove paying investments of one's time."[28]

Evangelist Sam Jones brought the Methodist tradition of religious enthusiasm and moral reform into an urban setting with huge, interdenominational revivals in Atlanta and Nashville during the 1880s and 1890s. Jones spoke pointedly to the newly rich in these cities and demanded that they demonstrate their religion by doing good works among the poor, the intemperate, and others left to suffer amid the wealth and progress of the New South cities. "You love money more than your souls," he scolded Nashville's rich at one revival. During the mid-1880s, Jones helped galvanize powerful temperance crusades that enlisted many of the wealthy women and men of Nashville and Atlanta. Though members of the business class often disagreed over the best means of advancing the cause of temperance, the cause itself was widely approved. Often wealthy women drafted their husbands, who saw in temperance reform one of many practical expressions of their self-image as examples and benefactors to the community at large. Temperance, in their hands, became a "symbolic crusade," a campaign to impose not simply abstemious drinking habits, but a more encompassing culture of self-discipline and improvement that lay at the heart of the social code championed by the business class. "If Nashville was made what it ought to be," exhorted Jones on one occasion, "there would be no use in going to heaven. God would run the streets of the New Jerusalem in front of your houses."[29]

On a more personal level, the Methodists, along with the Presbyterians and other southern Protestant denominations, offered a code of living that was very much in tune with the ideal of the New South urban elite. Their code emphasized self-denial and a disciplined life of hard work, frugality, temperance, and honesty. It was a moral code that denied impulsive, pleasure-seeking behavior and interpreted worldly wealth as the honorable reward of virtue. Wealth, according to this view, was also the means, as much as the reward, for good works of philanthropy and charitable service. It was a code well suited to those on the rise.

No one offered a better example of this translation of "old time religion" into the modern values of the New South than Edmund Cole, the Nashville railroad and banking magnate. Young Cole's "very pious, good Methodist" mother had taught him "that moral character is the basis of all true success" and urged him to join a church when he left the family farm at the age of eighteen and went to Nashville. "Instead of going out 'skylarking' of [*sic*] nights with the town boys, young Cole went to his room and read and studied to improve himself. The result was that he never danced a step, never was intoxicated, and never gambled." Cole later claimed he only wanted to "make a little money, so I could get a good education and fit myself for the ministry." Picking up the skills of a bookkeeper, young Cole went to work for the Nashville and Chattanooga Railway in 1851. From there he worked his way up to president of the road and then went on to an extraordinary career as a southern railroad magnate. By the 1880s, "King" Cole had put together two schemes for a grand trunk line connecting the Midwest and southeastern ports through Tennessee. He died in 1899 one of the wealthiest men in Nashville, a major philanthropist, particularly of Vanderbilt University (where his bust stands outside the college dean's office), one of his favorite Methodist charities. Reflecting on his early dream of becoming a preacher, Cole once mused, "I suppose I have been able to do more good by giving to the church from the store I have been allowed to collect than I could have done as a minister of the gospel."[30] The New South's evangelical zeal for regional uplift and material salvation offered an ideal channel for the religious impulses that compelled Cole and his peers.

Atlanta's Leading Men

The group portrait examined thus far comes into sharper focus when we look more closely at a few individuals. All followed different paths in their individual business careers, but those paths usually traced the major avenues of opportunity that opened in the postwar economy of each city. Some were new industrial paths blazed by pioneering entrepreneurs. Others were well-worn conventional pursuits in wholesale merchandising, where hard work, aggressive marketing, and initial advantage gave a few the edge. Table 4.3 shows the distribution of occupations for all the board and company directors of 1880 and the more select group of business elites in Atlanta and Nashville. The business leadership of each city was drawn from diverse sectors of the city's economy, and their occupations represented the most promising opportunities of the postwar scene. All these men of wealth and standing, whatever the personal virtues to which their admirers credited their success, also had to have a combination of business acumen, a capacity for innovation, and an abundance of luck and timing.

George W. Adair, postwar Atlanta's leading real-estate developer, may offer

Table 4.3 Occupations of Directors and Elites, Atlanta and Nashville, 1880

	Atlanta		Nashville	
	All Directors	Elites	All Directors	Elites
Agricultural, extractive	3.2%	4.9%	2.4%	5.1%
Manufacturing, construction	18.9	24.4	17.1	15.4
Wholesale merchants	17.8	29.2	31.7	23.1
Retail merchants	9.5	9.8	8.9	7.7
Transportation, communication	21.1	12.2	11.4	7.7
Finance	22.1	14.6	16.3	20.5
Professional, government	7.4	4.9	12.2	20.5
Total	100	100	100	100
N =	(95)	(41)	(123)	(39)

Sources: See table 4.1.

Note: Retired persons and those whose occupations are unknown are not included.

the best example of the close link between individual striving and city building that propelled so many careers. He began life in rural Georgia and entered business as a store clerk in Decatur, just east of Atlanta. He spent several years trying out different roles—reading law, working as a railroad conductor, and doing business in Charleston—before he settled in Atlanta in 1854, when he was thirty-one years old. There he began what his biography describes as a "general auction" business. The R. G. Dun and Company credit reports record him for the first time in 1857, in partnership with W. A. Chisolm and listed as "Negro Brokers"—slave traders. The firm was estimated to be worth about $6,000 to $8,000, and Adair and Chisolm were described as "keen and shrewd traders, good for all contracts." During the war, Adair published a Confederate newspaper in Atlanta, speculated in cotton, and later served as aide-de-camp to General Nathan Bedford Forrest.

At the end of 1865, Adair resumed his business in auction and commission sales, now specializing in Atlanta real estate rather than slaves. By 1870 the R. G. Dun reporter estimated his worth at $10,000 to $15,000, and he was said to be "doing well and making money—has the confidence of the community, prompt and reliable." That year he launched the Atlanta Street Railway, a mule-drawn streetcar system that would open up the new suburb of West End, Adair's first major subdivision. In 1872 the R. G. Dun reporter claimed that Adair was now worth $200,000, "an active energetic man."

The panic of 1873 hit Adair broadside and quickly deflated the Atlanta real-estate boom. "This party is embarrassed, had run with money and has been unable to meet paper [his loan notes] promptly." By 1877 Adair, swamped with high-interest loans borrowed against declining assets, had to declare bankruptcy and assign his property to creditors. "His failure is considered an honest one, and his integrity is not in question," the Dun agent concluded. Indeed, Adair retained the confidence of wealthy allies like Richard Peters and soon recovered with the resurgence of the Atlanta real-estate market in the 1880s. With his four sons joining him in the business, Adair and Company rode the boom in Atlanta real estate with great success by specializing in the subdivision of suburban property that was quickly taken in by the expanding city.

Like so many others of the economic elite in Atlanta and Nashville, Adair shifted from private entrepreneurial ventures in his initial line of business into public enterprises in which he joined with other Atlantans to promote the local economy. Among Adair's favored projects were the Atlanta Cotton Factory, the Kimball House Hotel, the Georgia Western Railroad, and the Piedmont Exposition. "No citizen has been more prominently identified with all the agencies which have been conducive to the growth and development of Atlanta," his biographer wrote. At his death in 1899, Adair's personal estate was estimated to be worth almost $98,000, most of it in the valuable Atlanta real estate that he had been so zealous in promoting.[31]

James R. Wylie of Atlanta built a more modest fortune as a wholesale grocer, a profession that became one of the leading enterprises in the New South as self-sufficient farming gave way to cash crops and sharecropping. Born in Chester County, South Carolina, in 1831, Wylie had left the family farm at age twenty to clerk in a country store, then to work as a drummer for a Nashville wholesale grocery firm. His peripatetic youth typified that of many New South business leaders. During the war he worked as an agent for the Western and Atlantic Railroad in Calhoun, Georgia. After the war Wylie followed the rails into Atlanta, where he began a wholesale grocery business in partnership with two other men, one of whom, a wealthy landowner back in Calhoun, apparently financed the firm. By 1867 Wylie was in business on his own, and the Dun agent knew little about him. "Can get [nothing] very accurate about him. He has the reputation of being a high-toned, honorable, honest man and to possess good business capacity, and is also said to have capital." By 1871 Wylie had accumulated real estate worth $16,000 and had bought unspecified stocks worth another $15,000. The firm itself was estimated to be worth between $50,000 and $60,000 by 1873 and was able to ride the depression that year without disaster. At the end of 1875 the Dun report glowed with admiration for Wylie. "Removed to Atlanta ten years ago when he embarked on the grocery business which, though small at first, has by close attention to same built up to present standard. In commercial circles he is regarded as a high-toned, honorable man of sound judgment and undoubted integrity. In a social point, he is respectably connected."

Wylie, like Adair and many others in his cohort, transcended his individual success in one line of business to engage in a variety of entrepreneurial ventures in cooperation with other Atlanta businessmen. He was a principal promoter and director of the State National Bank, later the Merchants Bank, and was its president beginning in 1889. He was a director of the Atlanta Street Railway, served on the board of the International Cotton Exposition in 1881, was a member of the executive committee of the 1887 Piedmont Exposition, and was director of the Cotton States and International Exposition in 1895. Wylie invested heavily in Atlanta real estate and in several railroad and stock-breeding ventures as well. "Without means, save as he created them," his biographer wrote, "Mr. Wylie has had solely to depend on his own exertions for all he has attained in life."[32]

Like Wylie, Edwin W. Marsh exploited Atlanta's growing importance as a wholesale distribution center to develop a thriving business, in this instance in the dry-goods trade. Born in rural North Carolina, Marsh had moved with his family to LaFayette, North Carolina, where he worked in his father's store.

Marsh came to Atlanta during the war when he was thirty-nine years old. During the latter part of the war, he worked on Henry Watterson's newspaper, the *Southern Confederate*. At the war's end he stayed on in Atlanta and joined with William A. Moore, another newcomer from East Tennessee, to open a whole-sale dry-goods business. Moore and Marsh came in on the ground floor and rode the postwar recovery rapidly upward to become Atlanta's largest firm in the dry-goods line. By 1872 the Dun credit report entry said "Moore and Marsh are men of families, each are 40 to 45 years old. Stock in trade worth $200,000." "Have made $. Excellent character, very close and cautious," the 1878 report added. By April 1879, the partnership was described as "the leading commercial house here. Came to Atlanta immediately after the War and established this business, which has grown to . . . sales of $1 million annually." The firm was estimated to be worth up to one half million dollars net by this time. Moore and Marsh, the R. G. Dun agent went on, "are in independent circumstances, are both high-toned, honorable gentlemen, enjoy the confidence of the community."

Marsh's will showed that he had invested liberally outside his business in a variety of Atlanta properties, in bank stocks, and in the Trion Manufacturing Company, a large cotton mill in Chattooga County, Georgia, along with iron lands in northern Georgia and a hotel in Salt Springs, Georgia. His pattern of diversified investments in Atlanta and north Georgia was common among these men of wealth, who, as capitalists if not as entrepreneurs, linked their fortunes to those of their community and its hinterland. Marsh's partner died in 1891, and Marsh himself retired from business three years later. By that time he was regarded as "one of Atlanta's wealthiest citizens, who has been closely identified with her growth since he made the city his home."[33]

Few Atlantans cut a wider swathe than Samuel M. Inman, head of the leading cotton business in the city. He was locally acclaimed as "an ideal citizen of Atlanta." Born in rural East Tennessee in 1843, Inman was raised in a "strong, earnest Presbyterian family." His father, described as a prosperous planter, sent young Inman to Princeton, which he attended until the war broke out. He returned home to serve as a lieutenant in General Johnston's cavalry. During the war, his father had to leave East Tennessee, where Union sentiment was strong and people were hostile toward pro-Confederate neighbors. The elder Inman entered the cotton trade in Augusta and later in Atlanta. Sam joined his father in the cotton business in Atlanta in 1867. The credit agency described the son that year as "a young unmarried man of fine business capacity, but I think limited means. . . . Doing a small, safe business and stick close to it." Within a few years, Inman was regarded as "the leading man in the cotton line here . . . previous rating too low." Sam Inman alone was estimated to be worth a quarter of a million dollars by the late 1870s, and the firm was worth much more, with a huge volume of business, handsome profits, and plenty of cash to lend.[34]

By the early 1890s, S. M. Inman and Company was regarded as the largest cotton house in the world, handling a half-million bales a year and employing over five hundred people. With brothers John, of Inman, Swann, and Company in New York City, and Hugh, a rich Atlanta capitalist, and relatives William and Walker, the Inman clan was easily "one of the strongest families in this country." Their cotton business stretched from its branch headquarters in Houston across the cotton belt, with connections in New York and Bremen, Germany. This was only a part of Sam Inman's empire, which included large interests in several railroads making up the Inman System, the *Atlanta Constitution,* and large parcels of Atlanta real estate. Though cosmopolitan in his business and investment interests, Inman was a zealous patriot of Atlanta. He was credited with launching the Georgia Technological Institute in the 1880s, an institution to which he gave liberal support as an advocate of "practical education." He also figured prominently in Atlanta philanthropy, having offered substantial contributions to an orphanage, Henry Grady Hospital ("for white and colored" patients), and the Y.M.C.A. "A pillar of Atlanta's prosperity and a gentleman of stainless honor . . . high-toned, magnanimous . . . he is loved by every station of society," one generous biographer summarized.[35]

The career patterns and business strategies followed by other Atlanta elites varied, of course. But the above examples do illustrate some common themes: mobility, ascendance from inauspicious backgrounds, and calculating efforts to advance one's fortunes and one's community together.

Nashville's Leading Men

While Nashville did not enjoy the spectacular boom atmosphere of Atlanta, its leading businessmen cut similar figures as men emerging from the middling levels of white southern society to grasp new wealth and position in "the new order of things" after the war. Most of the Rock City's business elite in 1880 had built their own fortunes, and, on average, they commanded every bit as much or more individual wealth as their more braggadocian counterparts in the Gate City.[36] As in Atlanta, the main avenues for entrepreneurial ambition in Nashville involved the new opportunities that had opened in wholesale trade, finance, railroads, and manufacturing.

One of the most successful areas of the latter category was the iron industry, the source of several Nashville fortunes in the 1880s. Launched in the antebellum era and stimulated during the initial stages of the Civil War, the iron industry of Middle Tennessee flourished after the war due to the combination of new corporate organization and new technology. It was an industry that centered on Nashville as the major source of capital and entrepreneurial skill but rapidly grew beyond the city to benefit other parts of Middle Tennessee and also Birmingham and northern Alabama.

James Cartwright Warner, the "iron master of Tennessee," was the major figure among several Nashville business elites who built their fortunes in iron manufacturing and its ancillary industries. He was born in 1830 in Gallatin, Tennessee, a small town a few miles upriver from Nashville, where his father was a tailor. Warner left home at seventeen to begin his business career as a clerk in a Nashville wholesale grocery firm. About 1852 he left for Chattanooga, then a small city full of promise as an industrial center, where he began a wholesale hardware business. There he became active in politics and served briefly as mayor of Chattanooga and as representative in the state legislature. He spoke for the former Whig industrialists and opposed secession. When war came, Warner did not enlist on either side, invoking as justification his chronically poor health and his desire to stay at home and protect his young family.[37]

Sometime in 1863, as Union forces besieged Chattanooga, Warner returned to Nashville, reportedly with no resources, and decided to make a new start there. He worked for a time as a cashier in the Bank of Union before it dissolved in the chaos of postwar financial crisis. In 1868 he joined Arthur S. Colyar in a small coal-mining company located south of Nashville in the Cumberland Mountains. Tennessee Coal and Railroad Company, which had been started in the 1850s, was struggling to revive after being nearly destroyed by the Confederate and Union armies during the war. Colyar, a lawyer, newspaper editor, and former Whig political leader, brought to the company a zeal to provide cheap coal to fuel industrial development in the New South. He found in Warner a skilled manager who could execute that dream. "Married, sober, and reliable," the R. G. Dun agent reported in recommending Warner in 1870, "a live man" who "will in all probability make a success" of the enterprise.[38] Under Warner's management, the company repaired the dilapidated mines, rebuilt the railroad connecting the mines to the Nashville, Chattanooga, and St. Louis line, and brought the whole operation into good working order by the early 1870s.[39]

Anxious to find new uses for an abundance of "slack" coal, Warner enlisted the aid of an English ironmaker, built a cheap temporary furnace, and demonstrated for the first time in Tennessee that the slack coal could be turned into coke suitable for the production of pig iron. He then built a plant with two hundred coke ovens, the first of its kind in the South. Soon coke production led to the expansion of a southern iron industry. New iron furnaces emerged at Chattanooga and a few miles away at Rising Fawn, Georgia, both important customers of Tennessee Coal and Railroad. By 1876 the company erected its own iron furnace south of Nashville at Cowan, Tennessee, and purchased a furnace begun by English ironmakers a few miles away at South Pittsburgh, Tennessee.[40]

Warner left as general manager of the company in 1874, and, after recovering his frail health at his home across the river in Edgefield, he returned to the nascent southern iron industry on his own. For a time he gained control of the furnaces at Chattanooga and Rising Fawn, the latter in partnership with Atlanta's Joseph E. Brown. He turned both into profitable operations, then quickly sold his interests in 1882. Next Warner shifted his energies to the development of a charcoal-fueled iron industry in western Middle Tennessee, in the old western iron belt where charcoal iron of high quality had been produced since the 1790s. In 1880 Warner, backed by a quarter of a million dollars from Nashville capitalists, built the first modern plant in the area—a model of scientific efficiency that introduced new methods of testing ore, steam shovels to mine the surface ore deposits, and new economies of scale in pig iron production. Near the furnace, Warner built company-owned homes, schools, churches, and stores for his work force. Six years later Warner opened the Aetna Furnace, another highly profitable operation located west of Nashville. At the same time, Warner served as president of the reorganized Tennessee Coal, Iron, and Railroad Company (1882–85) and became a major investor in street railway systems in Nashville, Chattanooga, and Birmingham.

By 1889, his health failing again, Warner sold all his iron interests to the Southern Iron Company, formed that year mostly by Nashville capitalists to take over Warner's iron empire. The days of charcoal iron were numbered as steel manufacturing gained ground, and this company was "driven to the wall" in the 1890s.[41] Warner retired to a fashionable town house on Spruce Street and to a summer country estate, "Renraw," in East Nashville. He died in the summer of 1895, one of the wealthiest men in the city. His estate was worth nearly $1.5 million, and he was said to have already given away much to schools, churches, and other charities before his death.[42] The city honored him by naming a school for him, and at his death the eulogists held him up as a model of enterprise and virtue. "He amassed a large fortune, and there was not a dirty dollar in it. His life was one to be studied and emulated; it was an illustration of practical Christianity."[43]

Nathaniel Baxter, Jr., was another of several Nashville business leaders in the 1880s whose wealth came primarily from the iron industry. Born in Columbia, Tennessee, in 1845, young Baxter moved to Nashville four years later when his father was appointed circuit judge. Though his father was a strong Whig and pro-Union man, Baxter enlisted in the Confederate army at sixteen and served with General Joseph Johnston. Baxter returned to Nashville after the war and began a career in law. In the 1870s he moved into banking as president of the Merchants National Bank, whose merger into First National Bank he negotiated. When John Inman, the New York financier (and brother of Atlanta's Sam Inman), took over Tennessee Coal and Iron in 1891, he invited his friend Baxter to serve as president of the company, a position Baxter held almost continuously until 1901, when he retired. Baxter was a fierce competitor who, with little previous knowledge of the iron and coal industry, demonstrated uncanny skill in managing the company during a period of rapid expansion.[44] Though Baxter's role at the helm of Tennessee Coal ultimately benefited Birmingham more than Nashville, much of his personal fortune, worth over $280,000 at his death, flowed back home, where it was invested primarily in local banks, railroads, and real estate.[45]

As the southern iron industry expanded beyond Nashville, local manufacturing became concentrated more in food processing, particularly flour milling and meat packing, both products of Nashville's position as a distribution center in the expanding L&N system. Oscar F. Noel was one of several in this industry who took a prominent role in Nashville's business leadership. Born in 1821 in rural southern Kentucky, Noel worked on his father's farm until, at age seventeen, he came to Nashville and began clerking in a wholesale grocery firm. By 1851 the R. G. Dun reporter found him in business with his brother in a retail grocery. "Only have small means," the report warned, but added the next year, "pretty fair credit, industrious young men." By 1858 Noel claimed $28,000 in real estate and another $11,000 in personal property, according to the Dun agent. The war was good to Noel, and to the grocery business in general, as Nashville became the chief supply center for Union armies in the western theater. "Rich and doing a large business," an 1871 report went. "Noel worth an estimated $100,000, owns large real estate, bank stock, etc." A year earlier Noel had bought Jackson Mills, a flour mill, and he later built the Noel Mill, both on south Nashville's "roller mill hill." Noel also had erected one of the first grain elevators in the region and worked tirelessly to make Nashville the "Minneapolis of the South."[46]

Noel's fortune in milling flowed into numerous other Nashville and Tennessee enterprises, including Cumberland Telephone and Telegraph, East Tennessee Telephone Company, and the Glendale Park Railway. He also invested heavily in city and suburban property. As the Dun agent had reported in 1874, he "makes money at anything he turns his attention to."[47]

Henry Hart was one of several industrialists who made Nashville an important center of meat packing for the region. He came to Nashville in 1850 from Clarksville, a small tobacco town downriver. He had been born in Robertson County twenty-eight years earlier. In Nashville he entered the wholesale grocery line in partnership with William Phillips. When the war came, Hart apparently remained in business and prospered with the great demand for food, first from the Confederate and then from the Union armies. In 1867 he formed a partnership with Henry C. Hensley to open a pork-packing plant. Within a few years the Dun agent described them as "men of the most unquestioned character," with "credit as good as any house in the city." Hart inherited a large estate worth $100,000 from his father-in-law sometime before 1871 and became a capitalist and real-estate speculator of some standing in the city. Hart, too, diversified his investments in a variety of ventures linked to Nashville's burgeoning economy. Beyond his own pork-packing plant, Hart invested in the Fourth National Bank, on whose board he served as director, the Nashville Cooperage Company, and the Union Stockyard Company and put large amounts into country property at the fringe of the city. By 1885 the Dun agent reported that Hart and Hensley were in the "best of standing personally" and were "good influential citizens."[48]

James Whitworth's career exemplified the growing importance of Nashville as a financial center in Tennessee after the war. Born in nearby Sumner County in 1816, Whitworth endured a childhood of poverty. When he was thirteen his father, a farmer, died, leaving a widow and eleven children. "By assiduous and persistent toil," one laudatory source recounted, "he contributed to the support of the family and worked out for himself a meagre [*sic*] education." At twenty-six he came to Nashville, "with neither money nor friends," and began reading law.[49] Whitworth practiced law and ran a large farm outside the city. By 1856 he was appointed county judge, a position he held through the Union occupation, testimony to his strong Unionist sentiments. After the war, Whitworth sold his farm, moved to town, and soon emerged as a major force in Nashville's postwar economy. By this time, according to R. G. Dun and Company estimates, he was worth between $125,000 and $150,000. In 1867 he was instrumental in launching the new Fourth National Bank and served as its president for the next fifteen years. During that time, the Fourth National emerged as Nashville's leading bank, amassing nearly $2 million in assets by 1880.[50] "Controlled by men of known financial ability," the Dun agent reported in 1878. "We have no institution in which more confidence is felt." The stock, which had issued a 12 percent dividend for years, was worth $125 per share and "none can be bought."[51] Whitworth may have been one of the most versatile among the business elite in either Nashville or Atlanta. He resigned as bank president in 1882 in order to rescue the ailing Tennessee Manufacturing Company, a Nashville textile mill that had been the hope of local industrial promoters. Whitworth also took on the role of capitalist and adviser-at-large to numerous Nashville enterprises and charities before his death in 1899.[52]

Other models of enterprise were northern imports. Their acceptance in Nashville was testimony to the lack of serious sectional animosity surviving in the city. Gates P. Thruston was a Union officer who married into Nashville society and became a leading figure in business and cultural affairs. Born in 1835, Thruston hailed from Ohio but often stressed his "old Virginia" lineage among his new southern neighbors. He studied law in Cincinnati before serving in the Union army, where he was promoted from captain to lieutenant colonel and finally to brevetted brigadier general. He married Ida Hamilton, daughter of a prominent hardware merchant, and made his own way as a lawyer, banker, and partner in the State Insurance Company. The latter was described by the Dun agent as "a live money-making institution" run by "men of the best character."

Whatever residual prejudice against the northern conquerors may have survived in Nashville, it did not inhibit Thruston from becoming an influential citizen in the community. A member of the First Presbyterian Church and a leading figure in several important societies, Thruston was especially noted as a devoted benefactor of cultural endeavors, a guarantee of social distinction in the "Athens of the South." He left generous portions of his "handsome estate" to Vanderbilt University, the Tennessee Historical Society, the Nashville Art Association, and numerous charities. To his only son, Charles, he left one thousand dollars, to be given on his twenty-first birthday, provided "he has not used tobacco in any way or form, or any intoxicating liquors to excess up to that time."[53] This equation of money and personal piety was not new to Nashville.

Nashville's major function in the new economy, like Atlanta's, was to serve a growing territory of retailers and consumers as a wholesale distribution center linked by rail and river to its hinterland. Many of the business elite built their fortunes in the various lines of trade spawned by each city's development. John Kirkman made his money in the lucrative wholesale hardware trade and moved into banking on the side. A native of Nashville, Kirkman was born in 1813 and opened the first wholesale hardware business in the state at the age of sixteen. By 1858 credit agents noted his "good moral and business habits" and described his firm as "a first class house with large means and credit . . . estimated worth $200,000." Kirkman was by this time also president of Union Bank, and he later headed the Third National and American National banks. He suspended his hardware business during the war but resumed it afterwards with J. M. Gray, in a business considered by credit agents to be the "largest hardware business in town . . . none better." By 1871 Kirkman was said to be "considered one of the wealthiest men in Nashville." By 1880 the business, now styled Gray, Kirkman, and Fall, alone was worth $300,000 to $400,000, and Kirkman also owned real estate and bank stock, though much of it had cautiously been placed in his wife's name following the panic of 1873.[54] When he died in an accident in 1888, tributes from the Merchants Exchange and business leaders testified to his role as a vital figure in Nashville's banking and merchant community.[55]

William H. Morrow offered Nashville one of its more spectacular displays of new money, wrung largely from the forced labor of leased convicts in this case. A native of Edgefield, a suburb across the river from Nashville, Morrow was born in 1837, studied medicine in his youth, and served in Confederate hospitals during the war. Although engaged in the saddlery business with his father before the war, he afterwards relocated in Knoxville and in 1871 returned to Nashville. In that year, Morrow was said to "own nothing," but his political connections with the Conservative Democrats won him a position as state treasurer. Morrow became a partner and eventually a majority share-holder in Cherry, O'Conner, and Company, which had been granted the right to lease convict labor from the state. The company manufactured Tennessee wagons and subleased the convicts to Tennessee Coal and Iron, of which Morrow owned a substantial share. The costs for convict labor were so low that Morrow amassed an enormous fortune within a few years. By 1881 his half share in Cherry, O'Conner, and Company was estimated to be worth $300,000 and rising rapidly. Thomas O'Conner died in a duel in Knoxville in 1882, and William H. Cherry followed him to the grave three years later, leaving Morrow as the sole surviving partner. An upright member of Tulip Street Methodist Church, where he taught Sunday school, Morrow was an active supporter of Methodism in Tennessee. An 1879 credit report cast this prosperous entrepreneur as "an honest Christian gentleman in high standing in the community." He moved to an ostentatious Victorian mansion overlooking the city from high on Rutledge Hill and lived until 1895 as one of the city's richest men.[56]

The men of Atlanta and Nashville who served as economic leaders at the opening of the 1880s were by no means all "new men" who emerged untouched by the war and the passions that had led to war. They were, at least at the beginning of the decade, a bit too old for that, even in the young, dynamic city of Atlanta. Many had come to Atlanta and Nashville well before the war. Among the southern-born elite, they or their fathers were usually identified with the Whig tradition, favoring industrial progress and opposing secession. Although some of these men fought for the Confederacy from a sense of duty, more sat out the war or profited from the business opportunities it offered, particularly in occupied Nashville.

Whatever their experiences before 1865, these men entered the postwar era with the economic wind at their backs. Their cities were favored by the new system of railroads and by their strategic geographic location. Atlanta stood at the gateway between the Southeast and the Northeast, Nashville at the crossroads between the Midwest and the South. But their success was not inevitable, not even in the robust economy of postwar Atlanta and Nashville.

Out of a world that had been shattered by rebellion, invasion, destruction, and emancipation, the new elite sought, first of all, wealth for themselves and their families. Some operated entirely within these narrow interests and viewed their lives of sumptuous luxury as a reward for their business acumen. Others, embracing a vision of the New South, saw themselves as harbingers of a new order, which they would help to build out of the wreckage of the old.

5 | *Patrician and Parvenu*

Inquiring of a young stranger, it is asked in Boston "How much does he know?"; in New York, "How much is he worth?"; in Charleston, "Who was his grandfather?"
—*Charleston proverb*

"As for Charleston," Francis W. Dawson grumbled in the editorial columns of his *News and Courier,* "the importation of about five hundred Yankees of the right stripe would put a new face on affairs, and make the whole place throb with life and vivid force."[1] He recommended a cross between the Boston and Chicago species, a mixture that would bring the best of refinement and aggressiveness to his adopted "ancient city." For Dawson and other critics, it was never a question that Charleston's dismal economic fate was explained by the lack of such ambition and talent. Though the area's external problems were legion, it was, in their view, a failure from within—a failure of human will— that doomed the city.

Both Charleston and Mobile entered the New South era with business leaders who, as a group, had little cause for optimism about their cities and, therefore, less inclination toward bold, risky responses to the challenges—and the opportunities—they confronted. The relatively stagnant economies of both cities allowed a well-entrenched older group of men to continue in positions of leadership and influence in the business community without significant chal- lenge. These were, for the most part, men with strong ties to the plantation economy, foremost among them being the cotton factors and commission merchants who, in both cities, continued to command great prestige even as the economic base of their wealth eroded in the new order.

As in the previous chapter on Atlanta and Nashville, a collective biography of the business leaders of Charleston and Mobile around 1880 provides a useful description—both as a group portrait and in individual details—of the men who dominated economic affairs in the two seaports.[2] Though the available information was spotty in many cases, the following sample of sixty-eight men in Charleston and sixty-one in Mobile offers a close view of the types of men who commanded positions of leadership and influenced the direction of their cities. In each of these cities there were also a few wealthy men who remained outside the board rooms and commercial associations.

Businessmen who had acquired sufficient wealth and standing in the community to be elected to the board of directors of a major bank or to an office in the chamber of commerce were, as a rule, mature, successful, and well established. But Charleston's business elite, among those of the four cities studied here, was particularly skewed toward older men. The average age was fifty-seven in 1880 (see table 4.1).[3] This was only seven years older than the corresponding average in Atlanta, which had the youngest business elite, but the age range was narrower in Charleston. Only 5 percent of Charleston's business leaders were forty or younger, compared with the 18 to 20 percent in the other three cities. More than 37 percent of the men who directed Charleston's economic affairs in 1880 had passed their sixtieth birthday.

The experience and wealth that came with age were important assets to any business community. But in a declining economic environment the dominance of older men could also bring to the board rooms and the meeting halls a legacy of defeat and timidity. This was often frustrating for younger men who were, by circumstances, more open to risk and more ambitious for the future, if only because a longer future lay before them. It was that sense of impatience that William Trenholm touched upon bluntly in his address to the Charleston Board of Trade in 1869 when he pleaded: "We must forget to defer to senility, we must learn to respect and to make use of youth."[4] But as Charleston's economy continued to drag in the postwar era, many young men from the city's leading mercantile families found it necessary to search for opportunities in the South Carolina upcountry, northern Alabama, and other parts of the North and South.[5]

As a group, Mobile's business leaders in 1880 were younger than those in Charleston—the average age was fifty-two.[6] Though a similar portion (36 percent) were over sixty, Mobile's business elite included more young men than Charleston's, with 18 percent being forty years or younger (see table 4.1). As in Charleston, the economic decline drained the city of much of its youthful talent. Peter Hamilton described "an exodus of young men to New Orleans, Memphis, Texas and other places," particularly following the panic of 1873. "Losing so many young men," he added, "sapped much of the energy of the city."[7] By 1886 the *Mobile Register* attributed the loss of "many of her young men" during the last twelve to fifteen years to "the falling off of business . . . and to some extent to the want of interest in our young men on the part of merchants and others."[8]

The loss of young men through war and migration might easily have been replenished in more dynamic settings, but the business leaders of Charleston and Mobile found few newcomers to refresh their ranks after the war. Among the entire pool of 1880 directors initially examined in this study, more than 77 percent of those in Charleston and 61 percent of those in Mobile were listed earlier in the city directories for 1860 (see table 4.2). In Atlanta the figure was only 19 percent. Even in the more settled environment of Nashville, only 44 percent of the 1880 directors had been residents twenty years earlier.[9]

The insular quality of the business classes in Charleston and Mobile in 1880 is more striking when one examines the smaller sample defined here as the business elite, for whom there exists more precise information on birthplace and date of arrival in the city. Nearly 95 percent of Charleston's 1880 business elite had been living in the city when the war began at Fort Sumter. On average they had lived in Charleston fifty-two years. A majority (57 percent) of the 1880 elite had been born there, and many were descended from Charleston and low-country families whose lineage stretched back several generations.

While the rising cities of the New South recruited their business leaders from the small towns and farms of their hinterlands, Charleston's business leadership was almost entirely sealed off to newcomers. Less than 10 percent of the 1880 elite claimed a South Carolina birthplace other than Charleston, and another 10 percent came from other parts of the South. In striking contrast to the other cities, where northern-born businessmen constituted a significant minority within the business elite, Charleston had no such leaders in 1880. The dearth of newcomers, whose presence dominated the business leadership of Atlanta and Nashville, was both symptom and cause of Charleston's economic decline in the New South.

On the other hand, Charleston, among the four cities, had the largest share of foreign-born (24 percent) in its general population, a circumstance due to the city's access to European immigrants coming down the eastern seaboard and to the draw of its prosperous German and Jewish communities. All of the foreign-born among the 1880 elite were Germans, and several of these were Jewish. These men often qualified for entry into the ranks of the elite as directors of ethnic banks like Germania Savings and other corporations dominated by their own people.[10] The Germans had gained a foothold in the grocery trade, frequently beginning with small shops that catered to blacks and were known locally as "Germans." They also found a niche in the King Street retail stores where Jewish merchants concentrated, lending the sobriquet "Little Jerusalem" to their district. Initially, at least, the German and Jewish businessmen worked outside the prestigious cotton and rice trade dominated by old Carolinians. During the postwar era they expanded into wholesale commerce, banking, cotton trading, and most every other part of Charleston's business life. A sizable Irish population also formed in the city, but most of the Irish filled unskilled occupations and worked their way upward through political circles, winning patronage from city officials and eventually capturing city hall with the triumph of John Patrick Grace in 1911.[11] Of Charleston, a local proverb claimed, "the Germans own it, the Irish control it, and the Negroes enjoy it" (a similar adage described Mobile: "owned by the Jews, run by the Catholics, enjoyed by the Negroes").[12] Such sayings certainly exaggerated the state of affairs on all counts, but they acknowledged the assertive role of the immigrants as well as the obtuseness of whites in their view of local blacks.

Mobile recruited more of its business elites from outside the city, typically from the rural plantation districts of Alabama or from South Carolina and other land-worn eastern states. Only 14 percent of the city's 1880 elite had been born in Mobile; another 46 percent came from Alabama and other southern states (see table 4.2). The cosmopolitan heritage that came with Mobile's role as an outpost for northern cotton traders persisted after the war. Though criticized before the war as "birds of passage" who flew away with Mobile's wealth, northern-born businessmen still made up 21 percent of the elite in 1880, forming a larger presence than even their counterparts in Atlanta. A foreign-born population also contributed significantly to the business elite, particularly those German and Jewish merchants who occupied positions similar to their counterparts in Charleston.

Whatever their origins, most of the 1880 elite had been in Mobile for a long time. About 76 percent had been in the city before the war, and on average they had lived in Mobile for thirty-one years. As in Charleston, the business elite of Mobile was dominated by a group whose careers had been shaped in the antebellum era, when both cities served as entrepôts for a prosperous plantation economy. Now their world had been disrupted by war, blockade, and the traumas of emancipation and Reconstruction. They faced the postwar South as older men whose experience and business habits did not always equip them to adapt to new conditions.

The economic sectors from which the leaders of Charleston's and Mobile's business communities were recruited reflected the prosperity of the past rather than the opportunities of the new order. In both cities, the cotton factor and commission merchant, who had served the plantation economy with great profit from the cities' earliest history, remained, in 1880, a ubiquitous feature in the board rooms and commercial associations of these old seaports. As table 5.1 shows, in Charleston about 28 percent of the entire pool of 1880 directors were factors and commission merchants, and nearly 32 percent of Mobile's directors reported similar occupations. Among the more select group in the business elite, the factors' presence was even more pronounced. One-third of the business elite in Charleston and over 44 percent in Mobile were reported to be factors and commission merchants.

The cotton trade, and in Charleston the rice trade, had been the heart of each local economy for a long time, and it was only to be expected that factors

Table 5.1 Occupations of Directors and Elites, Charleston and Mobile, 1880

	Charleston		Mobile	
	All Directors	Elites	All Directors	Elites
Agricultural, extractive	4.3%	1.5%	1.9%	1.7%
Manufacturing, construction	10.0	12.1	9.6	10.2
Wholesale merchants	14.2	13.6	15.4	18.6
Factors, commission merchants	27.9	33.3	31.7	44.1
Retail	5.0	7.6	6.7	5.1
Transportation, communication	14.3	7.6	3.8	3.4
Finance	20.0	18.2	24.0	16.9
Professional, government	4.3	6.1	6.7	—
Total	100	100	100	100
N =	(140)	(66)	(100)	(59)

Sources: See table 4.1.

Note: Retired persons and those whose occupations are unknown are not included.

should play such a large role in the business leadership. After the war the economic foundations of the factor's business may have decayed, but the social props of his status remained in place.

The factors of Charleston had been the mainstays of the city's commercial life since the eighteenth century, when they began marketing the planter's crops and supplying provisions for his slaves. The factor's business connections to the planter were frequently reinforced by blood ties, since most great landowning families had at least one relative working as a factor in the city. Prominent planter family names like Ravenel, Middleton, Huger, and Lesesne were still represented among the city's factors and commission merchants as late as 1880. The invasion of the southern ports by New York cotton buyers, which Robert Albion describes as occurring in the 1820s, met with stiff resistance in Charleston, where native Carolinians prevailed in the cotton and rice trade.[13] The loyalty of planters to the old established firms, usually led by members of the old Anglo-Huguenot-Episcopalian upper class, remained strong after the Civil War. Though English, Scots, and northern businessmen dominated other lines of Charleston's trade in the early nineteenth century, the factors, noted Harriott Horry Rutledge Ravenel, an informed observer, were "the only gentlemen of native birth except the bankers who did any kind of business." To be engaged in "buying and selling cotton" remained one of the few respectable occupations aspired to by prominent Charlestonians. The factor, Ravenel explained, "furnished the money with which the crop was

Workers at a cotton warehouse, Charleston, 1879. (Library of Congress)

planted; made all needful purchases for the country family, from plantation supplies to pocket handkerchiefs; received the rice and cotton when sent to market; got the best possible price from the merchant to whom he sold it; kept all the accounts; and, as one gentleman said, 'Relieved them of the necessity of thinking about disagreeable things.' "[14]

Retail activities and the selling of wholesale dry goods, groceries, and hardware, on the other hand, were regarded as the province of German, Jewish, and other businessmen who stood outside the social elite of old Carolinian families. "There were only certain occupations that a gentleman could follow in Charleston without sacrifice of family dignity," noted DuBose Heyward, an astute insider, writing of a tradition that persisted into the early twentieth century. Banking, brokerage, cotton, and commission wholesale, along with the phosphate and fertilizer industries, were socially acceptable endeavors for the Charleston elite. "But a gentleman seeking a livelihood in the early nineteen hundreds could not engage in any branch of the retail business without imposing upon his humiliated family the burden of incessant explanation."[15]

The Business Culture

The business culture that took form in the declining cotton ports of Charleston and Mobile bore faint resemblance to the obsessive energy that Atlanta displayed to visitors. The erosion of commerce, and of the family fortunes built upon it, hardly allowed an aristocratic life of leisure, but neither did it encourage the style of confident, ambitious entrepreneurship that thrived among the arrivistes of Atlanta or Nashville.

In postwar Charleston and Mobile, some men of wealth and accomplishment emerged despite the stagnation around them. But their influence within the business community of each city was, until the early twentieth century at least, muted by the presence of an older corps of merchants, usually cotton factors, whose local prestige rested on a family's name and its accomplishments in the remote past. In Atlanta or Nashville, the *nouveau* easily won influential places in business and civic leadership and had schools, hospitals, streets, and parks named in his honor. But his counterpart in postwar Charleston and Mobile operated within a culture and social structure that did not fully embrace the nineteenth-century American adulation of material success, which automatically awarded social status and authority to those "self-made" men whose wealth was equated with virtue. In Charleston, especially, there persisted instead an exclusive elite that protected the foundations of its own social status against economic erosion by stressing genealogy, manners, cultural refinement, old homes, and a shared, precious past as the basis of honor and authority within the community.[16]

In Charleston the business culture was subjected to some self-critical evaluation in the aftermath of the war and Reconstruction. Some critics believed that the city was suffering from a pathological community disdain for commerce and industry—a product, they thought, of its subservience to the plantation economy and to the wealthy planter class who attached superior status to land and slaves. In the postwar era, Charleston's dampened business climate, now more apologetic and ambivalent, became linked to the city's inability to compete effectively in the New South. While Atlanta's Henry Grady glorified the New South's love of work and the pursuit of wealth, among conservative Charlestonians, one observer noted, "it was almost bad form to be rich." The "persistence of the disdain of business and also the good sense that conquers it" was revealed in the story of one upper-class Charleston lady who was forced to go into business on her own. Her sign used only the initial of her maiden name, bringing a rebuke from an in-law, who admonished her to spell it out in order that her family "take their share of this disgrace."[17]

"The honest truth is," William L. Trenholm, Charleston's most astute critic, told the chamber of commerce in 1884, "commerce was never heartily appreciated in Charleston, nor have the merchants of this ancient city done what they might, and, if I may say so, what they ought to have done, to influence its destiny and that of the state." Charleston's businessmen, Trenholm went on, had long accepted a "subordinate place" in affairs of the city and state, in deference to the planters. A constant "exodus of capitalists" depleted Charleston of experienced entrepreneurs and capital and further undermined the respect successful elder business leaders normally attracted. "In an old community like this," Trenholm admonished, "conservatism prevails in all things and is eminently respectable. . . . [B]ut conservatism is out of place . . . when it clings to antiquated methods of business and shuts its eyes to modern improvements and the requisites for progressive prosperity."[18]

The torpid spirit of enterprise that Trenholm excoriated was apparent in daily habits of work in the city. The R. G. Dun and Company agent was so struck by the diligence of James Reed Boylston, a dry-goods merchant, that he noted: "[H]e has been, for a Charlestonian, a remarkably hard working, close man—he means to be rich, he is tight. If he were a Yankee he would be called mean."[19] When George Walton Williams, a hard-driving Methodist wholesale grocer, came to Charleston from north Georgia, he was appalled at the lethargic pace his fellow merchants set during the work day. None opened their doors before nine in the morning, and by ten o'clock most merchants had drifted into one of the many coffee houses along Broad Street and East Bay for a "work break." It never seemed to occur to Charleston businessmen that, if they "could make a living beginning the day's work at 9 o'clock," they could "make more than a living starting some hours earlier." Williams's example of opening the business day at sunrise did nothing to change local custom, even after he amassed a fortune from his labors. Even after the work day finally commenced, by early afternoon the bells rang from porches, calling the men home for the traditional two o'clock dinner, a large meal and family gathering that could not be hurried. These meals were often accompanied by good wine from the prized collections that were found in all the city's "best homes."[20]

These habits of leisure only became more confirmed as the local economy entered a prolonged depression after the war. In 1899 a sympathetic observer admitted, "Charleston people only have about five hours a day in their business. They get to work about 10 o'clock, stop at half after 2, eat a heavy dinner, which knocks all the energy out of the rest of the day, and the day is over. They cannot compete with people who work ten hours a day." New opportunities awaited those willing to seize them, he felt certain, but too many Charlestonians "have given up hope and are really incapable of responding to energetic progress."[21]

The long afternoon break amounted to a kind of siesta or *mezzogiorno* common to Latin culture. As a custom among businessmen, it may well have been imported from Barbados and other parts of the West Indies, from which many old Charleston families had originated and with which many continued to do business well into the nineteenth century. The restful interlude was also a practical accommodation to the withering heat and humidity that plagued the city during a good part of the year. Mobile had a similar tradition of mid-day family meals that persisted until the early 1910s; Nashville businessmen abandoned the custom in the early 1900s, due to the expansion of distant suburbs and the growing preference for downtown business clubs that served lunch. Atlanta's higher elevation afforded a cooler climate, which was widely credited as the basis for the city as a southern exception. But if "altitude plus attitude" was the formula for the Atlanta spirit, the same may be said of the more languid Charleston style. For Charlestonians the afternoon dinner was a cool respite within high-ceilinged, dark, shuttered homes, or on breezy side verandas, for two hours or more during the enervating heat of the low country day. But even during the cooler fall and winter months, when trade was at its busiest, the Charleston gentleman was seen sauntering on foot from his home near the Battery to his office on Broad Street or East Bay and back again with a kind of deliberate lassitude that displayed his sense of priorities. His relaxed gait was reminiscent of the English gentleman who warned a quick-paced friend to slow down lest someone think he was "in trade."[22] In the evenings, the family promenade along the Battery was another Charleston custom also reminiscent of Latin culture that accommodated the heat and gave expression to a view of life that accepted leisure and sociability to be as important as the art of making money was in Atlanta. "On this battery," one visitor noted, "in summer, from half past six until dark, you may see almost every one of any notability in Charleston."[23]

The relaxed pace of business took its cue from the factors, whose prospects depended less on aggressive pursuit of new business than on the geographic dominance of the seaport and the special relationship they enjoyed with their customers, the cotton and rice planters. In antebellum times, before any significant competition from railroads and country merchants challenged their command of the upcountry hinterland, factors in the City by the Sea could rightfully count on a steady flow of business from planters who had no other realistic outlets for their crops. Habits died hard, even as the conditions that first warranted them changed. There was, upcountry people complained, a kind of arrogant assumption that the South Carolina trade would all naturally flow to Charleston. "The Charleston factors and brokers," one 1880 account had it,

> are with few exceptions, still wedded to the old fogy idea that Charleston is
> the State, and when Charleston takes snuff the whole State will be compelled

to sneeze. Instead of inviting trade by personal efforts and liberal commissions, they remain in their counting-rooms taking from the farmer 10 per cent commission with an air that amounts to indifference. The up-country merchants are satisfied with 5 per cent and less and they spend annually large amounts in traveling through the country buying futures and offering liberal inducements for shipments on commission.[24]

Business dealings with the planters required a long-term, highly personal relationship that involved the factor in nearly every aspect of the planter's affairs. Often these business attachments were reinforced by blood ties because, as noted above, many of the factors came from the great planter families in the low country. Such relations logically placed personal loyalty above aggressive competition as the basis for the factor's clientele.

The factor's business was, like that of the plantation, highly seasonal, and the rhythm of urban business kept tune with that of the country. When the planters came to town, as they did for long periods in the "sickly season" when malaria or "country fever" threatened the white population, Charleston and Mobile became resorts for pleasure, not work. The season in Charleston began as early as January, and normally by May, for most planter families and continued until the first killing frost, usually in late October or November, when the "sparrows" returned home. Particularly in Charleston, the planters built splendid town houses—indeed, they were grand urban mansions that rivaled their plantation homes in size and finery. A steady round of horse races, card games, gambling, concerts, fancy balls, theater, lavish dinner parties, and evening promenades on the Battery imbued the city with a gay, fun-loving atmosphere.[25] In such an environment, the lines between business and pleasure for the factor and his client, the planter, blurred quite easily—all the more with the wine and punch consumed on these festive occasions. This culture of leisure, which took form originally amid the opulence of the slave regime, survived in shabby dress amid the ruins.

In both Charleston and Mobile, the pursuit of pleasure, enhanced by both cities' roles as planter resorts, was less inhibited by the pietistic religious ethos that the Methodists, Presbyterians, and Baptists had stamped on Atlanta and Nashville. The religious preference among the social elite in these older seaports was the Episcopal church. In the "Holy City" of Charleston it was the tall, white spire of St. Michael's, at the corner of Church and Broad streets, that served as the symbolic center of the city. St. Phillip's, jutting imperiously into Church Street a few blocks away, shared the honors. St. Paul's, farther up the Neck, was the choice of many planter families during their summers in Charleston. Charleston's French Huguenot population had become an important element of the local upper class, but these French Calvinists had trans-

St. Michael's Church at Meeting and Broad streets, Charleston, 1910. (Library of Congress)

ferred their allegiance to the Episcopal churches, and the old Huguenot church, close by St. Phillip's, had dwindled to little more than another historic curiosity by the late nineteenth century. Surrounded by graveyards filled with Charleston's illustrious past heroes, St. Michael's and St. Phillip's were the embodiment of the city's traditional culture. In Mobile it was Christ Church

Episcopal that was favored by the Anglo-Saxon upper class. If the Methodists and other pietistic Protestant churches articulated the earnest pursuit of self-improvement and personal discipline among the business class of Atlanta and Nashville, it was the Episcopalian sense of self-assurance and traditionalism that set the tone for the leading families of Charleston and Mobile.[26]

Charleston's Business Leaders

The place to begin any study of the business communities of the old seaports is with the cotton factor. Although the factor played an increasingly marginal role in the economy of the postwar South as a whole, he remained at the center of affairs in Charleston and Mobile. Swimming against the tide of the new order, the factor was not the most likely guide to prosperity for either city.

Charleston's cotton and rice factors typically organized in small, family-based firms of one to three partners and dealt with the same clientele of planters year after year. Though some individuals and firms displayed a striking ability to adapt to the new conditions of the postwar era, there were many who, in the face of commercial adversity, took a conservative course, eking out smaller profits from a dwindling volume of trade. Others, desperate to regain their wealth after the war, took dangerous risks by speculating in futures sales and advancing credit to planters according to the old standard, with nothing more than the debtor's family honor as collateral. Their failures encouraged a conservative business strategy among the survivors.

Henry Gourdin, one of the most respected men in Charleston's cotton trade, was director of the Bank of Charleston, the South Carolina Railroad, Charleston Gas and Light, and two other companies in 1880. As early as 1846, R. G. Dun and Company reported his cotton-factor firm, Gourdin, Mathieson, and Company, as "one of the wealthiest and best regulated houses" in Charleston, with unspecified "large means." The company survived the war with $25,000 in capital and a "good reputation." By 1878 the firm had opened a branch in Savannah and was estimated to be worth $75,000 to $100,000, but business was described as "much depreciated," and the partners were noted as "close, conservative, give little evidence of activity." The next year, the South Carolina Railroad failed to meet its bond payment, and Gourdin, one of a syndicate of five Charleston merchants who had endorsed the debt, faced the prospect of losing all his assets. He died insolvent in June 1880, and the firm was carried on by relatives.[27]

William Ravenel's firm of cotton factors, Ravenel and Huger, was described in 1854 as "an old house." Following the war, Ravenel formed Ravenel and Company with a New York partner. By this time he needed Yankee financial support; the R. G. Dun agent reported losses of $200,000 during the war.

Ravenel managed to hang onto another $100,000, mostly in real estate, and was said to be "perfectly responsible." He became an agent for a New York steamship line, which was dismissed by the Dun reporter as a collection of "old hulls and not making much money." Ravenel's son, J. R. P. Ravenel, came into the business in 1872 with no additional capital. By May 1874 the company had failed "on account of the heavy endorsement by the Senior, William Ravenel, of the paper of J. R. Pringle & Co.," another Charleston factor. The Ravenels "acted honorably," settled with creditors at 25 percent, and cleared their debts by November 1875, but they never recovered fully. By December 1881 they claimed only $5,000 to $6,000 in capital and, it was reported, "do but a small business, just making a living. Have no means outside."[28]

William J. Middleton brought his venerable family name to the Union Bank and South Carolina Loan and Trust. He began his career as a Charleston cotton factor with R. D. Mure and Company in 1860. Mure, a Scotsman and an "old merchant of first-rate standing," enjoyed the support of "strong friends" in Europe in the 1850s but "suffered greatly by the war" and died in 1871. Middleton continued in business with Mure's son, and they struggled along until 1878, when Middleton split off with his own business as a commission merchant dealing in cotton and naval stores, a growing postwar industry in coastal South Carolina. By 1881 he was described as a "middle aged man of family, stands well as to character. Very steady with good capacity. Has nothing except capital of $2,000–3,000 and just making a living."[29]

His former partner, R. D. Mure, Jr., a director of two Charleston companies, fared no better. In 1879 Mure bought future cotton crops on speculation and could not meet his bills in March when prices had dropped. He compromised with his creditors and managed to get an extension to resume business the next fall. Henceforth, he bought only on orders from New York or Europe and "by close management has paid in full and has but little now," it was reported in 1881. "A young man of good character, energetic, and fair capacity," Mure struck out in 1882 for greener pastures in Atlanta, along with a steady stream of the old port's youthful talent, as well as much of its cotton trade.[30]

William C. Courtney, director and, later, president of the Bank of Charleston, began his career in the hardware business in 1845 and built a sizable fortune. He "lost heavily by the war," then tried to resume trade and moved into cotton factoring—a fall-back business for many in Charleston—in 1868 with a wealthy partner in New York and another in Columbia, South Carolina. In that year, Courtney claimed to be individually worth $50,000 to $60,000, but his business languished, and by 1877 he had "no means of consequence and little capital." The next year the firm failed, and Courtney became president of the Bank of Charleston, the city's oldest bank.[31]

These cotton factors were only a few among many leading businessmen who weathered hard times in the new order. They continued to enjoy reputations for "good character" and "strong friends" and family, as the Dun agent always noted. They maintained positions on the boards of Charleston's leading banks, railroads, and other important companies. Some, like E. Horry Frost and William Ashmead Courtenay, both cotton factors with declining fortunes, were elected as officers of the Charleston Chamber of Commerce and other commercial associations. These honors were not awarded to wealthy capitalists or dynamic entrepreneurs. The board rooms of Charleston were frequently filled by men with little capital to spare, and their own demoralizing experiences in business hardly inspired an ebullient enthusiasm for Charleston's opportunities in the New South.

Not all of Charleston's business leaders, however, suffered a decline in the postwar years. Even the most devastating economic shifts created opportunities for those with the skill and luck to profit from them. Among the twenty wealthiest directors (belonging to firms worth at least $100,000 in the Dun records around 1880) few belonged to the old Anglo-Huguenot-Episcopalian planter-class families. Yankees, Germans, Jews, and a few upcountry southerners, on the other hand, appeared frequently among the rich and successful Charlestonians in the New South. Some were cotton factors and commission merchants, but most of these rising men of wealth made money in less traditional lines such as wholesale groceries, hardware, lumber, phosphate mining, and fertilizers. Lewis D. Mowry, a director of Union Bank and three other local companies in 1880, began business with his father as a wholesale grocer sometime before 1845. His father was described with grudging admiration as "an old Rhode Island Yankee who knows how to make a dollar and how to keep it." "Lewis," the report went on, "is falling in the old man's footsteps, very fast in business quality." The father died a month before the war began and left Lewis a "handsome estate" of at least $100,000 in the business. Mowry and a partner who may have been his brother "engaged in blockade running during the war but lost heavily by it," according to the postwar Dun report. Nevertheless, they emerged from the war worth $150,000. Mowry's son joined the business, which now engaged in cotton factoring, and helped build it up to a capital worth of $250,000 by 1875, when Lewis Mowry and Son were described as "one of our most reliable and prudent houses."[32]

Herman H. DeLeon, a director with South Carolina Loan and Trust and Charleston City Railway, started off in 1855 as a young partner with Isaac Moise in an auction and ship brokerage firm. After Moise's death two years later, DeLeon continued on his own and built up a steady business buying and selling securities. When the war broke out, he was reportedly worth $75,000 and prudently converted $60,000 to gold. "An honest and respectable Israelite," DeLeon was a member of Charleston's prosperous Jewish community. By 1882 he was reported to be worth $125,000 and was "considered one of the shrewdest men in his line."[33]

David D. Cohen was another of Charleston's successful Jewish businessmen. In 1855, after serving for years as a clerk, he became a partner in Hart and Company, a wholesale hardware firm made up of Jewish merchants and described as "one of the oldest in the city." The firm did well after the war, and in 1877 Cohen took his share of the firm's $100,000 worth and split off to organize a new company to manufacture a new cotton tie fastener invented by a Charleston mechanic. He raised another $100,000 from investors in Charleston, New Orleans, and New York and began manufacturing the fastener in the North, with Charleston as the principal outlet for sales.[34]

William P. Hall, another of Charleston's postwar success stories, had been involved since 1853 in the Cuban sugar trade, a business that required "immense amounts of capital" and, according to the Dun report, was "regarded by old fogies as hazardous." He survived the war with only $5,000 to $10,000 in capital, but he soon expanded his ventures to include a cotton commission business in the 1870s. His individual net worth ran up quickly to $125,000 by 1877 and to $300,000 by 1882, much of it in the Atlantic Phosphate Company, for which he served as director in addition to serving on the boards of the Bank of Charleston and the Union Cotton Press.[35]

James S. Gibbes, one of Charleston's most prominent postwar businessmen, was the director and president of the People's National Bank, director of South Carolina Railroad, Gas, and Light, and vice president of the Home Insurance Company. Gibbes began as a cotton factor and, in 1857, was reported worth $20,000. He "has made all he is worth himself, middle aged, family, considered a good business man," the R. G. Dun agent pointed out. Before the war Gibbes claimed $200,000 in personal net worth, much of which was invested in stocks and real estate. Though he reportedly "lost very heavily by the war," Gibbes soon rebuilt his fortune by buying and selling cotton "on English credit," and he retired worth $200,000 to $300,000 in 1881.[36] It was this fortune that provided the endowment for the locally famous Gibbes Art Gallery, founded after his death.

William L. Trenholm, the son of the Confederate treasurer, George Trenholm, joined his father in a private banking business in 1868. Both had been active in John L. Fraser and Company, one of the largest cotton-factorage firms in the South, which flourished during the war by running the Union blockade around Charleston en route to its branch office in Liverpool, England. When the federal government pressed claims against Fraser and Company in 1867, the firm folded with liabilities of $2.5 million, the biggest single blow to the city's economy after 1865. Creditors went after the Trenholms, claiming that both were active partners in the firm. The Trenholms shifted their assets to other members of the family to protect their fortune, but the government filed a claim totalling more than $35,000 against their firm, Trenholm and Son. While the legal battle dragged on, the Trenholms moved strictly into cotton factoring. By 1873 they claimed capital of over $1 million. The father, it was said, "has more influence than any man in the city" and was one who "controls through his influence several corporations, also a large portion of our wharf property"—the "wealthiest man in this section." George Trenholm died in 1876, and William inherited his role as a major force in postwar Charleston: "one of the best businessmen of this city and enjoys confidence of all." In addresses to the local chamber of commerce and other business associations, young Trenholm became a sharp but constructive critic of the conservative Charleston business community and a firm advocate of the New South spirit. Typical of so much of Charleston youth and talent, Trenholm left the city in 1885 to explore better opportunities elsewhere. He accepted an appointment from President Cleveland as comptroller of the currency and then pursued a career in finance in New York City.[37]

Another of Charleston's postwar models of business success was Robert Adger, who began his career as a cotton factor with his father in James A. Adger and Company sometime before 1848. Worth at least $1 million, the company was described as "one of the best and oldest houses in this place." The Adgers were "the Rothschilds of Charleston," according to the R. G. Dun agent's report. Adger's grandfather came to Charleston from County Antrim, Ireland, in 1790 and joined a small, prosperous cohort of Scots-Irish Presbyterian merchants and bankers in the city.[38] By 1858, when his father died, Robert Adger alone was worth $400,000. After the war Adger, with the aid of David Lopez, a local Jewish mechanic, became the first Charleston capitalist to enter phosphate mining in a big way. He organized the Coosaw Mining Company in 1873 with $200,000 in capital from Brown Brothers of Baltimore (Adger's allies in the cotton trade since the 1850s). The Coosaw's board of directors included Charleston's "most wealthy and influential businessmen." Coosaw soon became the leading river-mining company in the industry and the most prosperous example of Charleston's postwar enterprise. By 1881 the company assets were estimated worth $1 million, and a small group of local stockholders had already grown rich from its generous dividends. James A. Adger and Company, in the meantime, continued to prosper as cotton factors and agents for a New York steamship line.[39] Though one of the richest men in the city, Robert Adger sat on no board of directors for the city's major banks during the 1880s and was not even a member of the chamber of commerce.[40] There are no hints in the rare public notices of this man as to whether his isolation reflected a single-minded pursuit of his own affairs or a failure of the Charleston business community to enlist him in larger fields of enterprise.

Francis J. Pelzer, a prime representative of Charleston's wealthy German community, offered further proof that Charleston was capable of cultivating men of talent and ambition. He had entered the city sometime after 1848 and emerged in the late nineteenth century as a major force in the local economy. Like many of the German immigrants, Pelzer started out as a grocer in partnership with a compatriot, E. H. Rodgers, sometime before 1851. Rodgers died during the war, and Pelzer went into business as a cotton factor with his former partner's son, Francis S. Rodgers. They must have prospered during the war years, as they were reported to be worth at least $100,000 by 1867. Their capital assets rose steadily to $.5 million in 1875 and then to $1.5 million in 1879. "Doing largest cotton factorage and commission business here, are enterprising firm. Stand well in every respect," the Dun agent reported. By 1883 Pelzer, Rodgers, and Company were estimated to be worth $2.5 million, "one of the strongest houses in the South," with large outside interests, including the Atlantic Phosphate Company and several upcountry textile mills organized by Pelzer and Rodgers. Pelzer was an active member of the Charleston Chamber of Commerce and was serving on at least six local boards of directors by 1880.[41]

Charleston's German enclave nurtured many other models of success in the New South era. John C. H. Claussen was among a group referred to by the Dun agent as Charleston's "industrious" and "pushing" German entrepreneurs. Claussen was a member of four boards of directors in 1880. Beginning as a baker sometime before 1855, he had made money supplying bread to Confederate troops during the war. "I suppose if the Confederate money he handled was put into a pile it would be more than his ovens could hold," the Dun agent speculated in 1866. Claussen branched out to establish a flour mill after the war, and by 1871 he claimed at least $100,000 in assets.[42]

Frederick W. Wagener, another German, began a small grocery and liquor business in Charleston before the war. He served as captain of the Confederate German Artillery of Charleston during the war. In 1865 the firm Wagener, Heath, and Monses was described as without "much means," but the proprietors were "said to be industrious and honest men of families," with $20,000 to $25,000 worth of capital invested in the firm by 1869. "Active pushing fellows," a later report warned, "but not cautious enough and blow too heavy." By 1876 Wagener had built a large warehouse on East Bay—"one of the finest buildings in the South"—and expanded into the cotton business. The firm's net assets rose from $195,000 in 1876 to $415,000 by 1880, but R. G. Dun and Company still warned that "they are too much extended or too liberally." The firm continued to deal in groceries as well, claiming the largest business among all Charleston firms in that line by 1881. Wagener invested heavily in land on the Charleston Neck and in the Royal Bag and Yarn Manufacturing Company, one of the city's few ventures into the textile industry. Wagener also launched a prosperous tourist resort for northern visitors in Summerville, outside Charleston. In 1901 he was the moving spirit behind the South Carolina Interstate and West Indian Exposition. But for all his wealth and drive, Wagener was one who, during the 1880s, held no positions on the city's boards of directors and was not even a member of the Charleston Chamber of Commerce until 1883. Despite his major efforts on behalf of Charleston's exposition, among many other contributions, Wagener, like most of this city's new men of wealth after the war, remained a nearly invisible man in the annals of the city's history.[43]

The richest man in postwar Charleston, George Walton Williams, was yet another who came from outside the Charleston "aristocracy," amassed great wealth, and was an active proponent of the community's fortunes, yet remained an obscure figure in local society. Williams came to Charleston from the upcountry of northern Georgia, by way of Augusta, in 1852. He was a wholesale grocer in partnership with Daniel Hand of New York. A temperate Methodist, Williams took pride in his role as the only house in his line that did not carry liquor. Williams rose before sunrise and put in long hours at his Charleston business, and by 1858 he had built a personal fortune of $250,000. Before the war, Williams "saw what was coming, immediately moved up his business, converted everything into Real Estate, gold, cotton, and exchange," and managed to save somewhere between $100,000 and $200,000 in foreign exchange, plus real estate and securities, when the war ended. It was Williams, white flag in hand, who greeted the federal troops as they first entered the city in February 1865.[44]

After the war he quickly bought up land in the city's desolate burned district and constructed fifteen brick warehouses for cotton, merchandise, and fertilizer. He also rebuilt the Charleston Iron Works and put up a large cotton press. In order to move the huge shipments of cotton received at Charleston, his company needed more currency, so Williams organized the First National Bank in 1865 with $.5 million in authorized capital. His firm's total assets, apart from the banks and other enterprises, were estimated at over $1 million, free of debt. George W. Williams and Company was touted as "the strongest house in the city," with at least $2 million in capital by 1873. In 1879, after an embarrassing venture in speculation on the New York Cotton Exchange, Williams sold out his interests in the grocery and cotton business and went into banking full time. In 1874 he had opened the Carolina Savings Bank under state charter, also with $.5 million in authorized capital, and since then had devoted most of his time to banking. Williams joined Pelzer, Wagener, and Trenholm as an outspoken advocate of Charleston's potential in the New South, but his frustrations kept pace with his efforts to turn around the city's declining economic fortunes.[45]

Williams and other men of wealth in postwar Charleston gave proof that ambitious men could wring prosperity out of what seemed nothing more than a chronically stagnant city. But their material fortunes never matched the moral capital controlled by the old families, whose inertia, if not opposition, left Charleston in the backwater.

Mobile's Business Leaders

As in Charleston, Mobile's cotton traders and commission merchants were the heart of the city's business community. Over 40 percent of the 1880 elite were in this line, and many of the others took part in buying and selling cotton either at some phase in their career or on the side. The cotton factors occupied key positions on the boards of the city's leading banks, insurance companies, and corporations of all types, and they enjoyed great prestige, though the foundations of their wealth eroded in the late nineteenth century. As the cotton trade declined after the war, many Mobile traders shifted into other occupations, often into the many new fire, commercial, and life insurance companies that cropped up in the 1870s when new state regulations favored home-owned companies. But for most of these men, buying and selling cotton was all they knew, and it was still a prestigious line of trade even as the profits from it withered.

None embodied the spirit of the Mobile cotton men more fully than Daniel E. Huger. Born in South Carolina and raised in Louisiana and Kentucky, he had migrated to Mobile in 1856 at the age of twenty. He became a leading figure in Mobile's cotton trade over the next half century before his death in 1904. Regarded as the "Father of the Cotton Exchange," he was serving his fifth term as president of that venerable body when he died. But Huger's reputation derived more from his social than from his business acumen. He cut a wide swathe in Mobile's lively society circles, where he made a mark as a founder of the Manassas Club, a prestigious men's social club, and of the Gulf Fishing and Hunting Club, where he indulged his favorite hobbies. He was also a leading figure in the city's Mardi Gras mystic societies, in which Mobile's cotton factors played a central role, and was locally known as having served as the celebration's first Felix, Emperor of Carnival. A member of Christ Church, Mobile's most prestigious Episcopal congregation, Huger was a convivial, well-met fellow, generally popular and known for his gregarious sociability. Huger had served in the Confederate army and had been promoted to colonel.

Mobile's Cotton Exchange and Chamber of Commerce, 1890s. (University of South Alabama Photographic Archives)

Generous in defeat, however, Huger welcomed as honored guests of the Manassas Club General Ulysses S. Grant and Major General Canby, whose forces had occupied Mobile at the end of the war. In Mobile, it seemed, visiting conquerors offered yet another occasion for festivity.

After the war, Huger returned to his cotton-brokerage business. The R. G. Dun agent reported that he was in partnership with a man named Batre (an old French family in Mobile) in 1867, worth about $25,000 and "doing fair business, considered reliable." Later, Huger went into partnership with Charles J. Michailoffsky and by 1871 was reported worth only $3,000 to $5,000. Soon, though, he was said to be "doing a large brokerage business," and by July 1873 his worth had jumped to "fully" $15,000, with "the largest business in his line the past season. Stands very high as a broker." But by 1876 there were warnings of Huger's expensive taste for good living. "Are supposed to be in receipt of a large income, but they live fast, entertain grandly and perhaps spend their earnings and more besides." By 1879 his partner had withdrawn, and Huger continued alone, described as "a good reliable broker but weak financially," with "old matters hanging over him."

Huger later joined with other partners and continued, on a declining scale, until his death. From his home on St. Francis and Jackson streets, Huger walked or drove his carriage to the Cotton Exchange or to his office on St. Michael, where most of the cotton factors worked in second-floor offices connected by ornate iron catwalks that bridged the street below. Indeed, the elderly Huger was seen on the floor of the Cotton Exchange just hours before he took ill for the last time. He died at home a few days later—on Mardi Gras, as chance would have it.

Huger died intestate, and the probate records reveal only portions of his estate: some unappraised real estate in town and a few nearly worthless shares in two textile mills and a Mexican gold mine, all together valued at less than $700. By all accounts, even in his salad days, no one would have mistaken Huger for the kind of hard-driving businessman so celebrated in Atlanta and other cities. Yet he represented a certain style that combined honorable business dealings with an affable sociability, marks that stood well among Mobile's business community in the postwar era.[46]

Louis Touart was another of Mobile's old-line cotton factors, and his career paralleled Huger's in many ways. A native of Mobile, Touart was born in 1835 to one of Mobile's many Catholic families. Educated locally at Spring Hill College, he entered the cotton business at seventeen, beginning a career that would span more than half a century. Touart was an early member of the Cowbellions, a young man's social group that presaged the postwar Mardi Gras mystic societies. Following service with the Confederate Mobile Cadets, Touart resumed his career in the cotton trade. By 1866 he was reported in partnership with a man named Lawler in a firm worth $10,000: "good honest and reliable young men," they were thought to be "energetic and enterprising." By 1868 Touart had reorganized in partnership with James Touart, apparently his brother, and over the next few years they built the firm up to an estimated worth of close to $50,000. "Lewis Touart has fine business capacity," the Dun agent observed in 1876. By then he was president and major stockholder of Washington Fire and Marine, one of several new insurance companies in Mobile. He continued in the cotton business but split from his brother "because of the dissipated habits of James," according to the credit report. Lewis was, by 1881, worth $50,000 personally and was regarded as an "exceptional, upright, high-toned man . . . not at all speculatively inclined," with solid holdings of real estate among other investments.

Touart continued as a cotton factor until shortly before he died, when he transferred the business to his sons and son-in-law. "Mr. Touart is one of the old-fashioned factors, of that type with which it was a pleasure to transact business," the *Mobile Register* noted at the time of the transfer. "Conservative, careful of the interests of clients, his trained knowledge of market conditions and problems made his advice and services most valuable to the planters and interior merchants who were and are his consignors." His death in 1904 was mourned by the men of the Cotton Exchange, who flew their flag at half mast in tribute to one of the brethren whom they remembered as being "straight as a die."[47]

While Huger and Touart survived and even maintained a modest competence amid the declining cotton market, others among Mobile's cotton traders fell to ruin. Andrew Jackson Ingersoll, a vice president of the Cotton Exchange, had been in business for some time before the war. He served as a lieutenant colonel in the Confederate army and was thought to have made money in business during the war as well, apparently from running cotton through the blockade. By 1866 the Dun report claimed that his firm, a partnership with H. O. Brewer, was worth at least $300,000 and later said that Ingersoll alone was worth $600,000. With Brewer in New York and with branch houses in New York and Boston, Ingersoll and Company was riding high until late May 1867, when a telegram reported that the firm could not meet payment on a million dollars in notes. The company "suffered heavily" with the failure of Fraser and Company in Charleston and barely survived without suspending payment altogether. By June 1872, Ingersoll and Company was reportedly worth only $30,000, and its credit rating had plummeted. "Ingersoll is an old merchant and highly respected," the 1874 report noted, "makes a good income and spends every $ he earns. Has a large and expensive family." "Lives high. . . . Lives expensively," the credit reports warned in 1875. "Looked upon as a man of high honor." "Has a few friends in the East who send him occasionally orders for cotton," an 1877 report explained. Ingersoll was elected vice president of the Cotton Exchange around 1877, but his fortune and business capacity were rapidly deteriorating by that time. "Appears to be dwindling down," the agent reported of the firm in 1880, "owing mainly to the habits of A. J. Ingersoll who is a heavy drinker and cannot attend to business as he ought to." The situation only got worse, and the next year Ingersoll was described as "very dissipated. . . . It is thought by his best friends that his mind is affected in consequence. . . . [C]annot be regarded as safe to do business with." By 1890 Ingersoll had picked up a minor post as vice consul for Brazil, but he stayed on in Mobile until his death in 1894; he was a sad reminder of the bad times that afflicted Mobile's once prosperous cotton trade.[48]

Sober newcomers to Mobile often fared no better in the cotton trade. Cornelius E. Thames came in from Selma and started out in a grocery firm with two others in 1866, when he was about forty-seven years old. He moved into cotton within a year. Estimated to be worth close to $40,000 on his own, Thames was the chief backer of the firm and thought to be "a man of fine business qualities." He did a strong business until 1873, when the panic hit the firm and forced it into liquidation in the face of $135,000 in liabilities. By the beginning of 1874 Thames's firm was "totally broke." Like many in the cotton trade, however, Thames had moved into Mobile's growing insurance business a few years earlier and was president of the Alabama Gold Life Insurance Company. Beginning with $200,000 in paid-in capital, the stock rose dramatically to 150 percent of par. Thames was said to manage the company well and had invested nearly $750,000 of its assets safely in gold and "good reliable securities."[49]

Leroy Brewer was another newcomer to the Mobile cotton trade who managed quite well for himself in the postwar economy. Born in a log cabin in the piney woods section of Alabama in 1818, Brewer was one of Mobile's more notable new men of wealth who rose out of the Alabama yeomanry. During his youth, he shared the "hard drudgery of farm life" with his four older brothers, and in his limited spare time he attended rural common schools and the local Methodist church. "My father," he later recalled, "taught me industry, economy and honesty, my mother taught me all that and religion too."

Brewer entered mercantile life in a country store in Mississippi sometime in the 1840s and came into Mobile in 1851 to begin a career as a cotton factor. He lost heavily during the war and afterward resumed business in wholesale groceries and cotton. In 1869 Leroy Brewer and Company, a firm with three other partners, claimed a net worth of $100,000 and was described as "the largest business in city"; in 1875 it was the "largest business in state in their line." Brewer, by this time, had invested considerably outside the business in real estate, insurance and bank stocks, and federal bonds. In 1878 he reorganized the firm, withdrew from cotton brokerage, and concentrated solely on the wholesale grocery trade, with his nephew, Thomas P. Brewer, as managing partner and himself as the capitalist. The firm was burned out and suffered heavy losses in 1884, following which Brewer returned to cotton factoring and carried on until his death nine years later.

Brewer was thought to be worth up to $150,000 on his own by the end of the 1870s, and his company was regarded as "one of the oldest and most substantial firms here." Brewer was also president of the Planters and Merchants Insurance Company, a director of National Commercial Bank, and vice president of the Mobile Board of Trade. "Mobile needs but a few more wide-awake firms of this class to regain her pristine commercial activity," the *Register* said of Brewer and Company in 1880.[50] Brewer was a leading figure in Mobile politics as well, serving in the Redeemer cause as Mobile's representative in the 1872 legislature and as delegate to the constitutional convention in 1875. Brewer served in the legislature again in 1882 and was regarded as a serious candidate for governor at that time.[51] He died in 1893 with a modest estate of nearly $69,000, most of it in his cotton business and local real estate, state bonds, and insurance stock.[52]

Albert C. Danner was another of Mobile's postwar newcomers who brought uncommon energy to the business community. Born in Virginia in 1843, he spent most of his youth in Missouri. After serving in the Confederate army, Danner came to Mobile with no resources and "had difficulty making his way at first." He became a pioneer in Mobile's nascent lumber industry, one of the few dynamic new sectors in the local economy outside of cotton in the late nineteenth century. Danner also actively promoted Mobile as an outlet for Alabama coal.[53] He and his first partner, Captain Allman, were described in 1868 as "young men of thrift and energy," but with only $1,000 to $2,000 in capital. By 1872 Danner had found other monied backers in Mobile, particularly among the lumber interests of rural Alabama and Mississippi. He expanded his Mobile business and opened a branch in New Orleans. The Mobile firm was now considered worth $30,000 to $40,000, with "prospects excellent." A. C. Danner's company quickly became the largest lumber and coal firm in Mobile. Its net worth rose to between $75,000 and $100,000 by 1875 and about $200,000 eight years later.

Danner was regarded as a "very progressive, clever, energetic, economical businessman." He became a leading spokesman for a "new Mobile," urging more aggressive promotion of the city and attacking its complacency. Returning from a business trip that took him through Birmingham and other industrial towns in northern Alabama, Danner applauded their "energy and push," particularly in attracting new industries. In contrast, he complained, "our moneyed men seem to be perfectly satisfied with our present conditions" and say "'Oh! Mobile's doing well enough.'"[54] He had become a director of People's Savings Bank and in 1883 was elected president of the Bank of Mobile. Danner was still only forty years old, and his business career would carry well into the twentieth century before his death in 1921.[55]

Jonathan Kirkbride offers another example of a Mobilian rising outside the cotton trade. Born in New Jersey in 1818, he arrived in Mobile in the late 1850s, beginning as a mason and builder. Kirkbride invested in local real estate and was described as a "prosperous mechanic" in 1859. The next year he joined Ira W. Porter in a sash and door wholesale business, selling northern-made goods on consignment. By the time the war came, Kirkbride was worth $50,000, most of it in real estate. During the war, he and Porter became involved in the cotton trade and came out with forty bales of valuable cotton at the end. They went into wholesale hardware after the war and thrived. Within ten years, Kirkbride had established an individual net worth of $150,000, now diversified in real estate, railroads, and bank stock. He served as vice president of Mobile Savings Bank and was widely involved in affairs of Mobile's business community before his death in 1895.[56]

Adolph Proskauer was one of Mobile's Jewish merchants who emerged as an important element in the local business community after the war. He first appeared as a bookkeeper for William H. Leinkauf's variety store in 1860, and after the war he was recorded as a partner with George F. Werborn in a "family grocery." This was a small firm worth only $4,000 to $5,000, but it was backed by Lehman Brothers of Montgomery, forerunner of today's well-known New York brokerage house. Proskauer moved into cotton factoring sometime before 1870 and became an agent for the Prattville Factory, a textile manufacturer. He rapidly built a personal fortune of $107,000 by 1873. Two years later he was described as "one of our rising men. . . . Has lately added to his real estate by purchase of an Elegant Residence."

The depression hit Proskauer hard, and in 1876 he chose to "lay quiet a while in the full endeavor to straighten up all he has lost." His real estate lost value, and he was now regarded as worth only $75,000 net. He allowed his own cotton-factorage business to decline and became a buyer for Lehman Brothers, now of New York, and for their branch in Liverpool. Proskauer, an 1880 Dun agent confided, "is an old and well-known citizen, regarded as a man of first class financial ability and shrewd in the management of his business." But he went on to provide evidence that it was not only old regulation southerners who gave in to the sybaritic air of Mobile. "He is said to be a man of expensive tastes and lives high." His income of $15,000 to $20,000 a year "he exhausts as he is a high liver and some what given to extravagances in his tastes." His net worth was now down to $20,000. By June 1882 Proskauer's expensive life-style led to financial catastrophe. After quietly shifting assets to his brother-in-law, Manuel Forcheimer, and to William H. Leinkauf, both prominent merchants in Mobile, Proskauer sold two bills of exchange against Lehman Brothers to Mobile banks, and both were "dishonored" in New York. Proskauer, facing some $100,000 in liabilities, suspended payments and "took dangerously ill." At the end of the year his debt had been reduced to $40,000, but it was 1883 before he was completely clear.[57]

For many of the business elites in the old cotton ports of Charleston and Mobile, the changed conditions of the postwar South undermined the foundations of their wealth. Often, older men, unable to adapt to the new order, clung tenaciously to their established mooring as the economic tide ebbed. Others, more able and willing to respond to whatever opportunities confronted them, built impressive personal fortunes amid the decay. But in both cities, these ascendant men of new wealth found it difficult to overcome the powerful economic undertow that pulled against these cities. Their hopes and ambitions played to great advantage in the building of private fortunes, but their numbers were too few, and their powers of organization and influence too weak, to enable them to transform personal ambition into community enterprise.

6 *The Atlanta Spirit*

We have raised a brave and beautiful city.
—Henry Grady, 1886

A businessman visiting Atlanta passed outside a banquet hall in the Kimball House Hotel and stood transfixed by a spectacle of community enterprise. "Why during the hour I stood by that door I saw and I heard more enthusiasm than I have ever observed in all my life apart from a Confederate Veterans' meeting." Some four hundred businessmen inside, described as "the cream of the business element in Atlanta," were gathered to launch an industrial exposition and were being treated to speeches on Atlanta's past and future. They cheered lustily on every occasion their city was even mentioned. "It was the one word—'Atlanta'—that set the gathering to making a noise, a sort of talisman for a Babylonian confusion." The visitor was amazed at the excitement a city could inspire: "To me it seemed that it was Atlanta alone every one in the banquet hall loved. For the time being at least every man present appeared to have forgotten his wife, his home, his father, his mother, his sweetheart. Atlanta was the all in all." "Nothing on earth," he concluded, "can delay the advancement and the growth of a town which has such loyal, loving, devoted citizens as were gathered in that banquet hall last night."[1]

What the visitor saw at the Kimball House was an example of the typically boisterous celebration of local patriotism that flourished in the New South and developed to its fullest in Atlanta. Boosters expressed the community's faith in its capacity to shape its own destiny. This faith sprang from a set of common goals capable of uniting the business elite who were the major stockholders and directors in this enterprise of city building. At the same time, the booster ethos countered powerful forces of competition and factional conflict that divided the business class. City boosting subordinated the pursuit of self-aggrandizement to the collective task of city building and demanded organized rather than individual entrepreneurship. Whatever the booster spirit actually did for the building of cities, though, it was a powerful adhesive in the making of the business class.

Foremost among the common goals that united the business elite was the pursuit of growth for their city. It was an article of unquestioned faith that bigger was better, and that the faster a city grew the more successful were its promoters. Sentimental pride in small-town intimacy was for the losers in the race for urban greatness. Romantic nostalgia about protecting historic landmarks and controlling reckless growth was the mark of "old fogy" defiance of progress. The true city booster looked to the census of population as his measure of success, and he took pride in the rapid obliteration of old landmarks and old ways. The successful city was viewed as a dynamic growth machine, with every citizen and every component—commerce, industry, transportation, government, even schools and churches—contributing in some measure to the pursuit of expansion.[2]

Nineteenth-century urban promoters recognized the importance of "natural advantages," particularly the role of a central location to markets and resources, and they never tired of extolling the beneficence of nature's blessings to their community. Many were obsessed by a kind of geographical determinism that, they believed, destined some cities to play a dominant role in the region or nation. Much promotional literature was devoted to elaborate maps and statistics describing the ideal location of the chosen city in the larger scheme of commerce and the healthiness and beauty of the environment. But natural advantages were not regarded as sufficient; human effort was essential to capitalize on nature's blessings, to publicize them at the very least, and to overcome whatever adversities geography and rival cities presented to the ambitious city. "Altitude plus Attitude" was the formula to which Atlanta booster Ivan Allen attributed his city's unique success.[3] Except for its healthy and cool elevation, and of course its central location, Atlanta's natural advantages were not obvious. A Nashville editor contrasted the prosperous farm lands and river system that surrounded his city with Atlanta's "sparsely settled . . . plain of sand ridges dotted with scrub and black-jack thickets," with "no navigable stream of any kind" within a dozen miles. Atlanta's booming growth, this admiring rival concluded, simply proved "there's more in the man than there is in the land."[4]

At a time when most businesses still took the form of small family firms and partnerships, the city-building enterprise brought businessmen together in a large-scale enterprise. There were rough parallels between these community enterprises and the strategies that successful businesses in nineteenth-century America were following as they formed large, multi-unit corporate enterprises that required a new managerial hierarchy to administer them.[5]

The changes in nineteenth-century capitalism affected the capacity for cooperation among business leaders in contradictory ways. The trend toward specialization in marketing fragmented the local business community by separating wholesale from retail and different lines of trade from one another. But this trend also reduced the kind of direct competition that was pervasive among small-scale general merchants. At the same time, the growing influence of agencies outside the community, particularly railroads and the federal government, demanded a collective response from local businessmen. A common enemy—usually the railroads, who were accused of freight rate discrimination—provided the essential rallying cry for local businessmen.

Though much of this cooperative effort among businessmen took place in ad hoc organizations formed to meet narrow, short-term goals, it was the chamber of commerce or board of trade (these and other terms, like "merchants exchange," were used without meaningful distinction) that became the permanent base for an organized business community in most American towns and cities. Only a handful formed before 1860, and few of those survived the war. It was in the late nineteenth century, with the emergence of a national economy, that businessmen everywhere felt a new urgency to organize.[6] By the end of the century, about three thousand local chambers of commerce, going by various names, had been formed in towns and cities at every level of the urban hierarchy. With the proliferation in numbers, there was also an elaboration in the functions these commercial bodies performed. During the late nineteenth century, chambers in the larger cities evolved from rudimentary merchants exchanges, which provided members with a regulated market, into large, powerful agencies through which the local business class could advance its views on civic affairs as well as business matters.[7]

In southern cities, it was cotton buyers and wholesale merchants (usually in foodstuffs) who typically formed the core of the early commercial associations, which centered around the telegraph ticker and the price board. Retail merchants were drawn to wholesale sellers operating within a regulated market where prices, weights, and other measures were guaranteed by all members to meet certain standards, and where arbitration committees, vested with the power of law in some cities, resolved disputes and discouraged unfair practices. Commercial associations also took it upon themselves to collect economic statistics, issue trade reports, and advertise the favorable prospects of their cities in a multitude of pamphlets. Beyond these market and promotional services, the chambers came to serve as organized pressure groups through which local businessmen could speak with one voice to promote their interests. Whether protesting freight rates before a railroad corporation or representing local business interests before government agencies, the chamber of commerce became the businessman's lobbyist.

Organizing the Atlanta Spirit

Atlanta at first had difficulty in constructing a platform upon which businessmen could work together. But in comparison with other southern cities, Atlanta's commercial associations displayed great strength and continuity, and its Chamber of Commerce played a decisive role in converting the renowned "Atlanta spirit" into an effective program for city building.

Founded in 1860, the first Atlanta Chamber of Commerce aimed at fighting railroad rate discrimination, a perennial issue, and sustaining commercial relations with the North. After secession it turned to promoting direct trade with Europe, part of a larger southern aim of gaining economic autonomy from the North. This chamber foundered during the war, and in 1866 wholesale merchants reorganized under a new Board of Trade, "for the purpose of establishing uniformity of action in the promotion of its mercantile interests." The board's primary function was to provide daily quotations on commodity prices, a service of immense value to cotton brokers and to wholesalers purchasing western grain and meat. Under president William J. Lowry, a leading banker, the Board of Trade held daily meetings, and its membership increased rapidly.[8]

In 1871, amid a booming economic recovery, Atlanta's businessmen formed a new Chamber of Commerce. The new organization was led by a group of "merchants, millers, and business men of Atlanta," who were dissatisfied with the narrow base of the Board of Trade. They put out the call to every sector of the local economy, from wholesale and retail merchants to "all business men having the welfare of Atlanta at heart," to meet in Skating Rink Hall and form a new commercial body. The center of attention was the railroads. "Atlanta," Jonathan Norcross told the assembled crowd at the first meeting, "was large enough to speak to the railroads and other corporations. . . . She would be heard if she spoke through a Chamber of Commerce."[9]

The new body moved beyond providing market quotes to address a range of issues affecting the local business environment. It established standing committees on internal improvements, transportation, manufacturers, taxes and finance, insurance, legislation, real estate, market reports, and statistics. For several years, the chamber held daily meetings at eleven each morning to issue commodity price quotations "and for consideration of such general matters as might be brought before the body."[10]

Heading the new chamber as president was Benjamin E. Crane, a thirty-six-year-old wholesale grocer and commission merchant, who played a major role in the chamber's formative years. A native of Georgia, Crane was trained in civil engineering in New York and served the Confederacy as quartermaster during the war. He entered what soon became a prosperous wholesale grocery and commission business in Atlanta with T. L. Langston in 1866. By 1871 Crane was a rich young merchant with a successful business that brought him into contact with all the problems and opportunities Atlanta merchants faced. Rather than rotate the office of president as an honorific post, Atlanta's chamber kept Crane at the helm continuously from 1871 until his untimely death in 1885. Crane not only brought greater visibility to the chamber in Atlanta and in Georgia, but as the elected chair of the National Commercial Convention at St. Louis in 1872, he brought notice to Atlanta within a national forum.[11]

The new Chamber of Commerce focused, as had its predecessors, on the issue of railroad rates and assumed the role of lobbyist for Atlanta's merchants. The major point of contention involved the western grain trade. One rival was Nashville, which was favored by the L&N as a grain and flour distribution center for the South and was given lower rates than Atlanta on northeastern imports as well. The other culprits, in Atlanta's view, were the Georgia railroads that favored Augusta, Savannah, and other rivals by giving them much lower through rates. The Chamber of Commerce offered to contract with any railroad that would offer the lowest fares and promised the road a monopoly on all business with chamber members. Soon the Georgia Railroad and the Western and Atlantic agreed to work with the chamber's Committee on Transportation. At the same time, the chamber persuaded the city to use its powers as stockholder in the Georgia Railroad to force concessions on freight rates. In 1872 the chamber launched a full investigation into "the abuses practiced by the railroad companies engaged in carrying freight to this city, and to devise remedies for same."[12]

The chamber quickly moved beyond issues directly affecting their present business operations to promote Atlanta's general economic development. It was the Atlanta Chamber of Commerce that led the movement in 1872–73 for the Atlantic and Great Western Canal, a spectacular project that would have connected the Tennessee River and Atlantic Ocean by way of Atlanta. Inspired by fantasies of a southern version of the Erie Canal, the city sent off representatives to lobby Congress on the subject, and the Chamber of Commerce called for a major convention of governors from all states interested in the project. Atlanta played host to the convention, held in May 1873, and its businessmen and political leaders took a leading role in promoting the dream of a grand canal for the South. The panic of 1873 cast a dark shadow over further plans for a canal, aside from the practical problems and expense of such a project. But Atlanta's aggressive role in championing it drew attention to the Atlanta spirit.[13] Beginning in 1871, the chamber also successfully lobbied the federal government to make Atlanta a port of entry and to erect a new federal customhouse. Later the chamber led a campaign to establish a U.S. mint at

Atlanta. On the local level, during the early 1870s the chamber investigated the high property insurance rates in Atlanta and pushed city officials to improve water and fire service "in the mercantile portion of the city."[14]

The Chamber of Commerce continued to meet daily, even as the depression of the 1870s descended and its membership dwindled. But when Atlanta's economy began to recover, the chamber failed to expand beyond the stalwart corps of grocery merchants and bankers that had led it since the 1860s. Meetings became infrequent, and membership withered to less than 140 individuals representing 50 firms.[15] The annual dues were barely enough to cover rent. Though the chamber played a supporting role in Atlanta's successful International Cotton Exposition of 1881, the city had outgrown the old chamber, and by 1883 another major reorganization was essential.

By that time, President Crane admitted, the Chamber of Commerce was moribund, "held together only by the efforts of a few grocery merchants and provision dealers," who met infrequently above a store on Alabama Street in what one member complained was a "dingy little room . . . to consider questions of the gravest importance."[16] The chamber decided to raise the initiation fee to $50 (and to twice that after July 1 of that year), and it launched a membership drive that soon boosted the rolls to over two hundred "good and true business men." The revenues were invested in a new building, "in keeping," as one member put it, "with the dignity and acknowledged commercial importance of the organization."[17]

At the same time, Atlanta merchants tried to organize a commercial club as a "distinct" though "subsidiary" organization, designed purely as a club "intended to supply the social feature that a strict trade organization cannot start or control." This group would support the new Chamber of Commerce with "a club of influence and earnestness that will enlist the sympathy and support of all reputable classes of our people." It was "the social element"—good food, drink, speeches, and entertainment at lunches and dinner banquets downtown—one observer explained, "that our commercial organizations have always lacked, and lacking which they have always gone to pieces through indifference."[18]

By early 1885 the new Chamber of Commerce Building, a four-story brick structure, stood proudly in the heart of the city at the intersection of Hunter and Pryor streets. Worth an estimated $52,000, it was described as the "handsomest and most substantial structure in Atlanta." It was symbolic of the growing importance of the chamber in Atlanta's affairs that the building's ground floors were occupied by the city government.[19] Its opening, the *Atlanta Constitution* proclaimed, marked "a new era for Atlanta. . . . It means cooperation among her merchants, the organization of her trade, the systematization of her business." The board room was filled with a "jolly lot of merchants . . .

lunching, gossiping, applauding, listening to the tickers." This mix of business and sociability lay at the heart of the new chamber and its role in forging a coherent business class. "A light lunch set at 12 o'clock each day," the *Constitution* advised, would instill a "habit to go on 'change at noon," and "the business features would evolve rapidly from the social idea. . . . Fifty of Atlanta's businessmen never come together . . . without advancing Atlanta's interests in some way." In this manner, the chamber would become "the throbbing, pulsing heart of our commercial system."[20] And so it did: by 1890 membership had climbed to about 600 individuals, representing 350 firms.[21]

The earlier idea of an auxiliary commercial club with a purely social purpose did not bear fruit until 1892, when such a club opened its quarters in the upper floors of the new Chamber of Commerce Building. The club's founders took pains to promise a gentlemanly decorum, a prospect assured by the "older and matured business and professional men of the city" who dominated its membership. "There will be no feature in it," the club's new officers went on, "which would be found improper in any gentleman's private residence."[22] It was out of concern for the moral propriety of a men's club that wives were invited to the opening night gala.[23] While the Chamber of Commerce offered a mix of business and pleasure at lunch, the club's aim was to provide convivial social contact among men after business hours, "to effect through a pleasant medium an enlarged acquaintance, and promote a beneficial intercourse among the best classes of Atlanta citizens." More than that, the club promised to "aid in advancing the material interests and general welfare of the city."[24]

During the panic of 1893, the Chamber of Commerce took the lead in subduing the financial crisis by urging local banks to issue scrip from their clearinghouses. This emergency currency allowed Atlanta merchants to move the cotton crop that fall, and the chamber's decisive action shored up business confidence.[25] During the depression the chamber also sponsored a joint committee of businessmen, manufacturers, and laborers to stimulate "the consumption of home manufactures" and "bring to Atlanta a revival of business." This "plan of cooperation" between business and labor may have had little real effect on the economic slump, but it cast the chamber as spokesmen for the general welfare of the "working men of Atlanta" as well as for its business class.[26] In the nadir of the depression, it was the Chamber of Commerce that rallied the business community to promote a daring and enormously successful industrial exposition in 1895.[27]

At the end of the depression of the 1890s, the chamber launched several new membership campaigns and regained its former total of more than three hundred member firms. Initiation fees were lowered from $50 to $10, and a series of banquets with prominent speakers, "meant to revive the old Atlanta spirit" and "bring in new blood," were staged beginning in 1897.[28] So successful were these affairs that the chamber decided for a time to host them bimonthly.[29] "These dinners," an approving reporter for the *Constitution* wrote, "will give the membership an opportunity to become personally acquainted, and will serve in a measure to weld and strengthen their common interests." The speeches and the discussions that followed became "notable events; attracting the attention of business men in all parts of the country."[30]

The chamber made a special effort to bring in young businessmen who, one observer speculated, may have felt uncomfortable in an organization described as being dominated by "men who have grown old and gray in the service of the city." "Let the young men organize!," the *Constitution* cheered.[31] A Young Men's Business League formed in early 1899 under the chamber's tutelage and then flourished as an independent organization that soon exceeded the chamber in numbers. By the end of 1900, the league had merged into the chamber, bringing with it a new group of younger men and more manufacturers.[32]

Atlanta's enlarged Chamber of Commerce came to play a more visible and more instrumental role in directing the city's economic development and civic affairs after 1900. It worked directly with the city council to sponsor a number of innovative new measures for Atlanta's growth and social reform. The Greater Georgia Association, launched by the chamber in 1903, issued a stream of advertisements in western and northern journals, broadcasting the agricultural riches and industrial opportunities of Atlanta and Georgia. The chamber also sponsored a number of its own publications, mostly guides and picture books filled with favorable statistics and complimentary views of Atlanta. *Atlanta, a Twentieth Century City* (1903), *Sixty Views of Atlanta* (1906), and *Souvenir Album, Atlanta, Georgia* (1907) were all handsome promotional books. Earlier the city and the chamber had produced the *Handbook of the City of Atlanta: A Comprehensive Review of the City's Commercial, Industrial, and Residential Conditions* (1898), which contained a predictably flattering profile of the city.

The chamber claimed a larger public role in other ways as well. Under its guidance, the city established the Atlanta Freight Bureau. Beginning in 1904, the chamber pressured the city to suspend all concessions to railroads for right-of-ways and franchises until they came to terms on freight rates. It was the Chamber of Commerce, in league with city government, that made Atlanta the "convention city" of the Southeast in these years. The chamber led the way in attracting and entertaining an impressive series of national conferences, which became an important source of income and advertisement for Atlanta. To enhance the city's convention facilities, the chamber championed the movement to build a large auditorium-armory, which finally opened to elaborate fanfare in 1909. In that year, the chamber also began to steer public policy in such areas as public schools and public health. It took the lead in investigating health, hospital, and school conditions and successfully campaigned for a $3 million city bond that passed in 1910. The bond funded expansion of badly needed water and sewer systems, enlargement of Grady Hospital, and construction of several new schools.[33] Atlanta's Chamber of Commerce had come to embody the social vision as well as the material interests of diverse business leaders who, through the chamber, found a common voice.

Sinews of Commerce

The key issue before inland cities like Atlanta was transportation, and the railroad was the key to commercial prosperity. Business leaders pursued two strategies in dealing with the railroad: promotion of new projects and lobbying against discrimination by established railroad systems. The first involved supporting new railroad projects, either home-owned enterprises emanating from the city and controlled by local capital or lines projected from other points that might be lured into the local domain.

The other tactic used by the business community was to attack railroads accused of discriminating against their city. With masses of data on freight rates gathered from other cities, local shippers lobbied governments and corporations in a ceaseless campaign against freight rate discrimination. Before the panic of 1873, Atlantans struggled to control their own railroads, but they soon moved toward the latter strategy as more and more railroads fell under the control of large corporations in the hands of northeastern financiers.

Early in the city's history, Atlanta's business leaders eagerly promoted new railroads with the promise that local ownership would deliver the city from the monopoly of outside control. They promoted joint ventures between private investors and city or state governments, and Atlanta businessmen maintained a presence in both levels of politics. They brought to the political arena a Whiggish enthusiasm for government as an instrument for economic development.

Regardless of the extent of local private or government support, the prospects of Atlanta's building a railroad free of outside control were dim in the postwar era. The entreaties for local autonomy, however clamorous, were probably more important as a device for soliciting local subscriptions than as a realistic strategy for building a modern transportation system. In 1868 the Air-Line, a direct line to Charlotte and Richmond that had been promoted before the war, was revived with great fanfare at a series of mass meetings.[34] Atlanta investors, led by Jonathan Norcross, Alfred Austell, and S. B. Hoyt, raised over $200,000 and persuaded the city council to renew its antebellum pledge of $300,000 to the project. The state of Georgia put in another $240,000, but all together this amounted to less than one-tenth of the costs involved in building the road to Charlotte. It was a Richmond and Danville syndicate, backed by northern capital, that financed and controlled the Air-Line to Atlanta.[35]

The Georgia Western Railroad, launched at the same time as the Air-Line, was another scheme hatched by Atlanta boosters to tap the rich Alabama coal and iron fields and open an alternative route for western grain and Mississippi cotton. Its principal promoters, George Adair, Lemuel P. Grant, Campbell Wallace, and Richard Peters, touted the projected line as the key to Atlanta's industrial future as well as a rich commercial trade route. But this project foundered in the face of a city council that balked at underwriting a second project, opposition from the rival Georgia Railroad, and flagging support from Atlanta investors. When the panic of 1873 hit, only twenty-seven miles of roadway had been graded. A city charter revision in 1874 prohibited further aid to any railroad, and the project languished. When the Georgia Western was revived after the depression of the 1890s, it became a small pawn in a power struggle between the L&N and the Nashville, Chattanooga, and St. Louis and was finally completed in 1883 as the Georgia Pacific, financed and controlled by the Richmond and Danville syndicate.[36]

There would be other campaigns in Atlanta for new railroads. Beginning in 1886, there was a major campaign to build a railroad to the coast, the Atlanta and Florida. But after heroic efforts at local fund raising and years of construction, the road never made it to the ocean and was finally absorbed into J. P. Morgan's Southern Railway system in 1895.[37] As dreams of local control faded, Atlanta's business leaders focused more on a strategy of organizing, investigating, lobbying, and boycotting in order to receive more favorable treatment from the railroad corporate giants and to encourage more competition among them.

Atlanta, like many cities, was reacting to a national shift in railroad organization away from locally sponsored railroads, designed to expand the trading territory of a city, toward large, interstate systems controlled by financiers whose main interests were in corporate profits rather than in benefiting any particular community. The railroads led the way in the business revolution that reshaped small-scale, locally oriented entrepreneurial ventures into large, multi-unit, corporate enterprises in the late nineteenth century.[38] In earlier days, cities had built railroads through private and public investments; now railroads seemed to control the destiny of cities.

Atlanta's business leaders used the image of outsiders controlling the city's commercial fate with great effect. They, and the press, described railroad owners as people who were at best disinterested and at worst determined to thwart Atlanta's destiny as a great city. The depiction proved a reliable device with which to rally local businessmen and incite collective action against a common adversary. The railroads, Jonathan Norcross claimed in 1886, were engaged in "a cunningly devised and deep-laid scheme operating to dry up and destroy the business of a large and hitherto thriving city."[39]

With rhetoric, statistics, committees, petitions, and political lobbyists, the Atlanta merchants hammered away tirelessly at the railroads. When the Southern Railway and Steamship Association, a pool of southern railroads organized in 1875 to stabilize rates, rescinded a long-sought agreement to offer privileged rates on goods reshipped from Atlanta, an angry crowd of merchants met at the Chamber of Commerce. "For years we have been talking to the railroads," said Junius G. Oglesby, a prominent wholesale grocer and chamber leader, addressing the crowd. "[T]he time for talk [is] past." He called for Atlanta merchants to "make a pool to meet the railroad pool," form a committee, and give it complete control of Atlanta freight shipments. The motion passed without dissent. A. C. Wyly, chamber vice president and chair of the meeting, appointed a committee on the spot, calling on two representatives from each line of business.[40] On July 16, 1885, the chamber issued a long list of merchants' names below a pledge whose intemperate language recalled nothing so much as the fury of American patriots rising against the British:

> We, the merchants of Atlanta, whose interests have been trampled, whose
> energies and enterprises have been hampered and embargoed, hereby bind
> and pledge ourselves as business men and citizens, who value the welfare and
> prosperity of our city, to strictly conform to such rules and regulations as the
> "special committee on transportation" may adopt. And we further bind and
> pledge ourselves that we will patronize only such . . . lines . . . as said com-
> mittee shall direct.[41]

This was one of dozens of protests staged by Atlanta merchants against the railroads, and one of several attempts to boycott them.[42] The relentless attack met with a few piecemeal victories. In 1886 the state railroad commission ruled in favor of an Atlanta petition asking that it regulate rates on shipments originating outside Georgia once they crossed the state line.[43]

But the contest between Atlanta merchants and the railroads continued unabated. By 1902 "fifty of the most influential and representative businessmen" established a Freight Bureau. Its aim was to "promote harmony between and advance the mutual interests of the shipper and carrier," according to the conciliatory language of its charter. In truth, it was a full-time advocate of Atlanta's case against the railroads.[44] By 1904 the Chamber of Commerce and the city joined the Freight Bureau in a major confrontation with the railroads and the Georgia Railroad Commission. At the chamber's suggestion, the city used its power to refuse the railroads land-use privileges that they needed for expansion. "Atlanta is up against the fight for her

Atlanta's Chamber of Commerce greets a new passenger train, 1908. (Atlanta Historical Society)

commercial life," an editorial in the *Constitution* exclaimed.[45] The railroads finally compromised, and Atlanta received across-the-board reductions in rates.[46]

"Indeed, it is a mystery," an indignant Chamber of Commerce letter to the railroad pool admitted in 1888, "how the business of Atlanta has continued to occupy the place it has." Dismissing any credit to the railroads, it went on to say: "It can only be accounted for by the energy and industry [Atlanta merchants have] displayed, together with the very close margins at which the merchants do business."[47] Behind that mystery, behind all the rhetoric about railroad abuses and conspiracy, and behind all the numbing statistics on freight rates, Atlanta was thriving along with the railroads. It flourished because of its strategic location at the hub of what, by the 1890s, was no less than ten railroad lines radiating like spokes into the hinterland.[48] Though the railroads formed syndicates in an effort to reduce competition and uphold prices, Atlanta became a vital point of competition among rival companies, and freight rates dropped substantially over time.[49] The vigilance of Atlanta's Chamber of Commerce in fighting for more favorable rates was but one of many forces that enhanced the city's role as a railroad center. Whatever the measure of its influence, the Atlanta business class found in the railroad issue a common cause for organization and action.

The Pursuit of Industry

A city's commercial expansion involved building new railroads, lobbying the existing ones to serve the city better, and exhorting its merchants and drummers to compete with those of rival cities in the hinterland. Once the railroads were built and the frontiers of trade expanded, the limitations of a purely commercial economy became obvious to most cities. By the late nineteenth century urban promoters had come to see industrial development as the key to prosperity and growth. The cities of the New South were leaders and innovators in this movement, and they hailed industry as a means of rapidly overcoming decades of retarded economic development. They published advertising booklets and tracts advertising their cities, passed bond issues and tax exemptions to subsidize industry, and staged grand industrial expositions that set the standard for the nation.[50] Railroads, steam power, and, later, electricity loosened the ties of factories to water-power sites and gave every town and city the right to claim a place in the emerging industrial order.

No dimension of urban promotion seemed more amenable to human manipulation than industrial expansion, and no aspect of economic development appeared more in need of organized planning. Tax incentives, government or private subsidies, stock subscription drives, and more innovative techniques such as the introduction of technological schools, industrial training in public schools, and industrial expositions were all part of the tool kit industrial boosters utilized to bring manufacturing to their cities in the late nineteenth century.

Few cities in the South or North proved more adept at using those tools for industrial development than Atlanta. The Gate City entered the postwar era with the smallest industrial base of all four of the cities under study here. By 1890 it had surpassed all three, and in the succeeding years it expanded its industrial foundation even more substantially. In a city with no water power and no cheap coal close at hand, Atlanta's industrial revolution in the late nineteenth century was a triumph of entrepreneurship, both individual and collective.

Manufacturers and others interested in industrial development adopted the techniques of merchants by creating formal organizations to give a coherent voice to their cause and to apply pressure for its advancement. Several were formed in the early 1870s, beginning with the Atlanta Mechanics' Institute and the Atlanta Agricultural and Industrial Association, both founded in 1872, followed by the German Manufacturing Association three years later. It was the Atlanta Manufacturers' Association, formed in 1872, that became the leading force in the crusade for an industrialized Atlanta. "All manufacturers and all persons interested directly or indirectly" in Atlanta's industrial development

Table 6.1 Atlanta's Industrial Progress, 1870–1900

	1870	1880	1890	1900
Manufacturing establishments	74	196	410	390
Employees (thousands)	1.0	2.8	8.7	9.4
Capital invested (millions)	$.4	$2.5	$9.5	$16.0
Value of product (millions)	$2.0	$4.9	$13.1	$16.7

Sources: Francis A. Walker, *A Compendium of the Ninth Census, {1870}* (Washington, D.C., 1872), 812; U.S. Census Bureau, *Report on Manufacturing Industries in the United States at the Eleventh Census: 1890*, pt. 2 (Washington, D.C., 1895), 38–41; idem, *Twelfth Census of the United States, Manufacturers*, pt. 2 (Washington, D.C., 1902), table 2.

were welcome. The association worked first to encourage the Georgia Western Railroad's plans to build a new road to the Alabama coal fields. Because there was no water power and no other fuel supply nearby, this link would be the vital fuel line for industrial Atlanta. The association also successfully lobbied the city council to waive taxes on new and existing manufacturing companies. George W. Adair took the case to the city by arguing that local monied men were reluctant to invest in industrial ventures unless they could be assured of a high rate of return.[51]

The main achievement of the industrial crusade of the 1870s was the launching of the Atlanta Cotton Factory. Leading the company was the irrepressible Hannibal I. Kimball, the city's most flamboyant promoter. The Manufacturers' Association instigated the campaign for Atlanta's first cotton mill at a crowded meeting in the Mechanics' Institute in July 1874. The hall was packed with members of the Chamber of Commerce, the city council and mayor, and a large group of other Atlantans interested in this industrial experiment. Kimball delivered an impromptu blast of booster rhetoric that set off cotton-mill fever in Atlanta.[52] Later that year, at a formal lecture in the Kimball House ballroom, Kimball, at the invitation of the Mechanics' Institute, laid out his plan for a new mill in a full-blown essay filled with elaborate statistics to prove the irrefutable logic of bringing a cotton mill to Atlanta, the chief interior cotton market of the South. The only conceivable obstacle to Atlanta's success, Kimball warned, would be a failure of local support.

Atlanta had to launch this experiment in industrialization, Kimball announced, but—once it proved successful—outside capital would flow like a river to Atlanta and the South. Kimball set the pace with a pledge of $10,000 and challenged the city's other business leaders to match him. In the depths of a depression, Atlanta's capitalists were slow to respond, and subscriptions fell short of the requisite $250,000. When the depression lifted and the company was reorganized, the campaign was fulfilled, and the mill finally opened in the summer of 1879. By this time, the company was awash in scandal and litigation, mostly due to Kimball, but the cotton mill was a memorable milestone in Atlanta's industrial progress.[53] Indeed, this pioneer had its followers. By 1883 three more cotton mills had appeared in Atlanta. Despite the predictions of outside investments, they were largely the products of local capital and local entrepreneurial talent.[54]

The Atlanta Manufacturers' Association was revived again and again over the next thirty years, each time with renewed commitment to the idea that industrial development required aggressive planning from the business community for the good of the city. The association founded in 1872 dwindled and finally collapsed in 1875, but it was reincarnated, in various forms, in 1883, 1886, 1888, 1893, 1902, 1906, and 1913. Whatever Atlanta's industrial movement lacked in continuity, it certainly made up for in tenacity. Like religious revivals, which shared much of the same style and enthusiasm, the industrial crusade experienced a cycle of intense commitment interspersed with apathy and backsliding.[55]

The industrial revival of 1886 opened with a meeting at the courthouse, which was packed with Atlanta's leading men of business and industry. It was a rousing affair infused with evangelical fervor. Atlanta had been racked that year by a battle over prohibition, which left the press and the business community divided over an issue that set moral principles at odds with business interests and personal freedom. With the industrial revival came a deliberate effort to reaffirm the Atlanta spirit of cooperation and local patriotism as a healing balm. Grandiloquent speeches endorsing the reborn Manufacturers' Association met with repeated applause as the speakers appealed alternately to local pride and to fear of the city's industrial rivals, Birmingham and Chattanooga. The assembly appointed a committee of fifty to lay the groundwork for the new association. Their task was to elevate manufacturing to a plane equal to that of commerce and to promote industry as the key to Atlanta's future. "The progress of a city in population and wealth," their resolution dictated, "depends on a diversity of interests and pursuits." "Manufactures," it went on, were one of "the most direct and effectual" means to the increase of population, the extension of commerce, and, in a telling phrase, "the production of new values." The association would unite "manufacturers, merchants, bankers, and capitalists" in a cooperative effort "to use every effort in our power to sustain our manufactures, and the establishment of new enterprises."[56]

The new Manufacturers' Association began in 1886 by forming an information bureau designed "to familiarize capitalists with facilities in the city." The bureau courted outside industrialists and capitalists with considerable success and worked in every way to promote industrial Atlanta. Henry Grady of the *Atlanta Constitution* was a national publicist and local cheerleader for the cause:

"When Atlanta builds her factories to the stature of her stores, and fills the groves of her trade with her own products, she will then enter upon a growth on which the horizon constantly widens."[57]

Another major victory for Atlanta's industrial crusade came in 1886, when the state of Georgia decided that its new technological institute would be built in Atlanta. Samuel Inman and other local businessmen had championed the idea of a technological school to train an indigenous cadre of industrial engineers. Atlanta's industrial progress, a *Constitution* editorial noted, had been made despite the lack of "a native race of skilled mechanics and builders," so that for even the smallest enterprises "she has been forced to get her skilled labor from the north." Inman and other Atlanta industrialists had lobbied hard to convince the state to fund the school and then led the campaign to put together Atlanta's winning bid to host the new institute.[58]

The industrial strategy devised by Atlanta's business leaders aimed not at competing with Birmingham's or Chattanooga's iron and steel industries, but to foster a broad, diversified manufacturing base of textiles, food products, clothing, and other consumer "articles of daily use."[59] It was a plan designed to link industrial development to Atlanta's well-established commercial prowess by manufacturing a growing share of the city's export trade and by encouraging consumption of home manufactures. Atlanta boosters also proclaimed the advantages of diversity as a protection against economic depression. An overview of the city's industrial sector in 1886 revealed that it was producing watches, paper bags, candy, wire fencing, matches, cotton gins, razors, plows, brooms, fertilizers, shirts, furniture, cologne, and carriages, in addition to textiles, iron products, and lumber.[60]

The most famous example of Atlanta's quest for the production of "articles of daily use" was the enterprise of Asa Griggs Candler, which began inauspiciously during the industrial revival of the late 1880s. Candler, a druggist, bought the formulas to several patent medicines from an Atlanta manufacturer: Delectalave, Botanic Blood Balm, and, finally, Coca-Cola, a headache cure made from syrup and carbonated water (and originally laced with cocaine—it was popularly known as "dope"). Candler sold the potion out of his drugstore and soon discovered he had a popular, nonalcoholic beverage with tremendous appeal. By adopting aggressive advertising and promotion, Candler found a local, then a regional, and, by the early 1890s, a national market for Coca-Cola, on which he built one of Atlanta's most spectacular fortunes.[61]

Exhibiting the New South

The most impressive displays of the capacity of the New South business class for collective entrepreneurship came in a series of grand industrial expositions staged in Atlanta, Nashville, and other southern cities. No other enterprise could compare with their scale of organization, the extraordinary speed with which they were planned and carried out, and the numbers of people who were involved as managers, exhibitors, and participants.

Both Atlanta and Nashville had rehearsed the grand industrial expositions of the 1880s and 1890s in smaller agricultural fairs and industrial expositions during the 1870s and 1880s. These earlier fairs were aimed at the area immediately surrounding the cities, and they generally emphasized agricultural products and machinery rather than industrial development per se. Nashville had launched a series of small, annual industrial expositions in the early 1870s, and its centennial celebration of 1880 anticipated the grander models that were to follow.[62] The Georgia State Agricultural Society fairs, held at Atlanta's Oglethorpe Park during the 1870s, were the closest that city had come to staging any kind of exposition.

But it was Atlanta's International Cotton Exposition of 1881 that defined the standard for the New South. If there was any single turning point in postwar Atlanta's history, any element that was crucial in galvanizing the city's business leadership, it was the rush of confidence that came with the successful staging of the 1881 exposition. More than any other event, the exposition launched the New South movement, both as a publicity crusade and as a campaign for economic development, and it placed Atlanta at the vanguard of that movement. Atlanta followed its own standard with the Piedmont Exposition in 1887 and the Cotton States and International Exposition of 1895. Nashville finally topped them all in size and attendance with the 1897 Tennessee Centennial Exposition. But it was the Atlanta show of 1881 that established the style and defined the meaning of these New South extravaganzas.

The initial inspiration for the exposition came from outside the South, as did much of the capital and some of the key organizers. Edward Atkinson, a Boston industrialist, first suggested an exposition in 1880, not, as he took pains to point out, to encourage a southern textile industry, but to demonstrate the improved methods of cultivation, ginning, and baling, in order to eliminate the "dirty, wet, muddy bales" that were sent north to the mills.[63] Henry Grady and Evan P. Howell at the *Atlanta Constitution* picked up on Atkinson's suggestion and began promoting Atlanta as the ideal site for such an exposition.[64] Already New Orleans and Louisville were making their own bids for the proposed exposition. Atlanta was considered too small and inexperienced.

When Atkinson announced his forthcoming tour of the South in the fall of 1880, Hannibal I. Kimball, a personal friend, arranged for him to deliver an address on the exposition in the Georgia senate chamber and to meet with Atlanta businessmen. At this point, Atlanta's business leaders mobilized a campaign to transform the idea of an exposition into reality. They called a public meeting at which a reception committee, made up of the city's business and political elite, was delegated to meet with Atkinson during his visit in mid-October.[65] In a compelling address, Atkinson abandoned his earlier proposal that New York sponsor the exposition and threw his endorsement to Atlanta. But local planning stalled after his visit, in part due to a preoccupation with state and national elections that November, followed by local elections in January. Atlantans were also uninspired by Atkinson's insistence that the exposition focus on cultivation and preparing cotton rather than on manufacturing textiles.[66]

Once again, the stimulus for further planning came from outside. James W. Nagle and J. W. Ryckman, representing the *Textile Record,* a Philadelphia trade journal, came to Atlanta in late November 1880 to promote the exposition with help from the *Constitution.* The Chamber of Commerce, acting to facilitate rather than directly organize the plan, sponsored a series of meetings to consider the feasibility and aims of an exposition. Out of these meetings a preliminary organization, the International and Cotton States Exposition Association, was formed, with an organization committee led by Joseph E. Brown, Samuel Inman, and Ryckman. It was Ryckman who helped broaden the scope of the exposition by insisting that it should serve as a showcase for southern manufacturing. "In a few years," he told the *Constitution,* "Atlanta will be the Manchester of America."[67]

The exact focus of the exposition remained unclear. For Atlanta promoters, keeping their purpose vague may have been a shrewd ploy. They had to enlist the support of northern industrialists and cotton merchants and New South proponents of industrial development, along with local boosters, all in the same cause. Their exposition would be, for some, a lesson in improved production of raw cotton. For others, it would be a beacon of the New South's industrial promise, and for still others a symbolic occasion for sectional reconciliation.[68]

The *Constitution* continued to exhort Atlanta businessmen, and by February 1881 the exposition association sponsored a series of informal meetings at the Chamber of Commerce. Ryckman reported great enthusiasm in the North. Kimball urged that Atlanta "be definitely organized at once and proceed to adopt a methodical plan of action."[69] Atlanta's business leaders went ahead with incorporating a joint stock company to finance and plan the exposition. Made up of Atlanta's wealthy businessmen and some key figures in the cotton brokerage and textile industries in the North, this company was to be the vehicle for organizing an elaborate exposition that would open just eight months later and run for nearly three months.

The company's executive committee, dominated by the leading figures in Atlanta business and finance, elected Hannibal I. Kimball chairman and later "director-general" of the company. Kimball, the Yankee entrepreneur and politician, had a reputation as one of the more notorious carpetbaggers of Governor Rufus Bullock's regime. In Atlanta, however, he was regarded by many as a local hero, and he was credited with bringing the state capital to town and with the construction of the mammoth Kimball House Hotel. Kimball had left town under a dark cloud of political and financial scandal in 1872 but returned two years later to be feted by Atlanta's elite at a "reconciliation" banquet in the Kimball House. His role in the mismanagement and corruption of his railroad companies during the Bullock era was excused, and Kimball became an exemplary proponent of Atlanta's New South entrepre neurial spirit, a confidant of Henry Grady, and a man of indomitable show-manship and ambition, both for himself and for his adopted city.[70]

As director-general, Kimball brought to the exposition his experience with railroad management and other large-scale enterprises. He also brought a compelling brand of flamboyant salesmanship that went a long way in promot-ing this brash venture in 1881. After the fund-raising campaign had been launched and a company was formally organized, Kimball laid out an elabo-rate structure of departments and committees that allowed the exposition company to carry out plans with remarkable speed. Kimball's job was that of a corporation's chief executive officer, with concentrated administrative powers that allowed him to take quick action in moving the project along. Reporting to Kimball were twelve administrative departments, each responsible for a spe-cific phase of the exposition, from finance to public comfort. Each department was headed by a salaried department chief who was part of a three-man committee from the board of management. As Kimball explained, the arrange-ment was designed to effect "the most complete and systematic organization, with every branch of the work under the immediate supervision of experts."[71] It was a corporate model that enabled each department to operate on a semiautonomous basis, with authorization to make small expenditures and the power to hire and fire personnel. This corporate model also allowed the director-general to approve department decisions without having to clear every point with the executive committee.[72]

The first task was to raise money, a campaign that preceded the formal organization of the company in April 1881. Atlanta had to prove to a skeptical world that this upstart young town with fewer than 40,000 residents was capable of sponsoring such an enterprise. The seed money was to be raised by subscription to the exposition company stock—1,000 shares at $100 each. Kimball and the executive committee decided on a daring strategy. They would begin in Atlanta with a blitz of the business community, an all-out, one-day canvass for subscriptions that would make a convincing demonstration of Atlanta's commitment and its strength. The executive committee divided the city into four districts, with members assigned to each and with a specific subscription target based on the number of hotels and other businesses that would benefit from the exposition. The total goal for Atlanta was one-third of the 1,000 shares of stock. At midmorning on March 15 the canvass began, and stock subscription books were opened in all the Atlanta banks. Atlanta businessmen had been thoroughly primed in advance by a stream of editorials in the *Constitution* goading them into supporting this great opportunity and warning of rivals who were all too anxious to take over should Atlanta falter. The subscription drive was a stunning success. By four o'clock that afternoon, in time for the regular meeting of the executive committee, the total Atlanta goal was met. The news of Atlanta's "first grand success of the Exposition" went out on the Associated Press wires that day.[73]

Kimball went north with Ryckman to solicit subscriptions in the board rooms of New York and other cities. Another representative was sent to southern cities, and a third was dispatched to Britain and other cotton manufacturing areas of Europe. While at home the exposition's promoters trumpeted the great benefits that would befall Atlanta, the tactic "abroad" was to play up the exposition as an opportunity for industrial development and an occasion for reconciliation and charity toward the defeated and reconstructed South. The most poignant response to the latter appeal was General William T. Sherman's offer to head the northern subscription drive and to buy twenty shares for himself.[74] In New York, John Inman, who with his brother Samuel served on the exposition company's board of managers, played a key role as Kimball's conduit to the financial community. Inman and other cotton merchants and industrialists formed a New York board of managers and conducted a "personal canvass" that found buyers for 253 shares of stock, most of them connected with the railways that operated in the South, or with Inman, Swann, and Company along with other cotton brokers.[75] All this activity was given lavish attention by the press, which Kimball and Henry Grady exploited to full advantage in promoting the exposition.[76] From his triumph in New York, Kimball toured Boston, Baltimore, Norfolk, Philadelphia, and Cincinnati, returning to Atlanta with another 508 shares sold.[77]

Support across the South was mixed. The *Mobile Register* ridiculed Atlanta's "elaborate puffery."[78] Nashville, recovering from its own, less ostentatious, city centennial exposition the previous year, had little enthusiasm for helping its ascendant rival. The Georgia legislature, fueled by a mixture of jealousy toward Atlanta and deep suspicion toward Kimball, refused to approve a bill to fund the exposition with $20,000. In early June, Kimball and others went on the road again to drum up subscriptions in the South, the Midwest, and the Northeast. He brought back another $9,000 in subscriptions and enormous publicity for the exposition in urban presses across the country.[79]

By mid-June construction of the exposition buildings and grounds began.

The site was Oglethorpe Park, sixty acres of landscaped grounds located two-and-one-half miles from the center of the city. It had been laid out in 1870 by the city and leased to the Georgia State Agricultural Society for their fairs. The agricultural society and the city granted use of the park to the exposition company without charge.

As a construction project alone the exposition was an unprecedented feat for Atlanta entrepreneurs. It consisted of twenty-seven buildings containing twenty-one acres of floor space, all erected within three to four months. The Main Building was shaped like a cross 720 feet long and 400 feet across and modeled after a modern cotton factory. It was filled with machinery, which was driven by three steam engines connected to power shafts that spanned the ceilings.[80] Separate buildings for exhibits of railroad technology, agricultural implements, art and industry, minerals and woods, all were built on a smaller scale. A two-story Judges Hall, housing the administrative offices and a two-thousand-seat auditorium, was erected to serve as a main assembly hall. As more exhibitors applied for space, most of them within a month of the opening, annexes were thrown up next to the Main Building to accommodate the overflow. Ultimately there were 1,113 exhibits, and thousands more had to be turned down.[81]

Fearing that Atlanta hotels and boarding houses were preparing to gouge visitors or would be unable to house them all, the company put up the Exposition Hotel, which had 500 rooms. In all, the exposition company spent over $120,000 on construction, and more buildings were put up by exhibitors.[82]

When opening day arrived on October 5, 1881, the buildings and grounds were not yet finished, but visitors seemed more stirred by what this young southern city had accomplished than by what it had not. A grand parade of bands and militia companies began the celebration with a march to the exposition grounds. There the organizers and visiting dignitaries gathered on the grandstand, and Kimball, Governor Colquitt, and others delivered speeches and listened to the lengthy tribute, "Exposition Ode," written for the occasion by Paul Hamilton Hayne. Later, in the Judges Hall, a painting of *The New South Welcoming the Nations of the Earth* was unveiled with "thrilling effect," as the band played and the audience cheered. The painting depicted the New South as "a beautiful brunette girl draped in the American flag." Above her was "Uncle Sam, his face beaming with satisfaction," and elsewhere in the picture "Uncle Remus" and "Old Si" looked on as other blacks picked cotton in the field, behind which scenes of cities and factories depicted "evidences of great wealth and prosperity."[83] A choir of eight hundred schoolchildren sang Handel's Hallelujah Chorus, and the exposition was declared officially open.

Amid all the industrial and agricultural displays, northern visitors seemed

Atlanta's International Cotton Exposition, 1881. (Atlanta Historical Society)

most impressed by the exhibit depicting the "new spirit in the South," with its "new born zeal for hard work" and its eagerness to learn from "the thrifty and industrious people of the North," as a *New York Times* reporter put it.[84] Another visitor representing the *New York Commercial Bulletin* concurred in enthusiastic reports of a South "ready to work for a living. . . . The most valuable part of the Atlanta exhibition will be . . . the southern people themselves, and the revolutionary change in their industrial character and attitude. . . . The south [*sic*] is being permeated with new men, new money, new ideas, new aims and new methods. . . . That old Japan of the Western world is now declared as open."[85]

Atlanta's exposition organizers seemed eager to conform to this ebullient, if patronizing, northern view of the New South. Henry Grady promised swarms of "business men and capitalists . . . spying out fresh fields for investment." "The impressions made," he went on, "will retard or advance the manufacturing interests of Atlanta more than ten years of natural progress or obstacle could do."[86]

Grady and the others seemed to understand that it was they and their city—their mansions, their boasts of new wealth, their attitudes and ideals, and, above all, their power to organize and effect change in their region—that were on exhibit every bit as much as the machinery and cotton. What they had to show visitors was a full performance of the "Atlanta Spirit," that force a *Constitution* editorial once described as "only the militant expression of Atlanta's personality—forceful, aggressive, intelligent, harmonious, with an abundance of that requisite indispensable in man or city—sleepless initiative."[87] The Atlanta spirit, in turn, was only a concentrated expression of the New South's program for economic development and social progress. What the organizers also put on public display was the directing agent behind that spirit, an increasingly organized and purposeful cohort of business leaders. It was a business class fashioned on the northern model and devoted to reshaping the South in the image of the North. "The exposition," Kimball summarized, "acts as a harmonizer of opinion, it conforms men and women to one another, it circulates intelligence and awakens a thirst for knowledge."[88] He was speaking of reconciliation between the sections, but the comment suited as well the melding of interests, purposes, and values that had been demonstrated among Atlanta business leaders and their counterparts in other cities, North and South.

7   *The Charleston Style*

{W}e must forget to defer to senility, we must learn to respect energy and to make use of youth.
—*William Trenholm,* 1869

The logic of business class unity rested on the idea that its members were stockholders in a collective enterprise driven by a shared desire for growth and by the promise that sacrifice for the common welfare would be rewarded. The Atlanta spirit soared on the wings of economic prosperity. The Charleston style, in contrast, was one of dignified repose in the face of chronic economic stagnation before the turn of the century. A legacy of failed efforts to break the serene apathy of Charleston's business leaders only reinforced the cycle of demoralization and decline. The tendency was for individuals, instead of lending loyal support to any and all local ventures, to either "croak" about the feasibility of such plans or to quietly mind their own business and not take risks for the collective good. For the young and ambitious, the alternative was to leave and pursue opportunities elsewhere. Faced with the choice of moving themselves (or their capital) to more promising fields, resigning themselves to a defensive allegiance to the status quo, or agitating for change, most Charlestonians had traditionally opted for one of the former two courses, ensuring the failure of those who chose the third path.[1]

Economic stagnation and impotent community enterprise were mutually reinforcing, in short. The *Charleston News and Courier,* under Francis W. Dawson and, after 1889, John C. Hemphill, generally did its best to break that cycle, as did a number of civic-minded business leaders. According to their analysis of the problem, Charleston did not lack resources in the way of natural advantages, investment capital, or *individual* entrepreneurial skill; what was failing repeatedly was a capacity for *community* enterprise. "This has been the secret of our decay," the maverick mayor John Patrick Grace protested in one of his irate attacks on the old aristocracy; "it is the answer to those who have come and inquired what has kept us back. That answer is OURSELVES."[2]

With all its troubles, Charleston's economy was still capable of generating sizable personal fortunes, as several biographical sketches in chapter 5 demonstrated. Probate records for the 1880 elite reveal that many of those with money invested aggressively in a wide range of ventures that were at the heart of the New South movement. "There is hardly an industrial enterprise in the State which has not received material assistance from Charleston," a *News and Courier* editorial cried in 1898.[3] Several upcountry cotton mills drew heavily on Charleston's capital and its exported entrepreneurial skills. Francis J. Pelzer, Ellison A. Smyth, and William A. Courtenay were among the most visible of those directly involved in the textile boom, and there were dozens of other Charlestonians who bought stock in various mills. Birmingham's iron industry also attracted Charleston capital and business skill. Robert Adger, J. Ellison Adger, Augustine T. Smyth, and others formed the DeBardeleben Coal and Iron Company in 1886, to cite just one Charleston venture launched in the "Magic City." Atlanta's economy attracted money from the elderly seaport as well. Numerous Charleston portfolios included stocks in banks, transit systems, and utilities, and, typically, stocks and bonds from the rising cities of the New South.[4] But although wealthy Charlestonians prospered from their investments in the New South, home enterprises repeatedly failed for want of support from the "monied men" of the community.

This pattern did not change significantly until the late 1890s. Then a number of external and internal forces converged to arrest the cycle of stagnation and demoralization and gradually bring the old city closer to the currents of change that were shaping the modern South. Among the external changes, the intervention of the federal government in deepening the harbor and bringing a navy yard to the Neck were instrumental in resuscitating Charleston's economy. The reorganization of the railroads serving the city and their decision to offer better terminal facilities and improved service were also essential. An infusion of investments by outside capitalists in a new electric transit system, new waterworks, and other enterprises demonstrated a confidence in Charleston's potential that was rarely shared by local investors. Not least among these outside investors was the Virginia-Carolina Chemical Company, which bought out the fertilizer industry around Charleston, liquidating a large amount of locally held stock. But these external forces would not have had much influence, and perhaps none at all, had it not been for changes within the city that were effected primarily by a corps of aggressive young businessmen who emerged with more energy and organization than ever before beginning the late 1890s. They supplanted an older and more conservative generation, which had by that time died out or retired, with a generation that was self-consciously "progressive" and eager to catch Charleston up with the pace set by Atlanta and other New South models. This young cohort represented an alliance between the old "aristocracy" and the wealth and entrepreneurial talent of those outside the old families, particularly Charleston's German, Jewish, and Irish populations.

The Ancient Chamber

In 1884, while the commercial associations of Atlanta and Nashville were struggling to establish a presence in the affairs of their cities, Charleston's Chamber of Commerce was celebrating its centennial anniversary. Like so many of the city's public institutions and landmarks, the "ancient Chamber of Commerce" claimed distinction as the oldest continuous institution of its kind in America. It was typical of Charlestonians that on this occasion of their chamber's centennial, instead of filling the air with prophecies of the city's future greatness, they looked to the past.

William L. Trenholm's address at the banquet, held according to custom at the old Charleston Hotel, hardly provided the kind of nostalgic recollections of past glories such a celebration might have been expected to offer. Instead, he gave them a critical review of the city's, and—with more subtlety—the chamber's, historic failures. The son and partner of the former Confederate treasurer, Trenholm had built a fortune running goods through the Union blockade during the war. He spoke as well as any of his generation in the critical rhetoric of New South oratory, with a tendency to scrutinize the mistakes of his elders. In Charleston this style of critical self-examination was not balanced by the kind of confident booster ethos that more prosperous cities sustained, and Trenholm's after-dinner address to the chamber that evening in 1884 must have made a few coffee cups rattle.

Reviewing the early history of the city and its Chamber of Commerce, Trenholm noted Charleston's early rivalry with Boston, New York, and Philadelphia and its position as the leading port of the South Atlantic coast. "Why has so fair a promise failed?," he asked pointedly. "When and how was Charleston's career turned aside from so brilliant and assured a prospect?" This was more than just an academic historical inquiry, for, as Trenholm explained, "destiny is fond of presenting to communities the same problems over and over again."[5] A legacy of failure was still directing Charleston's course in the New South, and it had to be confronted.

Undergirding Trenholm's entire argument was an indictment not only of South Carolina's overwhelming dependence on agriculture, and the slave plantation economy in particular, but also of the business community for its inability to overcome those forces. Charleston merchants had failed at "building up structures" to support an enduring commercial community. The organization of the Chamber of Commerce in 1784 (actually a revival of a similar body that had formed at least ten years earlier as part of the nonimportation movement against Britain) was an effort toward that end, but Trenholm gently exposed its historical shortcomings. Established as a means of redirecting Charleston's shattered post-Revolutionary commercial life, the chamber amounted to a nativist, exclusive group fearful that British merchants were undermining the city's economic independence. Its rules included careful screening of members and a two-thirds vote to approve applicants. It remained a small and weak organization as a consequence. Despite the chamber's restrictions, in the early nineteenth century English, Scottish, and Yankee merchants regained preeminence in many fields of Charleston's trade, and natives "passed out of business," leaving the field clear to outsiders.[6]

The failure to nurture an indigenous business class, Trenholm insisted, was due to the "apathy, and occasionally . . . actual hostility" with which an agricultural society regarded men engaged in commerce. "'It was held disreputable to attend to business of almost any kind. All the merchants with a very few exceptions were from the Eastern states or Europe.'" Even as native Carolinians began to regain ascendancy in commercial circles following the nullification crisis in the early 1830s, the low regard for trade lingered with devastating effect: "[A]s soon as a merchant acquired a fortune in Charleston he invested it in lands and negroes, became a planter, and devoted his sons to the learned professions, or worse still, he moved away and carried off his gains as if they were plunder." The exodus of capital and talent was propelled also by Charlestonians' overriding fear of slave insurrections and their exaggerated concerns about the unhealthy quality of Charleston's climate. The city's many grand mansions were ample testimony to the affluence of Charleston's merchants, yet, as Trenholm noted pointedly, "hardly one of these is now occupied by the representatives of the man who built it." This was not due to the kind of suburban migration that pushed out New York's and Philadelphia's old elite families, but to the "shifting and drifting of our mercantile element" away from the urban origins of their wealth.

The result of these formative historical forces shaping the Charleston business community was a scarcity of seasoned capitalists with money, credit, and entrepreneurial experience, according to Trenholm. Such men might have helped Charleston to channel some of its profits from agricultural exports into home-owned shipping fleets, shipyards, insurance companies, and other spin-off enterprises that would have given the city a more solid and independent economic foundation. Their lack was particularly felt during the 1850s, when "a sunburst of prosperity" led inexperienced businessmen and city officials into a series of "speculative enterprises and . . . unwise investments in distant railroads," all of which failed disastrously.

Trenholm then moved into the more delicate realm of recent history. During the 1860s, he accused, Charleston's merchants "gave uncalculating support to the Confederate Government," and defeat left the city "like a wreck on the shore . . . every prospect was dismal." Now, following the "new departure" of 1865, and following the years of political turmoil and slow, painful progress, Trenholm pleaded, the "ancient Chamber should assume the leadership" in pushing Charleston forward in the New South. "There is need of just such an organization to unite opinion and effort, to formulate and to diffuse among the community enlarged and enlightened views and to influence those concerned to enlightened and effective action." But to assume its proper role, Trenholm warned, the chamber must do more than congratulate itself on its antiquity, it must engage in critical "self-examination."

> In an old community like this conservatism prevails in all things and is eminently respectable. . . . [B]ut conservatism is out of place and perverted from its proper sphere when it clings to antiquated methods of business and shuts its eyes to modern improvements and the requisites for progressive prosperity. Let it be the mission of the Chamber of Commerce to preach progress and to teach the art of commercial success in the times as they are. Its antiquity and its honorable history crown it with authority; let its future career help to clothe the community with prosperity, and reflect upon itself the splendor of successful effort in a noble cause.

Trenholm's penetrating exercise in self-examination may have upset some of the chamber's elder members, but it was only one of many calls for a new departure in Charleston, pleas that generally met with little response before the end of the century. Soon Trenholm took his own departure, leaving Charleston for a career as comptroller of the treasury under Cleveland and, later, as a financier on Wall Street. He followed the same path away from Charleston that he had criticized other successful merchants for taking.[7]

The Chamber of Commerce continued along its well-worn groove as a kind of prestigious old merchants' club, dominated by cotton factors drawn from the aristocracy of Charleston. Before it took up quarters in a building at East Bay and Broad streets in 1870, the chamber sought to refurbish the historic Exchange Building at the foot of Broad as its home. The gesture provides a telling example of the reverence for the past that so often ruled in Charleston. The venerable landmark, built before the Revolution and witness to several of Charleston's most memorable events (including the confiscation of abolitionist mail and the defiance of the tariff during the nullification crisis in the 1830s), became the object of the city's first historic preservation campaign. After the Civil War, when federal authorities considered razing the bombarded struc-ture, the chamber petitioned Congress in 1868, begging that the building be kept as a "place of common resort" for the "whole mercantile community. . . . We hope that the tide of prosperity is again setting upon us, and we wish in

Charleston's Old Exchange Building at Broad and East Bay streets. (National Archives)

every way to establish and strengthen the Commercial character of Charleston. Besides this, the building itself is one of the Institutions of our City. . . . [I]t is consecrated by many memories" ("of the Revolution of '76," they carefully added). This ancient landmark, the chamber argued with unintended irony, would serve as the ideal symbol of the city's commercial spirit.[8]

In the years following the war and Reconstruction, the chamber addressed the major issues that confronted the city and did its best to advertise whatever progress the city achieved. But there was a certain melancholy air surrounding the chamber. Its meetings were sparsely attended, and although most of them were devoted to serious matters, much time was also devoted to lengthy eulogies offered to departed members, replete with descriptions of their genealogies, their honorable business reputations, and their long-standing involvement with the ancient chamber. The chamber seemed older than it in fact was because so many old men were at its helm. An 1887 membership roll reveals that, although the overwhelming majority of the members (108 out of 132) had joined since the war, all of the officers—past and present, with the exception of a second vice president in 1885—had been members since at least 1859—in William Ravenel's case, since 1826.[9] Surely this is what William Trenholm meant when he criticized Charleston's tendency to "defer to senility."[10]

Judging from the attention devoted to it in the chamber's meetings, the club room, introduced in 1870, offered one of the chief attractions to members, and any connection it had to serious business went unmentioned. Well stocked with wines and liquors, the club room was open from nine in the morning until midnight and on Sundays from 11:00 A.M. to 2:00 P.M., closing in time for the traditional dinner.[11] In Atlanta and Nashville, the same type of amenities, including good food and liquor, even cards and billiards, became important attractions of successful commercial associations. But these luxuries were added much later, in the 1890s and early 1900s. They offered a social supplement to the serious work performed by these organizations and always were justified in pragmatic terms for their value to business class unity. In Charleston the club rooms of the chamber seemed to be a substitute for, rather than a supplement to, the tasks before it.

The chamber's membership grew steadily, from 142 in 1866 to 274 ten years later. But beginning about 1876, in the midst of the depression, the number of members sagged drastically and by 1886 stood at 118. In that year the chamber reorganized and launched a membership drive that met with limited success. Though by this time the chamber was made up largely of men who had joined since the war, it remained an exclusive club whose rules governing admission must have discouraged many from even applying. The 1886 constitution still required that applicants be endorsed by members with written statements giving the applicant's occupation and the "qualification of the candidate." The executive committee would screen nominees and bring those they wished to include before the general membership. Five negative votes meant rejection, and the candidate could not be reconsidered for a full year.[12] A few German and Jewish merchants began to enter the ranks of the chamber in the 1870s and 1880s, but the officers, with few exceptions, were still almost all from the old Anglo-Huguenot aristocracy and were typically in the cotton trade.[13]

The Board of Trade

There were challengers to the ancient Chamber of Commerce's position as the voice of Charleston's commercial spirit, but none managed to survive for long. Immediately after the war a new organization, the Board of Trade, sprang up. It spoke for a new crowd of younger men, mostly wholesale merchants outside the cotton trade. The new board elected officers for one-year terms, and they rotated in and out of office quickly, allowing a broad spectrum of the business community to participate at the head of the new organization. William S. Hastie (wholesale hardware), William L. Trenholm (banking), Henry Cobia (commission merchant), D. F. Flemming (wholesale boots and shoes), and Herman H. DeLeon (broker) were among the rising men of wealth who served as the board's first presidents.

The Board of Trade seemed determined to maintain a separate identity and in 1868 rebuffed an invitation to merge with the Chamber of Commerce. By this time, with 162 members, it was the larger of the two organizations and had every reason to see itself as the leading commercial association in Charleston's future.[14] The board adopted a tone of impatience with Charleston's older merchants, who seemed thoroughly demoralized by the Confederate defeat. "Sitting down upon the crumbling ruins of our ancient City with our arms folded and complaining of our lot will not give our children bread," the board admonished.[15]

Initially the new Board of Trade opened its doors to anyone willing to pay the dues, and, though it required endorsements from members, it avoided the restrictive system of voting and blackballing that were the hallmarks of the chamber. Within a few years the board's membership rose to 250. William L. Trenholm, enthused by the younger business community's show of strength, believed that the new Board of Trade would overcome the southern "defect" of individualism, a trait that had been painfully apparent in the "late war." "Combination and organization were always wanting to [*sic*] this commercial community," was his familiar refrain. With the new board, "we must each forget himself and stand by the common interest of all . . . [W]e must stand by our State, our city and our order."[16]

The board met monthly in somewhat Spartan quarters in a rented room at the Charleston Hotel. It pursued an energetic course by attacking each of the city's commercial problems, with special attention to railroad connections with the upcountry and Midwest. The board also became actively involved with the National Board of Trade, and local delegates to the annual convention reported with excitement on Charleston's future in the emerging national economy.[17] Their enthusiasm was fully in accord with the New South spirit of national reconciliation so visible in Atlanta: "We are no longer sectional. Our interests are identical with every Northern and Western State." "There is not a vestige of war feeling existing in this community," one board member asserted, probably with more hope than conviction. "There is no North, no South, no East, no West, but one country, with one Constitution and one destiny."[18]

Everything possible was done to appeal to northern capitalists and to advertise the opportunities for profit in Charleston. The board made strenuous efforts to repeal legislation that discouraged business and investment in Charleston, particularly the state bankruptcy and usury laws and the local practice of jailing visiting debtors. The board also investigated and attacked with zeal railroad rate discrimination, high wharf and warehouse rates, and other obstacles to Charleston's trade. At the same time, the board cheered new enterprises, such as steamboat lines and phosphate works, that exemplified Charleston's "race for the golden prize." In 1868 it especially welcomed recent developments in the phosphate industry and honored its entrepreneurs as the "native and adopted citizens of Charleston . . . [who] are entitled to the earnest support of the community and the applause of this Board."[19]

The Charleston Board of Trade also tried, with limited success, to awaken the "ancient Chamber of Commerce" to the need for "concerted action" in all these endeavors.[20] When, at the board's annual banquet in 1868, a toast was raised to "our elder sister," S. Y. Tupper responded graciously for the chamber, insisting that there was no rivalry between them and wishing that the "vigor and freshness of youth" would join the "experience and prestige of the past, which remains with the Chamber." Together, he added, they must "work out the regeneration of this ancient city; recuperate her broken fortunes, and restore to her that importance which locality, her past fame and traditions, so justly entitle her." But Tupper then revealed too much of the chamber's spirit by launching into a lengthy discourse on white supremacy, states' rights, and the evils of Radical rule, a diatribe that must have confirmed the board's determination to pursue its own course.[21]

As the Board of Trade matured, unfortunately for Charleston's ambitious young men, it took on more of the chamber's genteel and clubby characteristics. In 1870 it purchased the old Mowry house on Meeting Street, originally for use as a telegraph office and reading room in what was to be "the *Commercial Centre of Charleston.*" But it soon added a dining room, club room, and billiards room, complete with "elegant furniture and other appurtenances." Membership shot up. Many were clearly drawn by the new social amenities. One faction that lobbied to keep the club rooms open on Sunday did not give business duties as its reason. (A compromise allowed the rooms to be open all day, except from two to five in the afternoon, a concession to the obligatory two o'clock dinner and to families who expected the club members to be at home during that time.) New amendments to the rules also introduced a system for blackballing new applicants. The expense of the club rooms, combined with poor management, soon put the board under a heavy debt. As dues were raised and amenities in the club rooms were cut back, membership began to drop off. By May 1872 the board, which had begun with such eager promise just six years earlier, declared bankruptcy and disbanded.[22]

The Charleston Exchange

"Let us arouse ourselves from this morbid condition," the *Charleston News and Courier* implored as the Board of Trade was dying. "The trouble," the editor explained, "is want of purpose, want of earnestness and want of concert in action."²³ A new organization, the Charleston Exchange, emerged in the wake of the board's demise in 1872 and tried again to rebuild the commercial spirit of Charleston upon a broad platform. Designed to attract support from all of Charleston's wholesale merchants, the organization was originally called the Merchants' Exchange. Its purpose was to serve as a trading floor serving all of Charleston's major exports, from cotton and rice to naval stores, timber, and "heavy groceries." It also was meant "to serve as practical evidence of the Vitality of the commerce of Charleston and the Enterprise of her merchants."²⁴

The exchange's leaders insisted that the organization was not exclusively a cotton exchange, but cotton traders soon took over most of the offices and the board of directors, despite the protests of other wholesalers.²⁵ Those outside the cotton trade dropped out of the exchange, and it never acquired the necessary breadth or size to rival the Chamber of Commerce as a general commercial body. The exchange was, nonetheless, determined to become a modern trade association. It boldly made plans for a new building near Adgers' Wharf, hired Alfred Price (an "old citizen and merchant of Charleston") as full-time superintendent, and sent him to New York City to "acquire a knowledge of the interior management and detail of the kindred Institutions of the great Commercial Metropolis."²⁶ Price came back from New York brimming with new ideas, and the exchange eagerly followed his suggestions to build a vigorous commercial body on the northern model.

But the membership barely grew from seventy-three charter members, then fell to thirty-seven in the 1870s. This was thought to be due partly to the high entrance fees of $100 and the depression that began in 1873, but also to a stubborn indifference among many of the cotton factors and commission merchants along East Bay Street, in whose interest the exchange had been organized.²⁷ By the late 1870s it was difficult to muster a quorum at meetings. Expenses were cut, and the Charleston Exchange withdrew from the National Cotton Exchange. Membership picked up slightly in the more prosperous 1880s, but the Charleston Exchange was never more than a narrow association for a declining cotton trade. In the late 1880s the exchange was plagued by accusations of insurance fraud, perpetrated by a "ring" within the organization. The exchange conducted its own investigation without conclusive results, but the scandal exposed the slipshod leadership of the exchange (which, it was revealed, had not conducted a valid election of officers for nearly a decade) and cast, in the words of one member, "a broad shadow of guilt on the merchants of Charleston."²⁸

The Merchants' Exchange

The only other rival to the Chamber of Commerce before the 1890s emerged in 1883 with the organization of a new Merchants' Exchange. Formed by wholesale merchants, many of them Germans, Irishmen, and others outside the old Charleston aristocracy, this exchange was defiantly independent of the chamber and the Charleston Exchange.[29] Prominent among its leaders were Frederick W. Wagener, one of Charleston's wealthy Germans, who began as a grocer and became a leading industrialist, resort owner, and entrepreneur at large—a man who was to figure significantly in Charleston's economic revival in coming years.[30] J. A. Enslow, a commission merchant, Francis Q. O'Neill, and other members of the O'Neill family—prominent Irishmen who figured in banking, fertilizer manufacturing, and wholesale activities—were also actively involved in the new Merchants' Exchange.[31] William H. Welch, a prosperous wholesale grocer, who was to become a leading force in Charleston's affairs in the late 1890s, also made his first public appearance at the head of this new organization.

The Charleston Merchants' Exchange attacked the problems that plagued the old city with a refreshing spirit of criticism and irreverence. A special committee on trade and transportation, led by Frederick W. Wagener and including J. A. Enslow and William M. Bird, a hardware dealer, presented an ambitious report in 1885 that laid out a plan for centralizing trade facilities and included important recommendations for Charleston's physical planning. "Your committee is profoundly impressed with the conviction that serious errors have been committed in the past in the administration of business affairs in this city in almost every department . . . otherwise Charleston . . . might have attained magnificent possibilities." The "sad lessons" and "bitter experience" of the past ought not be forgotten, Wagener warned, but the exchange must not "sit idly brooding over past misfortunes."[32]

Instead, the committee laid out a bold plan for overcoming obstacles that had stood in the path of Charleston commerce for decades. To centralize the city's trade facilities, the committee members suggested routing the railroad tracks that came into the city from the north along the eastern waterfront and building a union station on the site of the current Northeastern Railroad station, with a freight depot, warehouses, cotton compresses, and a grain elevator next to it. The old route, these reformers advised, should be turned into an "attractive boulevard" with "handsome parks" along the way. They recommended that the Savannah and Charleston Railroad, which stopped far south of the Ashley River and then circumvented the city, be brought into Charleston along Spring Street to the proposed union station. Furthermore, the report went on, the swampy area around South Bay should be filled in, allowing for attractively designed ponds that would replace the "unsightly shanties" with an "attractive pleasure resort" surrounded by "handsome residences." Such a setting would "perhaps present attractions to Northern visitors in connection with our unsurpassed climate that would make Charleston a favorite resort for much of the winter travel that now finds its way to Florida through Charleston."[33] This was the inspiration for what became the Colonial Lake and Murray Boulevard developments in the southwest quarter of the city.

Interest in developing Charleston's much-vaunted potential as a tourist attraction became the focus of a major campaign in 1888 to launch construction of a modern hotel near the Battery. Though it was not officially sponsored by the Merchants' Exchange, Wagener and other exchange leaders were intimately involved in the scheme, and it seemed to excite the same enthusiasm among young businessmen that the exchange itself had sparked. About one hundred prominent business and civic leaders put out the call for a mass meeting in the German Artillery Hall, an event that closely resembled a New South revival. George W. Williams, the wealthy wholesale grocer and banker, spoke first and pledged $50,000 toward the $1 million he thought necessary for the hotel. The crowd "went simply wild with enthusiasm. Then shouted and applauded and rose from their chairs and waved their hats and applauded again until the band . . . played 'Dixie' . . . then there was another furor." Francis J. Pelzer and Frederick W. Wagener followed suit with their own subscriptions, and two days later at another enthusiastic meeting a company was formed to build the new hotel.[34]

The subscription drive became a crusade among the young businessmen of Charleston, who saw in it "an opportunity to make their influence felt and to show the faith they have in the future of Charleston." Francis W. Dawson's *News and Courier* applauded their zeal: "We need some new blood in the commercial and business veins of the city . . . and we require the ardor of youth in this great Hotel enterprise as a tonic to the older men who have borne the heat and burden of the day." The alternative, Williams noted, was the "melancholy sight" of "our best young men leaving in search of work elsewhere." Later, following a separate mass meeting of young men called to launch the subscription drive, a crowd of eager young Charlestonians poured out of the German Artillery Hall and formed behind the band in a torchlight parade through the city, stopping to serenade Williams, Andrew Simonds, Francis S. Rodgers, and Francis J. Pelzer, all prominent supporters of the project. The young men canvassed the city and raised $250,000 within three weeks. "There is no place and there is no time for stragglers and camp followers. We can make Charleston what we would have it to be, but we must all pull together," Dawson exhorted. "Untie the purse strings and let the golden current flow."

But the flow was not forthcoming, and Williams soon had to beg the city council for aid and go North to find investors. "I am greatly disappointed," Williams admitted to the *News and Courier*, "in not having responses from many who we had reason to expect liberal subscriptions." Wagener, too, registered his disgust with "our wealthy men [who] take so little interest in this great movement." To hurt matters further, owners of sites near the Battery were holding out for outrageous prices. The *News and Courier* suggested that the hotel could be built on Mars with less trouble than in Charleston. The hotel campaign soon died, having added only another episode of demoralization to the city.

The Merchants' Exchange took on a variety of other causes with mixed success, but the focus of their mission became the annual excursions that brought rural merchants into the City by the Sea. The excursion idea became the centerpiece of a determined campaign to recapture a hinterland which, in the exchange's view, had forsaken its natural metropolis, largely because Charleston merchants appeared to take the upcountry for granted or, worse, look upon it with contempt.

The exchange was organized simultaneously with a spontaneous movement among many small wholesale merchants, many of them Germans, which called for a major campaign to enlarge the city's trade. On their own, these men canvassed the city and organized a large meeting to address the issue. Pointing to Atlanta as a model, the merchants quickly accepted the notion that Charleston needed more than a single burst of energy; it required a sustained annual program of excursions to regain its hinterland.[35] The Merchants' Exchange sent a delegation to this meeting, including Frederick W. Wagener and J. A. Enslow, who persuaded the impatient merchants that their best interests would be served by joining forces with the new exchange to bring a combined effort to bear upon the railroads and the newspapers in planning and publicizing the excursions.[36]

"We need agitation," Dawson's *News and Courier* wrote, encouraging the new movement. "[A]bove all we need pushing, active, energetic business men, who will lead Charleston up to the full enjoyment of the great natural advantages which it possesses." The first "Gala Week" excursion came off late in 1883, but little more was heard of the idea until 1887. After the earthquake of 1886, an event that "shook the merchants together," according to one observer, they made the Gala Week excursions an extravagant display of their determination to rebuild. "On its success," the *News and Courier* stated bluntly in 1891, "the reputation of the city as a business community and as the home of hospitality is staked." "Instead of crumbling walls, falling columns and streets heaped high with rubbish," the paper proclaimed, "the visitor will find a bright, clean, vigorous city, full of life and activity, and with its wharves, its warehouses, its stores, its residences newly swept and garnished, and as fresh as work, and paint, and money can make them. . . . What was the old city is now the new city. It is the newest old city in the Union. There is nowhere any mark of decadence."[37]

A familiar eye could detect shades of the old planter resort in the entertainment that was now staged to lure country merchants to the city's counting houses. To a grand fare of fireworks, horse races, parades, concerts, and decorated streets were later added boat races, mock sea battles, baseball games, balloon rides, theater performances, and Civil War battle reenactments.[38] The Trades Display took place during the day, when merchants marched in groups organized by trade, carrying banners and accompanied by brass bands. At night the Fantastic Parade was a more raucous affair that should have dispelled any notions about the staid old city of Charleston. The men wore masks and dressed in "ridiculous costumes," many as women with exaggerated bustles and wigs, as they threw confetti and favors to the crowds that gathered along the torch-lit streets.[39] All were part of the campaign, inspired largely by the Merchants' Exchange and supported enthusiastically by Francis W. Dawson's *News and Courier,* to rebuild goodwill among the South Carolina small-town merchants following decades of erosion marked by upcountry jealousy and metropolitan indifference. "Howdy, Howdy, how dy do," the *News and Courier* welcomed country visitors to Charleston, which it described as "a great old town," if "a little old fashioned . . . in some of its ways."[40]

Depression and Revival

Before a massive hurricane swept across the low country in August 1893, there were plans underway for another Gala Week. The storm destroyed the bridge across the Ashley, wrecked wharves and ships along the waterfront, tore up trees and houses across the city, and inflicted severe damage on the people, farms, and industries surrounding the city.[41] Amid the disarray that followed, the annual festival was abandoned. The depression that also arrived that year prolonged the suspension, and three years passed before the celebration revived.[42] Coinciding with a multitude of old and new obstacles to the city's economic progress, the depression of the 1890s marked the lowest point in Charleston's postwar doldrums since Reconstruction.

In truth, the depression only aggravated the chronic illness of Charleston's economy and accelerated the decline of railroad service. One by one, the roads that had been built by Charleston enterprise in the antebellum era passed into the hands of large syndicates controlled by interests indifferent to Charleston's plight. This was the lot of many American cities by the end of the nineteenth century, but few suffered as much as Charleston. The South Carolina Railway had remained mired in debt since it was placed in receivership in 1889, and by 1892 it faced foreclosure. When the L&N proposed to buy the road and break the Richmond and West Point Terminal system's growing monopoly in the South Atlantic, it appeared for a time that Charleston might at long last have its western connection. But the L&N abandoned the plan after the panic of 1893, and "old reliable" was sold in 1894 to a New York syndicate and reorganized as the South Carolina and Georgia Railroad.[43] That same year, the Plant system bought the Charleston and Savannah Railroad and allowed it to serve Norfolk rather than "the city that gave it birth."[44] Four years later, the Atlantic Coast Line, another large railroad trust, bought the Northeastern Railroad and the Cheraw and Darlington Railroad. The Southern Railway, successor to the Richmond and West Point Terminal Company, swallowed the new South Carolina and Georgia the following year. In 1902 the Atlantic Coast Line absorbed the Plant system. Charleston's rail service had fallen completely into the hands of two large, distant railroad trusts, both seemingly indifferent to the city's deterioration. Moreover, both roads were north-south systems, and Charleston, along with most of the South Atlantic coast, was effectively cut off from any competitive trade with the West.[45] "The very life blood is being sapped out of Charleston's trade and commerce," the *News and Courier* lamented in 1896.[46]

If prospects were dimming for Charleston's railroad service in the 1890s, the city's maritime trade was finally picking up. The year 1895 saw the completion of the "national jetties," the culmination of a federal project that stretched back to the late 1860s. The harbor now held twenty-two feet of water over the bar at high tide, enough for modern steamships to pass safely. Further improvements in the years that followed would deepen the channel to thirty feet and more.[47]

Now, as the *News and Courier* put it, "with the swells from the open seas running unbroken to her wharves," the sea lanes were open.[48] What remained broken, as it had been since the 1830s, was the link between the main cluster of wharves along East Bay and the rail lines that terminated several blocks northward. Cargo still had to be transported by dray wagons, adding to the high costs and slowness of Charleston commerce. The prospects of bringing the rails to the water and modernizing Charleston's terminal facilities looked more hopeless than ever in the early 1890s. The South Carolina Railway had finally brought its rails to the water in 1882–83, when it extended tracks to the Cooper River and built a new freight depot and warehouse at the waterfront, but this was far north of the East Bay wharves where Charleston maritime commerce remained concentrated. Under pressure from a large group of East Bay merchants, the city council had approved the extension of rail lines down to the wharf front in 1884, presaging what the *News and Courier* eagerly predicted would be a "revolution in the old method of doing business at this port."[49] But the extension was obstructed by property owners and a lethargic city council, and the revolution did not come. In 1890 the East Shore Terminal Company, formed by a syndicate of outside railroad investors, received a thirty-year franchise from the city to build a waterfront railroad spur, and it quickly

Stevedores carrying rice on the Charleston waterfront, ca. 1891. (Library of Congress)

bought up most of the warehouses and piers along East Bay. That company failed in the depression and was taken over by the Atlantic Coast Line and Southern Railway. Merchants were urged to utilize the Terminal Company's services, but rates were so high that most continued to use the old drays. With Charleston commerce in decline and with the company's franchise in force until 1920, the railroads felt little pressure to reform the Terminal Company and, instead, allowed its wharves and warehouses to deteriorate.[50]

Added to Charleston's transportation problems were the devastating blows to the phosphate industry that hit suddenly in the early 1890s. The hurricane of 1893 caused severe damage to the industry, wrecking several expensive river dredges and plants. Governor Benjamin Tillman, who had built his career on upcountry resentment of Charleston, slapped a heavy royalty of one dollar per ton on river phosphate, substantially reducing the profit margin. Simultaneously, new, richer, and more accessible phosphate deposits were discovered in Florida and middle Tennessee, bringing a sudden end to the South Carolina monopoly.[51]

Tillman's populist movement aggravated the long-standing strain between Charleston and the upcountry. That tension further countered efforts to rebuild trade relations with the hinterland, and it put the city at a disadvantage in all dealings with the state government. The central issue of contention for Charleston became Tillman's dispensary law, which banned all liquor except that sold from state dispensaries. It was the revenge of a pietistic upcountry against the jaded habits of the city. Though the law was openly flouted by Charlestonians, who enjoyed their wine at home and their liquor in illegal "blind tigers," it placed severe constraints upon the city's hotel business and hurt efforts to build trade among tourists and visiting merchants. More important, the dispensary issue became an aggravating reminder of Charleston's beleaguered position within a state it had once dominated with ease.[52]

The New Charleston

"Charleston must do something to help itself," a desperate editorial in the *News and Courier* admonished in 1894. "It has worked its 'superior natural advantages' to death, it has played the dignified and independent and high-and-mighty role out, it has tried the waiting policy until the policy is worn out, and it must take a new start and take it quick, or it will lose whatever of commercial importance it has left."[53] Already, new sources of energy were beginning to move amid the stagnant economy of the 1890s.

The leadership behind Gala Week, and behind much of the new movement in Charleston's business community, passed from the Merchants' Exchange to a new organization, the Young Men's Business League. The league, organized at the nadir of the depression in 1894, included among its officers several German and Irish merchants and others who had helped to launch the Merchants' Exchange eleven years earlier. The league was driven by the same impatient and independent spirit that had marked the exchange. In creating an organization exclusively for "young" men, the league articulated what had been only implicit in the earlier movements of the Merchants' Exchange and the Charleston Board of Trade. The *News and Courier* editor, criticizing a suggestion that the league include representatives of the other business associations in its leadership, wrote: "[I]t has been the custom here for so long a time to pay deference to the ideas of older citizens that it will be hard to combat the influence that one or more of them would have if placed on the board [of the new Young Men's Business League]." Besides, the editor went on, the Chamber of Commerce and Cotton Exchange were already captives of "the older business men." This new organization needed to remain the property of "the more progressive young men" of Charleston if they were going to have any say in the city's affairs.[54]

The league began as an alliance of young men, many of them already members of one of the other commercial associations, and it emerged simultaneously with a movement to establish a freight bureau to investigate rates and speak with one voice to the railroads and maritime shippers. The Charleston Freight Bureau, the first fruit of the new movement, became an agency of the municipal government, reputedly the first city-sponsored agency of its kind in America, with representatives selected from the league, Chamber of Commerce, Cotton Exchange, Merchants' Exchange, and Fertilizer Exchange.[55] The Freight Bureau was conceived as a "central agency . . . to work under a kind of general welfare clause for the common defence [*sic*]." "The great trouble in Charleston," a *News and Courier* editorial opined at the initial announcement of the league, "has been that while the present commercial bodies have done very good and effective work in their own special spheres, they have not co-operated in any general work for the good of the whole community." The Chamber of Commerce pursued harbor improvements, the Cotton Exchange watched its own market, and the Merchants' Exchange looked after western grain and hay, along with the jobbing trade in the hinterland. What was needed was a more general commercial body to investigate "abuses" and lobby for reform.[56]

The Young Men's Business League's definition of "young" was never specified, but the name offered the organization's followers an identity with youthful energy and buoyant idealism—both rare in the Charleston of the 1890s. With no other restrictions to narrow its goals, the league came to form a broad-based, active force whose main purpose was to agitate for change and to confront the railroads, the city government, and the other seemingly intractable problems that plagued Charleston. The league itself did not attempt to establish permanent quarters but met periodically in crowded business meetings, often held at the German Artillery Hall.[57] Not the least of its roles was to embarrass the elders of the Chamber of Commerce, the Cotton Exchange, and city hall, to nudge them into action and to shame into silence the croakers who had always undermined confidence in any new Charleston venture.

By 1896 the *News and Courier* was hailing the league as "one of the most progressive trade organizations of this city." Though it had grown in two years to 250 members, it ought to have 1,000, the editor thought. "Think of it! One thousand men pulling together and working together for Charleston; talking for Charleston, planning for Charleston, thinking of Charleston day and night. There would be no room in this place for a croaker."[58] Indeed, the local press took the occasion to chastise the old Charleston style: "The community must pull together. It has been pulling apart for the last twenty-five years. The kicking and croaking and overreaching we have had in Charleston would have killed almost any other town long ago. We must think Charleston, talk Charleston, work for Charleston. If any man croaks, shoot him on the spot."[59]

The formation of the Young Men's Business League during the depths of the depression in Charleston marked the ascendance of a new generation of business leadership in the city. By 1900 more than 70 percent of the old 1880 business elite had died. Though some members of the young element that emerged in this period were the sons of the old-line Charleston "aristocracy," the business and political leadership of Charleston increasingly reflected the arrival of the Germans, Irish, and other "new men," many of whom had risen in occupations outside the cotton trade, often in wholesale trades. There were also important threads of continuity that tied the ascendant leaders to the Charleston establishment. J. Adger Smyth, who served two eventful terms as mayor from 1895 to 1903 and was a powerful ally of the young business leaders, was from an eminent family, had been prominent in the local cotton trade for years, and was former president of the Chamber of Commerce.[60]

The advent of this corps of new business leaders coincided with events that would resuscitate the chronically ill economy of Charleston and open new opportunities for enterprise. Many of the forces of regeneration that enlivened the "new Charleston," as some now styled it, came from outside and owed more to federal government largess and outside capitalists than they did to local entrepreneurship. Still, Charleston's new leaders in government and business were more than mere passive recipients of these benefits; they actively promoted their city as never before. They also learned to identify with the community interests they shared as a business class. Above all, they learned to work together effectively in large and elaborate voluntary organizations to advance those interests.

The first fruits of this learning experience came with a series of national conventions that were lured to the old city in 1899 and 1900. In themselves, these affairs were of fleeting significance to the economy, but their successful accomplishment was a major contributor to the confidence of Charleston's new business leaders. The idea of promoting Charleston's sultry climate and quaint charm as draws for tourism and conventions had been touted for years. But the closest Charleston had come to acting on this dream was the abortive hotel campaign of 1888. Governor Tillman's dispensary law and his efforts to enforce it through a state-controlled metropolitan police force put a cloud over the hotel business and discouraged any plans to develop tourism in Charleston.

An earlier movement to invite the United Confederate Veterans to meet in the city in 1896 was rejected by the city council, which did not want the men of the Lost Cause to "witness the city in its humiliation."[61]

The Young Men's Business League did bring a convention of South Carolina's Confederate veterans to the city in April 1898 (despite the lack of any "substantial help from some of the 'enterprising' business men of the city," as the *News and Courier* complained), and its success inspired a bolder move to draw the national Confederate veterans' reunion for 1899. The plan seemed a perfect marriage between Charleston's still unreconstructed image as the cradle of secession and its newly discovered, progressive interest in hustling business. A large meeting of businessmen gathered at the Chamber of Commerce in June 1898 to consider bidding for the reunion. The group included representatives of the city government and Freight Bureau, the railroads and steamship lines serving the city, and the local veterans' organization. The meeting dwelled on the multitude of obstacles Charleston would have to surmount to host such a convention. One impatient spokesman challenged the assembly in blunt terms: "Charleston will never move a peg if she don't quit getting in her shell and turning the cold shoulder on the world." After some hesitation, a committee of Charleston businessmen was appointed to bid for the convention at Atlanta, where the 1898 reunion was to be held the next month. Despite a heated contest with rivals from Louisville and Baltimore, the Charleston delegation came home with the prize.[62]

It was indeed a prize, but one that entailed frightening demands for concerted effort from the old city. Even the most successful Gala Week celebrations would look small in comparison to this event. The reunion would bring some 30,000 visitors to a city of less than 56,000, a city with deplorable railroad passenger facilities, decrepit hotels, and no adequate meeting hall. The hotel and meeting facilities had been the source of widespread complaint at the Atlanta meeting, and even though the Charleston organizers took their hosting of the next convention as a rare opportunity to upstage their young rival, they had not thought just how they were going to accomplish it.

The first step was to set up an elaborate corporate organization, with an executive committee composed of a chairman, prominent attorney Theodore G. Barker, and the heads of no less than twenty-five specialized committees responsible for everything from publicity and finance to badges and ice water. Another twenty men were added to the executive committee, providing broad representation from every business, profession, and neighborhood in the city. Though many active members of the Young Men's Business League, including its president, William H. Welch, and Frederick W. Wagener, and members of the other commercial associations played a prominent role in the preparations for the convention, the committee remained autonomous and was able to accommodate all constituents.

The executive committee presented its hopes for the convention at a crowded meeting, described as among the very "strongest and most representative meeting of business men" ever gathered in the city. It was held at the Chamber of Commerce not long after the successful delegation returned from Atlanta. Grave warnings of the public humiliation Charleston would suffer if this convention failed stirred the audience into cooperative action. The *News and Courier* remonstrated just before the meeting: "[L]ukewarmness in the present emergency will do the city more injury than anything, not even excepting the war or the earthquake, has ever done it." Charleston's "honor and dignity" were at stake, as George Swinton Legaré, a leading attorney, congressman, and bearer of an eminent Charleston name, warned the audience, and "failure and disgrace" would surely follow if the city faltered. The planning for the convention became a test of Charleston's will, likened on several occasions to the resolve of the Confederate troops who defended the city against the Yankees nearly forty years earlier. Another large public meeting was staged in early August at the German Artillery Hall. A band played "Dixie" as the crowd faced the executive committee members, who stood in front. Again Legaré spoke, evoking the poignant image of this "city of sad and historical memories, standing . . . like monumental evidence of our beloved lost cause." The city must, he admonished, "shake off the cloak of apathy, rise up in your might and let the world know that you are a live and energetic people."[63]

Working "arduously and harmoniously" throughout the year, aided by an energetic corps from the Ladies' Auxiliary Executive Committee, the organizers pulled off the Confederate reunion to the acclaim of the visitors and the national press and—not least—to the astonishment of Charlestonians.[64] Private homes and makeshift dormitories were thrown open to absorb the overflow from the hotels. For meeting space, the city government, rather than private enterprise, rose to the occasion. Using funds bequeathed to the city by the late John Thomson, a wealthy seed and farm-supply merchant, the city—despite strenuous opposition from those the *News and Courier* denounced as "croakers," including some who preferred that the money go toward a Confederate museum—quickly constructed a large auditorium with a seating capacity of eight thousand.[65]

This rare experience with success emboldened the city's business leaders and city officials, who quickly lured other conventions to town. Thomson Auditorium played host to the National Education Association the following summer, drawing five thousand teachers and school officials to the city. The Fire Chiefs of the United States and Canada and the League of Municipalities met, in smaller numbers, later the same year. The economic impact of these and other conventions was less significant than the publicity they garnered for the "new Charleston" and the expanded confidence these events brought to the city's civic and commercial elite.[66]

While Charleston was entertaining Confederate survivors of the Lost Cause, the U.S. Navy was preparing a second invasion of Charleston harbor. This one was both more friendly in its intention and more successful from both the navy's and from Charleston's points of view. The outbreak of the Spanish-American War in the spring of 1898 excited a surge of patriotism throughout the city. It was part of a general southern response to the war as a test of the region's loyalty. In Charleston the desire to demonstrate loyalty was only accentuated by the rich economic rewards the war promised to bring to the city. Charleston's strategic location on the South Atlantic coast and its "impregnable" harbor, well known to veterans of the last war, came again to the attention of military officials in 1898. A delegation from the city's commercial associations, joined by Mayor J. Adger Smyth, implored the military to make Charleston a rendezvous for the forces preparing to invade Cuba. The *News and Courier,* which had earlier opposed the war on principle, now issued a steady stream of articles publicizing Charleston's interest in serving the nation. "Send the Soldiers Here," "Pitch Your Tents Here," the headlines pleaded. Two days after the Fourth of July, which white Charlestonians celebrated for the first time since the Civil War, some six thousand Yankee soldiers entered Charleston—this time, unlike 1865, to effusive welcomes from city officials and the press.[67]

Charleston's openness to reconciliation even extended to Ben Tillman, now a senator from South Carolina, who, as a member of the Senate Naval Committee, was in a position to do his old enemy Charleston some big favors. That fall Mayor Smyth entertained Tillman lavishly at the Charleston Hotel, and the city's leading citizens treated the senator as a royal guest.[68] Tillman was being enlisted in a well-organized campaign to bring permanent navy facilities to Charleston. For a long time the navy had been dissatisfied with its station at Port Royal, which was exposed to frequent damage from big storms and whose port was too shallow to accommodate large vessels. The navy had alternately considered improving or abandoning that site until the *Indiana* ran aground there in 1899, bringing the issue to a head.[69] With the completion of the jetties, Charleston's harbor was now able to accommodate the ships of the new steel navy. Tillman, learning that the navy planned to abandon Port Royal and build a first-class dry-dock yard elsewhere along the coast, switched his position to favor Charleston. For their part, Port Royal backers, with the aid of former Secretary of the Navy Hilary A. Herbert, led a vicious attack on Charleston as a malaria-infested death pit whose harbor remained entirely too shallow.[70]

Mayor J. Adger Smyth and George B. Edwards, president of Exchange Banking and Trust, with strong support from the *News and Courier,* led the counterattack with testimony before the Naval Committee of the Senate and an all-out public relations campaign that put the best face possible on Charleston's past problems and its recent improvements in health and harbor. After years of lobbying in Washington for harbor improvements, Charlestonians were practiced in the art of persuasion.

The most worrisome issue for the navy and the city was the lack of sufficient pure water, a problem that had long plagued Charleston's public health and its prospects for growth. Business leaders and city officials had launched a water reform movement in 1898, with the aim of bringing an early end to the old waterworks system, which depended on artesian wells, supplemented in poor neighborhoods by easily contaminated cisterns that collected rain water. Following legal battles with the water company, and with the state over restrictions on bonded debt, Charleston arranged to replace the old system with a modern waterworks in time to satisfy the navy's concerns.[71]

The coming of the navy yard brought a huge stream of federal monies— estimated at $15 million—through the local economy during the years of construction; afterward a payroll of $.5 million flowed into the city annually. By 1913 the navy yard was said to support one-tenth of the Charleston-area labor force and to supply one-fifth of the wages.[72]

The yard also brought indirect benefits that may have been even more important. The federal government now had a strategic commitment to keeping the Charleston harbor in top condition; there would be no more begging in Washington. "Will not Uncle Sam protect his great interests with zealous care?," a promotional booklet asked in 1904. The navy yard would "make Uncle Sam himself co-guardian with the progressive element . . . for the city's future."[73] When the new Secretary of the Navy arrived aboard the cruiser *Charleston* in 1906, city officials presented him with a silver punch bowl, and the *News and Courier* announced "the resumption of diplomatic relations between the White House and Charleston."[74]

Improvements in the water supply and in the transportation system serving the navy yard opened new opportunities for growth and economic development. Beginning in 1912, along the Neck above the navy yard, an area once considered uninhabitable, a new industrial park and waterfront facilities were laid out in a five-thousand-acre development. A beltway rail line connected these sites to all the railways. North Charleston, as it came to be called, offered cheap land and labor and the stability that a large federal neighbor ensured. With the development of the new waterfront, the piers along East Bay were allowed to decay undisturbed rather than be renovated at the expense of what Mayor Robert G. Rhett called "the most historic and interesting section of the city."[75] This time historic preservation and economic development worked in perfect harmony.

An Exposition of Enterprise and Conservatism

With the military-industrial complex that came to Charleston following the Spanish-American War also came renewed dreams of a commercial empire in the Caribbean. This ambition inspired the South Carolina Interstate and West Indian Exposition, held in Charleston from December 1901 through May 1902. Boldly modeled after the Atlanta and Nashville examples, the Charleston exposition gave voice to the same New South vision of economic development and social progress. "What it is hoped to accomplish by the Exposition in this city is the introduction of new people, new capital, new industries," the *News and Courier* proclaimed.[76] This episode in Charleston's history revealed at once the energy of the new business leaders who had emerged in the late 1890s and the powerful undertow of conservatism that continued to check their role in Charleston.

In the wake of wartime mobilization and the Confederate reunion, the idea for a major exposition was first suggested in October 1899 by Col. John H. Averill, a railroad executive. William H. Welch, president of the Young Men's Business League, took the initiative, and, in the face of continuing doubt as to whether Charleston could carry off such an enterprise, he pressed the idea upon the city's business and government leaders. A public meeting in January 1900 drew support for the exposition from a larger circle of businessmen, who soon pledged sufficient funds for preliminary planning. In short order, all of the commercial bodies fell in line with the Business League and endorsed the idea, as did the city council and the governor of South Carolina. Early plans for a strictly local or state exposition were soon eclipsed by a grand vision of an "interstate and West Indian" affair on a scale in keeping with earlier exposi-tions in Atlanta and Nashville.[77] The plan was launched at a mass meeting in Thomson Auditorium in March 1900, and by June a permanent exposition company formed to gather subscriptions and organize the entire show.

The officers and directors bore the stamp of the "new Charleston" that had emerged in recent years.[78] Frederick W. Wagener, long a champion of Charleston's revival, was elected president of the exposition company, in honor of his entrepreneurial acumen and his extraordinary personal commitment to the venture. Wagener's lands in the northern reaches of the city were offered, free of cost, for use as the exposition grounds, and it was largely Wagener's capital that kept the exposition idea afloat in its darker days. John H. Averill, a Confederate veteran, railroad executive formerly with the South Carolina Railway, and active member of the city council, served as secretary and director general, a tribute to his role in inspiring the exposition. William H. Welch of the Young Men's Business League became vice president. John F. Ficken, a lawyer from Charleston's German community who had ties to the Tillman regime, served as general counsel. Samuel H. Wilson, treasurer, was a retail grocer who had recently been active in the development of the Isle of Palms as a suburban resort.[79] Joseph L. David, a King Street clothing retailer, served on the board of directors, as did Samuel Lapham, a city councilman and businessman connected with an ice company, the Charleston Hotel, and other enterprises. John Calvin Hemphill, an upcountry native who followed Francis Dawson as editor of the *News and Courier,* was also on the board and played a leading role in publicizing the exposition, both at home and abroad. Christopher C. Gadsden, a city councilman and an executive with the Charleston and Savannah Railroad and, more recently, with the Atlantic Coast Line, was one of the few representatives of Charleston's old aristocratic families actively involved in the exposition.

The company quickly set up an auxiliary Junior Executive Committee to engage the "splendid determination" of younger men in the exposition plans. J. Ross Hanahan, a fertilizer manufacturer, Montague Triest and P. J. Balaguer, both with the streetcar company, and M. Rutledge Rivers, an attorney, were among the young businessmen most involved in the planning.[80]

The exposition organizers had planned on collecting $250,000 in subscriptions, to come mostly from federal, state, and local governments; from railroads, banks, and other corporations interested in Charleston's development; and, finally, from individuals, particularly among Charleston's wealthy families. The city council gave $50,000 and graciously "placed the chain gang at the service of the project" to help defray construction costs. The state gave another $50,000, and three railroads serving Charleston subscribed another $40,000. The real blow to the exposition came when Congress—influenced by the Republicans' partisan resentment toward Charleston—rejected Senator Tillman's hard-fought campaign to win an allocation of $250,000. A smaller amount was later allotted, but only after the exposition ended.[81]

More disappointing for the morale of the exposition movement, and certainly more damaging to the public image Charleston wished to rehabilitate, was the tepid response from local capitalists. True, in all there were more than 2,400 subscribers, and most were from Charleston. Though many were of modest means, able to purchase only one share at five dollars, this was an encouraging symptom of popular support. However, many of the city's richest men, as John C. Hemphill remarked pointedly in his report, "did not take an active interest in the enterprise, and . . . some of those who were capable of large subscriptions made the smallest contributions."[82]

When stock subscriptions proved insufficient, the exposition company issued $150,000 in bonds at 5 percent interest. It also pledged a large share of the gate receipts and mortgaged the buildings to back the bonds. But Charleston banks and private capitalists still held back their support. Only when Wagener laid his personal fortune on the line by guaranteeing that the company would not fail before opening day did the bonds begin to move. Wagener, who had already donated his land, most of his time, and had invested heavily in the exposition stock, himself took $20,000 of the bonds. It was, Hemphill remarked with acerbity, "a fine example for the rich men of the community, which none of them followed." "The timidity displayed by the leaders in finance," he noted, "undermined confidence in the exposition, and the bond sale fell short.[83] When creditors lost faith in the directors, they forced the exposition company into receivership and brought great financial loss to Wagener and other investors.[84]

Whatever the ledgers showed, the exposition was a triumph of sorts for the new spirit that had come alive in Charleston. The official opening day ceremonies had been designated in the company charter for December 1. When they realized later that this was a Sunday, the organizers planned the event as a solemn occasion heavily mixed with religious ceremony, in keeping, it seemed, with the intensity of faith in the economic revival the exposition was to herald. The main auditorium was packed with visitors that day. Following prayers, patriotic music, lengthy addresses by officials, and an exposition ode, the audience joined in singing Handel's Hallelujah Chorus. On Monday morning, a "secular" celebration opened with a grand procession—the largest ever seen in Charleston—that began at Marion Square and moved slowly to the exposition grounds. Thousands of spectators followed the military bands, carriages, and floats, falling in "like water at the stern of a moving ship" and entered— more than 22,000 of them—through the gates of the "Ivory City."[85]

"This day marks the beginning of the new era for this staid old city," Mayor Smyth announced, to enthusiastic applause. Enthusiasm, however, was not enough to overcome all the problems the exposition faced. Aside from the financial problems resulting from congressional vindictiveness and the "indifference of some of the 'leaders' at home," as Hemphill put it, nearly everything that could go wrong did. The weather that winter was described as "the most forbidding that has ever been known in this city," and gate receipts suffered, along with Charleston's long-touted reputation as a winter refuge for northern tourists. Crop failures across the state, said to be "worse than at any time since 1865," hurt the local draw. To add to the disappointments, construction of several exhibit buildings met with unexpected delays. Even more deflating was the competition from a similar exposition in Buffalo, New York, which captured much of the attention from the national press that year.

Finally, the efforts by white organizers to patronize southern blacks with a special Negro exhibit, by this time mandatory at any southern exposition, blew up in a protest by Charleston blacks. The furor centered on a statue, which whites had commissioned for the exhibit and which blacks considered a demeaning portrayal of their role in the South. Following lengthy controversy, local blacks organized a boycott of the Ivory City that cut deeply into potential attendance.[86]

Despite all these problems, by the time the exposition closed five months later, attendance records showed that more than two-thirds of a million people had passed through the gates of the Ivory City. What they saw within those gates was not radically different from what visitors saw in the Atlanta and Nashville expositions. There were similar displays of industrial technology, natural resources, and commodities. The intended emphasis on the West Indian markets fell apart when a Caribbean Trade Congress failed to draw more than a handful of delegates. There were also the same Negro and Women's buildings, meant to demonstrate the potential of two yet-undeveloped resources of the modern South. The race track and the midway offered recreation, together with economic propaganda along the same lines as in Atlanta and Nashville. In like fashion, a round of special days honored political leaders, states, and organizers of the exposition. The oratory and the printed publicity evoked the familiar progressive faith in economic development, social progress, and American imperial expansion that had invariably marked earlier expositions.[87]

What was astonishing was that this event was taking place in Charleston, South Carolina, a city that only a few years earlier had been regarded—even by many of its own boosters—as, in Henry Grady's words, "the last bastion of the old regime," unable and unwilling to embrace the New South. That characterization may have been an exaggeration, but it was one firmly embedded in popular perceptions of the city. Mayor Smyth's prediction that the exposition marked a "new era" in the "staid old city" was more than rhetorical flourish. Two *Atlanta Constitution* reporters, visiting the city early in 1903, were struck by the "new element" of "brainy, pushing and progressive young men" who had given new life to the city.

> There is perhaps no city in the south [*sic*] where the turning of the commercial and industrial tides have been so perceptible or so encouraging as in Charleston. For many years it has been the custom of the people of this section to point out this good old town as the home of fossils and the breeding place of fogyism. Even the smaller inland communities were wont to compare Charleston with all that was slow and unprogressive.[88]

The personification of Charleston's "new element" was Robert Goodwyn Rhett, who took a leading role in local politics and business in this period. Less than forty years old in 1902, Rhett represented the new generation that had found a voice in the Young Men's Business League and had constituted the driving force behind the exposition. His family name, famous for its connection to Robert Barnwell Rhett (his grandfather's brother), the fire-eating secessionist, at the same time lent him credibility among the "aristocracy." Rhett attended the University of Virginia and returned to Charleston in 1884 to begin a prosperous law practice.[89] He became involved in a multitude of business enterprises and at one point was on the board of no less than twenty-five Charleston companies, from railroads and cotton mills to banks. In 1899 he became president of the People's National Bank, which became an important participant in Charleston's economic revival. His father had been a pioneer in the phosphate fertilizer industry, and Rhett came into a fortune when the Virginia-Carolina Chemical Company, a large fertilizer trust, bought out the family business in 1902. Young Rhett was actively involved in civic affairs and served as alderman from 1895 to 1903 before he succeeded J. Adger Smyth as mayor in the latter year, serving two four-year terms during what proved to be the high tide of business class progressivism in Charleston.[90]

Rhett and the "new element" that had organized the exposition found a permanent institutional vehicle in the Commercial Club. Established in the wake of the exposition in 1902, the club replaced the loose alliance of the Young Men's Business League with a more formal organization. The Commercial Club put up a magnificent four-story building on Meeting Street and established a clear identity as the modern alternative to the "ancient Chamber" and to all the other commercial bodies of Charleston. With its reading rooms, restaurants, bowling alleys, and card rooms, the club offered abundant social allurements. But it was primarily a serious, self-consciously progressive organization, whose mission included the economic development of the city, municipal government reform, and social uplift. It boasted special committees on advertising, new industries, good roads, health and sanitation, and suburban development.[91] "There are no laggards on the roster," the admiring *Atlanta Constitution* reporter concluded, "and as a place of pleasing retreat drones will find the Commercial Club distinctly unpleasant." Within a year, membership jumped to over five hundred of "the best and most aggressive Charlestonians."[92]

For all the changes Charleston had lately undergone, the new Commercial Club was still an unsettling force in a city that, until recently, had been quite unaccustomed to bombastic self-promotion, much less to success in the New South game. In a speech before the new organization, William C. Miller, Rhett's law partner, explored some of the reasons for the "apprehension" the club had awakened in Charleston. A rare display of self-examination, Miller's speech was reminiscent of William Trenholm's centennial address to the "ancient Chamber" almost twenty years earlier. Charleston, Miller explained, was a city ruled by family loyalties, ties to homes that were places "of household gods, . . . of hallowed memories, and traditions, set apart from the scenes of our business cares. . . . We have always been a home keeping people. We have made good husbands; we have entertained our guests under our own roofs and gone to bed early. There is a feeling in some quarters that the club is going to change all of that." Miller was referring to the Charleston wives and their suspicions toward a male reserve, but he had a more important point to make about the Charleston style:

> [W]hat has been a domestic virtue has been . . . a civil fault. . . . We have neglected the larger life which we had together as one community. We have made ample provision for our own family circles: we have not made our provision for the family circle of Charleston. And it has resulted that there has been no such circle . . . only segments of circles. The commercial blood of Charleston has not circulated. We have been accustomed to revolve each in his own orbit, and we have often collided or left each other on a tangent for want of a better understanding. From the house to the office or the store and back again, each absorbed in his own affairs, meeting his fellow citizens but rarely; knowing nothing of their plans and purposes, . . . sometimes defeating them . . . and having no community of ideas and interest.

The pattern of autonomy, Miller noted, also marked Charleston's relations with the upcountry, under the delusion that the City by the Sea was independent. The new Commercial Club, he went on, would serve as the "great heart which will keep the blood in circulation throughout the veins and arteries to the very extremities of our commercial life." This new blood would flow through the "community of interest" in Charleston and through the state, which would again see Charleston as its major metropolis.[93]

The Commercial Club, along with other emblems of the progressive energy that had come to Charleston since the 1890s, signaled the belated arrival of the New South. That many of the forces for change were brought to Charleston by outsiders should not conceal the eager role of collaborators among the younger set in the old aristocracy and among those rising from more obscure quarters of the city. Still, as the tide of the New South rose in Charleston, there remained a powerful, if increasingly quiet, undertow of tradition that softened the force of change in this resilient old city. Nothing spoke so forcefully for the old ways as the physical appearance of the city itself, which appeared much as it had before the war. The new Charleston took form on the Neck, leaving most of the old city on the lower peninsula undisturbed. It was as though the Yankees, who had been so frustrated in their earlier assaults on Charleston back in the 1860s, had now returned, surrounding the city not with cannon and blockade ships, but with huge military installations, ship channels, industry, and growing regiments of tourists. Old Charleston, besieged and subverted, retreated to the safe territory South of Broad, with its old mansions and its old ways. As the new century progressed, the old city became a museum, a sanctuary of artifacts and values that no longer ruled the South.

8 New Class

> *The South that is cultivating country-clubs is a South
> presumably . . . quite in the right.*
> —Henry James, 1907

In Atlanta and Nashville the leading businessmen rose on the strength of their individual wealth and accomplishments and learned to advance their collective interests as stockholders in the community enterprise of city building. Beyond their shared pursuit of purely economic interests, these men, together with their wives and children, came to form a coherent social class whose purpose went beyond narrow material benefit. Here it may be useful to employ the distinction adopted by E. Digby Baltzell, who identified the elite—in this case, businessmen whose status derived from their position in the economy—and an overlapping upper class made up of families whose status was determined by their formal and informal associations with one another.[1]

To be sure, one of the chief sociological functions of the upper-class institutions formed in the late nineteenth century was to acknowledge newly won economic success with the intangible but socially important reward of status. These institutions also became a means of recruiting and screening the other nouveau riche families who would follow. The entry requirements for this social class were not mere wealth or admission to the city's board rooms, but acceptance into a constellation of new associations that came with residence in opulent suburban neighborhoods, membership in exclusive clubs, participation in high-society charities, and patronage of elite culture and education. In these realms it was typically the wives of business leaders who took the initiative. Social settings, particularly the society balls, country clubs, and elite schools, also provided the backdrop for courting among the children of upper-class families, whose intermarriage worked at once to perpetuate, consolidate, and recruit new entrants into the local upper class, as well as to establish links with counterparts in other metropolitan centers.

In Atlanta an essentially new upper class emerged within an environment of dynamic growth. The ground was clear for the rising men of wealth, their wives, and their children to build their own set of associations with no old monied families to obstruct or exclude the parvenu.

Nashville's self-made men of the New South era rose within a slightly older community that was, at least in comparison to Atlanta, more dominated by entrenched families with established wealth and prestige. Some of these hailed from the landed gentry, whose grand plantations surrounding the city had been symbols of status and wealth in the antebellum era, while others represented old business, professional, and political elites based in the city. But in Nashville, too, the standards of social status after the war were largely defined by the merchants, financiers, and industrialists who ascended to the top of the postwar economy. Many of the older landed families that survived into the late nineteenth century merged with the newly rich through marriage and business ventures, and they often lent the symbols of their status to the rising class, as old plantations were converted to elite suburbs and the great houses to prestigious social clubs and academies. In both Atlanta and Nashville the most important social foundations for the emerging upper class included neighborhoods, clubs, charity organizations, and marriages.

Streets of Fashion

The select neighborhoods of Nashville and Atlanta took form within a radically changing urban environment. Rapid population growth and new urban transportation technology combined with upper-class social values to transform the social geography of these cities in the decades after the Civil War. Earlier, the prevailing pattern in American cities, large and small, had been for wealthy families to reside near the heart of the city in lavish town houses on streets of fashion, usually located at the edge of the central business district. This placed them within easy walking distance of where the men worked in the mercantile houses, banks, and offices, and close to the best retail stores, churches, and schools patronized by the women and children.

The growth of the urban economy in Atlanta and Nashville forced an expansion of the central retail and wholesale districts outward. As downtown property values rose, residential land use gave way to intensive commercial activity, eventually producing the skyscraper as the hallmark of the modern city. An interlude of real-estate speculation frequently turned the abandoned mansions of the rich into makeshift tenement apartments and otherwise created a zone of blight at the edge of the expanding business district.[2]

As commercial expansion pushed residential neighborhoods away from the downtown, new suburban developments drew residents to the periphery of the city. The task of daily commuting from home to work was eased by the advent of the streetcar, which appeared immediately after the war in Nashville and arrived in Atlanta in 1871. Drawn by sturdy mules, the streetcar provided convenient transportation within a range of a mile or two from the city center. By the end of the 1880s the arrival of the electric trolley (Atlanta and Nashville were among the first cities in the nation to adopt this new technology) increased the speed and range of public transportation and opened the suburban frontier to a land rush among real-estate developers and their middle-class clientele. Large-scale suburban development, linked to the interests of the electric streetcar companies, proceeded rapidly.

These new trolley-car suburbs pulled a growing portion of the wealthier middle class out of the compact, socially mixed environment of the central city into suburbs that were advertised as healthy, genteel, and ideal for raising the modern family. Within Atlanta and Nashville, as in most medium-sized and large American cities, the suburban migration also produced a number of exclusive neighborhoods for the wealthy and socially prominent. In both cities these areas emerged as a succession of suburban enclaves, each one farther from the city center. These elite suburbs evolved from strips of grand mansions that lined the major boulevards and adjacent streets into planned suburban parks that were more exclusively upper class and more insulated from the rest of the city. In Atlanta these two modes of suburban development were typified by Peachtree Street and Druid Hills, and in Nashville by West End Avenue and Belle Meade.

Elite neighborhoods were set off by opulent architecture, prestigious churches constructed on a grand scale, and private academies built to serve the rich. Within these neighborhoods, and in their accompanying religious and educational institutions, a distinctive class identity and a special style of life were nurtured as the hallmarks of the urban social elite. This upper-class subculture was largely derivative, despite certain regional distinctions; its values, manners, customs, and cultural institutions usually imitated standards set in New York City, or in Philadelphia or Boston. The rapid imitation of a distinctive upper-class subculture was evidence of the increasingly integrated national elite that E. Digby Baltzell and Robert Wiebe have described as emerging toward the end of the nineteenth century.[3] That it permeated cities like Atlanta and Nashville was a measure of the New South elite's growing affinity with its northern counterpart.

Before the 1870s most of Atlanta's wealthy families lived in unpretentious frame homes or apartments adjacent to the commercial center of the city that clustered around Pryor, Hunter, Whitehall, and Alabama streets, in the area south of the converging railroad tracks. Sherman's troops left the core of the city gutted. Initially, the rebuilding of Atlanta demanded slap-dash construction of makeshift shanties, and it was not until 1869 that "a more solid basis" for physical reconstruction began.[4] Most of the effort went into commercial

Atlanta, 1886. (Courtesy of James Michael Russell)

rather than residential structures, and domestic architecture remained undis-tinguished at best. As the city center was rebuilt it became densely commercial and expanded rapidly northward, straddling the railroad tracks and pushing residential land use before it.

Though some new residential construction for wealthy families took place on Washington Street south of the tracks, the residential center of gravity for Atlanta's rising rich was to the north, on Peachtree and Ivy streets and on other adjacent streets. Banker John H. James, a major figure in the rebuilding of Atlanta, set the pace when he constructed an elaborate mansion on Peachtree and Cain. It cost between $60,000 and $70,000 and was acclaimed the "finest

Atlanta's Peachtree Street, looking north from Ellis, 1907. (Atlanta Historical Society)

residence in Georgia" when it was opened for public tours on Christmas Eve in 1869. The next year James sold the house to the state for use as the governor's mansion in what was now Georgia's new capital city. James then built a second mansion down the street at Peachtree and Ellis.[5] These two homes were magnets for what became an "avenue of palaces" constructed during the 1870s and 1880s by Atlanta's merchant princes.[6]

Several prestigious churches also put up elaborate new edifices on, or near, Peachtree. In 1870 the cornerstone of the First Methodist Church was laid at Peachtree and Houston in a ceremony "embracing the beauty, the wealth, fashion and intelligence of the city," according to one report.[7] The First Baptist Church also replaced its old frame building in 1869 with a magnificent tall-spired church at Forsyth and Walton. St. Luke's Episcopal followed in 1874 with a new church at Spring and Walton and then, eight years later, left that to build a larger cathedral at the foot of Peachtree at Pryor and Houston.[8]

By 1872 Peachtree Street was served by a streetcar line extending from Decatur, just north of the railroad tracks downtown, to Pine, about a mile out Peachtree. Two years later the line was extended several blocks farther north and then east to Ponce de Leon Springs, a popular picnic resort about three miles from Atlanta's center.[9]

By the end of the 1880s Peachtree was the best address in Atlanta, a fashionable strip of "handsome homes" that extended all the way to the city limits at Sixth Street. A streetcar or carriage ride out this grand boulevard in 1890 brought the tourist past Atlanta's most prestigious clubs and churches and the mansions of its wealthiest families. They were set amid landscaped lawns and gardens, surrounded by ornate iron fences, and shaded by tall trees that lined the avenue. Driving past the First Methodist Church at the foot of Peachtree, one would see the Capital City Club at the corner of Ellis, and, farther up, the Executive Mansion, the Atlanta Female Institute, and the College of Music. The private residences of the leading merchants, bankers, professionals, and others who, for the most part, had made their fortunes in the postwar boom were lined up along Peachtree—the "Fifth Avenue of Atlanta"—in a bold display of new money. Tobacco and liquor merchant Robert F. Maddox, former governor and entrepreneur Rufus B. Bullock, grocer James R. Wylie, and lumber dealer Frank P. Rice were among those whose mansions adorned the lower section of Peachtree. Passing the monument to New South hero Senator Benjamin Hill that had been erected at the fork of Peachtree and West Peachtree, a visitor would go by the homes of dry-goods merchant Marion C. Kiser and the *Atlanta Constitution*'s executives, Henry H. Cabaniss, the late Henry Grady, and William A. Hemphill. Farther out were the mansions of industrialist George Winship and the widow of railroad and streetcar entrepreneur Richard Peters, along with those of lawyer and future senator Hoke Smith, industrialist Edward Van Winkle, cotton merchant Samuel M. Inman, and, at the corner of Peachtree and Kimball (later Ponce de Leon), the home of Hannibal I. Kimball.[10]

These were mansions done up in high Victorian style. The brick homes typically featured bold romanesque arches and facades decorated with baroque terra cotta insets. The frame homes bore elaborate Gothic towers, wide, sweeping porches, and gazebos, all adorned with lacy filigree and stick work trim at every opportunity. This was the ostentatious, occasionally garish architecture of a house-proud plutocracy eager to display its new-won fortunes in the most public way possible—in its homes. These and other fine residences built in postwar Atlanta were featured in the illustrated city guide books that were published for distribution to visitors and, no doubt, for local consumption among proud Atlantans. These exercises in what historian Edward C. Kirkland calls "architectural exhibitionism" were wonderful community advertisements for the great wealth the city had generated, and at the same time they served as a "visible bank balance" for the merchant princes who built them.[11]

As Peachtree's avenue of palaces spread northward, two other streetcar suburbs competed for favor from Atlanta's wealthy families. West End was

Atlanta's first real commuting suburb, but it never lived up to its early pretensions as the new home of Atlanta's upper crust. It began in 1867 as a small rural village outside the city limits, about two-and-one-half miles to the southwest of the city center. Served at first by commuter trains on the Atlanta and West Point and the Macon and Western railroads, West End offered a "rural, but at the same time sufficiently citified locality" in a "delightful suburban village."[12] By 1871 the first streetcar service in Atlanta brought easier access to West End commuters, but the village remained a sparsely settled community, and the streetcar company had trouble making the line pay. It was not until the mid-1880s, when West End built several churches and the West End Academy and after the streetcar line had been extended to the new West View Cemetery, that the suburb gained a solid footing.[13] By 1887 West End claimed 2,000 people, in a "very select" society with, one account added pointedly, a "limited population of negroes." Cheap, open land attracted more wealthy whites, and by 1890 several spacious country homes had been built, including those of Evan P. Howell, president and owner of the *Constitution,* and his son, Clark Howell, managing editor of the paper.[14] West End, a puff piece in the *Constitution* reported in that year, "is emphatically a residence community. There are no manufactures, with soot and dust, no paupers, but a thrifty well-to-do class of people . . . who, away from the noise and dust and strife of the great city, live in quiet comfort."[15]

Inman Park, on the east side of Atlanta, was first to take advantage of the speed and smoothness of the electric trolley. Real-estate developer Joel Hurt, in partnership with Asa G. Candler, the druggist and future Coca-Cola millionaire, Samuel Inman and his brother, Walker P. Inman, and several others, formed a syndicate in 1886 to integrate streetcar and suburban development. They cut a new road, Edgewood Avenue, from the center of town about two miles to the east and transformed it into a tree-lined residential boulevard. There on a large rolling plot they laid out gently curving streets and subdivided lots and designed a romantic, enclosed park with groves of trees and a small lake. This concept of a planned suburban subdivision, as the early publicity pointed out, was modeled after new designs introduced to the American landscape by Frederick Law Olmsted and developed in Riverside, Illinois, Detroit, and Cincinnati.[16] By August 1889 the Atlanta and Edgewood line, Atlanta's first electric railway, had its trolley cars gliding along the tracks to a modern suburban retreat. "This is a most delightful residence portion of Atlanta," an 1890 publication boasted of the new suburb. "A number of handsome residences have already been built and new ones are in the process of construction. A picturesque park . . . with groves, springs and a beautiful little lake . . . [make this] a most charming portion of the city." Among the "leading citizens" who took up residence in the park were Joel Hurt, Asa G.

Residences on Edgewood Avenue in Atlanta's Inman Park, 1895. (Atlanta Historical Society)

Candler, his brother, Bishop Warren Candler (a Methodist bishop and later head of Emory University), and several other branches of the Candler family, along with Ernest Woodruff, a young banker, Joseph E. Maddox, wholesale grocer and banker, Aaron Haas, wholesale grocer and liquor dealer, George King, hardware merchant, and P. H. Harralson, tobacco wholesaler.[17] If the castles of Peachtree represented the fortunes built before 1890, Inman Park represented the fortunes of the next era.

But this fashionable suburb was soon eclipsed by newer, more remote developments planned on a grander scale. The main residential thrust of Atlanta's white elite was now toward the northeast. In 1904 the city purchased the land for Piedmont Park, the site of the 1887 and 1895 expositions, and expanded the city limits in the process, opening a whole new section for development. "Atlanta's Chinese Wall Breached!," "North Side Dam Broken!," the excited realtors proclaimed following the first sale of lots. Ansley Park, once the "princely domain" of George W. Collier, was developed by E. P. Ansley at a cost of over $1 million. Laid out in the now-familiar curving streets and irregular blocks, it soon became the home for many "substantial Atlantans."[18] By 1910 Ansley Park was said to include a veritable "who's who" of prominent families. Among them were many former neighbors, refugees from the "old homes" near the city center that "have been usurped by the great tide

Nashville in the 1880s, looking south from the capital. (Tennessee State Library and Archives)

of business development that is now claiming portions of Atlanta, which only a few years ago were considered as the choicest of residential areas."[19]

No sooner was Ansley Park developed than Druid Hills opened on the northeast side where, earlier, Joel Hurt, in league with other Atlanta capitalists, had bought up nearly 1,500 acres of undeveloped land.[20] In the 1890s Hurt had invited the famous landscape architect Frederick Law Olmsted from Boston to design a suburban plan that would complement the natural beauty of the land. Later Olmsted's sons realized a plan that put Druid Hills in the forefront of modern suburban planning. Hurt sold the property to Asa G. Candler, Preston S. Arkwright, and Forrest and George Adair in 1908 for "a cool half million" dollars. The new owners announced plans for a grand auto driveway, eighty feet wide, that would continue from Ponce de Leon Avenue to the Atlanta Athletic Club at East Lake, past what would become "the handsomest residences in the south [*sic*]."[21] Druid Hills and, after World War I, Buckhead would remain the most prestigious addresses for the Atlanta upper crust.

Nashville's elite neighborhoods also followed a pattern of suburban migration as the city was transformed in the late nineteenth century. Compared with Atlanta, however, Nashville's fashionable addresses in the central city were

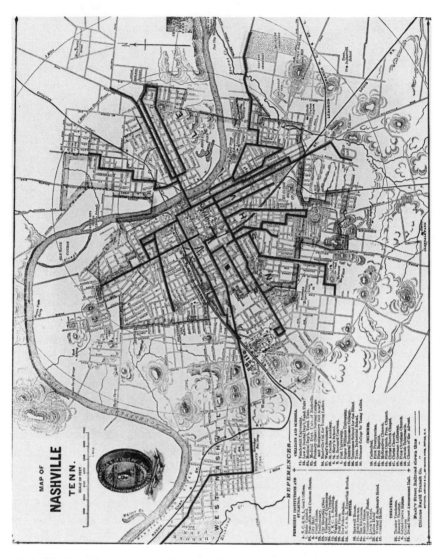

Nashville, 1897. (Tennessee State Library and Archives)

more firmly established by tradition, less disrupted by war, and more slowly pushed aside by an expanding central business district.

Capitol Hill, crowned by the proud symbol of the city's political authority, was flanked by fine brick mansions on Park Place to the east, Cedar Street on the south, and Vine Street on the west. Extending south from the hill along elevated ground, High Street, Vine, and Spruce were lined with handsome

Nashville's fashionable Vine Street, ca. 1900. (Reproduced from *Art Work of Nashville* [1894; reprint, Nashville, Tenn., 1981])

two- and three-story town houses, some old, others built since the war by the nabobs of Nashville. Capped by Polk Place, home of the former president and still home to his widow, the grande dame of Nashville society, these downtown streets were the most prestigious addresses in town at the opening of the 1880s. Many members of the Nashville economic elite in 1880 also lived after the style of the landed gentry, in large country estates along the major turnpikes that radiated from the central city, a tradition that remained a distinct feature of the Nashville elite well into the twentieth century. But among those who lived within the city in 1880, the largest number lived around Capitol Hill.[22] By tradition, men walked home from work each day for a lengthy midday meal before returning to the shops, banks, and wholesale houses a few blocks away, a custom that faded with suburbanization. Women shopped at the stores that faced the public square and, by 1900, lined Summer Street and Church. Here, too, were the city's most prestigious churches: McKendree Methodist, First Presbyterian, and Christ Church Episcopal, all on Church Street, and First Baptist at Vine and Broad.

The social world of Capitol Hill mixed eminent established families and rising New South parvenus in what became a gentle merger of old families and new money. An illustration comes from the Polk and Fall families, neighbors on Capitol Hill. J. Horton Fall, a successful hardware merchant, banker, and

Nashville's downtown, ca. 1910. (Photograph collection of the *Nashville Tennessean*)

leading member of the Nashville business community, built a new three-story brick home at Vine and Union in 1881. It was, his daughter Nell recalled, "very pretentious looking," with stone trim, bay windows on all three floors, and iron grillwork on the top. Inside, the decor was "as ornate as the late Victorian period would allow," with "seven or eight gilt-framed pier-glass mirrors" above the mantels, marble-top tables, sterling silver door knobs, "elaborate chandeliers," and a hand-painted fresco in the dining room.[23]

The Falls lived across the street from Polk Place, an estate that occupied the entire block between Vine and Spruce, south of Union. The Falls enjoyed a "slight connection" to the Polks by way of a cousin, George Fall, also in wholesale hardware, who had married Mrs. Polk's niece and adopted daughter, Sally. During Mrs. Polk's declining years, before her death in 1891, Sally became mistress of Polk Place and made the most of her affinity to the Polks. Sally "Polk Place" Fall, as she became known, "was not backward in letting people know about that relationship," according to one amused observer of this social climber. A "large buxom woman" who carried herself quite erect—her husband trailing behind her in striped pants, frock coat, silk hat, and gold-headed cane—Sally Polk Fall became the social lioness of

Annual dinner of the Executive Committee of the Tennessee Centennial Exposition.
(Photograph collection of the *Nashville Tennessean*)

Nashville.[24] Her daughter, Sadie, was a fetching belle, reported to have caused
"a sensation in the capital with her beauty and enchanting manners."[25] The
mother, according to one observer, "was exceedingly ambitious socially and did
everything to promote her daughter." She "was determined that she should
make a good marriage."[26]

Sally Polk Fall arranged a match between her daughter and Matt Gardner,
an older man, known to be "very moody," but "from a financial point of view
. . . a very eligible catch." He was the son of Robert Gardner, a wealthy dry-
goods merchant and industrialist who had left his son a large fortune at his
death in 1883.[27] The wedding took place a few months before Mrs. Polk's death
and was a great social event among the Nashville elite. But the match was ill-
fated; the marriage broke up not long after the wedding. However, when
Gardner learned of the exorbitant alimony his wife (and, doubtless, his mother-

in-law) planned to extract, he made amends, took her on a second honeymoon, and set her up in regal splendor at his country estate, Lynwood.[28]

As the Falls and Gardners ascended the social ladder—partly through their connections to the Polks—the symbol of the Polk family's presence in Nashville society met a rude end that revealed something of the city's soul in the New South era. For a few years after Mrs. Polk's death, Sally Polk Fall continued to maintain Polk Place as the center of Nashville society, but rival heirs of the Polks spoiled the scene. Eager for their share of the inheritance, they challenged the late president's will, which asked the state to support the home and permit the closest relative to live there. By 1897 the court forced a sale of the mansion and a division of the estate. An L&N tycoon from Philadelphia bought Polk Place and, in the face of a strenuous campaign by Nashville women to save it as a historic shrine, he razed the house in 1900 to make way for a more profitable apartment complex, which he named in dubious honor of the landmark he had destroyed.[29]

The Capitol Hill neighborhood grew south along Spruce and Vine, below Broad Street. By the 1890s it was hemmed in on all sides, on the north and west by steep inclines and the rough slums clustered around "Hell's Half-Acre" on the western slope, and by the railroad depots and the warehouses and industrial facilities that lined the tracks. To the southeast was "Black Bottom," a sprawling slum in a flood-prone area near the river. The retail business district grew westward, away from the public square along high ground, pushing back the once-fashionable residential districts along Deaderick, Union, and Church.

From within, once-fashionable residential streets were hard-pressed by the expanding business district. Mansions that had been built in grand style just a few years earlier gave ground to new department stores and office buildings or were converted to new uses as elite clubs, lodges, or, in many cases, boarding houses for lower-income tenants. The homes that remained on Park Place, Vine, and Spruce and had not been converted were occupied by old families left behind in the suburban exodus of Nashville's elite.[30]

Several new fortunes found a home on Rutledge Hill, a gentle rise about a half mile southeast of Capitol Hill, capped by the University of Nashville (later George Peabody College for Teachers), Vanderbilt University's Medical Department, and other educational institutions that gave a genteel tone to the neighborhood. The Rutledge family, descendants of the South Carolina Rutledges and Middletons, controlled a large tract of land north of the university until 1865, when it was subdivided and sold. The same year saw the opening of a new streetcar line that ran up the hill on Cherry Street, returning on College. M. A. Parrish, a wealthy commission merchant, bought up eight lots on Rutledge Hill and erected an elaborate Italianate brick mansion, topped by a magnificent tower and surrounded by a stone wall and iron fence. In 1877 the house was taken over by William H. Morrow, the industrialist, who bought more land, hired a French gardener to landscape it, and set his family up in "an elegant life style" on the hill overlooking the city. Next door to the Morrow home, steamboat captain Thomas Ryman built a grand estate in the early 1880s that sprawled over a full block and almost rivaled the Parrish-Morrow mansion in its Victorian bravado.[31]

By this time Rutledge Hill had become "a very select neighborhood," with less ostentatious, but very fine, brick homes lining South Market and College streets on the slope facing the city center. Arthur C. Hardison, wholesale grocer, Henry Metz, retail clothing, Charles Nelson, whiskey distiller and banker, William B. Reese, attorney, Horace G. Lipscomb, wholesale hardware, Ed Baxter, L&N attorney, and Morton B. Howell, attorney, were among the many well-off merchants and professionals who made their home in this fashionable suburb during the 1880s and 1890s.[32] Though many attended downtown churches, Rutledge Hill spawned its own with the Elm Street Methodist Church, Grace Cumberland Presbyterian Church, the Baptist Central Church, and the Episcopalian Church of the Holy Trinity.

Edgefield, across the river from Nashville, was another streetcar suburb that offered young, wealthy families a refuge from the "narrow, hot streets" of the city and cheap land on which to build large homes and spacious gardens. Streetcar service over the Woodland Street Bridge opened Edgefield to convenient commuting in 1872, and Russell Street, one block off the car line on high ground, became a showcase of rich-looking brick mansions. During the 1870s and 1880s, Edgefield had become the smart new suburb for young families seeking, as a puff piece in the newspaper put it, "a quiet, cozy comfortable retreat" with "plenty of air and light taxes."[33] By 1880, when Nashville's "little rival metropolis across the Cumberland" was annexed, Edgefield claimed over four thousand residents.[34] By the 1890s this suburb had become home to newly arrived merchants and manufacturers, several of whom owned factories along the river. Joining them were the sons and daughters of prominent Nashvillians who continued to reside downtown. Brick manufacturers William G. Bush and Thomas L. Herbert, wholesale grocers John and Samuel Orr, stove and tinware dealer William H. Webb, along with Michael Burns, Jr., William H. Weakley, and G. W. Stahlman, were among the many rising businessmen and sons of prominent families who lived along Russell Street in the 1890s.[35] Tulip Street Methodist Church, with its magnificent brick romanesque design, went up in 1892, and Woodland Street Presbyterian and St. Ann's Episcopal Church stood close by to serve Edgefield.

Neither Rutledge Hill nor Edgefield prevailed as exclusive enclaves for the Nashville elite, and they fell from favor almost as suddenly as they had risen. The center of gravity for elite Nashville's social geography shifted quickly to the west end. By the mid-1880s the city was experiencing a strong suburban building boom combined with downtown expansion, which displaced many Capitol Hill residents. From that point forward, Nashville's West End Avenue—and its extensions, Richland and Harding pikes—became the city's main line. From the foot of West End, where it intersected with Broad Street a little over one mile west of the Public Square, the road stretched west in a broad rolling boulevard graced with the lordly suburban palaces of Nashville's *haute bourgeoisie.*

The first West End elite neighborhood to form on the avenue, and on the adjacent streets of Belmont, Hayes, Church, and Elliston, clustered adjacent to the Vanderbilt campus. This area had gained status from the elaborate homes of suburban pioneers. Samuel Murphy had acquired portions of the former Boyd and Elliston estates in 1869 and 1871 and built a fine country estate surrounded by acres of trees and shrubs. Murphy was reputed to be the city's richest man, worth over one million dollars. A whiskey distiller from Cincinnati, he had made his fortune during the war and had married Anna Hayes, the daughter of a prominent Nashville merchant. A "man of marked personality," Murphy, it was said, "abhorred old money, and would never take a worn or crumpled bank note." But he saw to it that his niece and only heir (he and his wife had no children) married old money, and he even arranged for her to jilt one suitor in favor of Edwin S. Gardner, Jr., the son of a wealthy Sumner County stock breeder who was a close friend of Murphy's.[36]

Farther west along Church Street, then known as Richland Turnpike, Norman Farrell, a wealthy hardware dealer, took over Burlington, an antebellum mansion that had been in his wife's family.[37] Closer to town, Henry M. Hayes and his wife, an heir to the Boyd estate, sold off portions of her father's land to build an ostentatious mansion at the corner of Church and Boyd. Hayes' Folly, as it was known, became the home of Jacob McGavock Dickinson, a prominent railroad lawyer.[38]

When streetcar service was extended from downtown out Broad and along West End in the 1870s, one editor, noting several young businessmen who were planning "fine residences" there, saw "no reason why this broad thoroughfare should not be made the grand boulevard of the city and become famous for its handsome buildings."[39] In 1873 the Methodist church bought farm land adjacent to West End for the Vanderbilt University campus. During the 1880s and 1890s, new lots along West End, Broad and West Broad streets, Belmont, and Terrace Place filled up as the Vanderbilt campus developed and as streetcar service extended to its gate facing the avenue.[40]

The campus was a magnet for the new suburbanites. The principal founder, Bishop Holland McTyeire, had transformed fields of corn and hay into a parklike refuge planted with every variety of tree and shrub. For well-to-do

Nashville's West End Avenue, ca. 1900. (Reproduced from Nashville Land Improvement Company, *West Nashville* [Nashville, Tenn., 1900])

Nashvillians, a carriage drive along West End and through the campus was the fashionable recreation.[41] The university became a prestigious symbol that lent a certain tone to the West End neighborhood. Several of Nashville's monied men served on the school's board of trustees, and they and others made philanthropy to the university a guarantee of social recognition in Nashville. Except for the Episcopalians, who tended to favor the University of the South, Methodists, Presbyterians, and families in other denominations sent their sons and, by the 1890s, their daughters to Vanderbilt. A diploma from the school soon became a common feature, if not a requisite, of membership in the local upper class. At least one belle admitted that her father moved from Rutledge Hill to West End, having calculated that "it would be advantageous for his daughters to live near the fraternity houses near Vanderbilt."[42] When the university became open to women students in the 1890s, attendance at Vanderbilt often served as a substitute for the debutante parties and cotillions that had formerly been required rites of passage for Nashville belles.[43]

On and near West End, new churches emerged to rival the traditional claims of the downtown churches. Moore Memorial Presbyterian was located near the foot of the avenue on Broad. West End Methodist, at the intersection of West End and Belmont, replaced its modest frame church with an elaborate brick edifice in the 1890s. Close by was the ornate mansion that served as the rectory for Rev. Robert Anderson, who was also vice president of Vanderbilt.

By the 1890s this congregation claimed eight hundred communicants and represented, along with Vanderbilt University, the Methodist preeminence among Nashville's elite.[44]

During the 1890s, West End development extended beyond Vanderbilt's campus. The Tennessee Centennial Exposition, held on the grounds of the horse-racing track, West Side Park, in 1897, brought improved trolley service to West End and confirmed its place as Nashville's grand boulevard. Plans to develop the exposition grounds as an elite suburb yielded to public pressure for the development of Centennial Park in 1902. With its scale model of the Parthenon, symbol of the "Athens of the South," the park was a favorite resort of Nashvillians, and it greatly enhanced the value of West End real estate.

West of the park, Joseph H. Acklen, a wealthy lawyer and heir of a prominent antebellum family in Nashville, had developed West End Park, later called Acklen Park. Set on hilly land, with streets curving around spacious blocks, this suburban park seemed a promising counterpart to Inman or Ansley parks in Atlanta. Acklen built his own magnificent display of architectural exhibitionism in a luxuriant palace that set the tone for his development. Several ostentatious mansions went up along the West End border, but the interior remained unsettled, in part because of the sloping land.[45]

Farther out the avenue, about three-and-one-half miles from the city center, Richland emerged in 1905 as the latest development designed for the Nashville suburban elite. It centered around Nashville's first country club, the hallmark of the modern upper-class suburb. Chartered in 1901, the Nashville Golf and Country Club introduced a sport that was foreign to Nashville, but one that already enjoyed social prestige from its association with the leisure classes of the East and Britain. The country club offered social attractions for wives and children that had little to do with golf, of course. Soon it attracted many of the city's most eminent and wealthy young families, and Richland benefited from its proximity to the club, which laid out its course on the Whitworth estate.[46] Once streetcar service reached the neighborhood in 1905, the Richland Realty Company, a syndicate that included many of the city's leading businessmen, began selling lots in a strip two blocks deep along the avenue.[47] Again, the country estates of prominent citizens were advertised alongside the new suburban development to certify its status. Benjamin F. Wilson, a wealthy banker who had come to Nashville from Georgia after years in New York City financial circles, built an ostentatious country estate in the Richland district in 1902. Mrs. Wilson, touted as "one of the most popular and prominent women in Nashville," was said to have brought to her Richland "country seat" much of the same lavish taste she and her husband displayed in their "city residence" downtown on North High Street, "one of the most elegant homes in the city."[48]

Except for Acklen Park, Nashville's West End suburbs developed as strips

View of the Tennessee Centennial Exposition, 1897. (Library of Congress)

along the boulevard rather than as suburban parks set apart from the city, in the style of Atlanta's Inman Park, Ansley Park, and Druid Hills. Belle Meade, five miles out from the city center on Harding Pike, the extension of West End Avenue and Richland Pike, became Nashville's most opulent and enduring upper-class suburb. Here was a subcommunity insulated from the city, developed exclusively for wealthy families, and knitted together by a network of neighborhood, country club, churches, and schools. This suburb did not mature until after World War I, but it was begun in 1905 and was part of the same West End suburban thrust that began thirty years earlier.[49]

A Clubbable Spirit

New social clubs, along with charitable and cultural organizations that formed after 1880, became as important as neighborhoods in identifying and assimilating the members of the ascendant urban elite, and their wives and children, into an upper class. Affluent neighborhoods in the modern city, in effect, drew families by their wealth and gave expression on a daily level to the distinctive style of life that increasingly set apart the upper class. Social clubs and charitable organizations extended that process of defining a local upper class, and they brought residents of the proliferating neighborhoods of wealthy families together in metropolitan associations.[50] Several of Atlanta's and Nashville's most socially prominent clubs today had their origins in this earlier era when an ascendant New South elite was forming a durable upper class.

Metropolitan men's clubs, usually located downtown, offered the businessman "his peculiar asylum," as Dixon Wecter has put it, "from the pandemonium of commerce, the bumptiousness of democracy, and the feminism of his own household."[51] Some provided nothing more than social refuge; others, like the commercial clubs, took on roles in economic and political affairs. Before the 1880s Atlanta had no such men's clubs, or at least none that survived for any length of time. It was a point of local pride that Atlanta was an open city, free of social distinctions, welcoming the ambitious from all backgrounds. "There is no city in this or any other country more free from the domination of *caste*," Edward Clarke boasted in 1879.[52] But social clubs were a mark of urban refinement and luxury, as well as an aid to social advancement, and there were numerous calls to organize them. Atlanta, one reporter explained, "was too busy growing to stop long enough to crack a bottle of wine at the club." Most of the new clubs began among the younger men, bachelors looking for a convivial social setting. The Our Boys Club began about 1877, on the note that "Atlanta is sadly deficient . . . in her social organizations," but it died in 1882.[53]

Atlanta's Capitol City Club. (National Archives)

The next year a group of young men, finding their gathering place in the lobby and billiard hall of the Kimball House too crowded, launched the Capital City Club. They took up a subscription and fitted up club rooms in an "elegant residence" on Walton Street. The club, under the leadership of insurance man Harry C. Stockdell, attracted a large following among Atlanta's business elite and soon moved to more spacious quarters in the "palatial" James mansion on Peachtree.54 In both formal and informal ways, the club quickly became a center of Atlanta's high society. Presidents Grover Cleveland, William McKinley, William Howard Taft, and Jefferson Davis (C.S.A.) were among the dignitaries and celebrities who made a reception and banquet at the Capital City Club an obligatory part of their visit to Atlanta. Beginning with the first "ladies' reception" soon after its founding, this club became "a center of social life in Atlanta."55 The club's annual New Year's ball was a social event no prominent Atlanta family dared miss. The club also provided daily refuge with food, wine (no hard liquor was allowed at the bar), billiards, and informal conversation. Banker Robert J. Lowry recalled long hours spent playing pool with John Fitten while Henry Grady and Evan Howell talked politics and watched. Above all, as one club president put it, "membership in this club should be the insignia of a gentleman."[56] Indeed, membership did become an emblem of the Atlanta upper class—but not always one that worked to the member's favor. When insurance executive Livingston Mims ran for mayor in 1900, his affiliation with the Capital City Club became a target for democratic outrage.[57] This, as much as anything, was testament to the club's reputation in the community.

The Gate City's other prestigious men's club, the Atlanta Athletic Club, was typical of the new suburban resorts, centering around golf, that began to emerge in most large and medium-sized American cities around the turn of the century. Again young men, many of them the sons of leading businessmen, initiated the organization of the club, and it soon gained social eminence. It began inauspiciously in 1898 in rented space downtown.[58] Like its counterparts in other cities, the Athletic Club was devoted to "judicious cultivation [of] the physique" in a socially selective environment. Handball, tennis, baseball, and football were among the sports the club cultivated. Beginning in 1900, George W. Adair, Jr., urged the club to build a golf course, and when he became president in 1905 the membership, by then standing at about three hundred, endorsed his plan. By 1907 a small course had been laid out, according to the design of a noted golf course architect, in the rural area around East Lake. The new course was touted as a major attraction to wealthy northern tourists and was said to "be to all Dixieland what the Tuxedo and Westchester clubs of New York are to the east." By 1912 the Capital City Club, described by this time as a group of "staid, middle-aged business men," made a bid for the "younger men" by opening its own golf course, in conjunction with a major membership drive.[59]

The third of what became upper-class Atlanta's most preeminent social clubs began in 1887 as the Gentlemen's Driving Club, later known as the Piedmont Driving Club. It revolved around a clubhouse and a track for driving carriages and racing horses in a suburban resort on the northeast side of town. Earlier, racing had taken place at Oglethorpe Park, but, following the 1881 exposition, this track was ignobly sacrificed to New South enterprise when a cotton mill displaced it. Around 1887 a group of Atlanta's young business and professional men formed an association to buy up land and lay out a new driving course. About two hundred men, among them Henry Grady, Joel Hurt, Robert Lowry, John Keely, Hoke Smith, and Joseph Kingsberry, pledged $100 each and bought a large tract of two hundred acres on the north side of town. On this occasion, Atlanta's quest for industry joined hands with the pursuit of social luxury and recreation when Fulton County and the Richmond and Danville Railroad developed this site for Atlanta's Piedmont Exposition of 1887. The club opened, and the accompanying exposition offered a splendid

Atlanta's Piedmont Driving Club. (National Archives)

display of the Gate City's fashionable elite and the economic spirit that had spawned it.[60] As it evolved under its new name, the Piedmont Driving Club became one of Atlanta's most prominent and exclusive suburban clubs.

Nashville, too, had no men's social clubs before the 1880s, when several sprang into existence and quickly became emblems of the ascendant business class. Some men gathered regularly but informally in the lobby of the Maxwell House Hotel, constituting Nashville's counterpart to the Kimball House set. The absence of any club for "well-to-do men about town" was "a subject of chronic complaint" until 1881, when one of the complainers called a meeting at the Maxwell House to tap the "clubbable spirit" of Nashville. The Hermitage Club, as the new organization was christened, bought the stately Cunningham mansion on North High Street, a place long known as the former headquarters of the Union command during the occupation. The club added a ballroom and restaurant on the third floor and remodeled throughout. "Furnished with metropolitan taste," one smug account boasted, it was thought to be "second to none out of New York City for the completeness and elegance of its equipment, high personnel and the conservatism of its domestic government." The officers and members included the "cream of Nashville society," among them former governor James D. Porter, Godfrey M. Fogg, Van Leer Kirkman, Samuel J. Keith, William Duncan, Samuel Murphy, and James C. Warner.[61]

The club offered downtown businessmen a comfortable place for lunch and supper and an untroubled retreat from the world of office and home.

Women were allowed entrance only under strictly controlled circumstances during the day, but the club included the members' wives and daughters in its receptions for visiting dignitaries and in its annual ball, held on January 8, the anniversary of the victory at New Orleans, in honor of the club's "patron saint." The Hermitage Club also staged elaborate balls following horse shows, and it became a favorite place for debutante cotillions at which the belles of Nashville were presented to society.[62] Men in Nashville and Atlanta countered the "feminine dislike for [men's] clubs" by incorporating women into these and other "entertainments" and making club activities emblems of *family* status. "The Hermitage Club leads in point of wealth, influence and numbers," the *Nashville American* reported in 1890. Already it had exceeded its chartered limit of 150 resident members, and many prominent nonresidents also held membership.[63]

But the Hermitage Club suffered from some of the same instability that plagued Nashville's commercial associations in the 1890s and 1900s. In 1895, in the face of financial trouble, it merged with the less prestigious Capital Club, which had been organized a few years earlier in 1888. Three years later, this combined organization was forced into receivership during a dispute with a creditor and had to reorganize.[64] In 1905 the Hermitage planned another merger, this time with the rival University Club, an elite group of university graduates that had been founded in 1895. But this arrangement fell apart over a social flap in which Godfrey M. Fogg, one of the Hermitage's most venerable members, received a letter from the secret joint committee on membership for the two clubs asking him to resign. This, it seemed, was the result of pressure from relatives of his divorced wife. Fogg "placed the letter making this request in a conspicuous place at the Hermitage Club, which resulted in arousing other members." The members were appalled by this effrontery, and the merger plans collapsed amid the uproar. Two years later, the cost of maintaining the club rooms and restaurant forced the men of the Hermitage Club to reconsider the merger. The result was a club under a new name, the Watauga Club. This group planned a new clubhouse downtown, but their plans never materialized, and the members soon took up quarters in the old Hermitage Club and resumed the old name. As the downtown neighborhood that surrounded it declined, so did the Hermitage Club, and it eventually folded when the bank foreclosed its mortgage.[65]

Except for the Hermitage Club and the two clubs it combined with, Nashville had no large, prestigious men's clubs in the Atlanta style. The Cumberland Club served briefly as the social center of the "sylvan suburb" of Edgefield for a decade beginning in 1884.[66] The Standard Club was part of the separate social world of Nashville's well-to-do Jewish community. Organized in 1882 as a successor to the Concordia and Thalia clubs, which dated back to the 1860s, the Standard Club occupied the old Kirkman home on Summer Street until 1900, when it built lavish new quarters on Polk Avenue downtown. By 1910 it had added a suburban country club, a counterpart to the exclusively gentile Golf and Country Club.[67] But there was nothing on a metropolitan scale to compare with Atlanta's durable elite clubs.

Nashville did spawn several men's literary and discussion clubs, the most notable being the Round Table, founded in 1884, and the Old Oak, founded three years later. These were small clubs that engaged members of the business and professional elite in discussions of sometimes esoteric and often quite timely political and social issues. They were a part of the educated and genteel self-image the Athenians of the South pursued in the late nineteenth century. More than that, they provided one of the few explicit forums for discussions of ideas that were of compelling importance to business leaders in the New South. Papers on labor, race, government reform, and economic regulations were among those that informed and assimilated opinion among the business elite in Nashville.[68]

Nashville also boasted several sports clubs that drew younger men. The Nashville Athletic Club, founded in 1884, supported a swimming pool and gymnasium downtown. The Nashville Blood Horse Association involved a number of elite Nashvillians who enjoyed the "sport of kings" and the status attached to it. The most important club, socially, was the Nashville Golf and Country Club, predecessor to the exclusive Belle Meade Country Club. The club was begun by young golfers interested in bringing "the royal game" to Nashville. A group of leading business and professional men met at the Maxwell House in 1901 to formally organize a golf club and to acquire land on which to build a clubhouse and lay out a course. The club merged the next year with the Oakdale Hunt Club, a group organized a few years earlier to sponsor fox hunts and horsemanship. After its opening in 1902, the country club was the scene of a constant round of informal socializing and of frequent parties and "entertainments." Wives and children often socialized at the country club, with enough frequency to require an added men's wing with its own bar, lounge, and porch to afford a masculine retreat in the suburbs.

Society Women

The women of elite families played an especially important role in defining the local upper class. Their clubs, parties, debutante balls, and other social events acted as screening devices that allowed the wives of the elite businessmen to act as gatekeepers who passed approval on the newcomers and newly rich seeking entry into the intimate social world of the local upper class. These organizations and events sponsored by women also provided an approved setting for courting, with the ulterior motive of insuring proper, if not advantageous, marriages for the elite class's sons and daughters. Some women engaged in purely social activities, such as debutante balls, afternoon whist parties, and evening soirees, and others devoted themselves to the promotion of art, music, opera, and theater and other culturally uplifting programs. By the start of the progressive era, the upper-class women of Atlanta and Nashville were also increasingly involved in civic clubs devoted to charity, social service, and civic reform. For these women, the civic club became a means of justifying both the upper class and the "new woman."

Women also assumed the principal roles in setting the standard for manners among the social elite and in preparing their children for entry into a self-perpetuating upper class. The cotillion, or debutante ball, was one ritual imported from the Northeast that found its way into the upper class of the New South. The primary purpose of the debutante's *rite de passage* was to introduce the daughters of the elite to the sons of the elite, to encourage an endogamous, or in-group, marriage market and thereby consolidate wealth and perpetuate family status. Otherwise, as E. Digby Baltzell notes, "the democratic whims of romantic love often play havoc with class solidarity. . . . Romantic love as a reason for marriage . . . is deftly channeled within a relatively coherent sub-cultural circle."[69]

Nashville was old enough, rich enough, and pretentious enough to have established, well before the 1880s, a custom of annual debuts for the young belles of wealthy families. This tradition became amplified in the social context of new money in the Gilded Age. The city witnessed a constant round of debutante parties and cotillions, all reported in the newspapers by special society reporters. "There is a greater number of houses in Nashville to-day capable of entertaining on a liberal scale, more money at society's command . . . than at any time in its local history," one reporter boasted in 1888.[70] Atlanta could only admire the advanced state of high society in Nashville in 1894 when the *Atlanta Constitution* commented: "Nashville is, of course, the aristocratic center of elegance and culture in the State. It is a city of old homes and old traditions, combined with all that is intellectual and progressive in modern life, and it has produced a number of belles of national reputation."[71]

Josephine Elliston Farrell, daughter of an old Nashville family, recalled the elaborate preparations that were made for a Nashville debut.[72] The "coming out" was usually planned for the season after the conclusion of a young woman's formal education, usually when she was somewhere between the ages of sixteen and twenty. Gowns for the parties (and for the wedding such debuts were designed to precede) were often purchased in Europe during the obligatory grand tour that young ladies took with their mothers or chaperons. Otherwise, they might be purchased in the East or custom-made by local dressmakers. During the year a young lady was "presented" at thirty to forty parties, all hosted by friends of the debutante's family. The men at these affairs, Miss Elliston recalled, were not her own age but rather were older men, established in their businesses or professions and "ready to be married to the eligible daughters of Nashville people."

The major event was a cotillion put on by the family, often at the Duncan or Maxwell House hotels, or at the Hermitage or University clubs. Those families with large enough houses staged the cotillion at home. The Benjamin F. Wilson family opened their third-floor ballroom to guests, and Sadie Polk Fall's "brilliant" reception at Polk Place was said to be attended by "all of Nashville society."[73] No cotillion was complete without an orchestra, preferably Pellettieri's Italian Band, and a midnight supper. A favorite waiter, Irvine Brown, a light-skinned man thought to have black and Indian forebears, was "a must" at these events. A communicant at Christ Church and trusted servant of the Nashville gentry, Brown became an unofficial arbiter of society in Nashville, a bountiful well of gossip and a knowing critic of manners among the Nashville rich. After serving at a large party given by newcomers to the city, Brown reassured one old Nashville family that it was "nice, but they are not in our class."[74]

The debutante parties and cotillion balls were part of a busy round of events that filled the social season in upper-class Nashville during the late nineteenth century. It began with New Year's Day receptions or levees at several of the most prominent residences.[75] "In imitation, we suppose, of Parisian society," the *American*'s society reporter noted, the "fashionable calling hour will not begin until 12 m[idnight]," when "charming matrons and bewitching maids . . . will only await to extend happy New Year greetings to friends of the opposite sex." By the late 1880s, reports of these New Year's Day receptions included an extensive list of those receiving, descriptions of the decorations and the gowns, and an account of who visited each home.[76] Next on the social calendar was the annual Jackson's Day Ball, held at the Hermitage Club on January 8, followed by a series of parties and receptions that continued until Lent. Fashionable weddings were planned to come after the hiatus of the holy season. During the summer, the social pace slowed as women and children of elite Nashville families retreated to summer resorts. Some went to Saratoga and other fashionable spas in the Northeast, but many went to Beersheba Springs and Monteagle in the Cumberlands where they owned summer cottages. Here they mixed with one another in an isolated community that affected a rustic and unpretentious air. These summer resorts played an important role in reinforcing the group consciousness that was the essence of class formation. Here, and more often in the eastern resorts, Nashville's elites could also meet their counterparts from other American cities.[77]

In Atlanta, the trappings of upper-class culture evolved later than in Nashville, but in essentially the same form. Though individual families had long sponsored debuts for their own daughters, it was not until 1911 that the custom became an annual, formalized institution in which all families who were presenting their daughters participated. The Debutante Club made its first appearance that year in a lavish dinner and dance at the Piedmont Driving Club, described as "the first formal dance of the season."[78] A chatty account by the *Atlanta Journal*'s society columnist informed outsiders about each debutante, her gown, her dinner hosts and escort, and other guests at the affair.[79]

Each year the Atlanta debutantes formed their own club, and many continued to meet periodically, ostensibly to carry out some charitable mission. The Debutante Clubs of 1914, 1915, and 1916 joined in the latter year to form the Atlanta chapter of the Junior League, a branch of an upper-class charitable organization that began earlier in New York.[80] The debutantes' new commitments to charity and community service, beginning in the progressive era, offered a means of self-justification that was as important to these young women as patronage of the arts and education was to their parents.

In addition to the cotillion, the channels that facilitated upper-class courting in Atlanta and Nashville were formed by a whole system of social relations, from the country clubs, where children played, to the elite private academies they attended, the neighborhoods they grew up in, the cultural events they attended with their parents, and the parties they gave on their own. William Raoul, Jr., the son of a wealthy railroad executive, described his "aristocratic upbringing" in Atlanta in the 1890s, when he was in his twenties, as a lively social whirl. His mother, the daughter of railroad entrepreneur William Wadley, was one of Atlanta's premier hostesses, and the family mansion on Peachtree was the scene of a busy round of festive parties. Young Raoul was given a "made place" of employment at the Southern Iron Car Line and was no slave to his job. His cohort of young friends seemed as driven by the pursuit of social pleasure as his father's and grandfather's generations had been by work and money making. The younger set of Atlanta society used the Kimball House Hotel as their center in the 1890s, later gravitating northward to the new Aragon Hotel (built in 1892), then the Piedmont Hotel (1903), said to be "the symbol of everything that was modern and smart."[81] The Atlanta Cotillion Club, a "fashionable dancing club" for men, met at the Capital City Club, while younger people went to dances held by the Nine O'Clock German Club at the Kimball House, at which the champagne flowed freely.[82]

The social scene among "the best society" in Atlanta came in for some

Ball at Atlanta's Piedmont Driving Club, ca. 1910. (Atlanta Historical Society)

criticism in 1897 when Otis Smith, a cashier at an Atlanta bank who was described as "a society leader of the swellest set," was caught embezzling money at work. He needed more funds, according to one disparaging report, to "keep up the procession" on the social circuit. Reverend Landrum of Atlanta's First Baptist Church used the Smith case as an object lesson in social morals and fixed the blame on the wives of Atlanta's rich businessmen. He roundly denounced the "beautiful women" of Atlanta, who "belong to two, three or even four card clubs, and devote the greater part of every week to the wicked fascinations of games of chance." A Charleston reporter enjoyed the scandal as a revelation of Atlanta's decadence and vulgarity, as well as for the comical display of its moralistic preachers. "We are not surprised or shocked at . . . the ways of Atlanta society," he commented with the patronizing air of an older and wiser relative. "It is a new town with a new and, in some respects, sadly assorted society. It will grow better and more respectable as it grows older."[83]

Society events in Atlanta and Nashville provided a forum within which the sons and daughters of the upper class could find suitable marriage partners. To be sure, each city saw several notable weddings involving mates who came from outside the city, including those of two Nashville belles who married European royalty, but most matches typically joined local offspring from similar backgrounds. Intermarriage within the local upper class was the ulti-

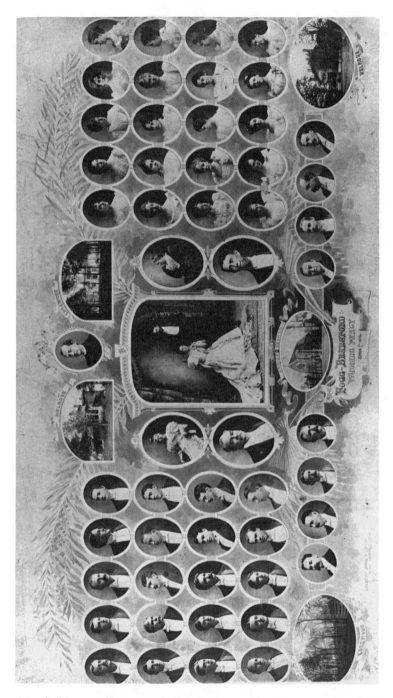

Bransford-Fogg wedding picture, 1896. (Tennessee State Library and Archives)

mate form of intimate association, which the elite neighborhoods, summer resorts, clubs, and society events all encouraged.[84] A well-arranged marriage ensured status, consolidated wealth, and perpetuated membership in an upper class that, as the second and third generations came of age, increasingly depended on birth rather than on personal wealth or accomplishments.

A photograph from the Elizabeth Bransford-Francis B. Fogg wedding in Nashville in 1896 reveals much about the marriage of families and fortunes that underlay this vital social ritual.[85] A central picture of the bride and groom is flanked by separate portraits of the parents. John S. Bransford, the bride's father, was a dry-goods merchant who had come to Nashville in 1856 from a small upper-Cumberland town and built a modest fortune. A Methodist, he lived in Edgefield with his wife, Mary Johnson Bransford, the daughter of a Nashville merchant.[86] Godfrey M. Fogg, the groom's father, was from an established Nashville family whose country seat, Melrose, was in the southern suburbs. His father was a wealthy lawyer who had made money in railroads, and his mother was sister to Vernon K. Stevenson, the L&N executive. Godfrey Fogg also became a prosperous railroad lawyer, an industrialist involved with Tennessee's phosphate fertilizer production, and a leader in numerous business and social affairs in Nashville.[87] The wedding of their children took place in the groom's church, Christ Church Episcopal. The groomsmen and the bridesmaids (twenty of each), flanked on each side of the parents, were the sons and daughters of Nashville's leading families.

Accompanying all of these society events was the publicity provided by the society columns of the local newspapers and other periodicals. Society reporters were a required feature on Nashville and Atlanta newspapers by the 1880s, and it is clear from the details included in their accounts that they received the full cooperation of hostesses who were eager to let people know everything from the flowers used in their decorations and the material in their gowns to the invitation lists for their parties. Surely one of the audiences for this kind of society reporting consisted of those outside the upper class, who may have derived a certain vicarious pleasure from reading about the lifestyles of the wealthy. Descriptions of receptions and weddings fed this appetite with gushing superlatives regarding the unsurpassed beauty of the women, the elaborately prepared decorations, and the "exquisite" quality of the entire affair. These public accounts were, of course, also a means by which members of the local upper class kept score and advertised their access to the intimate circle of association defined by these social events.

The appetite for social reporting was great enough in Nashville to support a separate weekly magazine devoted to accounts of the rich and prominent families of the city. The *Mirror,* "a journal of society, amusement and politics," appeared from 1892 to 1894 and kept up a running account of parties, personalities, and courting among Nashville's wealthy families. A rival magazine, *Chat,* appeared in 1893 and ran for about three years before folding. The product of a group of prominent young Nashville lawyers, *Chat* was filled with the usual laudatory reports on social functions, and in 1895 it ran a series of biographical sketches of leading citizens.

A more systematic means of demarcating status was provided by the "blue books," or social registers, that appeared in Nashville and Atlanta beginning in 1896. E. W. Crozier's 1896 *Nashville Blue Book of Selected Names* was more like a selective city directory. Published locally, it was intended for visitors to the exposition as well as for local consumption. It included over five thousand individuals, or about half that many families, and listed them both alphabetically and by street address. Crozier also included a list of prominent churches and clubs with the names of their officers. Four years later the Dau Publishing Company of New York City came out with *The Nashville Society Blue Book: Elite Family Directory, Club Membership,* which listed about 1,300 individuals and included their club affiliations and the ladies' "receiving days."[88] In 1901 the same company produced a similar book, *The Atlanta Society Blue Book,* which provided the Gate City elite with its first formal directory of the social elite and their clubs.[89] Dau came out with new editions for Nashville in 1903 and for Atlanta in 1904 and 1907. In 1911 a Nashville woman, Mrs. William W. Geraldton, published a new *Social Directory* for the city containing an expanded list of over 1,500 people.[90] By this time the Social Register Association of New York, publisher of the national *Social Register,* which had been produced annually since 1887, had come out with a combined register for several southeastern cities, including Atlanta, Richmond, Charleston, Savannah, and Augusta.[91] Atlanta's list included over eleven hundred individuals and half that many families.

Whatever their origin, these southern social registers were not as exclusive as those for New York and other large cities, if only because they had to include enough people to make them commercially profitable. Nor did their listings carry the same social importance as the ones in northeastern cities. But they were important in southern cities, as they were in the North, at a time when the economy was elevating new fortunes and new families. The social directories offered one more way for the patrician and the parvenu to identify one another and to facilitate the intimate circle of associations that helped transform the newly rich into a new upper class.[92]

High Culture and High Society

Patronage of the arts and education became an upper-class counterpoint, generally feminine in its inspiration, to the practical, masculine world of business. At the same time, financial support—if not appreciation—of art, music, opera, and theater became a mark of refinement. This was at least as important an emblem to the arrivistes of the urban South as it was to the more established upper class in the cities of the Northeast, where American standards of high culture usually originated.

Nashville had long claimed a place as an intellectual and cultural center in the South. After the Civil War, the city's image as the Athens of the South may have been temporarily disguised by the smoke and noise of the railroads, factories, and shops of the New South. But in the midst of its most prosperous years, Nashville's socially prominent women and their husbands sponsored a number of new cultural enterprises that became a mark of their class. The Nashville Art Association, formed in 1883, included many of the city's leading citizens. In the founding of this association and in other cultural enterprises, Jabez P. Dake, Gates P. Thruston, and, later, Herman Justi played key roles, but much of the support and a large portion of the membership came from the women. By 1886 the association had launched the Nashville School of Fine Arts, and it took the lead in planning the Fine Arts Exhibit at the 1897 Tennessee Centennial Exposition, which was housed in a replica of the Parthenon. Following the exposition, Nashville's elite women, led by Mrs. James C. Bradford, made the cultivation of art a prominent objective in social circles.[93]

Literary clubs also became important in identifying socially prominent women with cultural uplift programs. Nashville's Query Club, founded in 1885, originally was limited to unmarried women and was designed to offer a more serious alternative to the frivolity of debutante activities. The Review Club, founded in 1893, provided the same kind of outlet for married women. These two, among several similar groups,were the most prestigious and lasting. A like-minded organization, the Magazine Circle, was founded by Jewish women who, like their husbands, built a parallel society outside the gentile world.[94]

Nashville's performing arts found a regal home with the opening of the Vendome Theater on Church Street in 1887. The stockholders and box holders at the Vendome were among "the cream of society" who filled the theater on opening nights in "resplendent dress."[95] The Philharmonic Society was formed in 1892 to sponsor a series of recitals at the Vendome. In 1901 it brought a traveling opera company to the city. The turnout was so large that the performances had to be held at the Union Gospel Tabernacle (later known as Ryman Auditorium). The seats, a reporter for the *American* noted, were packed with music lovers, "the society element, . . . the business and leisure classes, and with representatives of the culture and refinement" of Nashville. "It was a truly metropolitan audience in the matter of elaborate dress," the reporter proudly observed, with men in tuxedos and "full evening suits" and women in "exquisite toilettes." Four years later, the Vendome played host to New York City's Metropolitan Opera Company, in what was claimed to be "the most colossal musical event in the annals of Nashville's musical life!"[96]

Atlanta's raw youth did nothing to discourage the self-conscious sponsorship of high culture and its symbols. The Atlanta Art Association, incorporated in 1905, had begun two years earlier in a Peachtree home where "art lovers" gathered. Led by Mrs. Isaac S. Boyd, the association began an art school, imported a director from the Chicago Art Institute, and staged a series of exhibits, essay contests on art, and public lectures.[97]

More spectacular than the stimulus to art appreciation were the efforts to cultivate musical taste among the Atlanta elite. Several small musical societies, beginning in the 1870s, promoted musical education and appreciation. DeGive's Opera House, the Grand Theater, opened in 1893, providing an ornate home for visiting musical and theatrical performances. The opening night gala filled the theater's boxes with Atlanta's select families, making it "an event in the social world of Atlanta as well as in the world of art," a reporter observed.[98] But it was the Atlanta Music Festival Association, founded in 1908, that established patronage of serious music and grand opera as a badge of upper-class culture in Atlanta. This was a movement that involved Atlanta's leading businessmen and their wives in herculean efforts to raise the necessary funds.[99] In May 1909, the inaugural performance in Atlanta's new auditorium (the product of an energetic chamber of commerce campaign) was to feature the famous Italian tenor, Enrico Caruso, backed by the Dresden Philharmonic Orchestra. Caruso had to cancel his Atlanta engagement, a disaster that might have crushed the city's nascent musical spirit, but five other opera singers were hastily recruited as substitutes. Atlantans, joined by visitors brought in by special trains from miles away, poured into the auditorium for five solid nights of opera.[100]

The remarkable success of this event encouraged its supporters to stage a festival of grand opera the following year. They not only rescheduled Caruso's visit but also invited no less than New York's Metropolitan Opera Company. Two hundred of Atlanta's leading citizens together pledged the $40,000 that the company had insisted upon as a guarantee. Caruso sang to a record audience of over seven thousand on one night, and the series of five performances drew over 27,000 people, more than the company had ever attracted in New York. The opera festival of 1910 offered a splendid showcase for the Atlanta elite, and the newspaper obliged with detailed descriptions of the ladies' gowns and jewels and a generous amount of name-dropping. It was the beginning of a continuing series of spring visits to Atlanta by the Metropolitan Opera.[101] This annual musical extravaganza was also the most poignant testimony to the eagerness of Atlanta's New South plutocrats to embrace the symbols of upper-class culture imported from the Northeast and Europe. That these eminently practical, business-minded men, whose backgrounds had offered little preparation for the appreciation of Italian opera, would invest so much in bringing it to Atlanta was also testimony to the influence of Atlanta women, who had managed to link high society to high culture.[102]

The Club Woman

During the progressive era, the society woman, preoccupied with her daughter's debut and her whist parties, yielded to the upper-class clubwoman, a civic-minded, serious breed given to a moderate brand of feminism. This upper-class version of the "new woman" often distanced herself from the self-indulgent society matron and called for a larger role for her sex in civic affairs. In response to the remarkable query by a *Nashville Banner* reporter who asked, "does society justify itself?," several Nashville women dismissed the "purely frivolous" activities of the former society woman and pointed to the new "club woman spirit" that had brought women to the serious business of philanthropy, cultural uplift, and "civic housekeeping."[103] It was this new sense of purpose that propelled women like Nashville's Ann Dallas Dudley, daughter of a wealthy industrialist and wife of a prominent hardware dealer and insurance entrepreneur, to take a leading role in the woman's suffrage movement.[104] In both Atlanta and Nashville, the most significant women's civic clubs sprang out of the New South industrial expositions of 1895 and 1897, events that helped crystalize a new understanding of the roles women would assume in the progressive era.

The Atlanta Woman's Club, founded in 1896 by a number of prominent women, was a product of the new consciousness aroused by the women's department of the 1895 exposition. The club's purpose was "good fellowship, better understanding and social contact," and, as the club's historian explained, "also to prove to the world that women could mean even more in their homes by participating in the civic philanthropic and legislative interests of their growing city and in standing side by side with the development of the times they could aid in the progress of a great city."[105] The Woman's Club met at first in the home of Rebecca Lowe on Peachtree and then, as it grew, moved to rented quarters before it found a permanent home in another mansion on Peachtree. The Woman's Club was devoted largely to charity and to educational programs for the disadvantaged in Atlanta. The same combination of civic concern and feminism inspired the formation of the City Federation of Women's Clubs in 1899, part of a state organization established concurrently. Not all members of the Woman's Club belonged to the social upper crust, but its rolls included the wives and daughters of many eminent Atlanta families.[106]

Nashville women had a longer tradition of organized philanthropy than their counterparts in Atlanta. Prominent women had taken a leading role in supporting the Protestant Orphan Asylum, founded in 1845. Its managers, all wives of leading business and professional men, represented the chief Protestant churches in the city. The asylum's fund-raising activities were treated as notable social events.[107] The Woman's Mission Home and the Nashville Relief Society, both founded in the 1870s, were other charitable organizations that occupied the wives and daughters of Nashville's business elite.[108]

It was the Tennessee Centennial Exposition of 1897 that sparked the formation of what became Nashville's first and most important women's civic club. The Centennial Woman's Board was dominated by Nashville women, all wives of wealthy businessmen, many of whom served on the exposition's board of directors. The exposition gave these women an unprecedented opportunity to examine the new social roles that would open to them in the coming era of reform. Though most of the women's exhibits and events at the exposition were devoted to the conservative celebration of the southern woman as belle, housekeeper, and mother, the exposition also offered glimpses of the "new woman" who would supersede those earlier incarnations. Chicago social reformer Jane Addams, a leading advocate of women as "civic housekeepers," was one of the guest speakers invited by the woman's department, as were suffragists Susan B. Anthony and Anna Shaw. Feminism, woman's suffrage, and a commitment to social reform, all of which might have been dismissed as the afflictions of crazed northern women, became less suspect—and even respectable—among upper-class Nashville women in the years following the exposition.[109]

Inspired by its accomplishments at the exposition, the Centennial Woman's Board tried to carry on its new organization and begin "some public work worthy of itself," but after 1900 the board stopped meeting, and it seemed that Nashville women were again limited to whist parties and cotillions.[110] In 1905, during a burst of enthusiasm for civic reform that centered on the "Greater Nashville" annexation movement, the Centennial Club, as it came to be called, was reborn.[111] Former members who had died since 1897 were replaced by relatives, usually daughters, of the deceased. But the Centennial Club rapidly grew beyond this group to mobilize more than five hundred Nashville women. The purpose of the club was "the cultivation of higher ideals of civic life and beauty, the promotion of city, town, and neighborhood improvement, . . . the promotion of hygiene and sanitary conditions." "We shall never have clean cities until the women undertake the job," the women resolved.[112]

With all the energy they had once devoted to cotillions and whist parties, the Centennial Club women threw themselves into an amazing variety of civic reforms. They organized neighborhood women's clubs in every quarter of town and launched an earnest campaign to clean up the streets, alleys, and private yards of the city, to plant spring bulbs, vines, and trees, and to press city officials to enforce laws regulating animals and public spitting.

Much of the initial emphasis on "city housekeeping" and public health reform was diluted in 1908, when the club reorganized into departments focusing on art, home, literature, music, and public interest. Despite its genuine commitment to social reform, membership in the Centennial Club was also a badge of upper-class status in Nashville. This was demonstrated at the club's first social function, an elegant reception at the Maxwell House attended by four hundred women. Described as "one of the most distinguished gatherings of women ever assembled in Nashville," the reception required "the most elegant clothes and sparkling jewels." The room was filled with floral bouquets sent by "prominent well-wishers," and Pellettieri's Italian Band entertained the guests. At the head of the receiving line, Sally "Polk Place" Fall, in a black velvet gown and diamond jewelry, acted as official hostess.[113]

Whatever their ultimate purposes, the wives of the South's ascendant business leaders played key roles in transforming an ambitious array of nouveau riche families into a coherent and enduring network of families and institutions. The metropolitan upper class that took form in Atlanta and Nashville in the late nineteenth century was identifiable not simply by the wealth of its members but also by the emblems of a common culture and style of life. In its homes and suburban neighborhoods, in its exclusive clubs and social rituals, and in its cultural institutions, the New South's urban upper class assumed its modern form for the first time.

9 Gentility and Mirth

I come from the old town of Charleston
Whose shrimp turn their nose up at cod;
Where Pinckneys recognize Ravenels,
But nobody worries with God.
—*Charleston's reply to Boston*

You have to live on Government Street, attend
Christ Church and go to the Striker's Ball.
—*anonymous observer of Mobile, ca. 1900*

While the "dollar aristocracy" of Atlanta won status in the social world largely through its success in the marketplace, Charleston's old families tried to preserve an aristocracy based on genealogy, gracious manners, cultural refinement, and reverence for a shared past in the face of a present and future that were less kind. As the nouveaux riches of Atlanta and Nashville formed more exclusive associations in anxious imitation of established upper-class institutions in older cities, Charleston's mild economic revival, beginning around 1900, actually opened the city more than ever to outsiders and to the rise of new money and leadership from within. Signs of this broadening of Charleston social life, as we have seen, were heralded in the business community by new associations and booster campaigns. Likewise, the boundaries that defined Charleston's social elite showed signs of expansion. But this change seemed to take place gently, with no outright challenge to the symbols of social status, which remained in the hands of the old families. The only overt and vehement expression of impatience with the old aristocracy during this period took political form with the rise in 1911 of Mayor John Patrick Grace, an Irish boss who, borrowing a page from Ben Tillman's book, built a popular following by verbally assaulting the Charleston aristocracy.

If the upper class of Atlanta and Charleston provide the sharpest contrasts among the four cities examined here, Mobile, like Nashville, fell somewhere between these extremes. Though the town was founded just thirty-two years after Charleston, Mobile's history as an American city extended back only to the 1810s. More of Mobile's leading men of wealth had been transient outsiders, not infrequently northerners. As a result, this city had not established the thick undergrowth of genealogy and deeply rooted customs of the type that persisted in Charleston. In Mobile, upper-class society after the Civil War took form around a cluster of exclusive Mardi Gras societies, whose celebrations underscored Mobile's image as a pleasure-loving resort. Whereas Charleston's elite answered the New South with serene gentility, Mobile's found solace in a mirthful response to the era's earnest pursuit of progress.

Manigault's Wine

Gabriel Edward Manigault was a perfect Charleston gentleman. The son of Charles Manigault, a prosperous merchant who had become a rice planter on the Cooper River, Gabriel had been educated at the College of Charleston and then sent to the Medical College of South Carolina and to Europe to study medicine. Though educated as a physician, young Manigault never practiced medicine, serving instead as curator of the Museum of Natural History at the College of Charleston and president of the Carolina Art Association while he maintained his father's rice plantation on the side. The museum and the Art Association, his obituary said, were "monuments to his cultivated taste and knowledge." He was, in addition, "devoted to the memory of his Huguenot forefathers" and contributed several useful documents to the history of the Huguenot Society.[1]

During the early 1890s, when he was around sixty years old, Manigault wrote a lengthy memoir and included in it a detailed account of a cache of wine his father had recovered in the aftermath of Charleston's bombardment and invasion at the end of the Civil War. It was the "choicest Madeira wine," the remnant of a two-thousand-bottle lot his father had purchased in 1838 or earlier. A favorite in Charleston since colonial times, when it was smuggled into the city in defiance of British restrictions, Madeira remained, Manigault explained, "a favorite wine here and no man of wealth and position in the city . . . felt that his social position was an assured one unless his garret was well stocked with that particular wine."[2] Until the federal bombardment began, the bulk of the wine was being stored in the old colonial powder magazine, within range of the Yankee cannons, and it had to be moved to safer quarters. At that time, Manigault's father discovered that much of the wine had been pilfered, apparently by Confederate soldiers who broke into the magazine. About six hundred bottles remained and were safely removed to the Manigault plantation outside the city. After the Confederates evacuated and Charleston was occupied by federal troops, Manigault's father managed to talk a Union officer into escorting him to the farm to recover the wine. At the plantation they were met by a crowd of raucous freed slaves, many of whom had themselves discovered the delights of Madeira and were not inclined to give up their supply to Manigault. The Union officer interceded on Manigault's behalf, helped load the remaining wine into the wagon, and was rewarded with a few bottles for his effort. The wine, about three hundred bottles remaining now, was brought back to the Manigault home, where it continued to supply the finishing touch to meals and parties, even as the family fortune declined.

After his father's death in 1874, Gabriel had to raise money by selling most of the remaining wine, now down to about twelve dozen bottles. This prized old wine brought a handsome price of five dollars or more per bottle—enough, Manigault mused, to cover his father's original investment in the two-thousand-bottle lot. In the years that followed, the Manigault Madeira was served at famous restaurants in London and New York—Delmonico's among them— and was said to have been offered at the White House during Chester Arthur's presidency.

The story of the Manigault wine provides a small but revealing glimpse of a people who aimed at preserving their way of life at a time when the economic support for that life was deteriorating. They held on to what they could and sold off or gave away some portions of their legacy in order to save the rest, or at least to postpone its eventual loss. This was the mentality that kept so many of the old Charleston "aristocracy" going in their decaying mansions South of Broad, paint peeling and brick and stonework crumbling. "Too poor to paint, too proud to whitewash," was the local adage. Old silver, antique furniture, and other family heirlooms were quietly taken to King Street pawn shops. Eventually, iron grillwork, fireplace mantels, and other fine architectural features of many of the old homes were sold in pieces to antique dealers from the North. It was this trend that had alarmed the Charlestonians who in 1920 formed the Society for the Preservation of Old Dwellings (later the Charleston Preservation Society) with the aim of protecting and restoring the remaining historic homes and artifacts of their ancient city.[3]

Charleston, to this day, is one of the most perfectly preserved cities in America, a reliquary of eighteenth- and nineteenth-century domestic architecture. In recent years it has been celebrated by promoters of tourism for its historic charm (touted as "America's Best Kept Secret"), but Charleston's stubborn indifference to the modern world was a source of great frustration to the city's more progressive advocates in the late nineteenth century. A visitor from Kansas City in 1898, enthralled by the antiquity and quaintness of the old city, recommended that "Charleston ought to be walled in and roofed over and kept for a museum!" But alas, he lamented, "the New South will soon push the Old South into the sea."[4] He—and also many of the ambitious men of the Charleston revival that began in the late 1890s—underestimated the powerful undertow of tradition in Charleston, which worked to postpone and compromise change even if it could not stop it. Charleston's old families guarded their homes and landmarks as symbols of their legacy. The Charleston Art Commission was founded in 1910 to preserve the "city historic" and to challenge the national fad of "city beautiful" in urban planning. But the Art Commission and

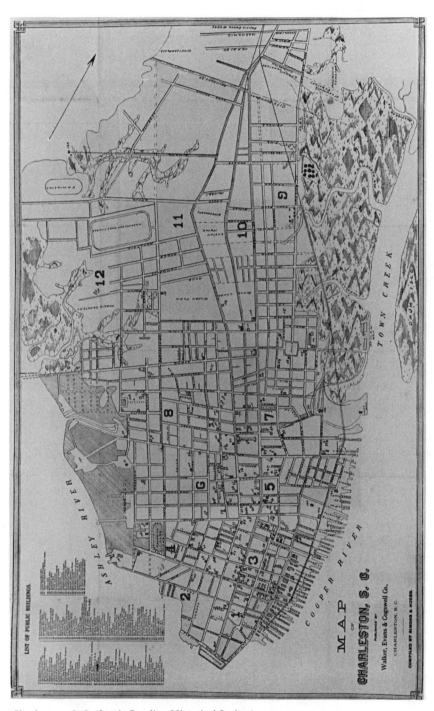

Charleston, 1898. (South Carolina Historical Society)

Charleston's Broad Street, ca. 1910. (Library of Congress)

the Society for the Preservation of Old Dwellings that followed it in 1920 only institutionalized attitudes that were already well developed in Charleston, and they did so precisely as that conservative mentality was challenged by the rise of the New South tide in their city.[5]

In other cities, as in Atlanta and Nashville, wealthy families rapidly abandoned their central city mansions in favor of spacious suburban neighborhoods that were joined to downtown offices and stores by streetcar lines. The central business district expanded into the old residential neighborhoods, then built upward with the advent of the skyscraper in the 1890s. Suburbs and skyscrapers became proud monuments to the modern urban life fashioned by the new business class.

Charleston, in contrast, "slammed its front door in Progress's face and resisted the modern with fiery determination," as one witness put it.[6] Before World War I only one skyscraper, Robert Goodwyn Rhett's People's Building, built in 1911, violated the city's skyline of two- and three-story structures punctuated by tall church steeples. The preindustrial urban form, in which the

Panorama of Charleston, from the belfry of St. Michael's. (Library of Congress)

wealthy upper class, mixed with some domestic servants, was concentrated in the city center while most of the poor and outcast lived on the edge of the city, persisted in Charleston. This arrangement was partly a consequence of slow growth, the isolation of the peninsula, and the swampy environs of the Charleston Neck, which confined the city. But Charleston's urban form and social geography were also the products of cultural choice among people who defied modernity in many facets of their lives.[7]

The residential patterns that concentrated the elite in the city center persisted into the late nineteenth century, in part due to the elite's disinterest in abandoning its old homes and neighborhoods in favor of commuting suburbs. Horse-drawn streetcars, introduced after the war, were met with defiant "prej-

Charleston's King Street, ca. 1891. (Library of Congress)

udice" among "conservative people . . . [who] preferred to go on foot, even under considerable discomfort from heat or rain, rather than patronize public conveyances that were so democratic." Aside from its social objections to mingling, Charleston had less need for streetcars because it remained largely a "pedestrian city." The physical pattern of residence, work, and shopping allowed most upper-class residents to commute by foot from homes between Broad and the Battery or a few blocks north of Broad. This preindustrial urban pattern remained virtually unchanged until the end of the century.[8]

Eventually, according to one account, even the "very best people . . . had become reconciled to the cosmopolitan horse car," only to strongly oppose the advent of the trolley in the 1890s.[9] Charleston was the last American city of any size to adopt the trolley in 1897, when it became a symbol of the "new

Charleston's Battery, ca. 1906. (Library of Congress)

Charleston" that the younger, more progressive business class promoted so earnestly. The trolley system was developed by an outside capitalist, J. S. Lawrence, who overcame opposition from the horse-car owners and built an independent line. Outsiders had great fun with Charleston's belated entry into the electric age. An amused reporter with *Frank Leslie's Weekly* attributed the "sudden revulsion in favor of modern ways and improvements" to "the younger business men . . . who pushed for it. . . . They protested that, on going home to dinner at 3 o'clock they sometimes had to wait full ten [*sic*] minutes." Local reactions to the trolley became a mark of distinction between the "ease and grace of bearing of the older men of a certain set" and the city's younger set, "said to be provincial and a little . . . wanting in drawing room graces." It would not be long, the reporter predicted, before the old city would become crowded with suburbanites, people would dine at seven instead of three, and some would even stop drinking cistern or artesian well water. The "picturesque survivals of the old regime seem out of key with the hustling trolley, and must give way."[10]

But Charleston's resistance to the modern had deep roots. The conservative frame of mind that prevented radical change in the physical layout and social geography of Charleston for so long was revealed in the aftermath of several catastrophic events that might have invited new departures. The massive destruction in the fire of December 1861, which burned one-eighth of the city's buildings, presented one unwelcome invitation to physical reconstruction of the city. The wartime shelling, a devastating cyclone in 1885, the great earth-quake of 1886, which leveled or seriously damaged about 7,000 homes and buildings on nearly every street of the city, and a disastrous hurricane in 1893 all afforded ample opportunity to redesign and modernize parts of the old city. But, with few exceptions, the city each time was restored brick by brick to its original condition. The narrow, crooked streets on the lower part of the peninsula, remnants of colonial days, were rebuilt without improvement. Following the 1886 earthquake, homes and other buildings were restored with no great innovations other than reinforcement with earthquake bolts.

Charleston's museumlike quality was as much a product of modern construction as it was of slow growth and preservation. The architectural styles of new structures rarely contradicted the antebellum and eighteenth-century neoclassical and Georgian fashions. Even the arrivistes conformed to the old Charleston style. Andrew Simonds, a wealthy banker originally from upstate South Carolina, built a magnificent mansion on South Battery in 1895. "Villa Margherita," as his wife named it later, had a massive portico supported by four elegant Corinthian columns that evoked antebellum Charleston architecture. In 1896 visiting artist Willis John Abbot remarked that this tendency stood in contrast to New Orleans and other southern cities, where rich families built their homes in imitation of the current fashion in New York or Chicago. "If a man having acquired wealth in Charleston determines to build himself a new house, he builds it in all architectural essentials exactly like the house which the oldest banker then in the city built some one hundred and fifty years ago. This loyalty of the Charleston of to-day to the Charleston of yesterday gives to the city a certain homogeneousness, a kind of self-content not to be found in any other historic American city."[11]

More typically, Charleston's wealthy families occupied the old mansions of antebellum and colonial vintage that predominated in the city's most desirable neighborhoods. Occasionally they "Victorianized" the facades with modern embellishments, as Frederick W. Wagener did to his home on Broad Street, but most restored the architecture and conformed to the Charleston mode. There were, however, exceptions who built ostentatious new homes in high Victorian style, with all the bravado of their counterparts in Atlanta and Nashville. George Walton Williams's massive Italianate-style brick mansion on Meeting Street was the talk of Charleston when it was built, beginning in 1876, at the extraordinary cost of $200,000. Williams outdid himself in 1892 with an ornate Queen Anne frame house at the foot of Meeting Street, built as a wedding gift for his daughter. The same spirit of conspicuous display inspired Francis S. Rodgers's monstrous mansion on Wentworth Street—a spectacular, four-story, brick extravaganza in ornate Second Empire style. Rodgers, a wealthy German who had made a fortune in cotton and phosphates, felt shunned by Charleston society and, according to local legend, promised to build the tallest home in the city so that he could look down his nose at the South of Broad crowd.[12]

The same self-content was evident when hard choices had to be made between economic development and the physical preservation of the old city. The inability of Charleston to modernize its waterfront facilities and bring its railroads into direct connection with the wharves was symptomatic of its bullheaded resistance to even the most compelling compromises with the modern world. Decisions about renovating the waterfront, too, were influenced by the preservation ethos. To enlarge and modernize the old waterfront, as Charleston's progressive mayor, Robert Goodwyn Rhett, admitted, "would cut into the most historic and interesting section of the city." Eventually the coming of the navy yard and the deepening of the harbor channel allowed the development, beginning in 1912, of modern waterfront facilities far up on the Charleston Neck, where they were linked to the city by a beltline railroad. The city—that museum of old architecture and old values—was saved once more from the enemy.[13]

Those who challenged the preservation ethos found they could provoke strong reaction to even the most innocuous efforts at improvement. When Mayor William A. Courtenay allowed the fifty-year-old trees in Washington Square to be cut down as part of his general plan to clean up the city and beautify the area around City Hall, he drew vehement protests. Courtenay responded defensively, assuring the citizenry he was not so progressive as to violate the Charleston code: "[W]ith some of our fellow-citizens we are thought to be ruthless iconoclasts, disrespectful of the past, and fixed in resolve to destroy what is *old,* desirous only for that which is *new.* This is a serious misapprehension. . . . [W]e value the past and the things of the past."[14] He had to defend his efforts to refurbish and clean the "dismal and unsightly prospect" surrounding the old City Hall at Meeting and Broad as an effort to preserve this prized Charleston landmark. "We do not envy our sister cities their costly hall, and only aim to imitate them in neatness and genteel business appointment for ours. So we preserve our old building, not because of the bare physical fact of its age and fourscore of years, but for its historic associations, its strength and its exterior beauty."[15]

Historic landmarks, it seemed, were to be defended with all the resoluteness displayed by the Confederates in the late war. When the new post office was built in 1896, Charlestonians rallied to protect its predecessor, the Old Exchange Building, built in 1772 at the east end of Broad. The *News and Courier* urged the federal government, rather than destroy the building, to "bestow it upon the city as a relic of Colonial and Revolutionary times."[16]

Throughout the late nineteenth century, when cities like Atlanta and

Nashville were busy building new central business districts, throwing up skyscrapers, expanding rapidly into their suburban frontiers, and busily keeping pace with everything that was modern and smart in Gilded Age America, Charleston's old families worked no less fervently at commemorating the past. Old landmarks and historic sites were carefully identified with monuments and plaques. Portraits, busts, and other "memorials to our illustrious dead" from the city's antebellum history were displayed in the city council's restored chambers.[17] Clubs, churches, and other associations commemorated their anniversaries with written histories and eulogized their departed brethren with tributes to the past they had shared. The *Charleston City Yearbook,* introduced by Mayor William A. Courtenay in 1880 with the intention of demonstrating the city's more progressive spirit, became increasingly devoted to lengthy historical appendixes with elaborate maps, manuscript facsimiles, and reprinted documents that dwelled mostly on Charleston's glory years in the colonial era.

Only a part of this historical consciousness was focused on the Lost Cause (which, paradoxically, became the obsession of New South cities, Atlanta and Nashville in particular). Great ceremony, for example, occasioned the return of General Beauregard's sword to the city he had "kept virgin to the last."[18] Most of the interest in local history concentrated on Charleston's halcyon days before the war. Harriott Horry Rutledge Ravenel's informative history of the city, published in 1906, filled more than five hundred pages with detailed descriptions of the colonial and antebellum achievements of Charleston's leading figures. Then, following a brief section on the war, the narrative stopped abruptly at the fall of Confederate Charleston in 1865 and ended with a resigned nod to the New South: "With the fall of the city and of the Confederacy went out the old life of Charleston. . . . If the new is, or shall be, better, purer, braver, or higher, it will be well."[19]

Whatever the stated object of this historical consciousness, its covert purpose was to instill a reverence for the past and for the city's social elite, whose status was rooted in the city of their ancestors. "Let us, then, fellow-citizens, draw from the store-house of our own recollections," pleaded one Charlestonian in 1889,

> let us relate to our children the deeds of their fathers; let us point out to them the houses where they lived and the streets through which they passed; let us show them the temples where they worshipped, and the pews in which they sat; let us familiarize them with the names of the good, the brave and the true, and as incentives to imitation let us unfold to them the beauties of their character; let us teach them to respect old age and revere its memory; to be proud of humble ancestry, if virtuous and honorable. . . . In a word, let us teach them to be true to themselves, true to each other, true to God; let us teach them to preserve their own records, to erect their own memorials, to write their own history.[20]

Charleston's cult of the past was at times strengthened by a self-conscious reaction to the New South ethos of Atlanta editor Henry Grady and others who saw the Civil War and Reconstruction as a break with all that was traditional, an opportunity to start anew and forsake the mistakes of their elders, and who saw history as the harbinger of progress. *Charleston News and Courier* editor Francis W. Dawson, though an enthusiastic advocate of economic development and a critic of his city's "old fogy" ways, reflected the Charlestonian irritation with Grady and the "new class who are rising into prominence in parts of the 'New South.'" Responding to Grady's atonement for the Old South, Dawson scolded: "it is not for the sons to apologize for their fathers, whose homes and honors they inherit."[21]

"New South," Dawson's successor, John C. Hemphill, added in 1890, was just a "cant phrase" that referred to "that part of the South which has adopted Northern ideas." Quoting Charleston author William Gilmore Simms, Hemphill warned that "after the conquest of arms came the conquest of ideas." But "the Old South, the true South, is too strong to be finally overcome."[22] The *News and Courier,* otherwise one of the most progressive forces in old Charleston, at one point dismissed the "'New South' cult" as the stuff of "sentimental young men, just out of college, who had not taken part in the war and knew nothing of the feelings of those who had. . . . [,] pimply youths, with a flow of curdled sophomoric volubility, [who] announced themselves as 'successors of Henry Grady.'" "There is no 'New South' in the sense of a departure from and a protest against an old South," the editor insisted. "The New South is a phantom. Its prophets are fakirs and fanatics."[23]

For the old families who were descending into a life of genteel poverty, the decaying mansions, the pawned silverware and furniture, and the threadbare gowns and tuxedos worn at their society balls all became proud badges of a declassé aristocracy who refused to answer the siren call of the New South. Those who did respond were often regarded with disdain. "I keep away from business men," William Heyward wrote from Charleston to a planter friend, "as I have found that a man is estimated by the quantity of money he has."[24] Another Charlestonian complained in 1878 that the New South materialistic spirit was corrupting the youth of Charleston, who were compelled by what he considered greed to work instead of study. "You can send the Boys to School but you can't make them study or learn—all say 'What's the use of Latin and Greek or Mathematics—let me go into 'business'—Business of course meaning the Making of Money—Smartness meaning the Making of it in some extra *cunning* way which no one can discover. You would be shocked to know the number of sons of your old acquaintances here, who have 'stopped school' at 13 or 14 years old to go 'into Business' as they call it." Charleston would need a "Noah Deluge again before we can be purified morally and physically."[25]

The Charleston upper class managed to survive by basing its status not on money and the things money could buy, but on genealogy, gracious manners, and loyalty to a certain code of life. It was a conservative, backward-looking philosophy dedicated to the preservation of standards that seemed to be discredited by the rising business class almost everywhere else in America. Charleston, one observer noted in 1917, "is unqualifiedly the aristocratic capital of the United States; the last stronghold of a unified American upper class; the last remaining American city in which Madeira and port and *noblesse oblige* are fully and widely understood." That upper class, he explained, was unified by a "vast cousinship," a thick growth of old and well-understood family trees that allowed nearly every prominent family to claim a near or distant tie of blood or marriage to the others in its social circle.[26]

The filial piety of the old "aristocracy" became, if anything, more pronounced after the Civil War, as the economic basis of the old social hierarchy disintegrated. Charlestonians, according to local proverb, are part Chinese because they live on rice and worship their ancestors.[27] "A man's position in Charleston society," one insider noted, "is not determined by what he wears, or the business he follows, or by his money or his looks. Brains do count for a great deal, but the chief factor in settling the question is his name, who his father and mother were and his grandfather and grandmother back perhaps for three or four generations."[28]

A letter from Henry Middleton to "cousin Alicia" illustrates how the "vast cousinship" came into play in even the most casual interaction and between those who obviously had not stayed in close touch. Middleton was writing to inquire if Cousin Alicia would sell some old family property on South Battery, a home where his relative, Russell Middleton, had lived, and he thought he had better drop a few names and relations. "Do you remember me? I was Ralph Izard Middleton's youngest son, and last saw you as a small boy. I married Betty Beirne Miles, daughter of William Porcher Miles, former mayor of Charleston, who moved to New Orleans. Cousin Langdon Cheves gave me your address."[29] The same point is illustrated in another way in the roster of the Huguenot Society, which listed the original families from which each member was descended. Thomas W. Bacot, for example, could claim lineage from the Bacot, Huger, DeSaussure, Peronneau, and Motte families.[30]

A cult of genealogy and an antiquarian interest in local history gained firm hold among the scions of Charleston's old families in the postwar era. The South Carolina Historical Society, organized originally in 1855 and moribund since the Civil War, was revived in 1876 to promote the collection and study of local and state history. The Huguenot Society of South Carolina was formed in 1885 to "perpetuate the memory, . . . promote the principles and virtues of the Huguenots," and to "discover, collect and preserve" materials relating to their genealogy and history. Open to all direct descendants of Huguenot immigrants before 1787 and to students of Huguenot history, the society was intended, as its president, Daniel Ravenel, explained, to instill "pride of birth and ancestry" as "an incentive to higher life."[31] With or without formal organizations, genealogy apparently became a hobby for many old-guard Charlestonians. In the fall of 1870, Wilmot G. DeSaussure, then a forty-eight-year-old attorney and insurance company officer, wrote to a fellow Charlestonian in exile: "During the comparative leisure of the summer, I have busied myself in some 'Old Mortality' work. . . . In other words, I have been drawing some genealogical trees and thus endeavoring to rescue from the ruins and from oblivion, some of those things which unless now saved, will go forever."[32]

For some, like DeSaussure, who later served as president of the Huguenot Society, pride in their lineage was nearly all they had left. When DeSaussure died in 1894, according to probate records, he "left no estate of any value, his personality not exceeding the value of twenty dollars."[33] For the Trenholms, who were rising in wealth, an elaborate family tree proved a distant connection to the prominent Legaré family and thereby conferred a crucial element of ascriptive status.[34] It was this inverted ambition, which sometimes sought to find status through one's ancestors instead of one's own accomplishments, that an anonymous wag sought to parody in the following verses:

> I thank thee, Lord, on bended knee
> I'm half Porcher and half Huger
> With holy pride my heart doth beat,
> I live at nineteen Lamboll Street.
>
> With grateful tears my eyes are wet,
> My uncle's J. Le Boutillier Rhett.
> For other blessings thank thee too—
> My grandpa was a Petigru;
> Simons and Waring and Legaré
> Appear upon my family tree
>
> Dear Lord, look down on those in pity,
> Who dwell outside the Holy City
> And when I die, save me from hell—
> I go to church at St. Mich-a-el[35]

Family lineage and gracious manners were also the criteria for entrance into the constellation of exclusive social clubs that set apart the upper class. Among the most prestigious old associations were those organized in the eighteenth century as mutual aid societies for particular colonial-era immigrant groups. The South Carolina Society was founded by French Huguenots in 1736, and by the late nineteenth century its club rooms on Meeting Street had become one of the preeminent social resorts in the city. The Hibernian Society, an Irish Protestant and Catholic fraternal order, built a grand hall on Meeting Street in 1840, in which the society hosted a number of Charleston's most prominent social affairs. The St. Andrew's Society and the St. George's Society, both organized in the eighteenth century, revived after the war and continued to serve as social centers for descendants of Scots and English settlers. Other prestigious social organizations included the South Carolina Jockey Club, sponsor of the annual Race Week and Race Ball, at the end of January, which in antebellum times had been the highlight of the social season.[36] The races at Washington Race Track on the Neck died out in the 1880s, due in part, one critic noted, to "the contrast between modern race track gambling and the gambling of ante-bellum gentlemen." The Jockey Club, nevertheless, continued until then as an important remnant of the old order.[37]

Another antebellum holdover was the Charleston Club, made up of prominent lawyers, professionals, cotton factors, and businessmen of varied types. Founded in 1852, it established a fine clubhouse on Meeting Street and enjoyed a reputation as a prestigious male refuge during the 1850s. It dissolved in the face of hard times in 1866, and many members moved over into the Carolina Club at Broad and State streets. This latter group lasted until 1881, when its membership was invited to join a reconstituted Charleston Club with quarters in a home at the foot of Meeting Street. Theodore D. Jervey, a prominent cotton factor, was "induced to serve {as president of the club] merely to give the prestige of his name and position to the newly formed Club."[38] It soon attracted 119 members, among them many of the leading figures in Charleston business, professional, and political life. Early in 1887 the club relocated at its old home at 45 Meeting Street.

Notorious for its "Charleston Club Punch," a "famous brew" of green tea, brandy, and rum, the club enjoyed its "halcyon days" in the early 1890s, as the city's economy was sinking into a demoralizing depression. "The Club-rooms were crowded of an evening," the official history recalled, "and the bottle was passed freely. There was a life, a camaraderie, which make those days unforgettable in retrospect. There was much gaiety and occasionally with it a little disorder. Play ran high at times, exaggerated, perhaps, by rumor. . . . [N]ever was social life more delightful." By 1896 the harsh reality of the depression intruded on this gaiety; membership in the club declined steadily, despite efforts to suspend the entrance fee and solicit new members. Joseph W. Barnwell, a prominent lawyer and political figure, took over as president, but the decline continued, and the Charleston Club slowly faded.[39]

The most elegant and socially important of Charleston's clubs was the St. Cecilia Society. It was "the centre about which the social circle is drawn," the standard by which other invitation lists were drawn up within the closed sphere of the old elite.[40] A rare account in the *News and Courier* described it as "the great bulwark of society in this quaint old city, which defends it from the onslaughts and inroads of the nouveaux riches and the self-asserting."[41] The St. Cecilia Society, one member admitted, "does Charleston more harm than she can possibly have done good" because it excluded from social acceptance worthy men "who are wealthy enough if that were all."[42]

Beginning in 1737 and formally organized in 1762 as an amateur concert society, St. Cecilia became famous by the 1820s for the highly formal balls and dinner parties it sponsored in January and February each year. It was a male club that invited wives and unmarried children to its dances. After the Civil War the sixteen-member board of managers continued to be "representative of each large family connection in the city." Some of the family names engraved on invitations in the late nineteenth century—DeSaussure, Huger, Miles, Rhett, Barker, Ravenel, Frost, Jervey, Lesesne, Prioleau, Pringle, Drayton, Middleton, Fraser, Legaré, Porcher, Pinckney, Stony, Barnwell—were much the same as those listed as board members a century earlier.[43] Membership was not, strictly speaking, inherited, but "if a man's father or grandfather, or any of his immediate kindred, have belonged before him, there is little doubt that he will be chosen," Harriott Horry Rutledge Ravenel explained. "Nevertheless," she went on, "blackballs (two suffice to exclude) have fallen, when the applicant was a notoriously unworthy scion of his family tree."[44] Someone from outside the old family network, "of a family recently brought into notice," would meet careful "inquiry, perhaps hesitation, and a good backing will be desirable." Good reason would have to be given for his approval: "This might be because of his talent and character," explained St. Cecilia manager and president Joseph Barnwell, "or possibly because he had already found entrance into most of the houses of Charleston whose families were invited to the balls."[45] Nonmembers might be invited to the balls on the recommendation of a member, but these invitations also required careful scrutiny. "A stranger must almost belong to the *livre d'or*" to receive an invitation, one appreciative visitor gushed.[46]

Exclusion from the St. Cecilia invitation list could unsettle the normally serene social climate of the City by the Sea. In 1870 the managers refused to invite any northerners "who had not, during our late war, . . . expressed decided sympathy with us." This condition excluded the daughter and son of a Mr. McCall who, in addition to having "resided at the North during the War," had carried on a feud with the Middleton family of Charleston, the result of an incident obliquely referred to as "a scandalous affair which occurred in Philadelphia some years ago . . . in which a near connection of theirs was involved."[47] According to ancient tradition, no actors and no divorced persons (divorce remained illegal in South Carolina) could be invited. The entire list had to be approved by the managers, who, Barnwell explained, "naturally selected those who would in their opinion have the manners and traditions of the majority of the Society."[48]

The membership and invitation lists, and indeed all news of the St. Cecilia Society, were kept "strictly private and did not come before the public in any way." So discrete were the managers that invitations to the St. Cecilia balls were never sent by mail but always by a "responsible Negro" messenger. Edmund, the servant who delivered the invitations for nearly half a century, was, by one account, a veritable "social register for Charleston 'quality.'"[49] But no coverage of the balls was allowed in the press, so instead of serving to publicize family status, an invitation to a St. Cecilia ball was a secret shared only by the in-group.

The St. Cecilia balls themselves remained a unique ritual of archaic social customs and manners. They were held in Hibernian Hall, where the rooms were lighted with candelabra (electricity was finally allowed sometime before 1917) and the tables were set with the society's own silverware, china, and linen. Ladies always attended with chaperones and had their dance programs carefully filled in advance. A promenade followed each dance. No smoking was allowed, and no cotillion or "German" dances were permitted. Outsiders who were invited sometimes found the strict decorum of the affair unbearable. "Why, this is not a social dance, but a rite," complained one New York lady who was invited to her first (and last, one assumes) St. Cecilia ball.[50]

The St. Cecilia Society was the finest expression of Charleston's declining aristocracy in its proud, resilient effort to preserve a code of chivalry and gracious manners against what it saw as a vulgar world that awarded status to "mere wealth." No one put this better than Theodore G. Barker in his 1893 eulogy to a departed St. Cecilia member, C. Richardson Miles:

> Though conservative in his views and disposed to stand upon the ancient ways he yet well knew that times change and men change with them, bending his best efforts towards preserving the essentials of good breeding and polite intercourse in the midst of change. He recognized and acted upon the principle that membership in this Society is not founded upon birth except as a probable presumption of gentlemenlike [*sic*] conduct, nor because of wealth, nor success in life, nor talent; but the possession of the manners, instincts, and feelings of a gentlemen [*sic*], and however difficult the task of applying this standard he held it a duty which the officers and members of this society must perform.[51]

The St. Cecilia Society, perhaps more than any other institution of the Charleston old guard, served as the gatekeeper to an exclusive realm that socially ambitious families could not ignore. Granted, "wealth, power, genius, ambition, in a great horde are not knocking at the doors of that ultra-refined

Carolina city for admission," a Philadelphia society woman noted condescendingly in 1905. Still, "the person who is not on the list of the St. Cecilia is not 'in society' in Charleston."[52] We are allowed a rare glimpse of the process of social selection in Charleston through DuBose Heyward's discerning novel, *Mamba's Daughters*. It begins before World War I, at a time when Charleston was beginning to open, if a bit reluctantly, to new talent and wealth, both from within and from outside the community. Written by an insider of the Charleston aristocracy, Heyward's novel observes the rites of passage into Charleston society with a detail that could not easily have been documented except in fiction.

Heyward's novel centers on Mrs. George P. Atkinson, the wife of a solid, wealthy cotton-seed-oil manufacturer from the Midwest, who desperately wants to be accepted by the "High Goddesses" of the "social Olympus" in Charleston, their adopted home. The Atkinsons have refurbished a grand old mansion on Legaré Street, South of Broad, which has become the scene of a steady round of luncheons, bridge parties, and afternoon teas staged for the wives of the native aristocracy. But, Heyward explains, "she had made the fatal mistake in the beginning of assuming that wealth was, as a matter of course, an effective weapon, not realizing that, with a number of the old families in straitened circumstances, simple living had become the criterion for good taste, and the ostentation had become, by contrast, mere vulgarity." Despite, or perhaps because of, her social ambition, Mrs. Atkinson has remained "outside of the fatal line, [where] one was always more or less a stranger stopping temporarily in the city," sometimes for generations.

It is George Atkinson, though he "did not have a single social aspiration upon him," who realizes that the way to the St. Cecilia ball is not over a lady's teacup, but over a glass of cold whiskey with the men down at the South Carolina Yacht Club after work. "Nice chaps, these," Atkinson muses over cocktails, "not too greatly concerned with the opinions and behavior of the insignificant residue of the globe lying to the north of Magnolia Cemetery and the south of the Battery. . . . Younger ones . . . secure in breeding . . . older men who knew a horse, a mint julep, and a gentleman when they met one—men who, like himself, were quite content to leave teas, the Sunday concerts, the Poetry Society, and the Episcopal ritual to their wives." Atkinson's more worldly familiarity with the realm of business and big government makes him useful to the Chamber of Commerce crowd, who send him with a committee to Washington, where he testifies on Charleston's behalf before the Interstate Commerce Commission on a matter involving freight rates. Atkinson's "clean, hard drive of his brain against a problem always brought concrete results," and he is able to "talk to the Yankees in their own language." Returning home on the train, with the sought-after concessions in their pockets, and with "genial comradeship in the air," one of the old boys in the "hereditary aristocracy" broaches the subject of the upcoming St. Cecilia ball and casually asks Atkinson if he and his wife would like to attend. Atkinson coyly accepts the invitation. His wife, who was already in New York City shopping for ball gowns for herself and her niece, returns to Charleston in time to receive an envelope from an "elderly negro who had the bearing of an ambassador to the Court of St. James's. She lifted the missive from the tray and, with shaking fingers, removed it from its two envelopes—'The Managers of the St. Cecilia Society request the pleasure. . . .' "[53]

Though the Atkinson family is finally accepted, at least partly, into Charleston society, Heyward is more interested in showing how their quintessential bourgeois values are submerged within the dominant culture of Charleston's "hereditary aristocracy." More accurately, Atkinson's northern background and business savvy are utilized in exchange for social recognition within a society with quite different measures of success. The St. Cecilia Society, according to some reports, did eventually open slightly to newcomers, people like the fictional Atkinsons and others who had come to the city along with the navy yard and its accompanying economic revival. "In late years," one visiting reporter noted in 1901, "the city has added new wings, . . . it is hustling more for business, but driving out ancient customs is slow, tedious work."[54]

It was an indication both of the gradual opening of the St. Cecilia Society and of its still-exclusive reputation when the *Charleston American*, John Patrick Grace's maverick newspaper, took the unprecedented step in January 1917 of publishing the names of those attending a society ball. This caused "a great stir in the city," which prompted an editorial, said to be written by Grace, mayor of Charleston since 1911 and outspoken enemy of the "aristocracy." Dismissing the "unwritten law" that proscribed press coverage of this "ancient society," Grace expressed mock concern that secrecy had spawned "in the vulgar mind weird stories of what went on behind the scenes." The article proved only that the St. Cecilia was "about the same as every other social collection of human beings." Grace went on to describe the society, once "the extreme limit of social exclusiveness," as "an anachronism on American soil, a matter of pure heredity. . . . Now, however, since the society, in keeping with the spirit of the age, has relaxed its rules to admit from year to year (if, indeed, only a few now and then) members whose blood is far from indigo," the press ought to feel free to "invade the quondam sanctity of its functions which are now being OPENED to all classes."[55]

Grace was exaggerating the new openness of the St. Cecilia Society as a way of criticizing the "un-American" character of this "threadbare aristocracy" and its persistent exclusiveness, which had limited Charleston for generations. Ludwig Lewisohn, who grew up in Charleston's German-Jewish community during the 1890s and 1900s, remembered it as "a city of very rigid social groups," in which a Protestant family with education or wealth "would tend to withdraw from its original friends and social life and try, by any means, to be reckoned among the small, conservative group which consisted of the members and descendants of the old Southern slave-holding aristocracy."[56]

When Henry James visited Charleston in 1905, he found in it the last remnants of the Old South, an emasculated survivor able to resist, but hardly to counter, the vulgar materialism of American culture. But James also discovered during his brief but insightful visit elements of the "new Charleston," particularly in the presence of a "kindly country club installed in a fine old semi-sinister mansion." It was, he thought, a symptom of "rude northern contagion." But "the South that is cultivating country-clubs," in contrast to the fire-eating secessionists who were proven wrong by the war, was "presumably . . . quite in the right."[57] Housed in a century-old plantation mansion north of the city limits, the Charleston Country Club was founded in 1901 next door to the exposition grounds. Both were harbingers of the new spirit among the eager crowd of young businessmen and professionals who were determined to bring Charleston into the New South. Indeed, golf and the amenities of the country club were thought to be essential to the tourist trade Charlestonians hoped to lure southward, to say nothing of the needs of the young local business elite that was, in so many ways, striving toward the modern. Though its membership, and particularly its chief officers, including president Edward Simons, an insurance agent, and vice president Francis Q. O'Neill, president of Hibernia Trust and Savings Bank, represented this new element, there were enough Rhetts, Porchers, Ravenels, and other venerable Charleston family names on the club's roster to lend an aura of status to this fashionable club.[58]

The economic blight that had afflicted Charleston in the past guaranteed what James called its "social shrinkage," but this also protected the city's old upper class from the full force of the changes that had reshaped most other American cities. But with the economic revival that began in the late 1890s, Charleston at last experienced the invasion of the New South. The younger, "pushing" business leaders included more of the ethnic element from within Charleston and some outsiders, but, with few exceptions, it was the traditional elite who defined the symbols of upper-class status in this city. The business leaders of the new Charleston also included in their central group the scions of old Charleston families. As the twentieth century progressed, this venerable city, surrounded by new military and industrial development, remained a museum of "quaint" artifacts and customs, products of people whose values, though they no longer ruled the South, yet retained symbolic power within Charleston.

George S. Leatherbury, a Mobile lumber dealer, and his family, ca. 1905. (Erik Overbey/ Mobile Public Library Collection, University of South Alabama Photographic Archives)

Mobile's Upper Class

The upper-class culture that took form in Mobile after the Civil War was, compared with that of Charleston, less pretentious, less exclusive, and less tied to antebellum traditions. Mobile society reflected the absence of a strong antebellum upper class whose families persisted in the new order. It also gave evidence of the more relaxed traditions of a city that responded to the challenges and reversals of the New South with drink and festivity, rejecting both the aristocratic pose of Charleston and the earnest busyness of Atlanta.

A visitor to Mobile at the end of the summer "dull season" in 1883 savored the "gentle flavor of mild decay" that economic decline had brought to the old city. "The rush of commercial prosperity is not favorable to the cultivation and growth of social life, of taste in literature and the arts, of genuine elegance and refinement of thought, feeling and manners." Recalling the Mobile of thirty years earlier, when "Cotton was king . . . and Mobile was clad in royal robes of fleecy staple," he remembered a "tinge of brassiness inseparable from *les nouvelle richesses* and crude social conditions." Comparing the city to Athens, Rome, and Venice, none of which "became exemplars of aesthetic taste and social culture until they had declined," this observer claimed that Mobile's "gentle declivity" had brought a "gain in the 'minor morals' of life."[59]

If economic decline was a prerequisite to social refinement, Mobile society had every advantage in the postwar years. Although there was little in the way of *nouvelle richesses* to upset the social hierarchy, neither was there much formal continuity of elite institutions from the antebellum order. The principle institutions and many of the customs that defined upper-class society in Mobile came into being after the war.

The Manassas Club, which had been founded in the fall of 1861 to honor the Confederate victory, became one of the city's more prestigious social clubs among Mobile's leading business and professional men.[60] Housed in the former building of the Mobile Bank, which had failed in the 1880s, the club seemed a fitting symbol of both the city's economic decline, which the 1883 visitor had so extolled, and the social grace that he supposed to have supplanted prosperity. The club's annual ball in January 1880 was "one of the most brilliant entertainments ever witnessed in Mobile," described as "*the* affair of the season." The club's rooms were "elegantly fitted up for the occasion," with the parlor and billiard rooms reserved for dancing, the floors covered in white cloth, and the ceilings "festooned with cedar" boughs. The supper was "one of the most elegant ones ever served in Mobile."[61] The annual ball of the Manassas Club became an important part of Mobile's pre-Lenten social whirl. During Mardi Gras parades, the Queen of Mardi Gras sat enthroned upon the club's balcony overlooking St. Joseph Street, where she was toasted by her king riding atop his float on the street below.[62]

Though less elegant than the Manassas Club in its decor, the Athelstan Club eventually became the more prominent of Mobile's male social clubs. It began in 1870 as a Masonic lodge and was converted to an independent men's social club beginning in January 1873. The reasons for the conversion were unstated and remain unclear. A likely cause, as the club's history hints, was the strict prohibition against alcoholic beverages in Masonic lodges, a rule that cramped the well-formed customs of Mobile's men.[63] As the Athelstan rule book explained, "the sublime Truths of Masonry can be . . . combined with the most innocent social pleasures."[64]

The club wasted no time in enjoying its new liberation from the confines of Masonic temperance. The next month, at a lavish opening-night gala held at club quarters on South Royal Street, the members were feted with French cuisine and wines. An air of jolly male camaraderie infused the club from the outset. The otherwise rather staid rule book allowed in 1873 for serenading recently married members "on the first convenient evening after the wedding;

provided however, that the members so honored shall not be allowed an expense of more than one glass of wine to each member of the serenade party."[65]

The club remained affiliated with the Masonic lodge, and Athelstan members were, at first, required to be lodge members. It later shared quarters with the lodge in a new building on the corner of St. Joseph and Dauphin. Athelstan began with seventy-four members and was limited to one hundred, but the hard times that followed the panic of 1873 forced the club to open its ranks. Several members had been suspended, perhaps for nonpayment of dues, and it was found necessary to widen the net and recruit beyond the Masonic lodge. By November 1875, the club cut itself off from the Masonic order altogether to become "a General Men's Club opened to membership by application." Applicants were required to be endorsed by two members and to have their names posted for ten days at the Club Room. The membership as a whole voted on applicants, and a rule that allowed one blackball to reject a member was modified early in 1876 to require three blackballs. The club's roster lengthened as the depression lifted, and Athelstan gained favor among downtown business and professional men, who found in it a delightful combination of social prestige and informal masculine fellowship, a refuge of relaxed sociability free of the decorum of late Victorian life.

The Manassas Club, at the same time, faded in social importance, and many old members shifted their allegiance to the Athelstan Club. In its declining years, the Manassas became a predominantly Catholic organization, and by 1914 it had passed from the Mobile social scene, leaving Athelstan as the unrivaled elite men's club.[66] The Athelstan Club's activities revolved around a very active and profitable bar, card tables where gambling was permitted, and the dining room. Bachelor members rented quarters there, and others could nap in sleeping rooms. The decor was rustic and decidedly unstuffy, according to recollections, yet it was an exclusive social group. Members were screened carefully through the use of endorsements and blackballing. Nonmembers and women were not allowed within the club rooms.

Its Masonic roots gave Athelstan a strong Protestant cast, and the club was considered closed to Jews, at least in its early years. Nevertheless, the membership list from the outset included several of Mobile's prominent Catholic business and professional leaders.[67] The social lives of Mobile's Jews were, as a rule, "completely separate" from gentiles. Even so prominent a family as the Proskauers, descendants of a Civil War officer who enjoyed close connections with the Christian community, remained excluded from Athelstan. Wealthy Jewish men founded separate clubs, Fidelia being the most notable. The Athelstan roster, however, eventually included Jewish family names such as Lienkauf and Forcheimer.[68]

By 1901 the Athelstan Club built new club rooms in a fine-looking two-story building on St. Francis facing Bienville Square.[69] It was, by this time, unrivaled as the premier social club of Mobile, and membership in it was virtually required as an entrée to Mobile's social elite.

Mardi Gras

The Athelstan Club took on added social importance as the visible hub for a number of secret "mystic societies." These organizations grew out of the annual revelry at New Year's and Mardi Gras, the latter of which became the central event in Mobile society in the years following the Civil War.

The Mardi Gras carnival was in many ways symbolic of Mobile's response to the New South. It embodied many of the contradictions that riddled the city in these years. As the climax to the social season that flourished from New Year's to Lent, Mardi Gras drew on Mobile's famous traditions as a pleasure-loving resort for planters in the days of high cotton before the war. Mardi Gras also romanticized the city's French and Spanish heritage and permitted a brief expression of light-hearted hedonism, with a Catholic flavor that was a notable relief to the earnest Protestant ethos of hard work and temperance that fueled the New South.

The early origins of Mobile's Mardi Gras celebration became a point of great local pride, particularly when compared with the more famous festivities of New Orleans, though local historians had to stretch a bit to establish the city's claim as "Mother of Mystics." The tradition actually grew out of one raucous New Year's celebration in 1830. A group of Mobile men led by a northern-born cotton broker named Michael Kraft, returning home full of an evening's entertainment, raided a hardware store and staged a rowdy procession through the town at dawn, armed with rakes, hoes, and noisy cowbells, on their way to make their New Year's Day calls. In mockery of their own juvenile behavior, they proclaimed themselves the Cowbellion de Rakian Society and continued the tradition with parades and masked balls each New Year. Membership in this secret club and invitation to its balls became a coveted mark of social status among the wealthy cotton brokers and other merchants and professionals of antebellum Mobile.[70]

Younger men, excluded from the select membership of the Cowbellions, formed their own society, the Strikers Independent Society, or S.I.S., in 1842. They took their name and much of their membership from the cotton trade, in which a striker was a clerk or apprentice who marked the bales for shipping. "Taste and lavish expenditure rapidly brought [the Strikers] close alongside the older club" in the richness of their New Year's parades and balls.[71] Like their elders, the Strikers maintained "absolutely inviolable secrecy as to their membership and intents" and invitations to the annual Strikers Ball, given each New Year's Day, were sent anonymously (like those of Charleston's St. Cecilia) to a select list of guests chosen by the membership. "Far less," Thomas C. DeLeon wrote, "could anyone of all that eager society, which waited in suspense for their annual invitation, sent out a week in advance, dream to what particular friend the grace of the valued card with the rampant goat upon the barrel [the Strikers emblem] was due." The Strikers Ball, he went on, "became the most noted and longed for social event of each year." Though membership in the Strikers was officially secret, and masks worn at the parade and the ball disguised identities, it was well known that both clubs, as DeLeon explained, "were composed of the cream of Mobile citizenry."[72]

Other clubs sprang up in imitation of these two before the war, but most were suspended during the crisis and never regrouped after 1861. Only the Cowbellions, Strikers, and a third group, the T.D.S. (variously known as the Terpsichore Dancing Society, Tea Drinkers Society, and The Determined Set), founded in 1844, managed to survive the war and resume their New Year's festivities. In 1866 the Cowbellions paraded through the occupied city on New Year's Eve for the first time since 1860.[73]

New Year's Day remained a significant holiday for Mobile's social elite, and the tradition of making calls on that day survived as an important ritual among wealthy families. "Receptions in the afternoon held equal place with the ball of the Strikers that closely followed them," according to one account. The women, who stayed home to receive, wore formal gowns. The men, dressed in Prince Albert coats, went by carriage or on foot, usually in groups of four, along Government Street and the other fashionable residential streets in the "calling area." Those who received in their homes on New Year's Day were reported faithfully in the newspaper, but those who made the calls had to know beforehand if they would be welcome in the homes of Mobile's prominent families. "In virtually every home was plenty of egg-nog, wine and kindred joy restorers, and all who came were invited to imbibe freely." Men were frequently induced to drink shots of liquor in the back room. The receptions began in midafternoon and continued well into the evening. By the end of the day, more than one caller was showing the effects. The code of upper-class Mobile, on this and on most social occasions, encouraged liberal drinking but demanded controlled inebriation. Palmer Pillans recalled one of his University of Alabama classmates who put away twenty-four drinks one New Year's Day, "but he was not a bit lit."[74]

It was after the war that Mardi Gras became the focus of Mobile's social life, giving rise to new mystic societies that cropped up to celebrate the occasion and to help define the social hierarchy of postwar Mobile. The annual revelry of this day was born of a defeated people in an oppressed city. Mobilians evoked a tradition from a distant colonial past as a way of escaping the burdens of their more recent, less glorious history. The celebration was initially inspired by a defiant mockery of the grim reality of defeat and military occupation. In 1866 a local character named Joe Cain showed up on Mobile's streets on Shrove Tuesday dressed outlandishly as "Chief Slackabamirimico." The "chief" declared an end to the gloom of war and led a contingent of "braves" down Dauphin Street, parading past astonished Union soldiers.[75] By 1870 Joe Cain and a group of men had formed a makeshift band, the Lost Cause Minstrels, which paraded through the streets in wagons "hideously masked and making music (?) more hideous still."[76] Veterans and younger men who had missed the war saw in Mardi Gras an opportunity to form new male groups as alternatives to their old militia companies, which were now outlawed. The new organizations were also blissfully devoid of any serious purpose.[77] The older New Year's societies, whose members were now elderly, gave way to these younger men. The Cowbellions, Strikers, and T.D.S. staged their last parade in 1881 and then faded from public view; only the Strikers continued their annual New Year's ball.[78]

The new postwar mystic societies, like their predecessors, were born in youthful exuberance and informality but soon evolved into prestigious and exclusive indicators of social status in Mobile. The Order of Myths (O.O.M.) put on its first Mardi Gras pageant in 1867 and thereby laid claim to being the first and oldest Mardi Gras society. It adopted the tradition of parading from the old New Year's societies and made Mardi Gras a public spectacle that attracted visitors from miles around. Following the public parade each year, the O.O.M. held a masked ball, with access by invitation only.

The Infant Mystics (I.M.) were said to have evolved from a young men's baseball team that answered Chief Slackabamirimico's call for celebration and followed behind the Lost Cause Minstrels on their Mardi Gras parade. In 1870 this group formally organized, initially as the H.S.S., a reference to their motto, Hoc Signo Sustineat, and to their nickname, the Heavy Samplers' Society, a testament to their "prowess at the punch bowl."[79] The H.S.S. staged parades on Mardi Gras night, with floats depicting such irreverent themes as a "Burlesque of Secret Societies in Mobile." Following the parade in 1873, the club held a fancy ball at the Battle House Hotel, a lavish affair that placed the members $1,500 in debt and ended their organization abruptly.

The Infant Mystics formed the same year the H.S.S. collapsed, absorbing many of its members and the entire debt of the defunct society. This group organized on a more formal basis now, requiring that members be "young men residents of this city, not under eighteen years of age and of good social standing." Steep initiation fees, monthly dues of three dollars, and fines for missing meetings and events screened out younger and less wealthy men. The

I.M. carried on a tradition of elaborate parades with more than a dozen floats attended by bands and banners, all producing an extravagant show for the public. Its masked ball, held incongruously at Temperance Hall, followed each Mardi Gras parade. The affair was strictly by invitation only, and the guest list was carefully controlled by the society's executive committee.[80]

As the older mystic societies became identified with Mobile's wealthy and prominent families, newer and less exclusive organizations cropped up in imitation. Some, like the Knights of Revelry (K.O.R.), founded in 1874, followed the tradition of the Strikers in being started by younger men who were excluded by the older societies. Another, the Comic Cowboys, founded in 1884, was begun by Dave Levi and was composed of Jewish men who were, with rare exceptions, shut out of the other mystic societies.[81] The Mystic Krewe of Mirth organized in 1887, and the Continental Mystic Crewe, another Jewish society, followed in 1891. There were several efforts to launch female mystic societies, but the Mobile Mardi Gras remained a social event dominated by male organizations, and therefore males continued to play the leading roles in controlling Mobile's social hierarchy.

Except for occasional generalizations about the elite status of the mystic societies, usually in reference to O.O.M. or I.M., the mist that obscures the internal workings of these organizations is impossible to penetrate. The secrecy of membership was inviolable, and even if the masks did not actually disguise identity, nevertheless the local newspaper, when it reported on the parades and balls, betrayed nothing. This practice stood in sharp contrast to the intricate and gossipy detail of the society columns that were standard fare in the Atlanta and Nashville newspapers. In those settings, news of upper-class doings provided a kind of public scoreboard on which socially ambitious families were eager to appear. In Mobile (and in Charleston, where a similar code of discretion was observed at St. Cecilia balls), the secrecy that enveloped elite social events revealed the more assured and relaxed assumption that those who deserved to know were already on the inside.[82]

As it evolved, Mobile's Mardi Gras revealed the ambivalence with which this city faced its economic decline within the New South. At all levels of local society, carnival gave an opportunity for an exaggerated expression of the traditions of drinking and frivolity that had long been a part of the city's legacy as a cotton port. It allowed at least a temporary inversion of the Victorian code of hard work, temperance, prudery, and rationality. All work ceased during Mardi Gras week, save in the saloons and other shops that catered to the tourist trade. "The Emperor had ordered closure and respite of money business, banking, and most especially of note-paying, upon the Day of Joy," an edict from Felix, the Emperor of Mardi Gras, proclaimed in 1877. "This is a hard world," the Felix of a few years later explained, "with but little to take the mind off the cares and anxieties of life. Life is entirely too practical with them unless, from time to time, their minds can be diverted from their daily occupations."[83] "All work and no play is not good policy," a *Mobile Register* editorial advised.[84] A later publication denounced "those who have been so deeply contaminated by sordid commercialism that work is permitted to interfere with the Mardi Gras spirit," and the article then praised a string of other local delights: "barbecues, dancing, the shooting of the wild doves, deep sea and fresh water fishing, year round golf and surf bathing."[85]

The Emperor of Joy sanctioned a general suspension of the rules of deportment that ordinarily confined social behavior. The masks, worn both by those in the mystic societies and by many of the spectators, permitted a degree of anonymity that encouraged misbehavior. During carnival, crowds thronged the sidewalks around Bienville Square and along Royal Street downtown. The saloons were brimming with people who consumed "floods of bibulants" during Mardi Gras and the days leading up to it.[86] Women entered the normally forbidden saloons and drank alongside the men. Though newspaper accounts generally tried to emphasize the "good order" and "good humor" of the crowds, there were enough protests about heavy drinking, including stories of people passing out on the sidewalks, to suggest that widespread drunkenness was a common part of the celebration.

The pre-Lenten tradition of overindulgence before a period of self-denial extended to sexual appetites as well (a true Mobilian, according to a local proverb, is "conceived at midnight on Mardi Gras under an Azalea"). An air of sexual liberty pervaded carnival, outraging whatever existed in the way of Protestant Victorian prudery in Mobile. Masked women wore daringly "short clothes" that exposed their legs and "gave a quite rakish look to the scene," according to one titillating *Register* report. Some of the women were prostitutes, who took full advantage of the libertine ambience to ply their trade. The costumes and masks allowed other forms of deviance to emerge from the Victorian closet at carnival. There were several accounts of men dressed as women. One described the astonishment of police who arrested a drunk and disorderly "female masker" and threw her in jail. "Then everybody was surprised to discover that the female was a male."[87]

The looseness of social restrictions also permitted the races to mix more freely during carnival. Though blacks were accorded no formal public role in Mobile's Mardi Gras festivities, they turned out in force to witness the white folks in their foolish revelry, and they joined as spectators in the celebration.[88] Again, costumes could conceal racial identity, a fact critics pointed out in efforts to outlaw masks and gloves. But whether or not skin color was actually disguised, the carnival atmosphere, heavy drinking, and the crush of the crowds encouraged a certain relaxation of the social etiquette that normally maintained a strict social distance between the races. "It was something of a colored folks' holiday yesterday," an amused *Register* editorial commented on the heavily black Mardi Gras crowd in 1888. Other accounts of fighting and pickpocketing suggest that carnival offered occasions for racial friction and for crime as well as for merriment.[89]

It was a measure of the power of postwar business values in the South that even the ribald spirit of the Mother of Mystics succumbed to the more sober and calculating goals of the New South's business mentality. Carnival quickly evolved from ad hoc celebrations, staged separately by rival mystic societies, into a public event that became linked to the business class's goals of advancing the city's commercial prospects.

The first step in this process was the formation in 1871 of the Carnival Association, a coalition of "some of the most prominent business men . . . [who] saw the advantage" of an "open and public concern." The association was designed to bridge the mystic societies, coordinate their activities, and turn the Day of Joy into a week, or more, of profit. The funds required to stage the Mardi Gras extravaganza were now drawn from the general business community rather than from the pockets of the mystic society members alone.[90] It was the Carnival Association that crowned Daniel E. Huger as Felix I, Emperor of Joy in 1872, beginning a tradition that gave the celebration dramatic focus. The emperor, his chosen empress (usually the unmarried daughter of a prominent family), and their court also provided a public display of the social elite outside their secret societies.[91]

A telling comment on Mobile's adjustment to the New South was the marriage between the mysticism and foolishness of the city's ritual of misrule and the business-minded, "practical" goals of bringing tourism and commercial advertisement to the city. The Carnival Association enlisted the aid of the railroads, which offered cheap excursion rates to country visitors. It also raised money, first among its members and then from the business community at large in a general subscription drive, and the money was used to advertise carnival throughout Mobile's trading area and beyond. During the fund-raising drive, carnival was promoted as a profitable community enterprise, "at once the busiest, merriest and best paying" week of the year. Aside from the short-term rewards, the "practical benefits" of Mardi Gras were thought to include a wonderful advertisement of a "largely unknown city" throughout the nation. "All that tends to show the taste, enterprise and energy of a city," an 1881 editorial instructed, "sets it further on in the march of progress." The annual Mardi Gras celebrations, another editorial boasted, apparently in all seriousness, "have added greatly to the reputation our city had already gained for taste and culture." Those who planned them "are public benefactors, for they add to the refinement of the community, and instill a thirst for informa-

Mobile's Mardi Gras court, 1907. (Erik Overbey/Mobile Public Library Collection, University of South Alabama Photographic Archives)

tion." "The country tributary to Mobile poured its people into the city," an 1880 editorial gloated after the annual carnival. "Our merchants who so liberally contributed to the enjoyments of the occasion, reaped golden fruits."[92]

The original commercial justification for the expansion of Mardi Gras into a public affair was that it offered an "inducement" for country merchants and farmers "to come to town in the early spring and make their purchases of goods." But business methods changed, and traveling jobbers—often from rival cities—began to visit the country merchants and slowly brought an end to the annual spring buying trips. Carnival increasingly became an occasion for hotel, restaurant, and retail businesses to make money off the visiting tourists. As in other areas of its economy, Mobile was reduced to taking the spillover from New Orleans, whose carnival drew a surplus of visitors from far and wide. Frequent attempts at making Mobile the main show were accompanied by the inevitable reminders that New Orleans was only copying the example of Mobile, but the Mother of Mystics remained a sideshow to the Crescent City's carnival. "This is an age of competition we live in, and we must use every endeavor, not only to gain new trade, but to hold on to what we have got." It

Mobile's Mardi Gras parade, ca. 1898. (University of South Alabama Photographic
Archives)

was this specter of competition, particularly from New Orleans, that continued
to fuel local interest in Mardi Gras. "A country merchant who is a regular
customer of Mobile desires to take a little recreation, we offer him nothing to
induce him to come here and he naturally goes elsewhere and as naturally buys
his goods there."[93]

The Carnival Association, with eager support from the *Mobile Register,* repeatedly pushed the mystic societies to make Mardi Gras a "public holiday" rather
than an exclusive celebration for local society. Daytime parades had been
added by the K.O.R. beginning in 1874, and the afternoon became a grand
spectacle. In an elaborate opening ceremony in 1883, Emperor Felix arrived by
boat up the bay, through a fleet of decorated tugboats and ships, disembarking
at the foot of Government Street and parading by horseback with his knights to
Bienville Square, where, before the Athelstan Club balcony, he took off his
mask, greeted his queen, and gave an address to his subjects. By the early
1890s, carnival spectators were also being treated to jousting tournaments and
public concerts in Bienville Park. In 1893 the Commercial Club took over the

planning and advertising of the celebration, with an emphasis on the practical benefits.[94]

During the depression of the 1890s, interest in Mardi Gras waned. The I.M. dissolved temporarily, and the *Register* complained of the "great deal of apathy" attending the 1897 affair. In the wake of this rather dull Mardi Gras, a new Carnival Association was formed, made up of "the foremost men of the city." With the economic revival that came to Mobile after the Spanish-American War, Mardi Gras became more than ever a public rather than a private celebration, and it was increasingly justified by business goals. "The street displays have been novel and brilliant . . . but the social features of the celebration were exclusive rather than comprehensive in character," the *Register* remarked in 1898. That year, the public events were stretched out over two days, beginning on Monday, and climaxed by a large fireworks display (a duplicate of the one given the previous year at the Centennial Exposition in Nashville). Two new mystic societies formed that year, adding to the number of parades, and Emperor Felix II reappeared, after several years' absence during the depression. "The aim is to create a popular carnival." The *Register* chided downtown merchants who questioned the practical value of Mardi Gras and, at the same time, ridiculed those dull citizens who were "continually on the run after the almighty dollar and . . . forget there is a time to play as well as to work." The carnival of 1898 was regarded as a new departure and a grand success. The next year, planning began early to raise the much larger sums of money now required. Though freezing weather ruined the 1899 celebration, the concept of a popular carnival remained foremost.[95]

The carnival soon became a three-day event, opening on Sunday with boat races, concerts, and "moving pictures." By 1903 Emperor Felix III began to sound more like George Babbitt than the Monarch of Mirth. He extolled the "gratifying evidences of . . . municipal developments," pointing to the "handsome new buildings," newly paved streets, and the growth of industry. Even as he declared the Day of Joy, he spoke forcefully of the need for further improvements in the harbor channel and for a new railway passenger depot.[96]

As Mobile's enlarged Mardi Gras celebration became linked to the city's struggle for economic revival after 1898, it also came under attack from moralists and reformers who saw the annual debauchery as a community disgrace. To the Reverend J. R. Burgett, Mardi Gras was but one symptom of a general moral laxity in Mobile society. "Pleasure seeking so largely prevails . . . that it seems to have become a business so extensively carried on as to be an actual hindrance often to the successful prosecution of what is legitimate and substantial," he argued in a sermon that was later published in pamphlet form and widely distributed. "There are," he continued, "regularly organized agencies in the form of mystical societies, social clubs, dancing clubs, card clubs, etc., etc., all of which take up so much time and so absorb the attention that they are greatly demoralizing in their influence and tendency." This went on not just for one or two days in the carnival season, he pointed out.

> From November till May, a period during which christian [*sic*] effort through the church ought especially to be made . . . there is an almost continuous round of dissipation, in the way of dancing and pleasure parties which begin at an hour when nature says we should retire for nightly sleep and rest, and which are kept up till the small hours of the night. . . . Those who are so engaged, at least many of them, well know that such dissipation,—and reckless pursuit of questionable pleasure and disregard of *natural* not to say *moral* laws utterly disinclines them for anything that is spiritual and soul-saving.

"Then there is the drink habit," he went on, which invaded every social gathering in Mobile. What bothered the Reverend Burgett was that these customs were deliberately encouraged by the social leaders of Mobile. "There is a large and influential element in our community that seems bent on making Mobile a sort of Paris or Venice where the pleasure seeker may find whatever is gratifying to his feelings, tastes and desires."[97]

In 1902 and 1903 the city council, in the face of growing pressure from Mobile women, the Ministers' Association, and the Chamber of Commerce, first enacted an ordinance that prohibited masking, then compromised with another ordinance that allowed masks for everyone before nine in the evening, and after that time only for members of the mystic societies, Emperor Felix, his escorts, and children. Masks were thought to be the source of much of the immoral behavior because of the anonymity they provided and because they disguised the wearer's sex and race. Those wearing masks were specifically prohibited, by the same ordinance, from wearing gloves. There was further debate, but no action, on amendments to prohibit women from entering saloons and to ban confetti throwing.[98]

The issue was still unresolved in 1907 when renewed pressure forced additional reforms. Baptist minister W. J. E. Cox, in his published sermon, *Some of the Immoral and Damnable Effects of Mardi Gras,* insisted that he was "not against fun," but he nevertheless made a case against carnival in stern language. "I never saw such flagrant indecency publicly exhibited as I saw in Mobile on Mardi Gras day." Referring to "shameless indecencies," "revolting scenes," and "unrestrained license," which apparently required no elaboration for his audience, he went on: "Disreputable women were permitted to parade our streets, clad in indecent garments, advertising their shameless character and dirty lives." One brandished a whip, others were in men's pants cut short above the knee, while others wore short ballet skirts. "Some unmasked men paraded the streets with them, going from bar room to bar room, and there engaged in such orgies as would have caused ancient Rome to blush."[99]

The expressions of moral indignation over the excesses of Mardi Gras were testimony to the earnest efforts of Mobile's business and religious leaders to turn the ancient revelry to the advantage of the business interests of the New South. But they also gave evidence of the persistent tradition of self-indulgence and gaiety that had shaped the city from its beginnings.

The business classes in all four of the cities examined in this study, though in strikingly different ways, had articulated in their social clubs, their churches, their neighborhoods, and their own special customs and manners a clearly defined identity as an exclusive upper class. In Charleston those institutions and customs were handed down almost without challenge from a waning aristocracy of old families, whereas in the other cities, including Mobile, a younger upper-class culture bore the marks of the businessmen who rose to prominence within the New South.

10 | *The New Paternalism*

{The South} must carry these races in peace, for discord means ruin. She must carry them separately, for assimilation means debasement.
—Henry Grady, 1887

They want the New South and the Old Negro.
—Ray Stannard Baker, 1908

Prophets of the New South joined their program of urban growth and economic development to an agenda for social progress. It was a vision that cast business leaders in the role of benefactors to former slaves and poor whites, not just as employers but also as civic stewards who promoted voluntary charities and government programs to aid health and education in their communities. The inspiration for such reforms came from a combination of genuine humanitarian sentiment, often grounded in religious faith, and a calculating grasp of the necessity of upgrading the South's human capital as a prerequisite to economic development. In the end, the New South's commitment to biracial social progress was compromised by the burden of racial prejudice.

Like their counterparts in northern cities, business leaders in the New South came to acknowledge the social disorder of their cities as regrettable byproducts of the very urban-industrial world they had championed. Drunkenness, prostitution, disease, poverty, crime, and political corruption were all understood as symptoms of the moral and physical chaos the lower classes fell into in the modern city.

It was the instinctive reaction of the business class to respond with efforts to bring order to the urban world they inhabited. Beginning in the 1880s, for example, powerful elements within Atlanta and Nashville launched temperance movements to control alcoholic consumption, first by moral suasion, then by government coercion. Beginning as a movement inspired by religious leaders, notably the evangelist Sam Jones, temperance became the center of a symbolic crusade that defined the social values of the business class.[1] It enlisted women and men in a cause that became linked to new efforts at organized charity for the poor, "fallen women," and other destitute casualties of urban disorder. Reformers also led campaigns to cleanse the city of corrupt political "rings" and bring in "good government," which usually meant a government under the control or influence of business leaders, who would run it according to "business principles." Reform, in all its social and political guises, became strongly allied to the city-building effort. A prosperous city was an orderly city, morally wholesome, clean and healthy, efficiently administered, well educated, and free of poverty.

The Negro Question

In their desire for a clean, efficient, and moral urban environment, southern business leaders shared the values and goals advanced by their northern counterparts. But for white southerners the issue of race, usually referred to as the "Negro question," became the salient point in any discussion of social policy. On this issue the confident, often naive, faith of reformers in the capacity for human progress ran aground on racism. For white businessmen the "Negro question" asked, What economic and political roles were blacks to play in the new order of things? What responsibility did whites have in preparing blacks for those roles? How were blacks and whites to coexist peaceably in a biracial work force?

The answers to the "Negro question" were not determined by white business leaders alone, but these men—with their allies in state and local government and in the press and with their wives, who were active in social reform—were instrumental in shaping the white racial policies of the New South's cities. What evolved was a pattern of race relations in which white supremacy was maintained by new measures of segregation enforced by episodic violence, while at the same time blacks were accorded limited public support to improve their health, education, and welfare.

Segregation, historian C. Vann Woodward has argued, did not come out of the traditions of the plantation and the Old South. In its modern form—rigid, systematic, and legalized—Jim Crow was an invention of the New South. The early experiments and applications of this system took place in the region's cities.[2] The urban environment presented a more fluid job market in which the races competed more directly for economic advantage than was normal in rural settings. Cities, especially fast-growing ones, also threw the races together in rapidly shifting neighborhoods where competition for housing presented another level of conflict. Of necessity, the city also forced the races to mingle on sidewalks and in streetcars, train stations, and other public accommodations. It is indicative of the close ties between the new order and Jim Crow that many of the segregation laws passed in the late nineteenth century were designed to regulate race relations in and around the very symbols of New South progress, in particular, railroads, streetcars, and public schools.

It was in the fast-rising cities of the New South, including Nashville and

Atlanta, that the modern forms of competition and segregation between the races appeared earliest. In the older cities of the Deep South, as we will see, traditions of intimacy and paternalism persisted, less disturbed by urban growth and economic change. In Atlanta and Nashville a stream of migratory blacks, drawn by more dynamic local economies, flowed into the city and vied with whites for jobs, housing, and political power. This more competitive mode of race relations produced friction of a type and on a scale rarely known before in the South, and it produced more vicious white reactions as a consequence. In these faster-growing cities, too, blacks and whites more often met as strangers with no personal knowledge of one another, no ties between them. In Atlanta, especially, the new order of race relations was less tempered by the traditions of deference and paternalism that had been nurtured under slavery, particularly between whites and their house servants.

Segregation, as it took full legal form in the 1890s and 1900s, was a system that deliberately deprived blacks of dignity and equality. But segregation measures were often defended by white moderates, who saw physical separation of the races as the only practical means of reducing racial friction. The alternative, in their view, was constant racial violence. Nashville had seen three blacks lynched in front of large crowds in a ritualistic revenge for alleged transgressions of the color line. In April 1892, a mob dragged accused rapist Eph Grizzard from the city jail and threw him over the Cumberland River bridge with a rope around his neck. Angry men then pumped Grizzard's dead body full of bullets and snapped it up and down by the rope while a crowd, estimated at 10,000 men, women, and children, watched the spectacle.[3]

Nor was Atlanta too busy to hate in September 1906, when a mob of whites, furious at reports that blacks were accosting white women, stormed the black business district on Decatur Street to begin one of the South's earliest and bloodiest urban race riots. At one point in the four days of rioting, whites dragged the corpses of two of their black victims to the Henry Grady monument. When they found another black man hiding behind Grady's statue, they beat him to death and laid his body with the others in a ghoulish tribute to this prophet of the New South.[4] Against these eruptions of racial violence, segregation was offered as an expedient reform essential to urban order.

Whatever the particular issue used as justification, white racial policies in the cities of the New South emerged from the ongoing debate over the innate capacities of blacks and their destiny in a modern industrial society. That debate ranged from outright advocacy of black extinction or emigration, based on the premise that the South did not need blacks, to optimistic programs for black uplift through public education and health reform, programs that stemmed from the assumption that blacks were an indispensable resource for the region.[5]

The "Negro question" arose during the Civil War, with the sudden influx of blacks to the cities in the wake of the Union invasion. The flight from slavery set off a steady migration into the cities, where blacks enjoyed greater autonomy and opportunity. The black population in Nashville jumped from under 4,000 in 1860 to nearly 10,000 in 1870, when blacks constituted 38 percent of the community. Atlanta's black population went from less than 2,000 to almost 10,000—46 percent of the total—in the same time span. Runaway slaves, and the freedmen who followed them, clustered in makeshift camps on the edge of town, alarming whites. Convinced that blacks would be a source of continual social disorder in their cities, whites joined the Freedmen's Bureau in urging the "surplus negro population" to go back to the country and work for their former masters.[6]

Many did return to the fields, but the black migration from farm to city continued to feed the growth of most southern urban black communities. As Atlanta and Nashville grew rapidly in the ensuing decades, the black share of the population kept pace until after 1900. By 1910 Nashville's black population had dropped slightly, from its 1890 high of 39 percent to 33 percent of the total; Atlanta's proportion of blacks leveled off, changing only from 46 percent in 1870 to 43 percent in 1890, but then fell to 34 percent by 1910. In both cities, blacks remained an indispensable part of the urban work force, even as their presence confronted white employers and civic leaders with unprecedented difficulties in adjusting from slave to free labor and in controlling a biracial work force.

Convinced that former slaves would never become reliable workers in a free labor market, many whites in Nashville and Atlanta were willing initially to endorse experiments in coercive labor. Convict lease labor was utilized across the South, in combination with vagrancy laws and other legal devices, as a postemancipation means of pushing blacks into forced labor. It was the basis of several fortunes among white businessmen in Nashville and Atlanta, but it never became a significant alternative in the urban labor market.[7]

New South advocates also tried to encourage blacks to migrate out of the cities and to replace them with white immigrants. As late as 1874, a *Nashville Banner* editorial, discussing ways of reducing friction between the races, suggested that the federal government acquire "the most Africanized State of the Cotton-belt, and make it wholly and entirely a negro State," populated by "voluntary colonization of negroes."[8] Yet when blacks tried to organize their own exodus from the South, local editorials reflected the ambivalence of whites who had not yet learned to live *with* free blacks but could not live *without* their labor. For the most part, reactions to black emigration and rumors of emigration took the form of apologies for white injustice, optimistic assessments of black progress in the South, and exposés of northern racial prejudice.[9]

Promoters of the New South at the same time placed great hope in their capacity to draw immigrants from abroad or from the North. They launched state agencies to advertise the opportunities available to newcomers and sent agents overseas or to the North to recruit immigrants. "Wherever reliable white labor can be secured, it will certainly supplant that furnished by the negro," a Nashville editorial confidently predicted a few years after emancipation.[10] "Unless there is a marked improvement in the quality of freedmen's labor," another threatened in 1870, "the necessity for the importation of Chinese or other laborers will be imperative."[11] But despite all efforts to make good this threat, the New South's immigration campaigns proved ineffective. The foreign-born population in the South actually declined between 1880 and 1910. Even the foreign-born share of the South's urban population went from less than 10 percent to below 5 percent (see table 1.1).

Coercion, migration, and replacement by white immigrants were among the several discarded, if not forgotten, alternatives to black labor that were considered in the years following emancipation. Most business leaders and editors of the New South eventually came to accept blacks as an indispensable source of labor and invited them to compete in a free-labor capitalist society. Like native white and immigrant labor in the North, blacks would be encouraged to join the American "race of life," though with more limited prospects of upward mobility. "The negro is here," a Nashville editor wrote in 1877. "He will remain here, acquiring skill and thrift as he goes along with the rest of society." Immigrants coming to the South should be warned, he added, not to compete with the Negro "in its [*sic*] own field."[12]

The blacks' "own field" was thought by most whites to be at the bottom of the social order, providing muscle on the farms and unskilled, low-wage labor in the cities. At the lower levels of the urban work force, blacks dominated the poorest-paid jobs in domestic and personal service and unskilled labor. Black women worked as cooks, nurses, laundresses, and maids with little competition from whites, and black men took a variety of mostly unskilled jobs as servants, porters, and common laborers. On higher rungs of the occupational ladder, a small cadre of black professionals and businessmen served an all-black clientele within the black group economy, where they did not compete with whites.[13] The middle levels of skilled and semi-skilled occupations, however, remained open to potential competition across the color line. This area of conflict was normally controlled by employment practices that segregated the work force, often by restricting certain industry sectors to one race. In Nashville and Atlanta, black factory workers dominated such industries as fertilizer manufacturing, lumber milling, and flour milling. Cotton textile factory workers, on the other hand, were exclusively white and mostly female.

Clerical and sales jobs were also dominated by whites, except those in black-owned businesses.

The vigilance with which whites defended the occupational color line allowed employers little flexibility. An experiment that introduced twenty black women into the all-white work force of Atlanta's Fulton Bag Company in August 1897 produced a violent series of strikes. Other white workers joined the strikers in protesting the hiring of black workers, a dangerous precedent that whites connected with recent wage cutting and layoffs during the depression. They forced mill owners to agree "to remove all negroes in direct contact with white labor," leaving only the black janitors and menial laborers.[14] A year earlier, white machinists at the Atlanta Machine Works protested that "they will not work with negroes and will resist with all their power any effort to place negro workmen in the machine shops with them."[15]

At the same time, white Atlantans and Nashvillians lauded the upward mobility of blacks, so long as it was not at the expense of whites. Because of their several black colleges and their generally strong local economies, both Nashville and Atlanta spawned a moderately prosperous black middle class of clergy, teachers, doctors, undertakers, and businessmen who generally catered to their own race. For whites, this black bourgeoisie served as a useful example in exhorting blacks to abandon collective political agitation and move ahead as individuals—a precept that Booker T. Washington also made the center of his program for black progress. An 1890 article in the *Atlanta Constitution* applauded the "thrifty negroes" of Atlanta who had "lived in the quiet pursuit of business achievements rather than to take an aggressive stand in political matters." They gave "conclusive evidence that the negro, so long as he follows with sober thrift and industry his different pursuits, is at home with his white friends in the south." Most successful blacks were reported to be "old ante bellum slave darkies" who had graduated from the "training school of their slavery" and with nothing but "faithful labor and thrift have laid up . . . snug little fortunes."[16] The same approving tone marked a Vanderbilt professor's report of his visit to several "comfortable and well-kept homes" of Nashville's successful black families. Their "example will inspire others to lift themselves up," he wrote, and "they are not only the best proof of the progress in civilization of the negro race, but they are also the best security of the welfare of the whites in property and in morals."[17]

These reports express the same ideal of the self-made man celebrated by white elites in their own biographies, based on models not unlike the "rags-to-riches" stories held up to northern workers. Tales of personal success, by implication, confirmed the potential of all blacks to advance on the strength of their individual characters and talents. They did so, however, without addressing the obstacles of the color line, a barrier that at once limited the mobility of the black masses and fostered the growth of a segregated black middle class.

In the same vein, the white press in post-Reconstruction Atlanta and Nashville began to openly refute the most pessimistic theories of inherent racial inferiority that were being aired in the late nineteenth century in favor of more open, even optimistic, assessments of black potential. Blacks, in this view, were not doomed to follow the path of the American Indian as a vanishing race overwhelmed by civilization. Nor were blacks any longer considered victims of the biblical "curse of Ham," assigned to perpetual servitude.[18] Their potential capacity was increasingly regarded as an open question. In filtering popular racial doctrines to the public, the local press usually embraced some form of evolutionary theory that portrayed the black race as slowly adapting to the new environment of freedom, with the ultimate outcome left undetermined for the indefinite future.[19] This stance avoided any admission of racial equality but at the same time held out the promise of some measure of advancement for blacks within a competitive society. "Suppose," a Nashville editor put it in 1877, "the negro is a stolid ape or a mere parrot, incapable of advancement. . . . On the other hand, suppose that by some strange madness we should conclude the negro was a very superior form of being, capable of the loftiest development. Between these two an infinite variety of opinions might be held. It is important, very essential to proper progress[,] to hold the right one."[20]

Black Progress, Southern Progress

It was within these more flexible parameters of racial potential that New South advocates formulated what historian George Fredrickson has called the "new paternalism." This doctrine countered the more vicious and pessimistic racial theories of the day with a program of white benevolence and black uplift joined to a vision of regional economic progress. Black progress was an essential prerequisite to southern progress, and the latter was the chief objective. Blacks were to be prepared, with white assistance, for entry into a competitive society, particularly through education and industrial training, but once prepared they were to rise—or fall—to their natural level of talent and ambition without the protection of permanent white guardianship. This was *bourgeois oblige,* to use Fredrickson's term, in which paternalism was to be implemented through public policy, not personal charity. It was a means to capitalist economic development and to a society stratified by class rather than racial caste.[21]

Advocates of this view invoked the paternalism of the old regime by recalling the loyalty of the former slave, an image warmly depicted in the Uncle

Remus tales of Joel Chandler Harris, whose characters invited fondness and amusement rather than fear. The new paternalists exalted the slaves' loyalty during the war and excused their "misbehavior" during Reconstruction as the product of encouragement by unscrupulous carpetbaggers. They also praised blacks' remarkable strides since, as one *Constitution* editorial put it, "in the swaddling clothes of freedom . . . the edict of emancipation stranded the blacks upon a shore bleak, and strange, and barren. . . . Dazzled and dazed by the freedom . . . they flocked to the cities . . . and then, helpless and forlorn, fell an easy prey to disease and wretchedness of their condition."[22] The new paternalism was articulated most clearly by the *Atlanta Constitution*'s Henry Grady and Joel Chandler Harris, and by Atticus G. Haygood, Methodist minister, author, and president of Emory College. In Nashville many of the same ideas were disseminated in print and public addresses, though by less prominent figures.

Nowhere was the racial ideology of the New South expressed more clearly than at the industrial expositions of Atlanta and Nashville. Atlanta's Cotton States and International Exposition in 1895 was the first to stage a Negro exhibit. Though it rapidly became a symbol of white philanthropy under the new paternalism, the idea was initiated by a delegation of Atlanta blacks, who implored Samuel Inman, chair of the exposition committee, to allow them exhibit space. Inman, "who had always taken a deep interest in the Negro," approved the plan, and the committee accepted it, in part because black support proved a shrewd political expedient for obtaining funds from Congress. Black spokesmen, including Booker T. Washington, pleaded with the House Appropriations Committee for an opportunity to exhibit the progress their race had made "under the new order of things." Congress responded with a generous grant of $200,000 and stipulated that the Negro exhibit was to be housed in a separate building, not in the U.S. government building as originally proposed.[23]

The Negro Building, built by black muscle and white capital, was described as "a monument to colored artisanry." It depicted on its pediments a slave mammy with a one-room log cabin and crude church on one side. On the other side was a picture of Frederick Douglass before a "comfortable residence, the stone church and symbols of the race's progress in science, art, and literature, all representative of the new negro in 1895." The Exposition Company, comprising Atlanta's leading businessmen, made a point of publicizing that it had paid for the building, waived the usual fee for renting exhibit space, and aided in the collection of exhibits from across the South. Filled with displays of the freedmen's skilled craftsmanship, inventions, art works, and educational achievements, the Negro Building was ample testament to black achievements and aspirations in the New South. I. Garland Penn, a Virginia schoolteacher and lawyer and chief of the exposition's Negro Department, noted with pride the evidence of his people's progress, which was on exhibit in "the first national panorama of negro progress," and expressed his hope that "the verdict of the dominant race be for the help of the deserving negro."[24] Earlier, Atlanta blacks had protested the small exhibit space granted to blacks, the use of Jim Crow railroad cars to bring black exhibitors and visitors to Atlanta, and the use of black convict labor in building the exhibit. Penn responded with a "long stirring and convincing speech," urging blacks not to spoil "the greatest chance the colored man had ever had to show just what was in him."[25]

It was in this setting that Booker T. Washington issued the famous speech that his adversary, W. E. B. Du Bois, later dubbed the "Atlanta Compromise." Conceding all present claims to political power and to social equality with whites, Washington linked black progress in agricultural and industrial labor to the future of the New South. The *Constitution* applauded the "sensible and progressive negro educator" as "a safe leader." It found the speech "in the very best of taste" and was pleased to report, "there was not a jarring note in it." "It was an address leveled at the whites," the editor observed, "and will go far toward narrowing, if not solving . . . the negro question." At the heart of the problem between the races, this account went on, was the erroneous notion among northerners that blacks should gain "social equality" with whites and challenge the rule of "property and intelligence." "The negro can only be advanced as he deserves to be advanced. . . . If he falls behind, well and good. If he advances, so much the better."[26]

Two years later, when the Tennessee Centennial Exposition was staged in Nashville, the white businessmen who organized it were determined to imitate and improve upon the Atlanta model of racial benevolence in their own Negro exhibit. Whites provided a much larger and more costly exhibit hall and set aside no less than eight special days for blacks, during which admission fees were reduced. The importance of the Negro exhibit, now regarded as "an essential feature" of southern expositions, was that "it determines their industrial status," Herman Justi wrote in the official history of the exposition. "This done, we shall be able, with each succeeding exposition, to measure their strides and determine their progress."[27]

Booker T. Washington was again among the several black speakers invited to Nashville to praise the accomplishments of his race and the generosity of white benefactors. "The negro problem in the South," he said in his Emancipation Day address on the steps of the Negro Building, "is fast passing from a question of sentiment into one of business, into one of commercial and industrial values." Slavery he credited as "an industrial school" that trained more men than in "the whole city of Nashville today." Striking the familiar theme of racial interdependence and economic progress, he went on to say:

"[W]e rise as you rise; when we fall you fall; when we are strong you are strong; when we are weak you are weak; there is no power that can separate our destiny."[28] A white editor echoed a similar theme when he wrote of the "new Negro": "[I]t should rejoice him to know that he has those innate qualities which enable him not to suffer but to profit by contact with a stronger race and a race in a much higher state of development."[29]

Education and Race

In areas involving education and health, the new paternalism acknowledged its obligation to use the power of local and state government to help fit blacks to their roles in the New South. Black education was a strong candidate for white support, if only because of the economic advantages and social control schools were thought to provide. In the North the public school crusade gained momentum from the 1830s forward, on the premise that schooling would prepare the work force for an emerging urban industrial society. Faced with an influx of immigrants into the North during the nineteenth century, school reformers also promoted public education as a device for Americanizing alien people and for instilling in children a discipline of work and an ambition to get ahead in life—values their parents were supposedly ill equipped to deliver.[30]

All of these goals seemed perfectly adaptable to the aims of the New South movement, faced as it was with a mostly rural, native work force of whites and blacks who were largely uneducated and unassimilated into a modern urban industrial society. Aside from the economic benefits associated with public education, the South felt a special urgency to train its newly enfranchised freedmen in citizenship. A Nashville educator put the case for public schools as well as any northern reformer could have: "Give to the children of poverty that portion of education which teaches them their own power and resources, and leads them to look onward with hope, and they will be no longer ready victims of destroying pestilence, nor the tools of designing demagogues, but the conservators of the social, political, and moral health of the State."[31] Whether they saw it as a means of black uplift or as an instrument of social control, advocates of the New South took up the cause of public education with enthusiasm.

But the rhetorical commitment to education and uplift was never matched by performance, even in the more prosperous urban centers of the New South, where sufficient public resources could more easily have been invested. Instead, public education in the South's leading cities, though more generous to blacks there than in the rural plantation districts, reflected the same sectional suspicion, racism, and general conservatism that characterized the region as a whole.

In the immediate postwar years it was northern missionaries, teachers, and Freedmen's Bureau officials who took the lead in providing the first schools for blacks. They followed in the wake of the military invasion in what amounted to an educational extension of the northern conquest. Driven by a combination of Christian duty toward the former slaves, denominational rivalry, and partisan interest in educating future Republican voters, these northern educators provided the first model for white assistance to the black race. That it was regarded by southern whites as an unwelcome and dangerous model imposed by meddlesome Yankees explains much of the difficulty faced by southern advocates of black uplift who tried to incorporate this model into the New South program.[32]

The main fruits of northern educational efforts were the establishment of a number of private schools and colleges for blacks in both Nashville and Atlanta. Nashville became a center of black education with the founding of Fisk University (1866), Central Tennessee College (1866), Roger Williams University (1866), and Meharry Medical College (1876). Atlanta rivaled Nashville as the black Athens of the South with Atlanta University (1865), Clark University (1869), Morehouse College (1879), Spelman College (1881), and Morris Brown College (1881).

Many of these schools opened as rudimentary grammar schools and continued to offer common-school education and manual training as their college enrollments increased. The freedmen and their children flocked to the schools. As early as 1862 Nashville had 1,200 black students packed into makeshift classrooms. Here many blacks seized their first opportunity for basic education, and these schools eventually turned out the first generation of educated black teachers, clergy, physicians, and others who would remain in Nashville and Atlanta to form the core of the local black elite.[33]

The white community resented the intrusion of northern missionaries and their dangerous experiments in racial egalitarianism, but after Reconstruction whites displayed a certain pride in these black colleges as symbols of black achievement and aspiration in the New South. No review of the city in newspapers or chamber of commerce publications was complete without a laudatory account of the black schools.[34] Nevertheless, financial support from local whites was meager. As the missionary societies began to wane in strength during the 1870s, black colleges had to seek funds from northern philanthropists. Well into the twentieth century, Atlanta's and Nashville's black colleges remained outposts of northern philanthropy, not genuine symbols of the New South's commitment to black progress.

It was in the realm of public education that southern white racial policy was most clearly demonstrated, though usually in ways that underlined the contradictions between the New South's rhetoric and its actual commitment to black progress. Public education was a new venture for most southern cities after the war, and its advocates met the same resistance from frugal taxpayers and suspicious parents that their northern counterparts had encountered thirty years earlier. Nashville established one of the region's first municipal public school systems in 1854, but the effort was a limited one, and wealthier families continued to favor the city's many private academies.[35]

Atlanta had failed in an attempt to launch a public school system in 1858 and waited more than a decade before making another, more successful, try. The rapid progress of black education after the war revived the movement to establish free public schools for whites. Elizabeth Sterchi, a missionary who taught whites in postwar Atlanta, complained in 1869 that there was "not a single city school for the whites, while it is done all for the blacks. . . . The blacks have a dozen schools . . . the whites beg at the door to be taught how to read."[36] The city appointed a committee on public schools, which reported in November 1869 that the "facilities for the gratuitous education for colored children are more extensive than those for . . . white children," whose "wants . . . are more immediate and pressing."[37] Later that year the city adopted what the council claimed was a "liberal system of public instruction, free for all [white] children of the City." A new board of education included many of Atlanta's most prominent businessmen.[38]

The premise that blacks were already being treated to free education at the expense of northern missionaries allowed officials of Atlanta and Nashville to maintain their schools initially for whites only. Nashville extended public education to blacks in 1867, when the city took over established northern missionary schools. This move, taken by white Conservative officials, preempted a Republican move to integrate white schools, reduced northern influence in the classroom, and enabled Nashville whites to exert their own influence over blacks. In Atlanta, on the other hand, Radicals on the city council led the move to shift black education to the public sector in 1872.[39]

In both settings, the ongoing effort to incorporate blacks into the public school system was inspired by an appreciation of blacks as an essential human resource in the postwar South and, simultaneously, as a dangerous class whose lack of education would put everyone at risk. "To make the negroes an element of wealth they must be trained in the ways of virtue, sobriety, and truth, and to habits of industry, frugality, and self reliance," a Nashville editor wrote in 1867 of the new city policy. "Though they may not now be able to return to the corporation the amount thus expended for their benefit, it will be a cheap expenditure to the whites in convincing the colored people of our justice and kindly disposition towards them, and our desire to see them elevated in the scale of humanity."[40] Later, when some whites threatened to slash the commitment of tax dollars to black schools, a Nashville editor responded: "To educate the children of the State is nothing more nor less than [an] act of self-protection. . . . Ignorance is the prolific mother of poverty, theft, adultery, prostitution, drunkenness, and general shiftlessness."[41]

Whatever their motives for extending public education to blacks, all whites agreed that they were to be educated on a strictly segregated basis. The social meaning of segregation after emancipation was not, in its initial stages, emphatically degrading to blacks. As historian Howard Rabinowitz has argued, the introduction of segregated facilities in the realms of education, welfare, and other public services and accommodations often meant a step up for blacks who had been entirely excluded before.[42] The justice of segregated public schools was occasionally debated in the early stages of public education in Atlanta and Nashville, but frequently such discussions became a means by which blacks extracted favors from white officials who preferred more equal benefits to any measure of integration.[43]

One of the occasions for such a debate came with the move to pass the federal Civil Rights Act of 1875, which in its original form would have prohibited segregation in public schools and other public accommodations. Nashville's superintendent of schools, Samuel Y. Caldwell, announced that integration flew in the face of intractable racial preferences and would force the city to shut down the entire system. "The co-education of the races in schools would scarcely be less repulsive to our people than their confraternity in the family," one editor argued in support of Caldwell. "To expect legislation to control such an instinctive prejudice is the dream of a lunatic, or a fool, or of one who is both; that is, a fanatic." In suburban Edgefield, whites were outraged at the prospect of sending their children to schools with blacks. Their superintendent echoed Caldwell's threat to close the schools and argued the case against integration in telling prose: "It takes six times as long to learn a negro any thing as it takes a white child, and mixing the races together in a school is like hitching a race horse in a wagon with an ox."[44]

Once the desegregation provision was, after strenuous pressure, jettisoned from the Civil Rights Act of 1875, the prospect of school integration was dead. The next step, initiated by black spokesmen, was to segregate the faculty and administration within the school system. Arguing that black teachers could better serve black students, the "colored teachers for colored schools" movement aimed at upgrading the quality of teachers and, in the process, opening opportunities for the growing supply of black teachers trained at the new black colleges of Atlanta and Nashville. The movement was also in keeping with the evolving strategy of black leaders who chose not to contest segregation outright but to turn it to advantage wherever possible. White officials, who had fought to remove northern influence from the black schools, were reluctant to yield control to blacks. They gradually relented, though, in part because they could further reduce the costs of black education by paying black teachers less than white ones. By 1887, following roughly a decade of experimentation and pressure, both cities had completed the transition to all-black faculty for black students.[45]

Up to this point, the acquisition of black schools with black faculties and administrations was a measure of the leverage blacks enjoyed in local affairs. But once segregated, black students and teachers became vulnerable to systematic discrimination, precisely at the time they were losing political power in both cities. Instead of redistributing public resources and bringing the disadvantaged up to par, the public school system in the New South actually reinforced the system of white supremacy. At the same time, it undeniably raised the quality of education available to both races. More than any other area of public policy, public education left a clear trail of evidence on racial differentials, and therefore it proves an unusually good indicator of racial policies that were better disguised in other areas. The evidence was particularly clear in data compiled by the Nashville Board of Education, which provides the material for most of the analysis that follows. If there is any place to test the New South's commitment to public education as an instrument of social uplift, it is in Nashville, the Athens of the South.

Aside from the city's role as an educational center in the postwar South, Nashville offers a revealing case study because blacks and Republicans retained considerable power in local politics well into the 1880s and beyond. It was largely due to black voting strength that Republican Thomas Kercheval was elected mayor twelve times between 1872 and 1887, a string of victories broken only twice by Conservative Democrats who were backed and led by the white business community. The competition for black votes initially strengthened the hand of black leaders in local politics. The attack on Republican and black political power in city politics began during the 1880s with the introduction of citywide elections for councilmen. But not until new state registration and ballot laws, aimed at the urban enclaves of Republican power, were passed after 1888 did Nashville blacks lose their local political strength. Even then, black voters regained a degree of leverage in Nashville beginning in 1909, when Mayor Hilary Howse built a durable political machine by soliciting their support. He acknowledged his debt to blacks by supporting new schools, parks, and health services and by carrying a black candidate for city council into office on his 1911 ticket.[46] If educational benefits for blacks reflected their political power, they should have fared as well in Nashville as anywhere.

When examined by themselves, Nashville blacks appear to have made remarkable gains in the late nineteenth and early twentieth centuries. The number of blacks regularly attending public schools (or "belonging," as school officials termed it) rose dramatically, from just over 400 in 1870–71, when systematic record keeping began, to over 5,200 by 1915. These numbers repre-

Figure 10.1 Nashville School Expenditures, by Race, 1871–1915

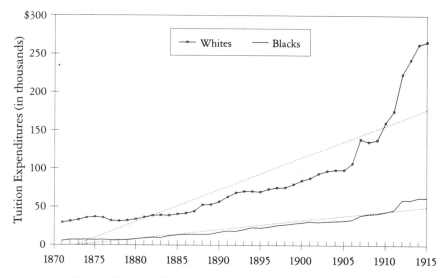

Source: Annual Report of the Board of Education for the City of Nashville . . . 1870–1915 (Nashville, Tenn., 1870–1915).

Note: Dotted lines represent trend lines. Expenditures include teachers' salaries only. All figures for expenditures are in 1913 dollars.

sented a growing proportion of the eligible population of black children, many of whom still had to forgo an education in order to contribute to meager family incomes. By 1910, 74 percent of Nashville's blacks ages six to fourteen were attending school, a rate only slightly less than that for whites (79 percent). As a new generation of blacks acquired basic skills, illiteracy rates declined to 22 percent by 1910. That rate was much higher than the figure reported for whites (1.6 percent), but given the starting point in 1865, when black illiteracy across the South was estimated at over 90 percent, this was a stunning achievement.[47] By every measure, when compared with their educational status immediately after emancipation, or when compared with their rural brethren, Nashville's blacks had made undeniable advances in the realm of education.

But to understand the racial policy of the New South as it was manifested in public education, one must look at how blacks fared in relation to whites. Such a comparison addresses the basic question that lies at the heart of any political and social order: Who gets what, and how much? The meticulous records kept by the Nashville Board of Education provide an answer, for they reveal with precision a systematic program of racial discrimination designed as much to channel resources toward the dominant race as to raise minimal standards for the subordinate race.

Figure 10.1 shows the small but steady gains in the tax dollars committed to black schools in the form of "tuition" expenditures (this meant teachers' salaries, which accounted for 80 or more percent of the annual school budget before 1905, when school construction and other costs began to rise). These gains roughly paralleled those for whites until the late 1880s, when, coinciding with the decline of black political power, more monies were directed to white schools. But this mild divergence intensified after 1905, when a massive spending program for new schools, new teachers, higher salaries, and free textbooks overwhelmingly favored whites. This trend continued even after the Howse machine took power in 1909, at which time Nashville blacks were supposed to have regained some leverage in city politics. The revival of black power was converted to gains in educational benefits, particularly in 1911, but the small improvements paled in comparison to the advances made by whites.

These crude budget figures do not account for varying numbers of students from each race being served at any given time. Figure 10.2 adjusts tuition expenditures for the number of students regularly attending the schools for each race. Black students began at, or near, parity with whites in the early 1870s. The drop in per-student costs during the 1870s came with the expansion of public education, when the city cut teacher salaries in an effort to control

Figure 10.2 Nashville School Expenditures per Student, by Race, 1871–1915

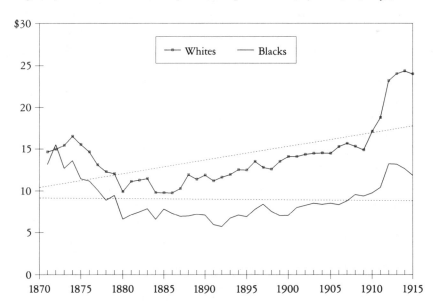

Source: See figure 10.1.
Note: Dotted line represents trend line.

costs.[48] To economize, school officials hired more women and less experienced teachers at lower salaries. The move toward "colored teachers for colored schools" after 1875 offered school officials yet another opportunity to economize, for black teachers were paid substantially less than whites with similar qualifications. Even when the faculties of black schools were predominantly white, as in 1880–81, for instance, teachers in the black schools received salaries that were on average 15 percent less than those of teachers in white schools. This was because less experienced, less qualified, and therefore lower-paid teachers were assigned to the black schools—one of the reasons blacks insisted on having their own teachers. Once faculties were segregated, the disparity increased. By 1890–91 the all-black faculty of Nashville's black schools was receiving an average salary 29 percent below that of white teachers.[49]

Whether they were black or white, the lower-paid teachers were placed in the black schools. One could argue that if the lower costs of black education resulted solely from salary discrimination against black teachers, black students would not necessarily have suffered significantly, all other conditions being equal. Tax dollars, in other words, would go further in black schools and provide equal education for less money, though at the expense of black teachers. But other conditions were not equal. Not only were teachers in black schools paid less, but their teaching load (as measured in student-teacher ratios) was far heavier in black schools and was another tactic school officials took to reduce the public investment in black education. In 1880–81, when the student-to-teacher ratio was forty-three in white schools, it was fifty-seven in black schools. Indeed, black schools would have been more crowded had not many students been turned away for want of seats in the classrooms.[50] These disparities increased during the progressive era. In 1906–7 there were forty white students per teacher and fifty-eight black students per teacher. By 1912–13 Nashville schools had one teacher for every thirty-three white students, while the black ratio was an incredible one teacher for every seventy-one students.

The pattern of discrimination in expenditures on teachers was underscored by the miserly allocation of resources to black school buildings and facilities. A Nashville Board of Education report in 1895 described the "gloomy proportions" of the city's black schools, with their "foul poison-ladened air; dim, insufficient . . . light." More critical was the chronic shortage of space for blacks. The report estimated that one thousand or more black children had been shut out of the public school system for lack of room in that year alone.[51]

The full effect of this policy of lower teacher pay and more crowded classrooms in black schools is shown dramatically in figure 10.3, which shows the money spent on each black student in relation to that spent on each white student. The graph reveals a choppy downward trend that, by 1892, allotted to

Figure 10.3 Nashville Black/White School Expenditure Ratio, 1871–1915

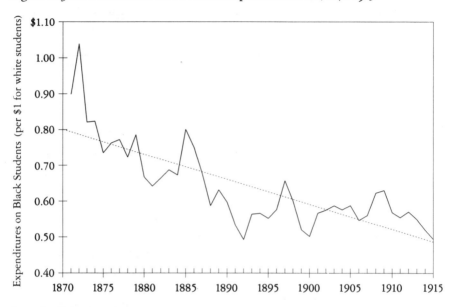

Source: See figure 10.1.
Note: Dotted line represents trend line.

blacks less than fifty cents for every dollar spent on white students. This ratio improved somewhat during the 1890s, apparently because many blacks stayed out of school during the depression. Once the depression lifted and black enrollments increased once more, the ratio of expenditures moved downward again to the fifty-cent mark. After 1900 blacks did make some gains relative to whites, only to see the inequality grow again with the new spending programs of the progressive era.

In the Athens of the South, the commitment to black uplift through public education was compromised by a policy that channeled limited public resources toward whites first. The gains in literacy and basic skills that blacks acquired within this system were undeniable. But those same gains also suggest the opportunities lost and the potential that could have been developed had greater investments been committed to black human capital during the crucial decades following emancipation.

Atlanta's school officials did not leave to the historian the same quality of data available for Nashville, but the points of comparison that can be made show that Nashville was not exceptional. In Atlanta black enrollment in public schools barely grew during the 1870s, largely because the city refused to accept responsibility for black education. Even the commitment to white education was jeopardized by the depression of the 1870s. In 1876 business leader Alfred Austell mounted a campaign to abolish the whole system of public education; for a time the schools had to charge tuition, and once they closed for a semester for lack of funds. The city's policy thereafter was to cut costs at the expense of blacks wherever possible, and that meant limiting the number of seats in black schools and turning away hundreds of eligible students.[52] By 1880 there were only 729 seats available for black schoolchildren.[53] Within the next decade Atlanta's black school population jumped to 2,373, which represented 43 percent of Atlanta's black children between six and eighteen years of age. The attendance rate for whites was 74 percent. The number of black children in school continued to rise, to 3,022 by 1890 and 4,440 by 1910, but black attendance percentage remained about the same as it was in 1880.[54]

Atlanta did not systematically compile data on its expenditures per student by race, but the disparity between the races is suggested by evidence extracted from reports by the Atlanta Board of Education for selected years. Student-teacher ratios, for example, began at equally high levels for both black and white schools. Indeed, in 1880 there were fifty-two students for every teacher in the black schools and fifty-three students per teacher in the white schools.[55] But the situation rapidly changed to the disadvantage of blacks: by 1890 the student-to-teacher ratio in black and white schools was sixty-eight and sixty respectively, in 1900 it was sixty-nine and forty-two, and in 1910 it was sixty-four for black schools and thirty-six for white.[56] The small improvements for black students after 1890 were insignificant in comparison to those for whites, as measured by this singularly important index of quality in education. Furthermore, even as black teachers shouldered a much heavier load, their salaries, determined by a fixed schedule, were set at about 40 percent less than those for whites with equal training and experience, a disparity that exceeded even Nashville's policy of inequality.[57]

Black teachers' salaries were only part of the story. An appraisal of Atlanta's school property, including lots, buildings, furniture, and apparatus, showed that the ten black schools in 1912 had a combined value of $129,470. This was a mere 7.7 percent of the total value of Atlanta's public school property, at a time when black students made up over 25 percent of the city's public school population.[58]

Public education constituted the most conspicuous failure of the New South's program of black uplift and regional progress. In Nashville and Atlanta, where both of these goals were enunciated with ostentatious conviction, the shortcomings appear all the more glaring.

Health and Race

Public health presented the new paternalism with an even stronger case for white benevolence than education. Like education, it spawned public policies and private charities compromised by racism and ambiguous in their effects. Unlike access to public education, however, the health resources and benefits allocated to each race are not easily traced. On the other hand, the *outcome* of public health policy shows with grisly precision in the data on mortality and morbidity compiled by city officials. The vital statistics of whites and blacks reflect more than the influence of government-sponsored health programs or private charity, to be sure. Occupation, income, education, housing, diet, and personal hygiene all affected the rates of illness and death among blacks and whites in a number of ways, but these factors only magnify the importance of mortality as a measure of the general welfare of blacks in a given community.

The health environment of American cities in the late nineteenth century proved quite amenable to improvement, and city officials everywhere wrought public health miracles through a few fundamental reforms. Before the 1880s, most American cities were filthy enclaves of pestilence with chronically high death rates, which periodically soared even higher as epidemics of cholera, yellow fever, and smallpox swept through the urban population. The introduction of pure water, modern sewers and sanitation, and the regulation of milk, meat, and other food supplies were among the key reforms adopted by municipal governments in the battle against urban disease. The dreaded epidemics had virtually disappeared by the end of the nineteenth century, allowing tuberculosis, the "white plague," to emerge as the major killer. Overall death rates dropped dramatically beginning in the 1880s.

Driving this revolution in public health was the germ theory, which gained acceptance among all but the most skeptical health professionals beginning in the 1880s. The germ theory challenged prevailing religious, moral, and racial explanations of disease and pointed to practical solutions for controlling, if not eradicating, many diseases. Like school reformers, public health crusaders promised civic leaders practical results that were utopian in their vision and, at the same time, warned of dire consequences if their pleas were not answered.[59]

Southern city boosters were especially sensitive to the health issue because death rates in their cities were generally higher than those in the urban centers of the North and West. Along with population growth, death rates were one of the important yardsticks by which cities measured themselves. Atlanta had long claimed its high altitude and mild climate as major health advantages over rival southern cities.[60] In Nashville, on the other hand, severe cholera epidemics in the 1870s highlighted a miserable health environment that caused the city's death rates to rank among the highest in the world.[61] The city worked diligently, and with notable success, to overcome its "sickly" reputation.

In every southern city mortality rates were strongly skewed by race, with blacks dying at 1.5 to 2 times the rate of whites during the period 1880 to 1910.[62] Separate reporting of death rates by race allowed civic promoters to point out the relative healthfulness of the white population, whose death rates were generally comparable to those of northern cities.

The excessive death rates among southern urban blacks (60 percent higher than those for southern rural blacks) were the source of anguished debate beginning in the 1890s.[63] Racial pessimists claimed that these high death rates supplied proof for their argument that blacks could never adapt to freedom and, particularly, to modern urban life. Frederick L. Hoffman, author of the widely cited *Race Traits and Tendencies of the American Negro* (1896), quantified the increased mortality among blacks since emancipation and attributed it to the "inferior organisms and constitutional weaknesses" of blacks and the "immense amount of immorality which is a race trait, and of which scrofula, syphilis, and even consumption are the inevitable consequences."[64] In 1900 Paul Barringer, a professor at the University of Virginia, addressed the Montgomery, Alabama, conference on race conditions in the South with confident predictions of black extinction. "There is a general drift of the Negro to the cities and towns, and once there the Negro seldom returns." Tuberculosis, syphilis, and typhoid cut down the black population almost as fast as it could migrate to the city, Barringer noted. He added a chilling prediction: "In the destruction of the race the city is to play a most important part."[65]

It was a natural extension of this pessimistic view to see segregation as a means of protecting the white race from contamination, a kind of racial quarantine that would at once take care of the "Negro problem," by sending blacks the way of the Indian toward a doomed future as a "vanishing race," and protect the health environment of whites. Thus William Lee Howard of Baltimore, in a macabre essay on Negro disease and degeneracy, pointed optimistically to segregation as the solution: "There is every prospect of checking and reducing these diseases in the white race, if the race is socially—in every aspect of the term—quarantined from the African."[66]

It was more than coincidence that the systematic reign of Jim Crow emerged in law and practice at the same time that the germ theory was gaining popular acceptance (a concurrence that is largely ignored by historians debating the origins of segregation).[67] The sanctions against interracial toilets, drinking fountains, restaurants, saloons, hotels, hospitals, railroads, and streetcars all served as symbolic means of insuring white supremacy, but they also had obvious links to practical health concerns. So did residential segregation, which accelerated with the movement of white families to the reputedly wholesome suburbs.[68]

Although many found the logic of enforced segregation as a racial quarantine compelling, Jim Crow provided at best a thin, permeable shield against disease. Germs, whites came to realize, were quite unprejudiced when it came to crossing the color line.[69] Formal segregation might lessen casual contact with diseased blacks, but there was no practical—never mind legal—way to truly isolate them within a city. First of all, the dependence on black domestic labor required intimate contact with black nurses, cooks, and servants of all types. Even those whites who did not have servants in the home depended on black washerwomen to do their laundry. Health officials expressed great alarm over the possibility that tuberculosis and other diseases might be transferred by way of laundry, one of several means by which disease could penetrate even the most sanitary home. One Nashvillian, calling for the sanitary reform of Black Bottom (the jumble of tenements, saloons, and brothels that sprawled along the low-lying areas between Capitol Hill and Rutledge Hill) in 1906, warned of the "microscopical demons" that "have a way of clinging to things—to clothes, to flies' legs, to particles of dust, to anything they can lay hold of—and that in this way they are transported by everybody and everything, even the wind and water that pass through Black Bottom." If, as he put it, Black Bottom were "full of wild beasts, there would be a mad hurrying and scurrying to get away from the city, and loud cries would arise for their immediate extermination. There would be no talk of expense. But Black Bottom is the breeding and feeding ground of creatures infinitely more dangerous than lions and tigers, because we can see and protect ourselves against the latter, whereas, the former are invisible, and their ways of killing are dark and cunning."[70]

Among those who understood the democracy of disease, the need for public health programs—far outweighing the need for public education—presented the clearest mandate for white civic leaders to take actions that benefited blacks, if only to protect their own race.[71] Moreover, the practical results of health reform were manifest, and the costs of ignoring the public health problem were more immediately visible than those caused by poor education. In the end, however, segregation as quarantine and health reform as protection for whites were embraced simultaneously as answers to this medical version of "the Negro question."

Again using Nashville as a case study in race and health policy, we find the same patterns that were revealed in the study of education policies. Blacks experienced undeniable benefits from the public health crusade, especially after 1900, but the gap between blacks and whites was widening. Figure 10.4 shows that death rates declined in the 1880s, rose during the depression-ridden 1890s, and dropped again after 1900. Board of health expenditures increased from less than $9,000 in 1892 to almost $35,000 twenty years later, but those sums represented only a fraction of the public and private resources that were committed to the improvement of the health environment.[72] The completion of a new city water system in 1889, the expansion of a modern sewer system beginning around the same time, and the introduction of the city hospital in 1890 were perhaps the most important events in Nashville's public health

Figure 10.4 Nashville Death Rates, by Race, 1875–1915

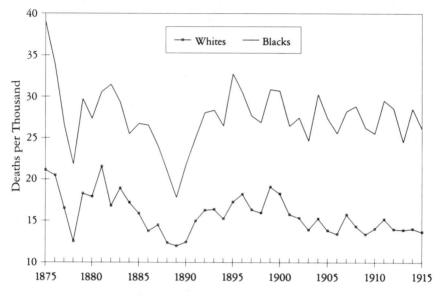

Source: Reports of Departments of the City of Nashville (Nashville, Tenn., 1875–1915).

movement. Crucial breakthroughs came in 1899 with the election of James N. Head, a progressive mayor devoted to health reform, and the introduction of a new city charter, which authorized a more powerful board of health staffed by paid medical doctors and nurses. During the progressive era, both public and private resources were concentrated on a number of public health reforms affecting the prevention and treatment of disease. Hilary Howse also made public health a major priority beginning in 1905 when, as a state legislator, he called for a new city-county tuberculosis hospital. Leading the health movement in the private sphere were Nashville's women, particularly the wives of business leaders in the Centennial Club, which, also beginning in 1905, made sanitary reform a major crusade.[73]

How did the public health movement affect the two races? How were the public health resources of the community allocated? As figure 10.5 illustrates, the disparity in mortality between the races actually grew as the health crusade mounted. Black death rates were 1.63 times higher than those of whites during the 1880s and 1.73 times higher in the 1890s. Even after the public health campaign of the progressive era was launched and death rates for both races began to decline, this racial disparity continued to increase, reaching about 1.83 in the 1900s and 1.93 in the early 1910s.[74]

City officials and health professionals who applied the lessons of modern

Figure 10.5 Nashville Black/White Death Rate Ratio, 1875–1915

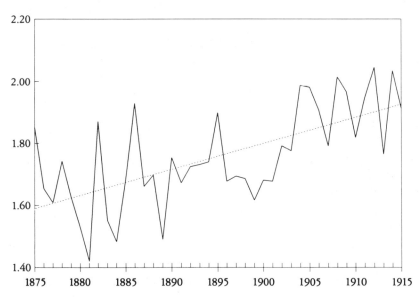

Source: See figure 10.4.
Note: Dotted line represents trend line.

sanitation and hygiene saw blacks not just as careless victims of disease but also as dangerous carriers of color-blind germs. The stricter system of segregation that took effect after 1890 helped insulate whites from casual contact with blacks. At the same time, racially segregated neighborhoods, public facilities, and health delivery services allowed the city to maintain higher standards for whites and to channel their growing (but still limited) public resources toward the improvement of white public health. Black public health could not be entirely neglected, but white officials gave it only secondary attention.

The crusade against tuberculosis (TB) offers a good example of racially influenced public health policy. As the chief epidemic diseases receded after the 1870s, TB became the foremost cause of death by disease in Nashville, where it accounted for 8,458 deaths between 1885 and 1915, or about 16 percent of all deaths.[75] TB was an endemic disease; it festered within dark, dank, cold, and poorly ventilated dwellings, often basement apartments in low-lying slums prone to frequent flooding. It was a disease that flourished amid the squalor of the urban poor in all American cities, and it became laden with moral and racial connotations. In southern cities TB afflicted blacks with cruel frequency (their death rates from the disease were about three times greater than those for whites).[76] Tuberculosis was the first disease proven to be caused by germs, and it came to be understood as a product of unhealthy living conditions, but moral and racial explanations of the white plague persisted. Nashville's health officer explained in 1899 that the "high death rate among the colored people is due to several well known and potent causes, which . . . affect the greater bulk of their number. Among these are improvidence, ignorance, lamentable neglect of personal cleanliness. . . . [B]ut over and above all, the negro has to contend with his marked racial susceptibility to all forms of tubercular disease."[77] Black TB, a scourge that appeared only after slavery, was a recurrent theme in anti-Negro literature of the day, for it served as evidence that blacks could not survive in modern urban society—at least not without the care of whites.[78]

While health officials condemned blacks for their unhealthy living habits, they also campaigned against the environmental causes of TB. Black TB was "due to their habits and mode of life, *which are in turn due to poverty and ignorance*," Nashville health officer Charles Mitchell argued in 1886. He pleaded for a tenement-house law to "prevent overcrowding and restrain avaricious land-lords in renting out damp basements, cellars, filthy stables, etc., for human habitations."[79] Other calls for housing reform and slum clearance met with mixed success, but most reformers showed great reluctance to challenge private property rights.[80]

The "municipal warfare upon the Great White Plague" focused instead on efforts to stop public spitting, to regulate milk supplies, and in every way to sanitize the city. It was the women of Nashville's Centennial Club who, in 1905, lobbied persistently for enforcement of a city ordinance aimed at banning the "evil of expectoration" in public places. Streetcars soon became a major target in the board of health's campaign to enforce the anti-spit law. Earlier, the board, noting that "streetcars are recognized as patent agencies in disseminating such diseases [consumption and others] through a community," had demanded that the trolley companies "disinfect and thoroughly cleanse each passenger coach as the same shall go out of service at the end of each and every day" and offered specific instructions on the procedure. Dr. Buist of the Board of Health complained in 1903, "no attempt whatsoever is being made by the conductors of the road towards enforcing the Anti-Spit Law." Indeed, the conductors themselves spat freely. The board continued to pressure the street-car company, requiring it to post copies of a new anti-spit ordinance on the cars and at downtown stations. By 1905 the streetcar problem was no better, and the Board of Health threatened (as it had in 1900) to require complete disinfection of each car every twenty-four hours if the law was not enforced.[81]

Jim Crow's connection with the public health movement is suggested by the coincidence of Nashville's battle to sanitize the streetcars with an almost simultaneous move to segregate public transportation, which remained one of the few public spaces where the races mingled. The publicly stated reasons for this extension of segregation were varied, inconsistent, and rarely developed with any precision. Most blamed growing black "impudence," and health concerns were invoked in vague ways, usually with reference to the alleged uncleanliness or bad smell of blacks.[82] "The impudence of negroes on the cars has already worn patience threadbare, and entire separation is the only alternative," one Nashvillian argued in 1904. Another asked, "[C]an you force Southern women to sit beside cooks, wash-women, carriage drivers and common laborers of the African descent—and scent as well?"[83]

Among whites there was little open debate over why segregation on the streetcars was desirable, but they did dispute how best to implement Jim Crow streetcars. The most extreme argued for completely separate cars, or "trailers," that would be attached behind the regular cars. A black editor in Indiana ridiculed Tennessee's legislators as they struggled to find "a measure that will save them from contamination." "Why not compel the building of parallel roads, under separate and distinct companies and entirely different cars . . . ? They might put up gigantic screens all along the line so the respective race passengers cannot see each other."[84] The compromise finally enacted in 1905 required separate sections for blacks and whites within cars, with signs designating the location of each. The Board of Health, in its continuing campaign to control spitting on the cars, required that separate but equal spittoons, filled with disinfectant, be fixed to the floor at each end of the car.[85]

Simultaneously with the movement to segregate the races and suppress the "evil of expectoration," the crusade against the white plague reached out to treat victims as well as protect the healthy. In 1905 the Nashville city council established the Division of Disinfection, which was charged with cleaning the homes and personal effects of diseased citizens. Four years later the city funded a bacteriological and chemical laboratory to help detect TB by examining sputum samples.[86] A local chapter of the Anti-Tuberculosis League, a citizens' volunteer group, joined forces with the Board of Health in 1910. Following several years of lobbying, a new city-county tuberculosis hospital opened in 1912.[87] "The necessity for this measure," the board had earlier assured the mayor and city council, "is not simply to show our humanity for them [pauper consumptives], but as protection against the dissemination of this disease among the population generally."[88] A special Tuberculosis Bureau, sponsored by the city board of health, began work the same year with a staff consisting of a medical doctor and two nurses, who were assigned to visit the homes of suspected TB victims, disinfect the premises, treat the patients, and educate the public about the causes of TB in order to convince people that it was a treatable, as well as preventable, disease. The board also sponsored several dispensaries to provide poor children with pure milk.[89]

Blacks benefited only marginally from this battle against the white plague.

The evidence is scattered, but it strongly suggests that a deliberate policy channeled public health resources toward whites first. The Board of Health's Department of Disinfection, which was responsible for fumigating and otherwise sterilizing the homes and belongings of all diseased persons, reported that it had disinfected over 4,374 homes between 1906 and 1912. Only 27 percent (1,169) of those homes were occupied by blacks, a number far below the black share of the tubercular population.[90] The Tuberculosis Bureau also recorded visits by nurses and physicians according to the race of the patients, and this list showed a similar bias. In 1912 the TB nurses—both specified as "white nurses"—visited 3,279 TB patients, about 35 percent of whom were black. This report also distinguished between "old" and "new" patients, thus revealing something about follow-up care for TB victims after they were diagnosed. The ratio of old to new patients was nearly 8 to 1 among whites, but only 4 to 1 among blacks.[91] Physician visits also heavily favored whites, with blacks receiving only 15 percent of a total 230 visits that year. Other statistics confirm that blacks consistently received a minimal level of public health services. The only statistic showing a higher rate for blacks than for whites was the death toll from TB.[92]

As health officials took pains to point out, the poor health service to blacks was not always due to an official policy of neglect. Blacks distrusted white health officers and were reluctant to admit to TB and other chronic illnesses for fear of losing their jobs or jeopardizing their insurance policies.[93] In response, public health professionals often evinced an impatience with the victims of disease, who were regarded as menaces to society if not to themselves. In some instances this impatience inspired draconian measures designed to help the victims in spite of themselves. The attack on smallpox in Nashville, for example, was waged by public officials who made house-by-house inspections, "vaccinating as they go." Likely victims of the disease were rounded up in a "suspect wagon" and thrown into a "detention house or suspect camp" surrounded by a "barbed wire fence . . . closely strung" and watched day and night by rotating guards. Suspects, and their clothing, were disinfected with sulfur or formaldehyde; after fourteen days of detention, they were released. The houses and all personal belongings of victims were to be sterilized, or, "if a hut or shanty of small value, it should be burned." Even these measures proved insufficient, because many blacks evaded the inspectors when they saw them coming. The campaign escalated with late-night sweeps through the black slums, during which health inspectors were accompanied by five or six policemen. "We could often vaccinate as many as four hundred in one night," one physician recalled.[94]

The new paternalism demonstrated the same kind of harsh benevolence when Nashville's society women concentrated their reform efforts on the slums

A slum apartment in Nashville's Black Bottom. (Reproduced from the *American,* August 8, 1909)

of Black Bottom. This "plague spot," filled with "low negroes" and "vicious" whites, became a symbol of all that threatened the physical, moral, and economic health of the "decent" white community. "No city in Europe or America can present a more sickening aspect of modern civilization," one reformer wrote of the neighborhood.[95]

Beginning in 1905, the ladies of the newly reorganized Centennial Club and its neighborhood auxiliary, the South Nashville Woman's Federation, made the "eradication of Black Bottom" the center of their campaign to sanitize and beautify Nashville. Their plan was for the city to purchase the property and transform it into an attractive park. Late in 1906 Mayor Thomas O. Morris, under constant pressure from the women, launched a major "cleaning out" of Black Bottom, sending police through the area to arrest vagrants and shut down the saloons and brothels. A law limiting all liquor sales to the downtown district struck another blow to the major line of trade in Black Bottom.[96]

But the goal was to eradicate, not regulate, the slum, and the women of the Centennial Club proved tenacious. They enlisted the aid of their husbands and

A Nashville tuberculosis nurse inspects a basement laundry. (Reproduced from the
Annual Report of the Departments of the City of Nashville, 1912)

associates in the board of trade and continued to lobby the city and state
governments for the legislation necessary to their plan. At a Monday afternoon
tea in 1906, held at the University Club, the subject of Black Bottom was
foremost. The Centennial Club, one speaker explained in revealing terms,
"wants better homes and more healthy ones for the good colored servants. It is
only the vagrant class of both races it wants to move." She further urged her
audience to "see to it that homes for the negroes should not be crowded, and
rendered as unsanitary as many of them now are." The women later broke up
into small groups and discussed the plight of Black Bottom. A reporter in the
society column described the scene, which transpired just a few blocks from
the teeming slums that were the object of concern that afternoon: "[W]hile the
members talked, chocolate, sandwiches, cakes and wafers were served," followed by a "charming group of songs" performed by a young woman.[97]

The New South's answer to the "Negro question" remained a strange
mixture of genuinely enlightened appeals for social uplift along with policies
that channeled public resources toward whites. The undeniable strides that
blacks made within the limits of white racial policies were often overshadowed
by the growing gap between the races, confirmed by the ascendance of Jim
Crow laws at the turn of the century. The ultimate failure of the new paternalism was its inability to transcend the region's traditional system of racial

caste and fashion a democratic, competitive society in which, according to the classic bourgeois formulation, individuals would rise to the level of their talent and ambition within an open class structure. If the prophets of the New South were correct in their argument that black progress was essential to regional progress, the burden of racism proved a heavy drag on the New South, one not borne by blacks alone.

11 | *Paternalism and Pessimism*

The whites are each of them fond of particular individuals among the blacks, but despise the race as a whole.
—Belton O'Neall Townsend, 1877

I would rather be an imp in hades than a Negro in South Carolina.
—Walter Hines Page, 1899

Bella, an elderly black woman, knocked on the door of her former master, Daniel Elliott Huger Smith, years after emancipation, when she and her husband, Nat, had left the Smith family. Nat had recently been killed by a train, and Bella needed justice from the white world. "'Mass, Judge,'" she implored in her rich Gullah tongue, "''enty yo' gwine mek de railroad pay me for Nat?'" When Smith recommended that she go to his lawyer friend to seek compensation through the courts, she made her expectations clear: "'Mass Judge, I ain' want no lawyer; I ain' want no co't I want [you] of' mek de railroad pay me of' Nat!'" Smith reassumed his traditional obligations, arranged for Bella's legal help, and explained to his lawyer that "she and hers had been slaves of ours . . . and that we owed her good feeling, in spite of the interference of the United States Government." Bella won her compensation from the railroad, and the lawyer "made her no charge for his kindness." This, Smith mused, "acknowledged fully the force of her plea that she had 'b'long to de family.'"[1]

If Atlanta and Nashville displayed the new order of race relations—with its competition, legal segregation, sporadic violence, and yet with its avowed commitment to black uplift and regional progress—Charleston demonstrated the persistence of a more traditional strain of white paternalism, which complemented the city's less sanguine accommodation to the New South. While the proponents of the new order advocated the improved social welfare of blacks as a prerequisite to regional progress, the more pessimistic view from Charleston focused on the burden blacks imposed on future progress. The same behaviors and attitudes also appeared, in less articulated form, in Mobile, but Charleston provides the clearest model of traditional white paternalism as it persisted in the New South. In the older seaports, a long history of urban slavery, suddenly disrupted by emancipation, was followed by a period

290

of interracial friction that was most antagonistic in the political arena. That interlude of racial competition and black defiance was countered by a white strategy of violence and intimidation that, at the same time, drew upon a paternalistic tradition of mutual duties and obligations between white masters and black servants.

Whites also took advantage of a traditional three-caste racial system that awarded distinctive status to mulattoes—"browns" or "colored" as they were known in Charleston.[2] The preservation of white supremacy in Charleston rested both on the perpetuation of paternalistic ties with a segment of favored black domestic servants and on the recognition of separate status for the browns. This acknowledgment of gradations of status among blacks, and between "full-colored" blacks and browns, was an extension of the fixed notion of social hierarchy that persisted among the white upper class in Charleston. This system withstood what historian George Fredrickson has described as a herrenvolk or master-race democracy that took root in most other parts of the South. By the herrenvolk doctrine, whites of all ranks were regarded as citizens of an egalitarian democracy, whereas all blacks, regardless of their individual talents and achievements, were regarded as subordinate. Charleston also resisted the corollary tendency in postemancipation law and custom to obliterate distinctions of color and class among blacks and relegate all those with even a drop of Negro ancestry to the inferior level of a two-race society.[3]

The preservation of customary patterns of race relations in Charleston meant that there was less friction and less physical segregation between the races, at least as compared with Nashville and Atlanta. To be sure, when the hierarchy of race and class was challenged, as it was during Reconstruction, the white upper class led what was at times a violent counterattack. White Charlestonians' rifle clubs and red shirts were the emblems of an embattled race fighting to restore its historic supremacy, and the city witnessed a number of armed racial clashes during Reconstruction. Once the rule of white "property and intelligence" was restored, however, Charleston's leading white citizens continued to defend a policy of conservative *noblesse oblige* toward black citizens, demanding only that blacks accept their inferior social position as fixed and allow their "natural superiors" in the white upper class to rule.[4]

Although family servants and the brown middle class in Charleston enjoyed protected status under white patronage, the black masses suffered callous neglect and deprivations of a kind that made racial policies in Nashville and Atlanta appear generous. By every measure of health, education, and welfare, blacks in Charleston were, as a group, much worse off than those in Atlanta, Nashville, and most other southern cities. Table 11.1 summarizes some of the key indicators that measure the relative condition of the races in the four cities.

The new paternalism, with its link between black uplift and regional

Table 11.1 Black Mortality, School Attendance, and Home Ownership, 1910

	Atlanta	Charleston	Mobile	Nashville
Black mortality, 1910	25.4	39.3	29.4	26.0
Black/white mortality ratio, 1910	(1.64)	(2.08)	(1.66)	(1.73)
Black school attendance, 1910	71.0%	65.1%	68.4%	74.0%
Black/white school attendance ratio, 1910	(.89)	(.80)	(.79)	(.93)
Black home ownership, 1910	13.0%	8.9%	15.1%	20.5%

Source: U.S. Census Bureau, *Negro Population of the United States, 1790–1915* (1918; reprint, New York, 1968), 320, 400–401, 473.
Note: Mortality figures represent deaths per 1,000; the mortality ratios are derived by dividing black mortality rates by those for whites. School attendance is based on the number of children between the ages of 6 and 14. The figures given for home ownership represent the percentage of all black households. Mortality and school attendance figures do not always agree with local data, presumably because federal census officials standardized these data for all cities.

progress, may have been based more in rhetoric than in reality in Atlanta and Nashville, but the rhetoric did give an intellectual foundation to a hopeful view of progress for both races in the South, and it motivated social policies designed to improve black welfare, even if those policies were not implemented with an even hand. The older doctrine of racial paternalism that prevailed in Charleston, on the other hand, accepted white patronage of blacks as a perpetual burden without offering any scenario for black and, concomitantly, southern progress, as prophets of the New South would have it. The Charleston press encouraged white philanthropy and black self-help on occasion, but members of the white upper class preferred to express their concern through personal acts of charity to black dependents rather than supporting public programs that invested in human capital to advance the welfare of the black masses. The presence of black street beggars, ubiquitous in postwar Charleston and immortalized in DuBose Heyward's pathetic portrait in *Porgy* (the inspiration for Gershwin's *Porgy and Bess*), offered daily testimony to the fatalistic acceptance of a permanently maimed, dependent race—a sharp contrast to the victimized freedman envisioned by the New South as a candidate for uplift and "scientific charity."[5]

The special features of race relations in Charleston derived from the negligible impact of economic development there and from the persistent traditions of the slaveholders, who had always been more dominant in antebellum Charleston than in cities like Atlanta or Nashville. Another critical factor was the unusual demography of race in Charleston and the surrounding low country. The single overwhelming characteristic of race relations in Charleston was that a privileged white minority held onto its precarious position amid a

Charleston street vendors, 1879. (Library of Congress)

sea of impoverished blacks. The low country, with its rich plantations and large slave population, left room for few of the white nonslaveholders who, elsewhere in the South, helped to balance the population and provided a source of slave control. The predominantly black population of the Charleston area was enlarged during and after the war when upcountry blacks flocked to the Sea Islands. The Union forces, and later the Freedmen's Bureau, had promised to break up the plantations there and distribute land to the former slaves. In 1880 Charleston County was 70 percent black; Colleton and Beaufort counties to the south were 67 percent and 92 percent black.[6] The most distinctive mark of the homogeneity and insularity of the low-country black population was the exotic Gullah speech, a creole admixture of African and English.[7]

Retrieving water from an artesian well, 1879. (Library of Congress)

Within Charleston, also, whites had long constituted a minority—or at times a bare majority—surrounded by slaves and free blacks. Even before Denmark Vesey's revolutionary plot in 1822, Charleston's slaves were vigorously repressed by an elaborate policing system. Drums beat at dusk, and the bells of St. Michael's rang to warn the slaves home. Those away from their masters were required to carry passes. Officials made strenuous efforts to repress a thriving underground life among slaves and free blacks, carried on in the grog shops, churches, and back alleys beyond the masters' eyes.[8]

The precarious position of the white minority became all the more attenuated after the war, when blacks were given political power. Within the city, the black population swelled with an influx of freedmen from the Sea Islands. The 1870 census, although an uncertain measure, showed that blacks had a majority of 53 percent of the population; by 1880 that majority had grown to nearly 55 percent.[9] Charleston whites found themselves in the perilous position of losing political representation in the state legislature while at home they were threatened with political impotence at the hands of a black-Republican alliance.

A Fragile Paternalism

In their struggle to restore white political power in Charleston and South Carolina after 1865, whites drew upon long-standing traditions of paternalism, which bound a small but politically crucial element within the black population to the former masters. Paternalism, at bottom, operated as an informal agreement between patron and client to fulfill a set of mutual obligations that went beyond the rational, contractual exchanges of the marketplace. Emancipation disintegrated these bonds between many whites and their former slaves, at least temporarily, but the paternalistic tradition survived, especially in the relations between upper-class whites and their house servants. The great townhouses of the planters and wealthy merchants of Charleston were brimming with black servants before the war. Daniel Elliott Huger Smith recalled no fewer than nineteen servants—all by name and with specific reference to their domestic duties—plus "sundry and various children" who lived in his grandmother's yard.[10] The necessary intimacy between the races under these conditions frequently created bonds of personal loyalty, which, according to accounts by whites, at least, appear to have persisted through the war with few attempts by blacks at desertion, escape, or sabotage.[11]

White Charlestonians were shocked by how suddenly and, in their view, how ungratefully those bonds were cast aside in 1865. When black Union troops marched through the streets and entered white homes to proclaim black freedom, many slaves dropped their work on the spot, walked out of their masters' homes, and never looked back. Free of their owners' protection, these former slaves, according to the abandoned masters, slid into a state of sloth, intemperance, and defiant insolence, open to easy corruption by the invaders.[12]

"Demoralization" was the word invariably used by former masters to describe the freedman's lack of discipline and deference under freedom. There was no better word to describe the mixed feelings of betrayal and humiliation Charleston whites experienced toward their former slaves. William Heyward, once a prosperous rice planter and descendant of an aristocratic South Carolina family, found it difficult to learn to live in Charleston without black servants. He took up residence at the Mills House Hotel and for a time ate his meals at the Charleston Hotel, but he complained that "the Negro waiters [are] so familiar and deficient in their attention." Rather than suffer these indignities, he bought a small kerosene stove and cooked for himself in his room, hired an "old Irish chamber maid" to clean his room, and did most of his own washing. "A part of the satisfaction," he wrote in 1868, "is that I am perfectly independent of having Negroes about me; if I cannot have them as they used to be, I have no desire to see them except in the field." Heyward found his accommodation a severe trial and admitted: "[W]e who have known so much better life, will find it hard to live. . . . I know that I am not prepared for the great change. . . . It will be hard ever to recover the privileges that have been yielded to the Negroes."[13]

Similar reports of insolent, ungrateful servants appear in the letters and diaries of other whites during the first shocking years of readjustment after emancipation. Henry Hunter Raymond wrote to his mother from Charleston in July 1865, advising her to hire a white servant and reporting that his three black servants are "not worth their feed and have not the slightest particle of feeling for us. All are bound for a common doom—a universal distinction of their race."[14] Henry W. Ravenel, abandoned by his personal servant, Edward, who told him he "had no further use" for his master, responded with disgust: " 'so much for the fidelity of indulged servants.' "[15]

But there were just as many testimonies to the mutual affection and dependency between the races—typically between older blacks and members of the white upper class—to suggest that the old ideals and much of the practice of racial paternalism had survived the war. "I have been very agreeably disappointed in the behavior of the negroes," Augustine T. Smythe wrote to his wife from Charleston in August 1865. "They are as civil and humble as ever. All I met greeted me enthusiastically as 'Mass Gus.' "[16] A more telling incident of persistent paternalism was recorded in John Berkeley Grimball's diary. When Maum Peggy, an elderly Charleston nursemaid, died in 1877, Grimball, her former master, arranged for full burial rites and supplied the coffin, a funeral carriage, and marble headstone. "She was with us throughout the War—and ... has been taken care of by us ever since," he wrote. The tombstone expressed the continuing fondness and sense of obligation that many whites sincerely felt toward their servants, feelings that were held up to public display with a certain pride: "Sacred to the Memory of Peggy Bonaparte, a nurse in the Grimball family for many years. . . . This stone is placed over her grave by John Berkeley Grimball and his Children in Grateful remembrance of her kind and faithful care of them during their Childhood."[17] It was not an isolated case. One white observer in 1882 noted with pleasure the "touching proof of the fidelity of old attachments, and of the still surviving power of the old personal ties," that led many blacks to ask to be buried at the homes of their former masters.[18] Whether this request was inspired by loyalty to whites or to black ancestors buried on the homesteads, or just by the expediency of gaining free burial privileges, matters less than the willingness of whites to see the practice as a mark of fidelity.

The same ambiguous mix of loyalty and expediency guided former slaves in choosing new surnames after emancipation. Maum Peggy Bonaparte took the heroic name her husband had adopted, but there were many other blacks who assumed the last names of their former masters, a point of amused pride among whites. For their part, blacks found that this practice strengthened the "family" claim made on white patrons in time of need.[19]

These brittle but enduring paternalistic relations were sustained by a curious mixture of genuine sentiment and shrewd calculation. In a stagnant local economy with a limited industrial base, the occupational opportunities for black men and, especially, black women were largely restricted to personal service and other unskilled labor for white employers. Black women, who constituted 81 percent of the female work force and 29 percent of the entire work force in 1890, were generally limited to jobs as servants, laundresses, or seamstresses in the service of white families. Among black males, who made up 56 percent of the male work force and 36 percent of the total work force in 1890, less than 10 percent were employed as servants, but most of the remainder depended on the goodwill of white employers for their livelihood.[20] A depressed local economy gave blacks less leverage than their counterparts in Atlanta or Nashville, if only because in the latter cities there was more competition for labor.

The inequality of justice, as well as economic disadvantages, required that poor and uneducated blacks secure white patrons to help them out of scrapes with the law and ease them through hard economic times. Charleston's race relations in the postwar era reveal the paradoxical truth that even the most oppressive and unjust social system rests on an intricate network of personal dependences, knitted together by hundreds of daily acts of kindness, as well as on the threat of brute force. It was this tradition of interdependence that drove Bella to approach her former master for help in receiving compensation when her husband was killed by a train. The same tradition compelled the master to carry out his old role as patron, as though Bella still, as she claimed, "'b'long to de family.'"[21]

The persistence of paternalism as a means by which blacks received protection from whites is suggested in *Mamba's Daughters*, DuBose Heyward's novel set in the early twentieth century. "In the Charleston of Mamba's day," Heyward explained, "the negro population might have been divided into two general classes: the upper, consisting of those who had white folks, belonged to the negro quality and enjoyed a certain dolorous respectability; and the lower class, members of which had no white folks and were little better than outcasts." Heyward himself was a scion of Charleston's white aristocracy, and his portrait of blacks was romanticized, to be sure, even if it was drawn from a close knowledge and sympathy. The value of his fiction is not in its accurate description of black reality, but in its depiction of the ideals of his own class.

Mamba, a destitute black woman in her late fifties, is determined to rise from that lower class, to "have white folks," as Heyward puts it. She attaches herself to the Wentworths, a declining aristocratic family, to establish her credentials as a house servant of the "Charleston quality." But Mamba understands that the Wentworths already have one servant and cannot afford to take care of her (and her daughter and granddaughter) in the manner to which she would like to become accustomed. Mamba explains her social ambitions to her astonished mistress: "'Ah gots tuh fin' uh white boss whut kin look attuh my chilen when dey meets dey trouble. Yo' an' Mauma [the rival house servant] here, yo' know Ah ain't a real house-raise' nigger, but dese w'ite folks what comin' tuh Chas'n now, dey ain't knows de different, and dey is want ole-time hous-raise' nigger what use' tuh b'long tuh de quality.'"

Mrs. Atkinson, the wealthy Yankee interloper who is on her own path to upward social mobility in Charleston, is the ideal candidate for Mamba's ambitions, and the Wentworths cunningly steer her to the Atkinson mansion. Introducing herself to the ambitious Mrs. Atkinson, Mamba shrewdly recollects that her father was "raised" by a wealthy planter family on the Cooper River that, by odd coincidence, bore the name Atkinson. Mamba quickly manages to convince her prospective mistress that the South Carolina family is a distant, aristocratic branch on her husband's family tree. Mrs. Atkinson, of course, is delighted to discover this claim to South Carolina aristocracy and to hire Mamba, complete with letters of recommendation from the esteemed Wentworth family, who have kept silent about Mamba's scheme. Mamba, Mrs. Atkinson tells her reluctant husband, is a splendid example of "'that fine old-fashioned loyalty that one encounters all too seldom in these days.'"

When Mamba's daughter inevitably falls into trouble with the law, Mrs. Atkinson begs her stolid midwestern husband to do his duty on behalf of "their negro." "'The right sort of people here do look after their negroes,'" she instructs knowingly. "'You're as apt as not to find a Ravenel, Waring, or Pinckney doing the same thing.'" "'Everybody knows,'" Mrs. Atkinson goes on, "'that Mamba's people used to belong to the Atkinsons, and now since the South Carolina branch of the family has died out, you are in a way the head.'"

George Atkinson, the personification of the bourgeois values Charleston has held at bay so long, finds himself caught up in the strange rituals of paternalism devised by the peers of those fictitious ancestors Mamba has invented for him, traditions carried on by his new Charleston friends in the early twentieth century. "'Was it,'" he ponders, "'the key to the puzzling attitude of the men he knew who could be so callous to the mass [of blacks], yet who responded with exaggerated generosity to the need of a known individual?'" Atkinson stands up in court for Mamba's daughter, saves her from an otherwise harsh system of justice for blacks, and comes away from the experience momentarily touched by having transcended the abstract "race problem" to help very human individuals who depend on him. Heyward allows Atkinson to comment on the central feature of Charleston's racial paternalism when he observes, through another character, "that the Yankee was all for the negro race, and hated him as an individual, but that in the South, we love the individual negro, while we hate, or at least fear, him as a race."[22]

Color and Caste

Just as ties between whites and their black servants were rejoined after the war, so the lines of demarcation that gave Charleston's browns their special status within the three-caste social system were also reaffirmed following an interlude of disruption during Reconstruction. The mulatto population, for the most part, traced its roots back to the old free black community of shop-keepers, artisans, and skilled workers who carved out a moderately secure and even prosperous niche apart from the slaves and the whites. As early as 1790 this group had organized the Brown Fellowship Society, a mutual aid society that became the mulatto equivalent to the St. Cecilia Society. Most of the brown elite married within the group, and most were members of St. Phillip's or St. Michael's, the white upper-class Episcopal churches, or of their own St. Mark's Episcopal. They emulated, in every way possible within a biracial society, the standards of the white elite.[23]

The affinity between whites and browns was disrupted for a time after emancipation, when free blacks suddenly lost their special status. In the fall of 1865, conservative whites in the newly reconstituted state legislature passed the

Black Codes, a harsh set of restrictions that applied to former slaves and free blacks—and on blacks and browns—alike.[24] Charleston's formerly conservative colored elite, seeing the shift of power, allied themselves with the black rural peasantry and urban proletariat. Indeed, the Charleston browns became a dominant force in South Carolina's Reconstruction governments. But this alliance between blacks and browns was filled with inner tension on both the city and state levels. The mulattoes enjoyed greater advantages in occupational skills, property, education, and the legacy of higher social status awarded to free, light-skinned Negroes, advantages that were resented by former slaves. Blacks and mulattoes, one observer noted, "have among themselves social rank and aristocracy outrageously severe and strictly discriminating."[25]

Nonetheless, as Charleston mulattoes joined political forces with the black masses, they withdrew from some of their connections to the white upper class. They followed other blacks, for example, in forming separate churches. St. Mark's Episcopal Church, originally founded in 1849, rapidly gained members after the war when mulattoes left the predominantly white congregations at St. Phillip's and St. Michael's. The St. Mark's congregation hired white ministers and remained exclusively mulatto in its membership. The white Episcopal establishment was ambivalent about the separation of the races and refused to admit St. Mark's into the Episcopal diocese, despite continued appeals into the 1890s. At the same time, Charleston's colored elite refused to identify with their black brethren. When the black-dominated Reformed Episcopal church entered South Carolina to recruit new black congregations, St. Mark's refused to join and persisted in its appeals to the white church. As one observer explained in 1888, this congregation "is composed of the crème de la crème of the southern light colored aristocracy and are as firmly wedded to the forms of the 'Henglish' aristocratic worship as their white brethren."[26]

The remaining ties between whites and the brown elite often worked to the benefit of whites. A. Toomer Porter, a white Episcopal minister, returned from the war with nothing to call his own. At the market he ran into George Shrewsbury, "a colored butcher [who] belonged to that respectable class of free colored citizens . . . who had always commanded the respect and esteem of the white population." George had insisted that his children all "be baptized, married, and buried by an Episcopal minister," and Reverend Porter had accommodated him on several earlier occasions. George had "acquired some wealth" and offered Porter "a roll of money" to allow him to stay in Charleston and begin his work toward founding Porter Academy. (It was Porter, incidentally, who later served as minister to St. Mark's.)[27]

The divisions of status between blacks and browns, and the ties of paternalism and interdependence between upper-class whites and their servants, played important roles in the collapse of Radical Reconstruction in Charleston and South Carolina. Conservative white Democrats, led by General Wade Hampton, who had been born in Charleston and had strong ties to the low country, carefully cultivated black support in the 1876 campaign that ended Republican rule in the state. Conservatives in Charleston, following the same strategy, had even joined fusion tickets with Republicans—white and black— against the more radical element. Conservative Democrats promised to protect black rights, including the franchise, and assured blacks that their best friends were their former masters. At the same time, white employers were urged to escort their servants to the polls to be sure they voted Democratic and to fire any who refused to cooperate.[28]

Once conservative white rule was firmly reestablished in the late 1870s, Charleston whites resumed a peaceable coexistence with the black majority.[29] Under Conservative Democratic rule, Mayor William A. Courtenay promised, "the policy of the whites to the negroes . . . will be . . . more free from irritation and more harmonious in every relation." Though effectively banned from the city council and most offices in local government, blacks maintained a presence on the police, fire, and street departments and received at least minimal public services in health, education, and welfare.[30] Whereas elsewhere in South Carolina and the South lynchings were used to terrorize blacks, Charleston boasted of never having witnessed a lynching. When Benjamin Tillman mobilized upcountry whites by his appeals to Negrophobia and resentment of the low-country aristocracy, many Charlestonians outwardly claimed to stand by the traditions of white paternalism and defended black citizenship. In reality, though, Charleston's conservative whites played an important role in disfranchising blacks through new voting regulations instituted in 1882, and they later joined forces with the Tillmanites to pass the constitution of 1895, the final blow to black political power.[31]

If the rhetoric of the new paternalism, promising uplift and progress for all blacks, rang false, so did the old paternalists' claims of benevolent protection. Still, the aristocracy of Charleston and the low country did not identify with the same brand of upcountry racism that fueled Tillmanism. Theirs was the confident ideology of white supremacy within a hierarchy of race and class that assured them of permanent black subordination, whereas Tillman and, later, Cole Blease exploited the anxieties of poor farmers and mill workers who saw in blacks a threat to their status.

A Familiar Mixture

Perhaps the most striking evidence of Charleston's confidence in white supremacy was the appearance of casual mixing between the races in everyday life, a practice that surprised many visitors. This was due in part to the large number of blacks in Charleston; their share of the population stood at over 50 percent until after World War I. More important was what an observer referred to in 1880 as "the proximity and confusion, so to speak, of white and negro houses."[32] Often this proximity resulted when live-in servants or renters occupied former slave quarters in the backyards of townhouses owned by whites. The mix of housing, in turn, produced what in the nineteenth century was called a "promiscuous" racial jumble in the streets and public places of the city. Fast-growing interior cities like Atlanta and Nashville adopted streetcars, then electric trolleys, and built spacious new suburbs that transformed their cities into increasingly segmented residential zones defined by class as well as race. Charleston's elite whites, in contrast, held fast to their central-city mansions and preserved the historical architecture of their city, at the same time maintaining a pattern of residential mixing by race that had persisted since the early days of slavery.

John Radford's careful study of the social geography of race and class in Charleston shows that, despite all the traumas of wartime destruction, emancipation, Reconstruction, and white redemption, the pattern of racially mixed neighborhoods changed remarkably little between 1860 and 1880. If anything, blacks became less concentrated as many left their quarters in their former master's yards to take up residence in different parts of the city.[33]

Nor did this pattern of racial mixing change significantly in the years after 1880. At the ward level, Charleston's index of segregation between blacks and whites was a mere fourteen in 1910 (simply put, 14 percent of either whites or blacks would have had to change wards to achieve even representation in every ward). This figure held even after the advent of the trolley and the expansion of suburban development on the northern edge of the city. At the same time, the segregation index in Atlanta stood at thirty-four, in Nashville thirty-nine, and in Mobile forty-four. Among Charleston's twelve wards, the smallest share of the population claimed by blacks was a little over 30 percent, and this was in the second ward, the wealthy neighborhood south of Broad and east of Meeting. The highest share of blacks, 72 percent, was in ward twelve, to the north of the city on the Neck.[34] This index does not mean that all of Charleston's blacks typically lived next door to whites. A map showing the racial concentrations in the city in 1910 revealed numerous heavily black neighborhoods interspersed with predominantly white areas. There was no large, solid-black ghetto of the kind that came to typify northern industrial cities and their younger southern counterparts.[35]

After emancipation, Charleston's color line in some ways appeared more blurred than ever as many of the restrictions of the slave regime fell by the boards. Around 1885 T. McCants Stewart, remarking on the changes that had occurred since his boyhood in Charleston, was struck that "the irrepressible

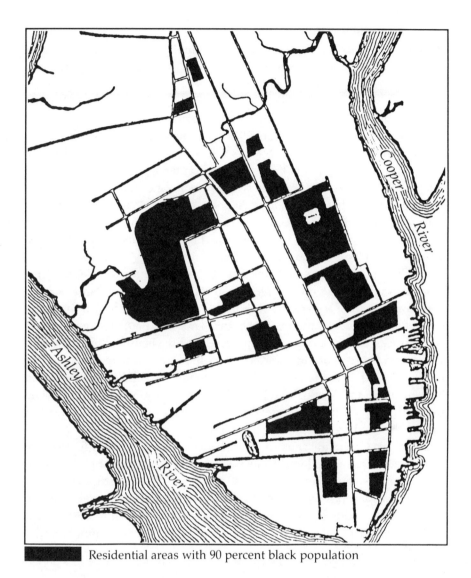

Residential areas with 90 percent black population

Charleston's black residential patterns, 1910. (Reproduced from T. J. Woofter, Jr., *Negro Problems in Cities* [New York, 1928])

Negro appears everywhere!" The benches of the once forbidden courthouse square were "full of colored people" and everywhere one could see "the laborers, white and colored, returning from their work side by side on the same street cars."[36] By custom, blacks, at least before the turn of the century, were allowed to attend public gatherings with whites. The Charleston Academy of Music and most Charleston theaters had no policy that discriminated against blacks. The main hotels, on the other hand, were all strictly for whites only. As the *Charleston News and Courier* explained, admitting blacks to hotels "would interfere with the accommodation and comfort of the white people—especially of the visitors from the North and West."[37]

In 1897, when South Carolina and Georgia were debating legislation that would require railroad segregation, the editor of the *News and Courier* spoke for many Charlestonians when he urged "leaving matters as they stand. . . . We have got on in this State for thirty years without a Jim Crow car, and have not missed it. . . . In every city of the State we ride in the small street cars with our colored fellow citizens and nobody is the worse for it so far as we know." He went on to imply that separation of the social classes was the more important issue: "To speak plainly we need . . . separate cars or apartments for rowdy or drunken white passengers far more than Jim Crow cars for colored passengers."[38] Within the following year Jim Crow was imposed on South Carolina railroads nonetheless, and the city of Charleston finally adopted legal separation of the races on its streetcars in 1912.[39] At the same time, a more pervasive pattern of segregation took form in Charleston, largely through the force of newly minted "customs" rather than laws. The Battery became forbidden to blacks, except during the annual revelry on the Fourth of July, when the segregation was temporarily reversed. Other public places were designated off limits to blacks as the reign of Jim Crow became established in Charleston between 1898 and World War I.[40] It was the "new Charleston," following standards set in the more "progressive" centers of the South, that accepted Jim Crow as the modern model of race relations.

Before Jim Crow's full entry into Charleston, a visiting reporter for the *New York Times* was astonished in 1893 by the ubiquitous presence of blacks in the city. "There does not seem to be any distinctly negro quarter in the city proper. They are everywhere." Though blacks were rarely found in white-collar jobs, he noted, "almost every avenue of employment is not only open to them, but if they were not there the work would not be done." The reporter summarized:

> The negro has a place in the social structure of Charleston difficult for a Northern man to understand. It is certain that there is no aversion to him as is often seen in the North. It is not that the necessities of the situation bring about a forced toleration. His presence is not an irritation. He gets his half the sidewalk as readily as the white man. . . . Each keeps pretty close to the path custom has assigned to him. . . . The negro in Charleston has his place as the white man has his. . . . [G]ood feeling exists on both sides when this distance is observed.[41]

Here was the key to race relations in Charleston as they existed in the late nineteenth century. The races could be close physically because they were so far

apart socially. Daily proximity, even familiarity, were tolerable—and necessary given the dependence on black labor—because the social distance was so
vast and fixed.

When that social barrier was breached, however, the relaxed attitude of
whites quickly gave way to violent reaction. When President Benjamin Harrison appointed the mulatto William D. Crum as Charleston's postmaster as
part of an effort to revive the Republican party in 1892, whites sent up a howl
of protest. Crum was a physician, well educated and a prominent Republican
spokesman. Nevertheless business leaders, acting simultaneously through the
Chamber of Commerce, the Cotton Exchange, and the Merchants' Exchange,
sent telegrams to the White House protesting this breach of the color line.
White Republicans, led by Episcopal minister R. W. Memminger, son of the
Confederate Treasurer, also brought pressure to bear on Harrison and finally
forced the withdrawal of Crum's nomination. The objections were neither
entirely partisan nor personal. It was the prospect of placing a man of color in
the position of supervising white postal employees that horrified Crum's
enemies.[42] In 1902 President Theodore Roosevelt tried to appoint Crum as
collector of customs at Charleston, and again white business leaders led an all-
out attack, even enlisting Charleston's old adversary, Senator Benjamin
Tillman, as leader of the opposition in Washington. Roosevelt forced Crum on
Charleston in the end, and Crum continued to serve at the customhouse until
1909, when President William Howard Taft and Booker T. Washington
persuaded him to step down in favor of a diplomatic post in Liberia. During
Crum's reign in office, the customhouse, long a reminder of federal authority
in Charleston, again became a symbol of the inversion of white supremacy by
distant powers.

Lady Baltimore, Owen Wister's romantic and insightful novel of Charleston,
published in 1906, places its proud hero, John Mayrant, in the humiliating
position of working in the customhouse under the supervision of a mulatto
collector. "John Mayrant and his kind were a band united by a number of
strong ties," Wister's narrator, a sympathetic northern visitor, observes, "but
by nothing so much as by their hatred of the modern negro in their town." But
Mayrant's fury at the "new Negro," who, in his eyes, had been placed in a
position of artificial superiority over him in the workplace, does nothing to
compromise his gracious paternalism toward the older black servants who
keep to their familiar place. Upon seeing Mayrant greet one of these representatives of the old tradition of subservience, the northern observer is fascinated
by "that particular and affectionate superiority which few Northerners can
understand and none can acquire, and which resembles nothing so much as
the way in which you speak to your old dog who has loved you and followed
you, because you have cared for him."[43] The alternating animosity and tender-

ness toward blacks were two sides of the same paternalistic coin. The white Charlestonian who accepted the obligation to care for a dependent race felt betrayed—and worse, threatened—when that race's dependent status was challenged.

Pessimistic Prognoses

More telling than the outbursts against rare violations of the color line were the pessimistic views of Charleston's white opinion leaders on the nature of blacks and their place in the future of the city and region. Many whites had seen slavery as a paternalistic shield that protected and educated a dependent race, and in the same way the freedman came to be seen as a menace to civilization and an unwanted burden.[44] The debate on the "race problem" among whites in Charleston dwelled on the most discouraging evidence of black degeneracy under freedom. In contrast to the more buoyant, though often naive, rhetoric of black uplift and regional progress that emanated from Atlanta and Nashville, Charleston's newspaper editors and intellectuals rarely gave hope for a substantial change in the capacity of blacks to become useful, productive citizens of a progressive region. Such pessimism was the racial counterpart to their despondent reaction to the New South and its promise of economic progress.

The *Charleston News and Courier,* whose editors, Francis W. Dawson and John C. Hemphill, were earnest advocates of southern industrial development and boosters of Charleston enterprise in particular, voiced an increasingly negative view of the place of blacks in the future of the city and region. Dawson, an Englishman who had arrived in the South in 1861, advanced the conservative platform of the former slaveholders and gave voice to the paternalism embraced by the followers of Wade Hampton. Assuring his readers that social equality between the races was impossible, as well as undesirable, Dawson nonetheless advocated protection of the minimal rights of black citizenship, so long as blacks remained under the control of white masters. Otherwise, he wrote, "the colored people . . . will be blind instruments for good or evil." Dawson acknowledged that blacks had some limited capacity for progress, but he saw their basic inferiority as an immutable fact. When a back-to-Africa movement began among South Carolina blacks in 1878, Dawson's *News and Courier* reported the planned passage to Liberia with sympathy and welcomed it as the first step in what might become a grand exodus.[45]

Carlyle McKinley, a reporter for the *News and Courier,* elaborated the more pessimistic view of black destiny in the South in his 1889 book, *An Appeal to Pharaoh: The Negro Problem and Its Radical Solution.* "Is it not a bare, hard fact, then, that the Negro in America has made very little progress, since his emancipation?," he asked. Reviewing evidence, from Charleston and else-where, of persistent poverty and deteriorating health among blacks, McKinley blamed both the inherent limitations of the race and the determination of whites to shun blacks and circumscribe their place in society. "Wherever he goes or stays, works or worships, plays or suffers, lives or dies, the lines are drawn sharply around and about him." Without the bonds between master and slave, the freeborn generation of blacks was growing farther apart from, not closer to, whites. "There is peace between them so long as the Negro 'knows his place' and keeps his place, and no longer." Yet blacks were multiply-ing rapidly and migrating to every corner of the nation, presenting a perma-nently alien presence within a white man's country.

The "radical solution" McKinley recommended was nothing less than deportation back to Africa of *all* blacks, and mulattoes, too, if they wished. Attacking the standard response that such a move was impractical, McKinley calculated the costs of a long-range plan that would require federal subsidies to cover transportation and resettlement in Africa. It would be a gradual program aimed first at women in their childbearing years, particularly pregnant women, in order to drastically cut the black birthrate. By the year 2000, McKinley confidently predicted, there would be "not a single black man, woman or child on these shores." Deportation may have sounded harsh, he explained, but the race problem, "is a case for the knife of the surgeon, not for philanthropical pills or political plasters."[46]

Others, less radical, urged expansion of the paternalist tradition and called for modest programs of black uplift and protection. Isaac DuBose Seabrook offered a more hopeful view in his treatise *Before and After, or the Relations of the Races at the South*. Seabrook, the descendant of an eminent aristocratic family, had been reduced to working as a desk clerk at the Mills House Hotel, an occupation that gave him idle hours to work on his manuscript. Written in 1895, when Tillmanism was at full tide, his book provides quiet evidence of the persistence of Hamptonian paternalism in Charleston, a counterforce to the main current of the times. Seabrook at once acknowledged black rights to citizenship and their lack of the requisite "qualities of the citizen." "If this is the disease, its removal consists in the Negroes' acquiring these qualities of the citizen." Alluding to McKinley, he added, "[T]his is the only solution which will be radical enough to merit the name of a solution at all." He went on to advocate raising the black population "to the plane of white life," a feat that would require close contact between the races and the elimination of any discriminatory obstacles to black improvement. Though it shared aspects of the new paternalism emanating from Atlanta and Nashville, Seabrook's agenda was motivated less by hopes for regional economic progress than by fears of social degradation. But his plea for an aggressive program of paternalistic uplift went unpublished, and regardless of the extent to which it represented the opinion of Charleston's old upper class, Seabrook's outlook was being eclipsed by more negative views of black destiny.[47]

With the death of Francis W. Dawson in 1889, the racial views of the *News and Courier* became hardened, perhaps under the influence of Carlyle McKinley. The editorial stance moved away from the Hampton tradition of conservative paternalism and toward a more virulent brand of racism more in tune with the Negrophobia of Tillman and the upcountry yeomanry. The new editor, John C. Hemphill, an upcountry native, came out strongly for colonization plans then being discussed in the U.S. Senate. "What shall we do with the negro?," an 1889 editorial asked. "If he remains here he will ruin himself and the South. . . . The only hope for the South is the dispersion or distribution of the excess of our colored population." "The race question in this country," another editorial concluded, "can only be settled permanently, with regard to the best interest of *both* races, by the gradual but complete and final separation of the races." Segregation of public facilities (which the *News and Courier* opposed as unnecessary in the 1890s) was not what was meant by this reference, for separation had more radical implications. "Send them back to Africa," another editorial urged.[48]

An editorial in 1892 blamed blacks for the poverty and industrial backwardness of the South. "The negro race is simply a parasite on the body politic and body economic in the South." Admitting that blacks could not forcibly be deported, the editor nonetheless suggested that "if they remain in the South," the alternatives were grim. Either whites would have to surrender the South to them, or the federal government would have to launch a second reconstruction program. Excluding these unlikely scenarios, "the negroes must occupy practically their present position and relations permanently." In 1899 the *News and Courier* was still advocating a "thinning out" of the black population by removal to Africa and touting McKinley's book as the blueprint for the "radical solution."[49]

When local industrialists launched the experimental use of black labor during the 1890s, the *News and Courier* took a more hopeful view, if only because of its zealous commitment to any enterprise that seemed to offer relief for Charleston's beleaguered economy. Though the newspaper had earlier denounced an experiment utilizing black labor in mills outside Charleston, it applauded when the Charleston Knitting Mills replaced its white female work force with black girls in 1896. The Charleston Cotton Mill and the Charleston Shoe Factory followed suit within a year. Though dubious about the ability of blacks to perform industrial labor, the *News and Courier* gave cautious encouragement to "an important, maybe a dangerous, experiment" as a "pioneer" effort to make good use of the city's surplus of black labor. Blacks, the paper said, must find work or become a "menace" as a pauper class. The black citizen "will remain ignorant, vicious, idle, until we assist him to work."[50] "Should Charleston discover that she can set a million spindles to humming in her midst by putting her colored population to work she will not only rid herself of an incubus, which has handicapped her hopelessly in the race for prosperity, but she will have blazed a way which her sister cities will not be slow to follow."[51]

But these experiments awakened hostile opposition from displaced white workers, who at one point threatened race warfare against the blacks who took their jobs. White managers also spoke discouragingly of the difficulties of training a raw, young work force, which they blamed on inherent racial incapacities. In 1899 the Charleston Cotton Mill, the largest area business experimenting with black labor, had to sell out to upcountry entrepreneurs, Seth Milliken and John Montgomery. Montgomery bought new machinery, reorganized the firm as the Vesta Cotton Mill, and recruited another black work force, this time with the help of Charleston clergy, who handpicked those people whom they thought would be the most reliable workers. But the next year the mill folded again, and the whole experiment in black industrial labor ended a failure. George Walton Williams, a major investor in the venture, criticized the black workers for shunning "the opportunity of their lives" in favor of skipping work to harvest oysters and, later, strawberries as each season beckoned. Williams acknowledged the good effort of Charleston's black clergy, "but they could not make efficiency where it wasn't." Black leaders pointed out that the wages paid to black mill workers were so low that they could make twice as much harvesting.[52] The failure of the Vesta mill seemed, to white Charlestonians, to end whatever slim hopes they had cherished for any substantial improvement in the condition of blacks and encouraged pessimists in their view of blacks as a detriment to the city's progress.

The Exposition

Pessimistic brooding over the "Negro question" in Charleston was the sour expression of paternalists who saw little hope for blacks outside of the discipline of slavery or something close to slavery. When Charleston's more progressive young business leaders began their ascent around 1900, the New South's program for black progress was articulated, alongside its hopes for economic progress, with all the conviction voiced in other cities. By the time Charleston staged the South Carolina Interstate and West Indian Exposition in 1901–2, the concept of a Negro exhibition had become an obligatory feature of such affairs, with similar expositions in Atlanta and Nashville setting the standard. The Negro exhibit offered an opportunity not only to display blacks' capacity for industrial labor, but also to give voice to the new paternalism as an expression of benevolent interest, on the part of white business leaders, in the progress of the black race. The exposition's board of directors funded the Negro Department in November 1900. They appointed Booker T. Washington as the official chief of the department, but local blacks, particularly William D. Crum, the assistant chief, were mainly responsible for organizing the Negro Department's exhibit. The Negro Building was filled with exhibits designed "to show the achievements of thirty-five years in morals, education and industrial activities."[53]

Standing in front of the Negro Building, the "Negro Group," one of several statuaries commissioned for the exposition, was meant to honor the exhibit. It was presented as a magnanimous gesture by the board of directors, who conceived of this statue as a tribute to the role played by blacks in the South's progress. But this sculpture immediately became the center of a furious controversy among black Charlestonians, a reaction that stunned their would-be benefactors. The Negro Group, designed by a white New York artist, depicted a black woman carrying on her head a basket filled with cotton and carrying a water pitcher in her hand. To one side and below her, looking up, was a shirtless black man with one hand on an anvil and another on a plow (his face was a likeness of Booker T. Washington). On the woman's other side was a young black male sitting on a cotton bale and happily strumming a banjo. Charleston blacks roundly protested what, in their eyes, was a degrading image of menial black labor, and some threatened to destroy the statue if it was not removed. The banjo player, one outraged black complained, looked like a "blank idiot." Others insisted that the white exposition directors put up a second group statue depicting Booker T. Washington and others, "showing the contrast between this ignorant vicious type and the intelligent cultural type." Failing in these efforts, a large mass meeting of blacks drew up a formal request that the offending statue at least be removed from in front of the Negro Building. The white exposition officers, astonished at the temerity of "the so-called 'new' negroes of Charleston," quickly obliged and deliberately moved it to "one of the most prominent sites" on the grounds.[54]

The incident set the tone for an exposition that, though intended to display a new appreciation for blacks in Charleston's future, became yet another discouraging testament to the alienation between the races. Local blacks, in effect, boycotted the exposition, and whites were miffed at what they considered an ungrateful response to their efforts. The board of directors, complained John C. Hemphill in his official report on the exposition, "manifested a far livelier interest in the success of the Negro Department than the negroes themselves displayed." Nonetheless, he concluded, "the practical results from the Negro Department were distinctly disappointing."[55]

The deferred, muted impact of the New South on Charleston allowed old manners and attitudes to wane slowly, even as Jim Crow brought the new modes of segregation to the city. In the face of black migration to the North, growing competition from industry and the military for black labor, and the upheaval that World War I brought to the black population, the advent of the "new Negro" was unavoidable. DuBose Heyward, whose novels *Mamba's Daughters* and *Porgy* recounted the transition with mixed nostalgia and respect, shared the ambivalence of many in his class toward the modern world of race relations that was now invading Charleston. Within a nation based on the "fallacious theory" of equality, Heyward argued, Charleston and the South had maintained a social order built upon the "cleavage between the ruling and servant classes." This was, in his view, a society bound by "pride of caste among the lowly" and "an obligation to respect the dignity of each other," a "bond which has held the two classes together in affection and mutual understanding through the vicissitudes of two and a half centuries."[56]

For Heyward and others in the old upper class, the most poignant expression of concern over the disintegration of these social relationships came after World War I with the founding of the Society for the Preservation of Negro Spirituals. Beginning about 1923, a small group of white Charlestonians began to gather informally to sing old Negro spirituals, which they later performed in public at a St. Phillip's Church fair. Like the Society for the Preservation of Old Dwellings, which saw its mission as the restoration of the architectural heritage of a museumlike city, the Society for the Preservation of Negro Spirituals saw as its task the preservation of a culture that was fast disappearing. That this mission was taken on by the white elite was, Heyward insisted, "not a gesture of patronizing superiority, but a natural and harmonious collaboration wrought in affection and with a deep sense of reverence." Elsewhere, the Negro "will be taken from our fields, fired with ambition, and fed to the machines of our glittering new civilization." But in the low country, according to Heyward, "where isolation and time have retarded the process," the premodern Negro survived, and with him an older tradition of relations between the races.[57] Ultimately, though, Charleston's white elite failed to preserve this aspect of their past with the same success they enjoyed in other realms of historic preservation.

As Charleston's older traditions of paternalism slowly gave way to the new order, the more modern vision of race relations articulated in Nashville and Atlanta, conversely, was compromised by deeply embedded assumptions. Coming as they did from different roots, the attitudes and policies that shaped race relations in the four cities studied here all represented variations on a theme of white supremacy. In each setting, the agendas that business leaders advocated for black uplift, racial harmony, and biracial economic progress represented both the most ambitious hopes and the most conspicuous failures of the New South. The squalid urban slums, poor health, impoverished schools, and especially the system of formal segregation and deprivation that came out of this era were among the most discouraging contradictions to the New South's claims of progress.

Epilogue

The new order of race relations that was incubated in the cities was one of the more peculiar legacies of the New South era. The inability to live up to its aims of black uplift, which it had proclaimed as an essential prerequisite to regional progress, was perhaps the most obvious weakness of the New South movement. Among its other bequests were a mixture of remarkable accomplishments and undeniable disappointments, all with lasting influence in the modern South.

Not least among the achievements of the New South was the creation of a vast network of towns and cities that had been integrated into a regional and national economy by rail, steamship, and telegraph. The number of southern towns and cities exploded between 1880 and 1910, particularly at the lower end of the urban hierarchy, providing a firm foundation upon which a regional urban system could build. With the proliferation of new towns, the South's population began a sustained shift from country to city that multiplied the urban share of the population almost three times in a half century, from less than 7 percent in 1860 to nearly 20 percent by 1910 and then climbing steadily to 68 percent by 1980 (see table 1.1). More than any agricultural reform programs from the New South era through the New Deal and more recent times, urbanization rescued a large number of country folk from the chronic misery of rural life in the South. Migration to the city was no guarantee of a better life, but the lure was sufficient to form the dissatisfied and the ambitious into a relentless stream of migrants from country to city. It was mostly urbanites living in the comforts of Nashville and other cities who waxed romantic about the agrarian world the South had lost.

As the towns pulled more people in from the country, an expanding urban commercial network simultaneously invaded the hinterland and drew the remaining rural inhabitants into a market economy in unprecedented ways.

The drummer, with his suitcase full of samples, carried the economy of the regional metropolis to the most remote crossroads merchant and his customers. Long before the South became an urban society, the city's commercial arteries had permeated the countryside.

Within the elaborate urban network that spread across the region, the growth and physical transformation of individual cities was no less impressive. In 1860 even the larger urban centers of the South were little more than simple depots through which cotton and other staple crops passed from the country to external markets. A slim consumer demand, emanating largely from the plantations, was fed by importing finished products through the region's sea and river ports.

That simple urban economy was rapidly transformed into an elaborate economic and physical complex during the late nineteenth century. The new cities boasted a concentrated downtown district that housed banks, insurance companies, retail shops, and department stores. Adjacent warehouse districts and industrial corridors filled out the contours of the modern urban form. From the downtown offices and stores, the new trolley cars glided smoothly out along grand boulevards that were lined with opulent mansions built by the merchant princes and industrialists of the New South. Later, planned suburban parks provided more exclusive refuges for the rich within metropolises that were increasingly segmented by class and race.

The physical achievement of building the modern city was more obvious, but hardly more important, than the social construction of a new urban business class within the cities. Although the new business elite may have had counterparts among the merchants and manufacturers of the Old South's cities, the antebellum business community had neither the size nor the influence to be recognized as a major force in determining the South's historical course before the war. What emerged beginning in the 1880s was a distinct southern urban business class whose upper strata rapidly formed a coherent social class. Its identity was defined not simply in economic terms by occupation, wealth, and interest, but also by the social marks of a shared way of life, a common view of the world, and a thick network of exclusive associations. Business associations like chambers of commerce and other booster organizations were instrumental in advancing the businessmen's shared interest in promoting urban growth and economic development. A multitude of other downtown lunch clubs, elite societies, suburban country clubs, and cultural institutions also gave form to the world within which the upper class identified itself and forged a set of bonds with institutional continuity. It was in this social realm that women played a crucial role in defining the boundaries and membership of the New South's urban upper class.

The New South's business leaders, with assistance from their allies in the press, the pulpit, and political forums, also created an ideological framework that enabled them to join their agenda for economic development to broad social reforms and to present their interests as those of the South at large. The New South creed provided a singularly powerful set of historical myths and forward-looking goals around which a broad group of business and industrial interests, along with a diverse array of other southerners, coalesced in the years following the war and Reconstruction.[1] According to this creed, it was time for southerners to accept the verdict of the battlefield and reconcile the South to its place in the nation. They could eulogize the Lost Cause as a heroic, but mistaken, event of the past. The maudlin celebrations of the Lost Cause and the pathetic monuments to Confederate dead, which seemed to deny defeat, were frequently sponsored by the proponents of the New South and were put on full display at the New South industrial expositions. This has been read by some historians as a measure of weakness in the southern bourgeoisie, a sign of its divided mind and its false identity with the old regime and the planter class that ruled it.[2] But the alternative strategy of repudiating the war and the old regime might have been more debilitating to the New South movement. The Lost Cause mythology was not simply a reactionary defense of the planter class and slavery. The war had been fought, at great sacrifice, by all classes of southerners, and it would have been self-defeating for New South advocates to launch an outright renunciation of the cause or to admit the moral superiority of the North's motives. Instead, tributes to Confederate heroism were often accompanied by subtle but deliberate disavowals of the basic principles of slavery and secession that had motivated the Confederates, and, most important, by the compelling admission that the cause was *lost*.[3]

More significant than the New South proponents' apologies for the war were their interpretations of its historical meaning. They accepted the defeat of the Old South as a blessing in disguise; it meant the emancipation of the New South, now free to fulfill its destiny unburdened by slavery. The New South creed offered for the region's future a program of economic development that would emulate the North in the pursuit of industry, urban growth, and scientific, diversified, market-oriented agriculture. Without mounting a frontal assault on the plantation regime, the advocates of the New South projected a vision of towns, factories, railroads, and mixed crops that would supersede the old order of the single-crop plantation. The New South vision was advanced as reform, not as revolution.

From the outset, the champions of the New South linked their agenda for economic development to programs for social reform that were similar in rhetoric and intent to those promoted by the middle class in the North. The New South creed advocated public and private investments in human capital, particularly in the realm of education, to upgrade the work force and prepare the region for economic progress. Joining the promoters of these practical concerns for economic progress and social efficiency were humanitarian reformers, who sought to ameliorate the harsher features of urban and industrial life for the poor while subjecting them to new forms of order and control. Women, religious leaders, and philanthropists—many of the latter from outside the region—usually took the lead in this area, but these reforms also enlisted the support of the New South's wealthy businessmen. During the progressive era, elements within the South's "new middle class" emulated the national movement aimed at bringing order, efficiency, and humanitarian relief to the world they had been so instrumental in constructing.[4]

A central feature of the program for social reform was its aims for black uplift. New South propagandists accepted racist assumptions about the limited capacity of blacks and their inferior destiny in the South, but they also espoused an ideology of regional development through white benevolence toward a deprived race. Despite lip service by reformers, though, public policy affecting the health, education, and welfare of blacks in the cities at best only partially lived up to the principles of the "new paternalism." Racism, like the Lost Cause, was a historical burden the New South failed—or refused—to repudiate. The deep racial animosity of the white South made it risky to implement even modest programs for black uplift. The political machinations that stripped blacks of power by the 1890s made it all the easier for whites to channel limited resources toward the favored race.

Despite compromises on the race question and the Lost Cause, the New South's ascendant business leaders were confident of their vision and certain that their program for the region would benefit all levels of the urban community and all elements of the South. But their agenda for economic development and social reform was not embraced by all southerners, and their claims to speak for the whole South were challenged with fury in the 1890s. The strongest protests against the New South came, not from the beleaguered planter class, but from farmers who joined the Populist revolt to express their hostility toward the new order.

As the urban nodes of transportation, commerce, finance, and manufacturing extended their reach into the hinterland, the rural response was initially compliant but later violently hostile. Farmers large and small calculated the risks of the market and entered it willingly to exchange cash crops for profits and the consumer goods that were its rewards. Others saw their main chance in the city and abandoned their farms, following the wagon roads and rail lines into the towns and into other, more novel forms of market relations in the urban world.

During the farmers' revolt that erupted in the late 1880s and 1890s, farmers, white and black, struck back at the market forces that had seduced them. They vilified the city and all it stood for; in their view, it was the city, with its banks, its speculators, its impersonal markets, its railroads, and its local agents in the country towns, that was responsible for corrupting the virtuous tillers of the soil. Beneath their rhetoric of invective was a frank challenge to the New South's "Gospel of Progress" and to the urban business class—North and South—that had proclaimed it.[5]

On another front, the industrialization of the New South brought sharp reactions after 1880. Mill workers in the Piedmont expressed resentment toward the plans of the town-dwelling middle class to transform fiercely independent rural migrants into a well-ordered force of workers under the tutelage of reformers. Efforts at child labor reform and compulsory education, both primary articles of faith among progressive-era reformers, met with a hostile reaction from workers, who defended the sovereignty of their families and integrity of their way of life against the claims of social uplift by their would-be benefactors.[6]

These challenges from farmers and mill workers were ultimately futile gestures against forces they could protest but not derail. The planters, for their part, continued to dominate within the plantation regions by virtue of their control of the land, but they mounted no effective political or ideological challenge of any significance to the new order of cities and factories that the urban business class busily constructed after the war. Planters' efforts to thwart the incursion of the market economy, with its accompanying competition for labor and merchants bidding against landlord, were at best only partially successful. Whatever hopes the planters may have entertained of controlling or limiting urban and industrial development, they posed no obstacle to the multitude of towns and factories that flourished in the New South. Indeed, the urban press never seemed concerned with the planters as opponents of the new order. They were treated as remnants of the past; the future of the South belonged to the cities.[7]

It is true that rural interests (not necessarily controlled by planters) continued to dominate the state governments of the South, and they often used their powers to check the influence of the urban South and its business class. Rural-dominated legislatures resisted reapportionment until the 1960s, when the U.S. Supreme Court required it. In many other ways, the rural South continued to slow the emergence of the modern South, but its power was gradually undermined by relentless migration to the cities and by the growing leverage of industrial and commercial interests.[8]

The New South's achievements in regional economic development and social reform were undeniable, but so were its shortcomings. Most notable was the chronic poverty of the region, unrelieved by the advent of cities and industry. The ostentatious mansions and opulent suburbs of the urban parvenus must be viewed in perspective beside squalid urban slums, austere mill workers' villages, and wretched sharecropper shacks before the New South's claims are evaluated. The region's late start behind a rapidly developing nation explained much of the persistent lag in southern development, as did the legacy of the plantation system and the isolation and immobility of southern labor. The persistence of racism, which deprived one-third of the population of political power, education, and economic resources, also continued to act as a drag on the South. The New South movement failed to undermine completely the foundations of the old regime, and it failed to fulfill its own promise of a new order across the region. But it was successful enough in both aims to open the road to the modern South.

Notes

Abbreviations

ADAH   Alabama Department of Archives and History, Montgomery, Ala.

AHS   Atlanta Historical Society, Atlanta, Ga.

BL   Baker Library, Harvard School of Business, Cambridge, Mass.

CLS   Charleston Library Society, Charleston, S.C.

GDAH   Georgia Department of Archives and History, Atlanta, Ga.

MCM   Museum of the City of Mobile, Mobile, Ala.

MPL   Mobile Public Library, Mobile, Ala.

SCA   South Carolina Archives, Columbia, S.C.

SCHS   South Carolina Historical Society, Charleston, S.C.

SCL   South Caroliniana Library, University of South Carolina, Columbia, S.C.

SHC   Southern Historical Collection, University of North Carolina, Chapel Hill, N.C.

TSLA   Tennessee State Library and Archives, Nashville, Tenn.

Preface

1. *Atlanta Constitution,* Aug. 15, 1880; *Richmond Whig and Advertiser,* Apr. 4, 1876; Mark Twain, *Life on the Mississippi* (Boston, 1883), 412; the latter two sources are quoted in C. Vann Woodward, *Origins of the New South, 1877–1913* (Baton Rouge, La., 1951), 151–52.

2. Woodward, *Origins,* 150–51, 179, 140–41.

3. C. Vann Woodward, *Thinking Back: The Perils of Writing History* (Baton Rouge, La., 1986), 62–63; Wilbur J. Cash, *The Mind of the South* (New York, 1941). For early interpretations of southern continuity, see also Broadus Mitchell and George S. Mitchell, *The Industrial Revolution in the South* (Baltimore, Md., 1930); U. B. Phillips, "The Central Theme of Southern History," *American Historical Review* 34 (Oct. 1928): 30–43.

4. See, for example, Henry Woodfin Grady, *The New South,* edited by Oliver Dyer (New York, 1890); Phillip Alexander Bruce, *The Rise of the New South* (Philadelphia, 1905); Holland Thompson, *The New South* (New Haven, Conn., 1919). See also Paul M. Gaston, *The New South Creed: A Study in Southern Mythmaking* (Baton Rouge, La., 1970), for an overview of New South thought and rhetoric.

5. The most explicit interpretations of the planters as opponents of bourgeois values, free labor,

and economic development are found in Barrington Moore, Jr., *Social Origins of Dictatorship and Democracy: Lord and Peasant in the Making of the Modern World* (Boston, 1966); Jonathan M. Wiener, "Class Structure and Economic Development in the American South, 1865–1955," *American Historical Review* 84 (Oct. 1979): 970–1006; idem, *Social Origins of the New South: Alabama, 1860–1880* (Baton Rouge, La., 1978); and Jay R. Mandle, *The Roots of Black Poverty: The Southern Plantation Economy after the Civil War* (Durham, N.C., 1978). Dwight B. Billings, Jr., in *Planters and the Making of a "New South": Class, Politics, and Development in North Carolina, 1865–1900* (Chapel Hill, N.C., 1979), argues that the planter class directed North Carolina's industrial revolution. Randolph B. Campbell, in *A Southern Community in Crisis: Harrison County, Texas, 1850–1880* (Austin, Tex., 1983), also makes the case for the continuity of a landholding elite. Crandall Shifflett looks at continuity and change outside the cotton South in *Patronage and Poverty in the Tobacco South: Louisa County, Virginia, 1860–1900* (Knoxville, Tenn., 1982). Michael Wayne, in *The Reshaping of Plantation Society: The Natchez District, 1860–1880* (Baton Rouge, La., 1983), accepts the idea of continuity among the large planters but shows that there were dramatic changes as landlords and tenants adjusted to a new market economy. For a good summary of this debate, see Dan T. Carter, "From the Old South to the New: Another Look at the Theme of Change and Continuity," in *From the Old South to the New: Essays in the Transitional South,* edited by Walter J. Fraser, Jr., and Winfred B. Moore, Jr. (Westport, Conn., 1981), 23–32.

6. Harold D. Woodman, "Sequel to Slavery: The New History Views the Postbellum South," *Journal of Southern History* 43 (Nov. 1977): 523–44.

7. Howard N. Rabinowitz provides a useful overview in "Continuity and Change: Southern Urban Development, 1860–1900," in *The City in Southern History: The Growth of Urban Civilization in the South,* edited by Blaine A. Brownell and David R. Goldfield (Port Washington, N.Y., 1977), 92–122. See also Rabinowitz, *Race Relations in the Urban South, 1865–1890* (New York, 1978); David R. Goldfield, *Cotton Fields and Skyscrapers: Southern City and Region, 1607–1980* (Baton Rouge, La., 1982), 80–138; Lawrence H. Larsen, *The Rise of the Urban South* (Lexington, Ky., 1985). Studies of individual cities include Michael B. Chesson, *Richmond after the War, 1865–1890* (Richmond, Va., 1980); James M. Russell, *Atlanta, 1847–1890: City Building in the Old South and the New* (Baton Rouge, La., 1988); Howard L. Platt, *City Building in the New South: The Growth of Public Services in Houston, Texas, 1830–1910* (Philadelphia, 1983). See also David L. Carlton, *Mill and Town in South Carolina, 1880–1920* (Baton Rouge, La., 1982); Gail Williams O'Brien, *The Legal Fraternity and the Making of a New South Community, 1848–1882* (Athens, Ga., 1986); Paul D. Escott, *Many Excellent People: Power and Privilege in North Carolina, 1850–1900* (Chapel Hill, N.C., 1985).

8. My use of this concept follows Robert S. Lynd and Helen M. Lynd, *Middletown: A Study in Contemporary American Culture* (New York, 1929), and Michael Katz et al., *The Social Organization of Early Industrial Capitalism* (New York, 1982). See also Stuart M. Blumin, "The Hypothesis of Middle-Class Formation in Nineteenth-Century America: A Critique and Some Proposals," *American Historical Review* 90 (Apr. 1985): 299–338.

9. E. Digby Baltzell, *Philadelphia Gentlemen: The Making of a National Upper Class* (1958; reprint, Chicago, 1971), 6–7.

Chapter 1

1. Daniel R. Hundley, *Social Relations in Our Southern States* (New York, 1860), 26.

2. U.S. Census Bureau, *1980 Census of Population,* vol. 1, *Characteristics of the Population,* chap. A, *Number of Inhabitants,* pt. 1, *United States Summary* (Washington, D.C., 1983), table 5.

3. Hinton Rowan Helper and J. D. B. De Bow were among the most outspoken southern

advocates of urbanization. On antebellum urban development, see David R. Goldfield, *Cotton Fields and Skyscrapers: Southern City and Region, 1607–1980* (Baton Rouge, La., 1982), chaps. 1, 2; Carville Earle and Ronald Hoffman, "The Urban South: The First Two Centuries," in *The City in Southern History: The Growth of Urban Civilization in the South,* edited by Blaine A. Brownell and David R. Goldfield (Port Washington, N.Y., 1977), 23–51; Goldfield, "Pursuing the American Dream: Urban Growth in the Old South," in ibid., 52–91.

4. Julius Rubin, "Urban Growth and Regional Development," in *The Growth of the Seaport Cities, 1790–1825,* edited by David T. Gilchrist (Charlottesville, Va., 1967), 6, 14–15. Rubin describes early America outside the plantation regions as being "90 per cent agricultural in an occupational sense . . . 90 per cent urban in a cultural sense," meaning that farmers were oriented toward urban markets.

5. Except in a few instances noted below, all references to the South are to the eleven Confederate states: Virginia, North Carolina, South Carolina, Georgia, Florida, Alabama, Mississippi, Louisiana, Texas, Arkansas, and Tennessee. The Census Bureau's definition of the South includes these eleven plus Maryland, Delaware, Washington, D.C., West Virginia, Kentucky, and Oklahoma.

6. David Ward, *Cities and Immigrants: A Geography of Change in Nineteenth-Century America* (New York, 1971), 11–50.

7. Goldfield, *Cotton Fields;* Carl Abbott, *The New Urban America: Growth and Politics in Sunbelt Cities,* rev. ed. (Chapel Hill, N.C., 1987); Rupert B. Vance and Nicholas J. Demerath, eds., *The Urban South* (1954; reprint, Freeport, N.Y., 1971); David C. Perry and Alfred J. Watkins, eds., *The Rise of the Sunbelt Cities* (Beverly Hills, Calif., 1977); Richard M. Bernard and Bradley R. Rice, eds., *Sunbelt Cities: Politics and Growth since World War II* (Austin, Tex., 1983).

8. Allan R. Pred, *Urban Growth and City-Systems in the United States, 1840–1860* (Cambridge, Mass., 1980), 109–17; William H. Pease and Jane H. Pease, *The Web of Progress: Private Values and Public Styles in Boston and Charleston, 1828–1843* (New York, 1985).

9. Pred, *Urban Growth,* 116.

10. Rudolf Herbele, "Mainsprings of Southern Urbanization," in Vance and Demerath, *Urban South,* 10.

11. Brian J. L. Berry and Frank E. Horton, eds., *Geographic Perspectives on Urban Systems* (Englewood Cliffs, N.J., 1970), chap. 3.

12. Kenneth Weiher, "The Cotton Industry and Southern Urbanization," *Explorations in Economic History* 4 (Apr. 1977): 120–40; Ward, *Cities and Immigrants,* 37–38.

13. Harold D. Woodman, *King Cotton and His Retainers: Financing and Marketing the Cotton Crop of the South, 1800–1925* (Lexington, Ky., 1968), 177.

14. Thomas C. Cochran, "The Business Revolution," *American Historical Review* 79 (Dec. 1974): 1449–66; Robert G. Albion, *The Rise of New York Port, 1815–1860* (New York, 1939), chap. 6, esp. 112–14; Harriet E. Amos, *Cotton City: Urban Development in Antebellum Mobile* (University, Ala., 1985), 29–30; Harriott Horry Rutledge Ravenel, *Charleston: The Place and the People* (1906; reprint, New York, 1922), 386–87; Frederic Cople Jaher, *The Urban Establishment: Upper Strata in Boston, New York, Charleston, Chicago, and Los Angeles* (Urbana, Ill., 1982), 337–39. Harold D. Woodman warns against blaming the factor for the problems in southern economic development (*King Cotton,* 129, 190–93).

15. Richard C. Wade, *Slavery in the Cities: The South, 1820–1860* (New York, 1964); Claudia D. Goldin, *Urban Slavery in the American South, 1820–1860: A Quantitative History* (Chicago, 1978).

16. Kenneth M. Stampp, *The Peculiar Institution: Slavery in the Antebellum South* (New York, 1956), 30.

17. Morton Rothstein, "The Antebellum South as a Dual Economy," *Agricultural History* 41 (Oct. 1967): 373–82; Gavin Wright, *The Political Economy of the Cotton South: Households, Markets, and Wealth*

in the Nineteenth Century (New York, 1978), 71; Steven Hahn, *The Roots of Southern Populism: Yeoman Farmers and the Transformation of the Georgia Upcountry, 1850–1890* (New York, 1983).

18. Eugene Genovese, *The Political Economy of Slavery: Studies in the Economy and Society of the Slave South* (New York, 1967), 155–239.

19. Goldfield, "Pursuing the American Dream"; idem, *Urban Growth in the Age of Sectionalism: Virginia, 1847–1861* (Baton Rouge, La., 1977); J. Mills Thornton, *Politics and Power in a Slave Society: Alabama, 1800–1860* (Baton Rouge, La., 1978); Robert E. Perry, "Middle-class Townsmen and Northern Capital: The Rise of the Alabama Cotton Textile Industry, 1865–1900" (Ph.D. diss., Vanderbilt University, 1986).

20. For differing views of economic historians on the experience of blacks after emancipation, see Roger L. Ransom and Richard Sutch, *One Kind of Freedom: The Economic Consequences of Emancipation* (New York, 1977); Robert Higgs, *Competition and Coercion: Blacks in the American Economy, 1865–1914* (Chicago, 1977); Gavin Wright, *Old South, New South: Revolutions in the Southern Economy since the Civil War* (New York, 1986); Michael Wayne, *The Reshaping of Plantation Society* (Baton Rouge, La., 1983).

21. David C. Roller and Robert W. Twyman, eds., *The Encyclopedia of Southern History* (Baton Rouge, La., 1979), 1018.

22. Woodman, *King Cotton*, 269–94, 327–29; Weiher, "Cotton Industry"; Philip Groth, "Plantation Agriculture and the Urbanization of the South," *Rural Sociology* 42 (Summer 1977): 206–19.

23. Donald B. Dodd and Wynell S. Dodd, *Historical Statistics of the South, 1790–1970* (University, Ala., 1973). Cf. Wright, *Old South*, 43, for figures on the census South.

24. As figure 1.1 indicates, the biggest jumps in southern urbanization were to come in the 1940s and 1950s.

25. On the New South campaign for foreign immigrants, see Rowland T. Berthoff, "Southern Attitudes toward Immigration, 1865–1914," *Journal of Southern History* 17 (Aug. 1951): 328–60.

26. Hope T. Eldridge and Dorothy Swain Thomas, *Population Redistribution and Economic Growth, United States, 1870–1950*, vol. 3, *Demographic Analysis and Interrelations* (Philadelphia, 1964), 204, 202.

27. Ward, *Cities and Immigrants*, 73–81.

28. Eldridge and Thomas, *Population*, 3:207.

29. Ibid., 3:90–91, 118. Between 1870 and 1910 the fourteen states of the South on which the Eldridge and Thomas study is based experienced a net loss by migration of 535,000 blacks and 279,000 whites.

30. Michael P. Conzen, "The Maturing Urban System in the United States, 1840–1910," in *Geographic Perspectives in America's Past: Readings on the Historical Geography of the United States*, edited by David Ward (New York, 1979), 253–74; Allan R. Pred, *The Spatial Dynamics of United States Urban-Industrial Growth, 1800–1914: Interpretative and Theoretical Essays* (Cambridge, Mass., 1966), 46–63.

31. Pred, *Spatial Dynamics*, chaps. 2, 3, 4. Some examples of the more recent work on selective growth and regional urban development include: Pred, *Urban Growth*; Edward K. Muller, "Selective Growth in the Middle Ohio Valley, 1800–1860," in Ward, *Geographic Perspectives*, 291–307; idem, "Regional Urbanization and the Selective Growth of Towns in North American Regions," *Journal of Historical Geography* 3 (1977): 21–59; Diane Lindstrom, *Economic Development in the Philadelphia Region, 1810–1850* (New York, 1978); Conzen, "Maturing Urban System"; James E. Vance, Jr., *The Merchant's World: The Geography of Wholesaling* (Englewood Cliffs, N.J., 1970); Ward, *Cities and Immigrants*; Kirby, "Urban Growth and Economic Change"; Timothy R. Mahoney, "Urban History in a Regional Context: River Towns on the Upper Mississippi, 1840–1860," *Journal of American History* 72 (Sept. 1985): 318–39.

32. Entrepreneurship is, in essence, a capacity for innovation and organizational skill that may be applied to a single business or to the grander enterprise of promoting a city. In its more

ambitious forms, entrepreneurship involves what economist Joseph Schumpeter described as the "creative response" to economic challenges, a propensity for innovation and risk taking, but it also entails a talent for administering such endeavors. See Thomas C. Cochran, "Entrepreneurship," in *International Encyclopedia of the Social Sciences,* edited by David Sills (New York, 1968–79), 5:87–90; Joseph Schumpeter, "The Creative Response in Economic History," *Journal of Economic History* 7 (Nov. 1947): 149–59. Wilbur R. Thompson examines the challenge and response syndrome in Boston, Pittsburgh, and Detroit in the twentieth century (*A Preface to Urban Economics* [Baltimore, 1965], 18–21). See also Arthur H. Cole, *Business Enterprise in Its Social Setting* (Cambridge, Mass., 1959), chap. 1. Cole insists on a definition of *entrepreneur* that takes into account the range of behavior, from pioneering innovator to routine management functions, that is required in business activity. See Burton W. Folsom, Jr., *Urban Capitalists: Entrepreneurs and City Growth in Pennsylvania's Lackawanna and Lehigh Regions, 1800–1920* (Baltimore, Md., 1981), 3, 7, for comments on economist Robert Thomas's argument that entrepreneurship "doesn't matter." See also the debate between Alexander Gerschenkron and those who advocate the seminal role of the entrepreneur, summarized in Cole, *Business Enterprise,* 99, 101, and in the journal *Explorations in Entrepreneurial History,* particularly Gerschenkron, "Social Attitudes, Entrepreneurship, and Economic Development," ibid. 6 (1953–54): 1–19; and Arthur Schweitzer, "Comparative Enterprise and Economic Systems," ibid. 7 (1970): 413–32.

33. Folsom, *Urban Capitalists,* and Carl Abbott, *Boosters and Businessmen: Popular Economic Thought and Urban Growth in the Antebellum Middle West* (Westport, Conn., 1981), are two exemplary recent studies of entrepreneurship and city building. Many of the South's railroads and most urban services, such as water and sewer systems, were typically financed by public bond issues, but these were usually sponsored by the business elite (John F. Stover, *The Railroads of the South, 1865–1900: A Study in Finance and Control* [Chapel Hill, N.C., 1955]; Carter Goodrich, *Government Promotion of American Canals and Railroads, 1800–1890* [New York, 1960]).

34. In one exceptional study, Anthony F. C. Wallace examines the ambivalence of early industrialists toward the tenets of capitalism (*Rockdale: The Growth of an American Village in the Early Industrial Revolution* [New York, 1978]). The work of French historians, suggesting a preference for family security over risky entrepreneurial behavior and a subservience among the business class to residual aristocratic values, may be instructive to students of southern history. See David S. Landes, "French Entrepreneurship and Industrial Growth in the Nineteenth Century," *Journal of Economic History* 9 (1949): 45–61; idem, "French Business and the Businessman: A Social and Cultural Analysis," in *Modern France: Problems of the Third and Fourth Republics,* edited by Edward Mead Earle (Princeton, N.J., 1951), 334–53; John E. Sawyer, "The Entrepreneur and the Social Order: France and the United States," in *Men in Business: Essays in the History of Entrepreneurship,* edited by William Miller (Cambridge, Mass., 1952), 7–22; idem, "Strains in the Social Structure of Modern France," in Earle, *Modern France,* 293–312. Cole, *Business Enterprise,* includes a good summary of Landes's and Sawyer's work.

35. See James Henretta, "The Study of Social Mobility: Ideological Assumptions and Conceptual Biases," *Labor History* 18 (1977): 165–78.

36. Abbott, *Boosters and Businessmen,* 4.

37. Clarence H. Danhoff, "Economic Values in Cultural Perspective," in *Goals of Economic Life,* edited by A. Dudley Ward (New York, 1953), 84–117.

38. Cole, *Business Enterprise,* 234.

Chapter 2

1. Jesse C. Burt, *Nashville: Its Life and Times* (Nashville, Tenn., 1959), 123.

2. [John M. McKee], *The Great Panic: Being Incidents Connected with Two Weeks of the War in Tennessee* (1862; reprint, Nashville, Tenn., 1977), 29–30; Walter T. Durham, *Nashville: The Occupied City* (Nashville, Tenn., 1985), chaps. 1, 2, 3; see also Durham's sequel volume, *Reluctant Partners: Nashville and the Union* (Nashville, Tenn., 1987).

3. *Chicago Tribune,* Mar. 7, 1862, quoted in Durham, *Occupied City,* 48.

4. Blanche Henry Clark, *The Tennessee Yeomen, 1840–1860* (Nashville, Tenn., 1942); Frank L. Owsley, *Plain Folk of the Old South* (1949; reprint, Chicago, 1965), 10–11, 213–25.

5. Maury Klein, *History of the Louisville and Nashville Railroad,* Railroads of America (New York, 1972), 27–29; Thomas L. Connelly, *Civil War Tennessee: Battles and Leaders* (Knoxville, Tenn., 1979), 14–15.

6. Stanley F. Horn, "Nashville during the Civil War," *Tennessee Historical Quarterly* 4 (1945): 2–22; Connelly, *Civil War Tennessee,* 14–15.

7. John Fitch, *Annals of the Army of the Cumberland* (Philadelphia, 1863), 631, quoted in Durham, *Occupied City,* 8.

8. Durham, *Occupied City,* 37–38.

9. [McKee], *Great Panic,* 20–23; Durham, *Occupied City,* 33–34.

10. Durham, *Occupied City;* idem, *Reluctant Partners.*

11. Thérèse Yelverton, *Teresina in America* (1875; reprint, New York, 1974), 246; Peter Maslowski, *Treason Must Be Made Odious: Military Occupation and Reconstruction in Nashville, Tennessee, 1862–1865* (Millwood, N.Y., 1978).

12. Alfred L. Crabb, *Nashville: Personality of a City* (Indianapolis, Ind., 1960), 66.

13. Durham, *Reluctant Partners,* 46–49.

14. *Daily Press,* May 3, 1864, quoted in Crabb, *Nashville,* 66.

15. Durham, *Reluctant Partners,* 156–61; Bobby L. Lovett, "Nashville's Fort Negley," *Tennessee Historical Quarterly* 41 (Spring 1982): 11; Howard N. Rabinowitz, *Race Relations in the Urban South, 1865–1890* (New York, 1978), 19.

16. Crabb, *Nashville,* 66–67.

17. Samuel K. Harryman to Maggie, Nov. 23, 1863, Harryman Letters, Indiana Historical Society Library, Indianapolis, Ind., quoted in Durham, *Reluctant Partners,* 68.

18. John Woolridge, ed., *History of Nashville, Tennessee* (Nashville, Tenn., 1890), 204.

19. Klein, *Louisville and Nashville Railroad,* 40–44.

20. Maslowski, *Treason;* Durham, *Occupied City;* idem, *Reluctant Partners.*

21. Durham, *Occupied City,* 88–89.

22. Crabb, *Nashville,* 72, 64; Jesse C. Burt counted 174 marriages to U.S. Army men in 1864 alone (*Nashville,* 60–61). Among the prominent former Union officers were Gates P. Thruston, Andrew Wills, and Pierre Drouillard (William Waller, ed., *Nashville in the 1890s* [Nashville, 1970], 186–87).

23. Woolridge, *History of Nashville,* 185. Anita S. Goodstein's book-in-progress on antebellum Nashville, "From Frontier to City," demonstrates a strong Whig presence in Jackson's hometown. See also Charles Sellers, "Who Were the Southern Whigs?" *American Historical Review* 59 (1954): 335–46; C. Vann Woodward, *Origins of the New South, 1877–1915* (Baton Rouge, La., 1951), 1–2, 27–28; J. Mills Thornton, *Politics and Power in a Slave Society: Alabama, 1800–1860* (Baton Rouge, La., 1978), 35–58.

24. *Nashville Banner,* Sept. 29, 1872.

25. Ibid., Oct. 20, 1871. Colyar was defending his role in founding the Reunion and Reform Association, a nonpartisan movement for sectional reconciliation and southern economic development.

26. J. T. Trowbridge, *The South: A Tour of Its Battlefields and Ruined Cities* (Hartford, Conn., 1866), 279.

27. Burt, *Nashville*, 66–67.

28. Woolridge, *History of Nashville*, 212–13; Gary L. Kornell, "Reconstruction in Nashville, 1867–1869," *Tennessee Historical Quarterly* 30 (1971): 277–87.

29. Don H. Doyle, *Nashville in the New South, 1880–1930* (Knoxville, Tenn., 1985), 135–42.

30. Quoted in James Reston, Jr., "You Cannot Refine It," *New Yorker,* Jan. 28, 1985, 53. Cf. Arthur Reed Taylor, "From the Ashes: Atlanta during Reconstruction, 1865–1876" (Ph.D. diss., Emory University, 1973), 24.

31. Quoted in Taylor, "From the Ashes," 24.

32. E. Y. Clarke, *Illustrated History of Atlanta* (1877; reprint, Atlanta, Ga., 1971), 23, 24, 28.

33. Ibid., 31; James M. Russell, *Atlanta, 1847–1890: City Building in the Old South and the New* (Baton Rouge, La., 1988), 14–37.

34. Grigsby Hart Wotton, Jr., describes Atlanta's subservience to Augusta, Savannah, and Macon and the failed attempt to establish an independent Atlanta bank in 1852–55 ("New City of the South: Atlanta, 1843–1873" [Ph.D. diss., Johns Hopkins University, 1973], 16, 22–26). Cf. Russell, *Atlanta,* 50–51.

35. Russell, *Atlanta,* chap. 2.; Wotton, "New City," 35–38.

36. Wotton estimates that one-fourth of the city's economic leaders (with known birthplaces) were northern born, one-third nonsouthern ("New City," 39–42). Russell shows that thirty-one business leaders in the period 1847–65 came predominantly from the South (52 percent), with a sizable minority (32 percent) from the North and 13 percent from foreign countries (*Atlanta,* 81, app. A, table 15).

37. Unless otherwise cited, all biographical information on business leaders in the postwar era is drawn from the collective biographical data discussed in chapters 4 and 5.

38. Russell reports that 20 percent of the population was black in 1850 and 1860 and that there were 373 slaveholders in 1860, 44 with more than 10 slaves (*Atlanta,* 70–71).

39. Thomas H. Martin, *Atlanta and Its Builders,* (Atlanta, Ga., 1902), 1:17, quoted in Russell, *Atlanta,* 72. See ibid., chap. 3, for a study of social mobility among Atlanta's antebellum elite. Russell argues convincingly for a tradition of aggressive entrepreneurship and mobility in Atlanta that transcended the war.

40. Samuel P. Richards Diary, Dec. 8, 1860, AHS, quoted in Russell, *Atlanta,* 4:4.

41. Russell, *Atlanta,* 92–100.

42. Ibid., 100–108.

43. Ralph B. Singer, "Confederate Atlanta" (Ph.D. diss., University of Georgia, 1973), 159, cited in Mary A. DeCredico, "Georgia's Entrepreneurs and Confederate Mobilization, 1847–1873" (Ph.D. diss., Vanderbilt University, 1986), 90–102.

44. Russell, *Atlanta,* 108; Clarke, *Illustrated History,* 52.

45. Clarke, *Illustrated History,* 56.

46. Richards Diary, July 30, Aug. 10, 1865.

47. Sidney Andrews, *The South since the War* (Boston, 1866), 340.

48. Whitelaw Reid, *After the War: A Tour of the Southern States, 1865–66,* edited by C. Vann Woodward (New York, 1965), 355–57.

49. John R. Dennett, *The South as It Is: 1865–1866* (1866; reprint, New York, 1965), 267–68, quoted in Taylor, "From the Ashes," 37–38.

50. Henry Deedes, *Sketches of the South and West; or Ten Months' Residence in the United States* (Edinburgh, 1869), 149.

51. Robert Somers, *The Southern States since the War, 1870–71* (London, 1871), 93–95.

52. Andrews, *South,* 340.

53. Quoted in Wotton, "New City," 208; see also George Augustus Sala, *America Revisited* (London, 1886), 264–65.

54. Edward King, *The Great South,* edited by W. Magruder Drake and Robert R. Jones (Baton Rouge, La., 1972), 350. Historian E. Merton Coulter echoed King and others three-quarters of a century later when he wrote, "Atlanta had no birthright to lose. . . . The force behind it was northern instead of southern" (Coulter, *The South during Reconstruction, 1865–1877,* A History of the South, vol. 8 [Baton Rouge, La., 1947], 256).

55. Franklin Garrett, *Atlanta and Environs: A Chronicle of Its People and Events* (Athens, Ga., 1969), 2:953–54; Royce Shingleton, *Richard Peters: Champion of the New South* (Macon, Ga., 1985), 155–58.

56. Russell, *Atlanta,* 176–81.

57. Eugene J. Watts, *The Social Bases of City Politics: Atlanta, 1865–1903* (Westport, Conn., 1978), 71–74, 115–19.

58. Quoted in Shingleton, *Richard Peters,* 160–61.

59. Alice E. Reagan, *H. I. Kimball, Entrepreneur* (Atlanta, Ga., 1983); Shingleton, *Richard Peters,* 183–85.

60. Russell, *Atlanta,* app. A, table 3.

61. Ibid., app. A, table 15. This table shows that 15 percent of sixty-six economic leaders in the years 1865–79 with known birthplaces were born in the North, declining to 11 percent of eighty-three in the years 1880–90. Wotton finds that 26 percent of the sixty-six wealthiest real property owners listed in the 1870 federal census were northern born ("New City," 225).

62. William H. Joubert, *Southern Freight Rates in Transition* (Gainesville, Fla., 1949), 181–84; Doyle, *Nashville in the New South,* 20–40.

63. Doyle, *Nashville in the New South,* 24–32.

64. Joubert, *Southern Freight Rates,* 177–80.

65. Ibid., 106–8.

66. *Annual Reports of Officers, Atlanta Chamber of Commerce at the Annual Meeting and Dinner, November 28th, 1905* ([Atlanta, Ga.], 1906).

67. Glenn Porter and Harold Livesay, *Merchants and Manufacturers: Studies in the Changing Structure of Nineteenth-Century Marketing* (Baltimore, Md., 1971), 214–27; James E. Vance, *The Merchant's World: The Geography of Wholesaling* (Englewood Cliffs, N.J., 1970).

68. *The International Cotton Exposition and the City of Atlanta,* Supplement of the *Textile Record of America* (Philadelphia, 1881), 11.

69. Thomas H. Martin, *Hand Book of the City of Atlanta* ([Atlanta, Ga., 1898]), 29.

70. Ibid.

71. Reilly and Thomas, *Atlanta, Past, Present, and Future* ([Atlanta, Ga., 1883]), 50; Nashville Merchants' Exchange, *Annual Report, 1884* (Nashville, Tenn., 1884), 29.

72. William F. Switzler, *Report on the Internal Commerce of the United States* (Washington, D.C., 1886), 597, 598.

73. Ibid., 688–89, 698; *Atlanta Constitution,* Aug. 31, 1890.

74. *Atlanta Constitution,* May 12, 1897.

75. According to data reported in city directories, in 1880 Nashville banks claimed a total of $1.4 million in capital stock invested and $6.79 million in total resources, as compared to $.9 million and $1.85 million in Atlanta banks.

76. *Nashville Daily News,* Apr. 25, 1902.

77. Garrett, *Atlanta and Environs,* 2:635–36; Walter G. Cooper, *Official History of Fulton County* (Atlanta, Ga., 1934), 607–8.

78. Thomas M. Deaton, "Atlanta during the Progressive Era" (Ph.D. diss., University of Georgia, 1969), 96–98, 21; Cooper, *Official History*, 783–87; Martin, *Hand Book*, 46.

79. Doyle, *Nashville in the New South*, 55–58.

80. *Atlanta Constitution*, Dec. 9, 1888.

81. *Manufacturers' Record*, Nov. 10, 1888; see also *New York Times*, Jan. 31, 1887, on the new spirit that was defeating "bourbonism" in Nashville.

82. U.S. Census Bureau, *Thirteenth Census of the United States, 1910*, vol. 9, *Manufacturers, 1909, Reports by States with Statistics for Principal Cities* (Washington, D.C., 1912), table 1.

83. Clarke, *Illustrated History*, 56.

Chapter 3

1. E. Milby Burton, *The Siege of Charleston, 1861–1865* (Columbia, S.C., 1970), 320.

2. Burton, *Siege of Charleston*, 252; Robert Rosen, *A Short History of Charleston* (San Francisco, Calif., 1982), 108.

3. Daniel Elliott Huger Smith, *A Charlestonian's Recollections* (Charleston, S.C., 1950), 96.

4. Burton, *Siege of Charleston*, 312.

5. Gregory Allen Greb, "Charleston, South Carolina, Merchants, 1815–1860: Urban Leadership in the Antebellum South" (Ph.D. diss., University of California, San Diego, 1978), 187.

6. Ibid., chaps. 4, 5; William H. Pease and Jane H. Pease, *The Web of Progress: Private Values and Public Styles in Boston and Charleston, 1828–1843* (New York, 1985), chaps. 2, 4, 5.

7. By the nineteenth century, Charlestonians and low-country planters were often taking to sea-island or mountain resorts during the summer as well (Lawrence Fay Brewster, *Summer Migrations and Resorts of South Carolina Low Country Planters* [Durham, N.C., 1947], 10–34, esp. 3–5, 8, 11, 13).

8. Harriette Kershaw Leiding, *Charleston: Historic and Romantic* (Philadelphia, 1931), 217.

9. Burton, *Siege of Charleston*, 263.

10. Robert G. Albion, *The Rise of New York Port* (New York, 1939), 102–3, 105. Harriott Horry Rutledge Ravenel, *Charleston: The Place and the People* (1906; reprint, New York, 1922), 404, explains that factors "were the only gentlemen of native birth except the bankers who did any kind of business." Cf. Greb, who shows that 62 percent of "merchants" and 69 percent of "professionals" in 1860 were native born ("Charleston Merchants," 7, 9, 34); see also E. S. Thomas, *Reminiscences of the Last Sixty-five Years* (Hartford, Conn., 1840), 1:34, 41; Frederic Cople Jaher, *The Urban Establishment: Upper Strata in Boston, New York, Charleston, Chicago, and Los Angeles* (Urbana, Ill., 1982), 337–39. Thomas and Jaher concur with the view that business was dominated by those with foreign backgrounds, particularly before 1832.

11. E. Culpepper Clark, *Francis Warrington Dawson and the Politics of Restoration: South Carolina, 1874–1889* (University, Ala., 1980), 147–48; Greb, "Charleston Merchants," chaps. 4, 5.

12. Jaher, *Urban Establishment*, 369–70; Steven Channing, *Crisis of Fear: Secession in South Carolina* (New York, 1970), 168–90.

13. Enid Ewing, "Charleston Contra Mundum," *The Nation*, Nov. 20, 1943, 579–81. Walter Edgar warns that the notion of South of Broad as the only elite neighborhood is a "twentieth-century conceit" of the modern "SOBs," as they are known in some circles (letter to author, Jan. 1988). Ansonborough, Wraggsborough, and other newer neighborhoods to the north of Broad and in St. Paul's Parish, not St. Michael's or St. Phillip's, were where many wealthy planters and merchants lived. John P. Radford shows some dispersion of planters and merchants above and below Broad ("Culture, Economy, and Urban Structure in Charleston, South Carolina, 1860–1880" [Ph.D. diss., Clark University, 1974], chap. 5, esp. 156–57). It was, nonetheless, com-

mon in this period to refer to an address below Broad, and especially on the Battery, as one carrying great social prestige. See also Dale Rosengarten et al., *Between the Tracks: Charleston's East Side during the Nineteenth Century,* The Charleston Museum Archaeological Contributions, no. 17 (Charleston, S.C., 1987), chap. 2.

14. *Charleston Mercury,* Oct. 27, 1860, quoted in Bayard Still, ed., *Urban America: A History with Documents* (Boston, 1974), 115–16; David R. Goldfield, "Pursuing the American Dream: Urban Growth in the Old South," in *The City in Southern History: The Growth of Urban Civilization in the South,* edited by Blaine A. Brownell and David R. Goldfield (Port Washington, N.Y., 1977), 88–99.

15. Greb, "Charleston Merchants," 187; E. Merton Coulter, *George Walton Williams: The Life of a Southern Merchant and Banker, 1820–1903* (Athens, Ga., 1976), 70–71.

16. Burton, *Siege of Charleston,* 263–65.

17. Coulter, *George Walton Williams,* 71.

18. Sidney Andrews, *The South since the War* (Boston, 1866), 1–2.

19. Whitelaw Reid, *After the War: A Tour of the Southern States, 1865–66,* edited by C. Vann Woodward (New York, 1965), 57–58, 68.

20. Anonymous letter, quoted in Robert Molloy, *Charleston: A Gracious Heritage* (New York, [1947]), 108.

21. Carl Schurz, *The Reminiscences of Carl Schurz* (New York, 1908), 3:165.

22. J. T. Trowbridge, *The South: A Tour of Its Battlefields and Ruined Cities* (Hartford, Conn., 1866), 513.

23. George Rose, *The Great Country; or Impressions of America* (London, 1868), 171.

24. Stephen Powers, *Afoot and Alone: A Walk from Sea to Sea by the Southern Route* (Hartford, Conn., 1872), 43–44. See also Thérèse Yelverton, *Teresina in America* (1875; reprint, New York, 1974), 44, 47, 63; Robert Somers, *The Southern States since the War, 1870–71* (London, 1871), 37–43.

25. For example, Owen Wister, *Lady Baltimore* (New York, 1906); Julian Street, *American Adventures* (New York, 1917), reprinted in *Colliers,* Nov. 1917; and the sharp critique of this genre in *Charleston American,* [Nov.?] 15, 1917, pamphlet, SCHS.

26. Clark, *Francis Warrington Dawson,* 146.

27. Coulter, *George Walton Williams,* 61; see also Jaher, *Urban Establishment,* 369–70. On Petigru, see Lacy Ford, "James Louis Petigru: The Last South Carolina Federalist," in *Intellectual Life in Antebellum Charleston,* edited by Michael O'Brien and David Moltke-Hansen (Knoxville, Tenn., 1986), 152–85.

28. Schurz, *Reminiscences,* 3:166–67.

29. Ibid.

30. Joel Williamson, *After Slavery: The Negro in South Carolina during Reconstruction* (New York, 1965), 22; Robert Goodwyn Rhett, *Charleston: An Epic of Carolina* (Richmond, Va., 1940), 305; David Duncan Wallace, *The History of South Carolina* (New York, 1934), 3:215; Leon F. Litwack, *Been in the Storm So Long: The Aftermath of Slavery* (New York, 1979), 177; Rosen, *Short History of Charleston,* 112.

31. Blacks made up 53 percent of Charleston's population in 1870, but an estimated 49 percent of the voting-age males. In Charleston County, blacks constituted 70 percent of the population (Rhett, *Charleston,* 291); see also William C. Hine, "Frustration, Faction, and Failure: Black Political Leadership and the Republican Party in Reconstruction Charleston, 1865–1877" (Ph.D. diss., Kent State University, 1979), 243.

32. Francis Butler Simkins and Robert Hilliard Woody, *South Carolina during Reconstruction* (Chapel Hill, N.C., 1932), 279–81.

33. City of Charleston, *Yearbook, 1880,* 2–14, provides an overview of the city debt and budget from 1870 to 1880; *Yearbook, 1881,* 1–5, discusses the state laws prohibiting further city stock

purchases and bond issues. During the 1880s the city's tax revenues went toward reducing the debt from $4.8 million in 1880 (down from $5.2 million in 1870) to $3.9 million in 1892; total expenditures actually declined from just under $800,000 to below $700,000 during this period (*Yearbook, 1892,* 1–3).

34. This was Burnett Maybank. Governor Hagood Johnson of Barnwell County, who served 1880–82, was, along with Wade Hampton (1876–79), a friendly ally of Charleston. Duncan Clinch Heyward of nearby Colleton County served 1903–5 (Wallace, *South Carolina,* 3:499–500).

35. Robert H. Woody, "Some Aspects of the Economic Conditions of South Carolina after the Civil War," *North Carolina Historical Review* 7 (July 1930): 353; Leiding, *Charleston,* 220; Herbert Ravenel Sass, *The Story of the South Carolina Lowcountry* (West Columbia, S.C., 1956), 226. William A. Courtenay estimates that one-fifth of South Carolina's entire white population served in the Confederate military during the war, and that one-fifth of those who served were killed (*The Centennial of Incorporation* [Charleston, 1883], 228–29).

36. Courtenay, *Centennial,* 228–29.

37. Rhett, *Charleston,* 322–23. David Moltke-Hansen notes that the declining fortunes of antebellum Charleston had discouraged ambitious youths a generation earlier (letter to author, Nov. 18, 1987).

38. Wister, *Lady Baltimore,* 51–52.

39. Henry James, *The American Scene* (1907; reprint, New York, 1967), 414–18.

40. Peter J. Hamilton, "Mobile: 'The Gulf City,'" in *Historic Towns of the Southern States,* edited by Lyman P. Powell (New York, 1900), 369–75; Walter L. Fleming, *Civil War and Reconstruction in Alabama* (1905; reprint, Gloucester, Mass., 1949), 69–71; Albert Burton Moore, *History of Alabama* (University, Ala., 1934), 436–38; Charles G. Summersell, *Mobile: History of a Seaport Town* (University, Ala., 1949), 41–42.

41. Quoted in Sidney Adair Smith and C. Carter Smith, Jr., *Mobile: 1861–1865* (Chicago, 1964), 45, 46.

42. Roberta Steele, "Some Aspects of Reconstruction in Mobile, 1865–1875" (M.A. thesis, Alabama Polytechnic Institute, 1937), 4.

43. Quoted in John Kent Folmar, "Post Civil War Mobile: The Letters of James M. Williams, May–September, 1865," *Alabama Historical Quarterly* 32 (Fall/Winter, 1970): 188–89.

44. Steele, "Some Aspects of Reconstruction," 5.

45. Quoted in Smith and Smith, *Mobile,* 38–39.

46. Steele, "Some Aspects of Reconstruction," 6–7.

47. William Howard Russell, *My Diary North and South,* quoted in Smith and Smith, *Mobile,* 3.

48. *Fourteenth Annual Report of the Mobile Board of Trade for the Year Ending November 1, 1882* (Mobile, Ala., 1883), 17; Harriet E. Amos, *Cotton City: Urban Development in Antebellum Mobile* (University, Ala., 1986), 21; Frances Annette Isbell, "A Social and Economic History of Mobile, 1865–1875" (M.A. thesis, University of Alabama, 1951), 30.

49. Amos, *Cotton City,* 23.

50. Ibid., 22, 213–17.

51. Albion, *Rise of New York Port,* 103–4. Mobile, J. D. B. De Bow remarked as early as 1847, had changed from "one of the most active cities in the South into a mere depot for the storage and transshipment of cotton bales." See Amos, *Cotton City,* 29, 51, for a description of urban leaders in general.

52. Allan R. Pred, *Urban Growth and City-Systems in the United States, 1840–1860* (Cambridge, Mass., 1980), 115.

53. Joseph W. Lesesne to John C. Calhoun, Sept. 12, 1847, quoted in J. Mills Thornton, *Politics and Power in a Slave Society: Alabama, 1800–1860* (Baton Rouge, La., 1978), 254–55. Mobile's booster

press complained at the same time that northern merchants were enriching themselves off the cotton trade without investing in local enterprises (Amos, *Cotton City,* 230–33; Thornton, *Power and Politics,* 254–57).

54. Quoted in Amos, *Cotton City,* 196.

55. Ibid., 196–204.

56. Both Mobile and Charleston preferred government rather than private financing of internal improvements, a solution that involved less risk for merchants but one that often resulted in projects that were politically, not economically, feasible (see Pease and Pease, *Web of Progress,* 56–58; see also Julius Rubin, *Canal or Railroad?: Imitation and Innovation in the Response to the Erie Canal in Philadelphia, Baltimore, and Boston,* Transactions of the American Philosophical Society, vol. 51 [Philadelphia, 1961]).

57. Amos, *Cotton City,* 235–37; Clarence Phillips Denham, *The Secession Movement in Alabama* (Montgomery, Ala., 1933), 101–3; Thornton, *Politics and Power,* 409.

58. Earl W. Fornell, "Mobile during the Blockade," *Alabama Historical Quarterly* 23 (Spring 1961): 36–37.

59. Fleming, *Civil War,* 183–87.

60. Henry Latham, *Black and White: A Journal of a Three Month's Tour in the United States* (London, 1867), 146; Hamilton, "Mobile," 368.

61. Quoted in Smith and Smith, *Mobile,* 19, 29.

62. Folmar, "Post Civil War Mobile," 190.

63. Quoted in Steele, "Some Aspects of Reconstruction," 17.

64. U.S. Census Bureau, *Population of the United States in 1860 . . . Eighth Census* (Washington, D.C., 1864), 9; idem, *A Compendium of the Ninth Census . . . 1870* (Washington, D.C., 1872), 115; Isbell, "Social and Economic History," 67–92.

65. Quoted in Mrs. Hugh C. Bailey, "Mobile's Tragedy: The Great Magazine Explosion of 1865," *Alabama Review* 21 (Jan. 1968): 41–42.

66. Quoted in Jay Higginbotham, *Mobile, City by the Bay* (Mobile, Ala., [1968]), 93–94.

67. Bailey, "Mobile's Tragedy," 47–48; Isbell, "Social and Economic History," 22–23.

68. Trowbridge, *The South,* 421.

69. Isbell, "Social and Economic History," 23–24.

70. Reid, *After the War,* 212, 213–14.

71. Ibid., 217, 226.

72. Greville John Chester, *Transatlantic Sketches in the West Indies, South America, Canada, and the United States* (London, 1869), 221, 224.

73. Hamilton, "Mobile," chap. 45; Fleming, *Civil War.*

74. Sarah Wiggins, "The 'Pig Iron' Kelly Riot 1867," *Alabama Review* 23 (Jan. 1970): 45–55.

75. Ibid.; Fleming, *Civil War,* 481–83. Horton had come to Mobile in 1835 from Boston (Hamilton, "Mobile," 230).

76. Fleming, *Civil War,* 580–82.

77. Isbell, "Social and Economic History," 46–47; Hamilton, "Mobile," 349–50.

78. *Mobile Register,* Jan. 12, 1879. Mobile offers a rarely cited precedent to the commission government reforms of the progressive era.

79. Ibid., Jan. 24, 1879, June 11, 1905 (for a good overview of the city debt problem), and Jan. 24, 1879 (on Duffee's Radical links); Hamilton, "Mobile," 358, 397; Summersell, *Mobile,* 45.

80. Mobile returned to a mayor-council form of government in 1886 and elected a more aggressive mayor, business leader Joseph C. Rich, who served from 1888 to 1893. But the legacy of fiscal constraint and limited government continued to restrict Mobile's most basic urban services (Hamilton, "Mobile," 386; Summersell, *Mobile,* 45).

81. Bernard A. Reynolds, *Sketches of Mobile* ([Mobile, Ala., 1868]), 39.

82. Rhett, *Charleston*, 322.

83. Simkins and Woody, *South Carolina*, 191–95; Edward King, *The Great South*, edited by W. Magruder Drake and Robert R. Jones (Baton Rouge, La., 1972), 364; John F. Stover, *The Railroads of the South, 1865–1900: A Study in Finance and Control* (Chapel Hill, N.C., 1955), 146–47; G. A. Neuffer, *Treatise on the Trade of Charleston* (Charleston, S.C., 1870), 20.

84. Duncan Clinch Heyward, *Seed from Madagascar* (Chapel Hill, N.C., 1937), 148–256; Woody, "Some Aspects," 352–53; Simkins and Woody, *South Carolina*, 284–85.

85. Samuel M. Derrick, *Centennial History of South Carolina Railroad* (Columbia, S.C., 1930), 230–81, quote on 250; Simkins and Woody, *South Carolina*, 195–200; Stover, *Railroads of the South*, 140.

86. Simkins and Woody, *South Carolina*, 208–22; Coulter, *George Walton Williams*, chap. 14; Stover, *Railroads of the South*, 75–79.

87. Stover, *Railroads of the South*, 116–17, 265–67. The Cheraw and Darlington road, which extended the Northeastern from Florence, was also the product of Charleston city and private investment in the 1850s and was taken over along with the Northeastern.

88. William and Jane Pease review the initial obstruction between rail and wharf in the early 1830s (*Web of Progress*, 60–62). See also George S. Rogers, Jr., *Charleston in the Age of the Pinckneys* (1969; reprint, Columbia, S.C., 1980), 161. Robert Goodwyn Rhett reviews the terminal company controversy (*Charleston*, 326).

89. Stover, *Railroads in the South*, 267–68; Rhett, *Charleston*, 324–25.

90. Rhett, *Charleston*, 324–26.

91. Jamie W. Moore, "The Lowcountry in Economic Transition: Charleston since 1865," *South Carolina Historical Magazine* 80 (Apr. 1979): 158; idem, *The Lowcountry Engineers, Military Missions, and Economic Development in the Charleston District, U. S. Army Corps of Engineers* (Charleston, S.C., 1981); Charleston Chamber of Commerce, *The Trade and Commerce of Charleston, 1865–1872* (Charleston, S.C., 1872), 6; King, *Great South*, 439; Simkins and Woody, *South Carolina*, 222–23. Steamship connections with northern ports were resumed after the war. By the early 1870s there were two lines to New York and one each to Baltimore, Philadelphia, and Boston, with connections to Florida, Savannah, and coastal South Carolina towns.

92. *Charleston News and Courier*, Aug. 27, 1885; City of Charleston, *Yearbook, 1886*, 1, 358–441; Anthony W. Riecke Scrapbook, 1:35–54, SCHS.

93. *Fourteenth Annual Report of the Mobile Board of Trade*, 17.

94. Isbell, "Social and Economic History," 37–40, 40–42; Thomas M. Owen, *History of Alabama and Dictionary of Alabama Biography* (1921; reprint, Spartanburg, S.C., 1978), 2:906. This road became controlled by the L&N.

95. Isbell, "Social and Economic History," 42; Owen, *History of Alabama*, 1:511, 2:1014–15.

96. Owen, *History of Alabama*, 2:1014–15; Hamilton, "Mobile," 364; Maury Klein, *History of the Louisville and Nashville Railroad*, Railroads of America (New York, 1972), 137.

97. Owen, *History of Alabama*, 2:1071–72; Hamilton, "Mobile," 362. A successor to this road did complete the line to Mobile in 1898.

98. Alma B. Weber, "Mobile Harbor: Problems of Internal Improvement, 1865–1900," *Journal of the Alabama Academy of Science* 39 (Jan. 1968): 13–20; Owen, *History of Alabama*, 2:1019–21, 1198–99; Isbell, "Social and Economic History," 49–50.

99. See, for example, *Memorial and Proceedings of the River and Harbor Improvement Convention* (Cincinnati, Ohio, 1886); T. G. Bush, *On the Harbor of Mobile: Address Delivered before the House Committee on Rivers and Harbors, February 6, 1888*, pamphlet, Mobile Public Library. For summaries of the expenditures and results of the river and harbor improvements affecting Mobile, see also Isbell,

"Social and Economic History," 49–50; Owen, *History of Alabama,* 2:1195–1200; Hamilton, "Mobile," 379–80; William E. Martin, *Internal Improvements in Alabama,* Johns Hopkins University Studies, ser. 20, no. 4 (Baltimore, Md., 1902), 52–63; Virgil S. Davis, *A History of the Mobile District U.S. Army Corps of Engineers, 1815 to 1971* (Mobile, Ala., 1975), 42–51.

100. Woody, "Some Aspects," 362–63; Simkins and Woody, *South Carolina,* 270–71; Charleston Chamber of Commerce, *Trade and Commerce,* 42–43.

101. David L. Carlton, *Mill and Town in South Carolina, 1880–1920* (Baton Rouge, La., 1982), 43–46. The probate records of the 1880 economic leaders (discussed in the collective biography of chapter 5, below) give evidence for the flight of capital from Charleston.

102. Isbell, "Social and Economic History," 56–57; King, *Great South,* 325; Hamilton, "Mobile," 373–74; Summersell, *Mobile,* 45–49.

103. Tom W. Shick and Don H. Doyle, "The South Carolina Phosphate Boom and the Still Birth of the New South," *South Carolina Historical Magazine* 86 (Jan. 1985): 1–28.

104. Hamilton, "Mobile," 382–84, 387, 401.

105. Even when the surrounding suburban population is included with historical estimates of what the federal census later defined as the Standard Metropolitan Statistical Area, the chart looks very much the same when the four cities are compared.

106. Alma Esther Berkstresser explains that 2,123 people were excluded by the 1879 adjustment of boundaries ("Mobile, Alabama, in the 1880s" [M.A. thesis, University of Alabama, 1951], 42–63). The city population in 1860 was 29,258; in 1870, 32,034; in 1880, 29,132.

Chapter 4

1. C. Vann Woodward, *Origins of the New South, 1877–1913* (Baton Rouge, La., 1951), chaps. 5, 6, esp. 150–54; Paul M. Gaston, *The New South Creed: A Study in Southern Mythmaking* (Baton Rouge, La., 1970).

2. *Richmond Whig and Advertiser,* Apr. 4, 1876, quoted in Woodward, *Origins,* 151.

3. The discussion that follows, in this chapter and the next, is based on a collective biography of a group of men who were identified as officers and directors of the major banks, railroads, corporations, and commercial associations, and who were listed in the city directories as living in each city about 1880. Initially, I compiled information on over one hundred of these directors and officers in each city; then, from this large pool, I identified a smaller "business elite" (forty in Atlanta, forty-two in Nashville) composed of those men who held two or more directorships and the directors of the most important banks, and I extracted these for more intensive analysis. I have pieced together the life histories for this select group of men from biographical sketches published in a multitude of sources including newspaper obituaries, along with confidential information on their business careers and fortunes from the ledgers of R. G. Dun and Company, a credit reporting agency and forerunner of today's Dun and Bradstreet. Finally, probate records, wills, and inventories of estates offered details about individual wealth and types of investments.

4. Woodward, *Origins,* 150–54; Gaston, *New South Creed,* 48 and throughout.

5. John S. Bassett, "The Industrial Decay of the Southern Planter," *South Atlantic Quarterly* 2 (1903): 112–13, quoted in Woodward, *Origins,* 152.

6. *Atlanta Constitution,* Jan. 15, 1887, June 6, 1890.

7. Alexander K. McClure, *The South: Its Industrial, Financial, and Political Conditions* (Philadelphia, 1886), 58–59.

8. Cf. James M. Russell, *Atlanta, 1847–1890: City Building in the Old South and the New* (Baton Rouge, La., 1988), app. A, table 17.

9. *Atlanta Constitution,* Aug. 26, 1877.

10. *Nashville American,* June 10, 1883.

11. U.S. Census Bureau, *Compendium of the Tenth Census* (Washington, D.C., 1883), pt. 1, 542. Cf. Russell, *Atlanta,* app. A, table 15.

12. The number of northern-born men was ten out of forty-two in Atlanta and eight out of thirty-six in Nashville.

13. *Atlanta Constitution,* Jan. 15, 1887.

14. *Atlanta Constitution,* June 17, 1887.

15. *Nashville Evening Herald,* April 28, 1891. Among the prominent businessmen the article mentioned were Sam J. Keith, Leonard and Thomas Fite, and John S. Bransford.

16. *Atlanta Constitution,* Aug. 15, 1880. See also the follow-up article on the "rules" that governed these men's rise to riches, in ibid., Aug. 19, 1880.

17. William Speer, *Sketches of Prominent Tennesseans* (Nashville, Tenn., 1888), 70–72; John Woolridge, ed., *History of Nashville, Tennessee* (Nashville, Tenn., 1890), 596.

18. *Memoirs of Georgia* (Atlanta, Ga., 1895), 867–68; *Atlanta Constitution,* Aug. 1, 1891.

19. Wallace P. Reed, *History of Atlanta, Georgia* (Syracuse, N.Y., 1889), 155.

20. *Atlanta Constitution,* Mar. 2, 1879. James M. Russell first brought this colorful account to my attention in his dissertation, "Atlanta: Gate City of the South, 1847 to 1885" (Ph.D. diss., Princeton University, 1972), 178–79.

21. For example, the *New York Tribune Monthly*'s 1892 list of American millionaires and the *New York World*'s list in its 1902 *Almanac,* both reprinted in Sidney Ratner, ed., *New Light on the History of Great American Fortunes: American Millionaires of 1892 and 1902* (New York, 1953).

22. *Atlanta Constitution,* Apr. 7, 1889, Apr. 29, May 6, 1888.

23. *Nashville Evening Herald,* Sept. 23, 1889, Sept. 28, 1890; *Nashville American,* Nov. 3, 1883.

24. Eighteen in Atlanta and eleven in Nashville could not be identified with any particular denomination.

25. On the Jewish communities, see *Atlanta Constitution,* Jan. 12, 1890, May 7, 1893; Steven Hertzberg, *Strangers within the Gate City: The Jews of Atlanta, 1845–1915* (Philadelphia, 1978); Fedora Frank, *Beginnings on Market Street: Nashville and Her Jewry, 1861–1890* (Nashville, Tenn., 1976).

26. Paul K. Conkin, *Gone with the Ivy: A Biography of Vanderbilt University* (Knoxville, Tenn., 1985), 17.

27. Myron J. Fogde, "Methodist Church," in *Encyclopedia of Southern History* (Baton Rouge, La., 1979), 815.

28. William S. Speer, *The Law of Success* (Nashville, Tenn., 1885), 5–8, 14, 19–20, 43, quoted in Woodward, *Origins,* 153–54.

29. Quoted in James Douglas Flamming, "The Sam Jones Revivals and Social Reform in Nashville, Tennessee, 1885–1900" (M.A. thesis, Vanderbilt University, 1983), 29, 37. Joseph Gusfield, *Symbolic Crusade: Status Politics and the American Temperance Movement* (Urbana, Ill., 1963), and Paul E. Johnson, *A Shopkeeper's Millennium: Society and Religion in Rochester, New York, 1815–1837* (New York, 1978), both deal with the role of temperance as a hallmark of business-class culture.

30. Woolridge, *History of Nashville,* 596–97; Speer, *Sketches,* 70–72; *Nashville Banner,* May 25, 1899.

31. Reed, *Atlanta,* 1; George W. Adair will and inventory, Drawer 115, Box 71, Book D, 742, GDAH (mf). R. G. Dun and Company Collection, Fulton County, Ga., 1:190, 206, 2:157, BL; Royce Shingleton, *Richard Peters: Champion of the New South* (Macon, Ga., 1985), 176–77; *Atlanta Constitution,* Sept. 28, 30, 1899, Oct. 2, 1892; James B. Adair, ed., *Adair: History and Genealogy* (Los Angeles, 1924).

32. Reed, *Atlanta,* 141–42; *Memoirs of Georgia,* 966–67; R. G. Dun and Company Collection, Fulton County, Ga., 1:170, BL.

33. *Memoirs,* 863; R. G. Dun and Company Collection, Fulton Co., Ga., 1:74, 76, 114, 2:283, BL; E. W. Marsh will, Drawer 115, Box 71, Book D, 773–76, GDAH.

34. R. G. Dun and Company Collection, Fulton Co., Ga., 1:43, BL.

35. *Memoirs of Georgia,* 834. Biographical information on Inman has also been drawn from Reed, *Atlanta,* 89–92; *Atlanta Constitution,* May 28, 1892, Apr. 23, 1893. Other clippings in the Inman Scrapbook, AHS, provide details on the Inmans and their place in Atlanta society.

36. Indeed, the analysis of probate records reveals that, on average, Nashville's business elites reported substantially larger estates at their deaths than did Atlanta's ($268,000 versus $98,000).

37. J. B. Killebrew, *Life and Character of James Cartwright Warner: A Memorial Volume* (Nashville, Tenn., 1897); Woolridge, *History of Nashville,* 636–39; James D. Richardson, *Tennessee Templars* (Nashville, Tenn., 1883), 232; *Nashville Banner,* July 22, 1895.

38. R. G. Dun and Company Collection, Davidson Co., Tenn., 2:56, BL.

39. Justin Fuller, "History of the Tennessee Coal, Iron, and Railroad Company, 1852–1907" (Ph.D. diss., University of North Carolina, 1966), 29–35.

40. Killebrew, *James Cartwright Warner,* 27–32; Anne K. Walker, *Life and Achievements of Alfred Montgomery Shook* (Birmingham, Ala., 1952), 70–73.

41. Killebrew, *James Cartwright Warner,* 69–70.

42. James C. Warner will, Probate Court Records, Nashville and Davidson County Courthouse, Nashville, Tenn., vol. 33, pp. 237, 270.

43. Killebrew, *James Cartwright Warner,* 80.

44. Fuller, "Tennessee Coal, Iron, and Railroad Company," 47–120 passim.

45. Nathaniel Baxter, Jr., will, Probate Court Records, Nashville and Davidson County Courthouse; John Trotwood Moore, ed., *Tennessee: The Volunteer State, 1769–1923* (Chicago, 1923), 2:786–88; *Nashville Banner,* Dec. 29, 1913.

46. *Nashville Banner,* Dec. 12, 1914; Woolridge, *History of Nashville,* 223; Moore, *Tennessee,* 3:550–51.

47. R. G. Dun and Company Collection, Davidson Co., Tenn., 2:362, 1:134, 241, 68, BL. The Oscar F. Noel will (Probate Court Records, Nashville and Davidson County Courthouse, Nashville, Tenn., vol. 38, p. 397) does not include a full inventory but does list property sold by the estate for nearly $200,000. An untold amount remained in the estate to be divided among survivors.

48. R. G. Dun and Company Collection, Davidson Co., Tenn., 1:389, 2:34, 40, BL; Richardson, *Tennessee Templars,* 93; *Nashville Banner,* Oct. 26, 1896.

49. *Nashville American,* July 7, 1899.

50. *Forty Years in the Life of a Great Bank: The Fourth National Bank of Nashville, Tennessee* (Nashville, Tenn., [1907]).

51. R. G. Dun and Company Collection, Davidson Co., Tenn., 2:66, 435, 477, BL.

52. Woolridge, *History of Nashville,* 641–43; W. Woodford Clayton, *History of Davidson County, Tennessee* (Philadelphia, 1880), 428; *Nashville American,* July 7, 8, 1899.

53. Gates P. Thruston will, Probate Court Records, Nashville and Davidson County Courthouse, Nashville, Tenn., vol. 38, p. 85; John Allison, ed., *Notable Men of Tennessee* (Atlanta, Ga., 1905), 1:99; Will T. Hale and Dixon L. Merritt, *A History of Tennessee and Tennesseans* (Chicago, 1913), 4:1080; "Gates P. Thruston," in *Who's Who in Tennessee* (Memphis, Tenn., 1911); *Nashville Banner,* Dec. 9, 1912.

54. R. G. Dun and Company Collection, Davidson Co., Tenn., 1:393, 353, 129, 125, 2:248, 368, BL.

55. *Nashville Banner,* Aug. 2, 3, 1888; Probate Court Records, Nashville and Davidson County Courthouse, Nashville, Tenn., 30:22, 653.

56. R. G. Dun and Company Collection, Davidson Co., Tenn., 1:214, 2:75, 376, 6, 202, 3:30, BL; *Nashville Banner,* Oct. 15, 1895; William Waller, ed., *Nashville in the 1890s* (Nashville, Tenn., 1970), 79n.

Chapter 5

1. *Charleston News and Courier,* Aug. 11, 1882, quoted in C. Vann Woodward, *Origins of the New South, 1877–1913* (Baton Rouge, La., 1951), 146.

2. See chap. 2, n. 3 for information on the collective biography of directors. This sample included 145 directors in Charleston and 109 in Mobile.

3. Average age is based on the fifty-nine whose birth dates could be determined.

4. William L. Trenholm, *The South: An Address Delivered . . . on the Third Anniversary of the Charleston Board of Trade, April 7, 1869* (Charleston, S.C., 1869). The quote is taken from an unpublished manuscript version of the same speech, entitled "The South since 1865," located in the Trenholm Family Papers, folder no. 1, SHC. Trenholm's suggestion of a struggle between generations in Charleston is an intriguing but slippery concept, given the difficulty of defining generational cohorts. See David Herbert Donald, "A Generation of Defeat," in *From the Old South to the New: Essays on the Transitional South,* edited by Walter J. Fraser, Jr., and Winfred B. Moore, Jr. (Westport, Conn., 1981), 3–20.

5. Robert Goodwyn Rhett, *Charleston: An Epic of Carolina* (Richmond, Va., 1940), 322–23; See also David Moltke-Hansen, "The Expansion of Intellectual Life: A Prospectus," in *Intellectual Life in Antebellum Charleston,* edited by Michael O'Brien and David Moltke-Hansen (Knoxville, Tenn., 1986), 40.

6. Average age is based on the fifty-five men whose birth dates are known.

7. Peter J. Hamilton, *Mobile of the Five Flags* (Mobile, Ala., 1913), 363.

8. *Mobile Register,* Aug. 22, 1886.

9. The city directories usually listed only household heads and those with occupations, so the figures on earlier directory listings underestimate the persistence of this group because many young men were unlisted.

10. Religious identity could be determined for only twenty-one members of Charleston's 1880 elite, and only one was identified as Jewish, but these numbers underestimate the Jewish presence in Charleston's business community.

11. Doyle W. Boggs, in "John Patrick Grace and the Politics of Reform in South Carolina, 1900–1931" (Ph.D. diss., University of South Carolina, 1977), tells the story of ethnic politics in the early twentieth century.

12. Robert Rosen, *A Short History of Charleston* (San Francisco, Calif., 1982), 128; Caldwell Delaney of the Museum of the City of Mobile is my source for the Mobile proverb.

13. Robert G. Albion, *The Rise of New York Port* (New York, 1939), 102–3, 105, 120.

14. Harriott Horry Rutledge Ravenel, *Charleston: The Place and the People* (1906; reprint, New York, 1922), 404.

15. DuBose Heyward, *Mamba's Daughters: A Novel of Charleston* (New York, 1929), 43.

16. George C. Rogers describes a turn to the past in the face of economic decline in antebellum Charleston (*Charleston in the Age of the Pinckneys* [1969; reprint, Columbia, S.C., 1980], 150–51).

17. David Duncan Wallace, *The History of South Carolina* (New York, 1934), 3:288, 285n. There is, of course, an issue of proper sex roles involved in this story, but Wallace is correct in seeing in it evidence of upper-class Charleston's low regard for certain business activities.

18. W. L. Trenholm, *The Centennial Address before the Charleston Chamber of Commerce, 11th February, 1884* (Charleston, S.C., 1884), 26–27, 41–42.

19. R. G. Dun and Company Collection, Charleston County, S.C., 1:197, 259, BL.

20. E. Merton Coulter, *George Walton Williams: The Life of a Southern Merchant and Banker, 1820–1903* (Athens, Ga., 1976), 30; George Walton Williams, *Advice to Young Men, and Nacoochee and Its Surroundings* (Charleston, S.C., 1896), 5.

21. *Charleston News and Courier,* Apr. 15, 1899.

22. The persistence of Charleston's leisurely habits are noted in Louis B. Wright, *South Carolina: A Bicentennial History* (New York, 1976), 7–8, and Albert Goldman, "Charleston! Charleston!" *Esquire,* June 1977. Walter Edgar is the source of information on Mobile's dining habits (letter to author, Jan. 1988); on Nashville, see Don H. Doyle, *Nashville in the New South, 1880–1930* (Knoxville, Tenn., 1985), 68.

23. William Ferguson, *America by River and Rail: Notes by the Way on the New World and Its People* (London, 1856), 114, quoted in John P. Radford, "Culture, Economy, and Urban Structure in Charleston, South Carolina, 1860–1880" (Ph.D. diss., Clark University, 1974), 203–4.

24. *New York Times,* Jan. 8, 1880; *Charleston News and Courier,* Mar. 19, 1896.

25. Lawrence Fay Brewster, *Summer Migrations and Resorts of South Carolina Low-Country Planters* (Durham, N.C., 1947), 3–5, 8, 10, 13, 14; Ravenel, *Charleston,* 385–86; Robert Molloy, *Charleston: A Gracious Heritage* (New York, 1947), 86–87, 183; Radford, "Culture, Economy, and Urban Structure," 211–13.

26. Radford, "Culture, Economy, and Urban Structure," 192–95; Molloy, *Charleston,* 119; Harriet E. Amos, *Cotton City: Urban Development in Antebellum Mobile* (University, Ala., 1985), 67. In Mobile, Government Street Presbyterian was also popular among the social elite (Caldwell Delaney, note to author, Mar. 1988).

27. R. G. Dun and Company Collection, Charleston Co., S.C., 3:22, 1:46, 283, 417, BL.

28. Ibid., 1:204, 292, 628.

29. Ibid., 1:123.

30. Ibid., 1:413.

31. Ibid., 1:30, 211, 2:452, 469, 566.

32. Ibid., 1:106, 2:448, 466.

33. Ibid., 1:242, 2:409.

34. Ibid., 1:30, 169, 2:382, 592, 274, 3:86.

35. Ibid., 1:175, 2:363, 360, 572.

36. Ibid., 2:311, 246. Gibbes's son, George, was more reckless and "too much disposed to do a risky business." He did a fair business trading on his father's name and his wife's wealth, but creditors were advised to be cautious (ibid., 2:587, 597).

37. Ibid., 2:41a, 649, 87; *The National Cyclopedia of American Biography* (New York, 1940), 28:376–77.

38. James Calvin Hemphill, *Men of Mark in South Carolina: Ideals of American Life* (Washington, D.C., 1907–9), 3:410.

39. R. G. Dun and Company Collection, Charleston Co., S.C., 1:77, 2:645, 646, BL.

40. *Sholes' Directory of the City of Charleston, January, 1881* (Charleston, 1881); *Roll of Officers of the Charleston Chamber of Commerce . . . 1884, Roll of Members . . . 1887* ([Charleston, 1887]).

41. R. G. Dun and Company Collection, Charleston Co., S.C., 1:143, 298, 399, 398, BL.

42. Ibid., 1:228, 509.

43. Ibid., 2:470, 579; *Roll of Officers,* 14; *The Exposition,* Dec. 1901, 501–2.

44. R. G. Dun and Company Collection, Charleston Co., S.C., 2:158, BL.

45. Ibid., 2:160, 341, 473, 546, 1:296, 419. George Walton Williams, *History of Banking in South Carolina from 1712 to 1900* (Charleston, S.C., 1903), 12–15; idem, *George W. Williams and Co., The 32nd Anniversary, May, 1874* (Charleston, S.C., 1903), 109–13; Coulter, *George Walton Williams.* See, in

particular, Williams's effort to promote a tourist hotel in Charleston (Coulter, *George Walton Williams,* 208–15).

46. R. G. Dun and Company Collection, Mobile Co., Ala., 1:168, 572, BL; *Mobile Register,* Feb. 16, 1904; Probate Court Records, Drawer no. 164, Mobile County Court House, Mobile, Ala.

47. *Mobile Register,* Jan. 23, 24, 1904; R. G. Dun and Company Collection, Mobile Co., Ala., 1:61, 360, 372, BL.

48. R. G. Dun and Company Collection, Mobile Co., Ala., 1:39, 308, 331, 330, 372, BL; Thomas McAdory Owen, *History of Alabama and Dictionary of Alabama Biography* (1921; reprint, Spartanburg, S.C., 1978), 3:883.

49. R. G. Dun and Company Collection, Mobile Co., Ala., 1:308, 2:424, BL.

50. *Mobile Register,* Sept. 1, 1880.

51. See the laudatory editorial touting Brewer as a candidate for governor (ibid., Apr. 21, 1882).

52. Ibid., Dec. 5, 1893; R. G. Dun and Company Collection, Mobile Co., Ala., 2:348, 443, 457, 458, 575, BL; Probate Court Records, drawer no. 40; Owen, *History of Alabama,* 3:212.

53. *Mobile Register,* Aug. 16, 1882.

54. Ibid., Sept. 20, 1889. See the follow-up in the *Mobile Register* editorial of Sept. 22, 1889.

55. Ibid., Mar. 16, 1883, May 6, 1921; R. G. Dun and Company Collection, Mobile Co., Ala., 1:8, 467, BL; Probate Court Records, drawer no. 79, contains no inventory.

56. R. G. Dun and Company Collection, Mobile Co., Ala., 1:284, 320, 571, 661, BL; Probate Court Records, drawer no. 189, shows an estate worth under $11,000, but this may have been after division among heirs. The Kirkbride home still stands on Government Street as host to the Colonial Dames Museum.

57. R. G. Dun and Company Collection, Mobile Co., Ala., 2:350, 351, 650, 695, BL.

Chapter 6

1. *Atlanta Constitution,* Dec. 3, 1905, Nov. 29, 1905; see also ibid., Nov. 7, 1905.

2. John R. Logan and Harvey L. Molotch, *Urban Fortunes: The Political Economy of Place* (Berkeley, Calif., 1987), chap. 3.

3. Ivan Allen, *The Atlanta Spirit: Altitude + Attitude* (Atlanta, Ga., 1948).

4. *Nashville American,* June 10, 1883.

5. Alfred D. Chandler, Jr., *The Visible Hand: The Managerial Revolution in American Business* (Cambridge, Mass., 1977).

6. The earliest American chamber of commerce appeared in New York City in 1768, followed by three other eastern seaports, including Charleston, before 1800. By the late 1850s there were about thirty local commercial bodies in the United States (Kenneth Sturges, *American Chambers of Commerce* [New York, 1915], 11, 41–42; Paul Studenski, "Chambers of Commerce," in *Encyclopedia of the Social Sciences* (New York, 1930), 325–29; Blake McKelvey, *The Urbanization of America: 1865–1915* (New Brunswick, N.J., 1963), 43–44.

7. Sturges, *American Chambers of Commerce,* esp. 43–50; Ryerson Ritchie, "The Modern Chamber of Commerce," *National Municipal Review* 1 (Apr. 1912): 161–69. For a comprehensive survey of commercial associations in towns of more than 2,000 population, see the report from the U.S. Department of Commerce, Bureau of Foreign and Domestic Commerce, *Commercial and Agricultural Organizations of the United States,* 62d Cong., 3d ser., 1913, Sen. Doc. 1109.

8. Wallace P. Reed, *History of Atlanta, Georgia* (Syracuse, N.Y., 1889), 440–47 (quotes on 446–47).

9. Ibid., 448.

10. Ibid., 447–49; Franklin Garrett, *Atlanta and Environs: A Chronicle of Its People and Events* (Athens, Ga., 1969), 1:866–67.

11. On Benjamin Crane, see his obituary, *Atlanta Constitution*, Jan. 15, 1885; Crane Papers, AHS; R. G. Dun and Company Collection, Fulton Co., Ga., 1:177, 2:109, BL. Crane's estate inventory showed that his net worth at the time of his death was approximately $76,000 (Book C, p. 210, mf, GDAH). Crane's business began as a branch of the Charleston firm, George W. Williams and Company.

12. Reed, *Atlanta*, 449–51 (quote on 451).

13. Ibid., 450, 451; *Proceedings of the Convention Called by Governor James M. Smith of Georgia for the Purpose of Considering the Best Means of Cheapening Transportation between the Great Producing and Consuming Sections of the Country, Held at Atlanta, Georgia, May 20, 1873* (Atlanta, Ga., 1873); Grigsby Hart Wotton, Jr., "New City of the South: Atlanta, 1843–1873" (Ph.D. diss., Johns Hopkins University, 1973), 172–73.

14. *Atlanta Constitution*, Feb. 1, 3, 1881, Mar. 13, 1878; Reed, *Atlanta*, 449–51.

15. *Atlanta Constitution*, June 22, 1890; Reed, *Atlanta*, 449–51.

16. *Atlanta Constitution*, May 15, 1883; Reed, *Atlanta*, 451–52; Walter G. Cooper, *Official History of Fulton County* (Atlanta, Ga., 1934), 340, 343.

17. Cooper, *Official History*, 340.

18. *Atlanta Constitution*, May 29, 1883.

19. Garrett, *Atlanta and Environs*, 2:406.

20. *Atlanta Constitution*, Mar. 8, 12, 1885.

21. Ibid., June 22, 1890.

22. Ibid., June 16, 1892.

23. Ibid., Dec. 22, 1892.

24. Ibid., July 3, 1892. Within a year the Dixie Club, made up of "the younger element of the businessmen of the city," merged with the Chamber (ibid., Sept. 24, 1893).

25. Cooper, *Official History*, 344; *Atlanta Constitution*, Aug. 15, 16, 1893.

26. *Atlanta Constitution*, Aug. 20, 1893.

27. Cooper, *Official History*, 344–45.

28. Thomas H. Martin, *Hand Book of the City of Atlanta* ([Atlanta, Ga., 1898]), 64; *Atlanta Constitution*, Sept. 9, Oct. 22, 1897, Apr. 23, 1898, Jan. 3, 10, 1901.

29. Martin, *Hand Book*, 64. Later these dinners were held twice a year (*Atlanta Constitution*, Jan. 3, 1901).

30. *Atlanta Constitution*, Jan. 3, 1901; Martin, *Hand Book*, 64.

31. *Atlanta Constitution*, Jan. 13, 1899.

32. Ibid., Jan. 13, 25, Mar. 10, 19, May 4, Dec. 12, 1899, Feb. 7, 16, Nov. 22, 1900. See also Chamber of Commerce collection, AHS, and Northen Scrapbook, p. 70, AHS, for more on the later chamber and its consolidation with the league. The latter came to be known as the Businessmen's League.

33. Cooper, *Official History*, 350–66; Thomas M. Deaton, "Atlanta during the Progressive Era" (Ph.D. diss., University of Georgia, 1969), 99–104. See George W. Doonan, *Commercial Organizations in Southern and Western Cities*, Department of Commerce, Bureau of Foreign and Domestic Commerce, Special Agents Series No. 79 (Washington, D.C., 1914), 10–11, for a description of the highly organized effort by the chamber to educate the public and get out the vote for the bond issue. See also Charles P. Garofalo, "Business Ideas in Atlanta, 1916–1935" (Ph.D. diss., Emory University, 1972), on the thought and policy of the later chamber.

34. *Atlanta Constitution*, Nov. 8, 10, 11, 1868.

35. Maury Klein, *The Great Richmond Terminal: A Study in Businessmen and Business Strategy* (Char-

lottesville, Va., 1970), 60–61. There were three Atlantans on the nine-man board directing the Georgia Air-Line, the link to South Carolina (James M. Russell, *Atlanta, 1847–1890: City Building in the Old South and the New* [Baton Rouge, La., 1988], chap. 5). By 1889 the only person representing Atlanta on the Richmond and Danville board was Samuel Inman. His brother John, of New York, was president of the company (Reed, *Atlanta,* 433–34).

36. Russell, *Atlanta,* chap. 5; Reed, *Atlanta,* 434. See the account of the Chamber of Commerce's celebrating the launching of the Georgia Pacific, in the *Atlanta Constitution,* June 6, 1881. See also Klein, *Great Richmond Terminal,* 91–92.

37. *Atlanta Constitution,* Apr. 7, 1886, July 22, 1888; Russell, *Atlanta,* 237–38.

38. Chandler, *Visible Hand,* chap. 3.

39. Jonathan Norcross, *Atlanta, Northern Georgia, and the Great Southern Railroad Pool* (Atlanta, Ga., 1886), 13, quoted in James M. Russell, "Atlanta: Gate City of the South, 1847 to 1885" (Ph.D. diss., Princeton University, 1972), 217.

40. *Atlanta Constitution,* July 11, 1885.

41. Ibid., Aug. 5, 1885. On the Southern Steamship and Railway Association's difficulties in maintaining rates in the competitive environment of Atlanta, see Russell, "Atlanta," 216–23.

42. Chamber of Commerce Minutes, July 24, Sept. 11, 25, Oct. 9, 1883, May 4, 1888, Chamber of Commerce, Atlanta, Ga. I am grateful to James M. Russell for making his notes from this source available to me.

43. *Atlanta Constitution,* Mar. 30, 1886; Russell, *Atlanta,* chap. 9, 16–17.

44. *Atlanta Constitution,* Jan. 30, Feb. 7, 1902; Garrett, *Atlanta and Environs,* 2:438.

45. *Atlanta Constitution,* Oct. 11, 1904.

46. Ibid., Apr. 25, May 5, 29, Aug. 27, Sept. 5, 25, Oct. 11, Dec. 1, 9, 1904, May 12, 1905; Garrett, *Atlanta and Environs,* 2:466; Dewey W. Grantham, Jr., *Hoke Smith and the Politics of the New South* (Baton Rouge, La., 1958), 132; Deaton, "Atlanta," 101.

47. Chamber of Commerce Minutes, Apr. 4, 1888, Chamber of Commerce, Atlanta, Ga.

48. Russell, *Atlanta,* 242–44. The eleventh and final railroad to enter Atlanta arrived in 1908.

49. William H. Joubert, *Southern Freight Rates in Transition* (Gainesville, Fla., 1949), 106–11; William F. Switzler, *Report on the Internal Commerce of the United States* (Washington, D.C., 1886), pt. 2, 343–44.

50. Charles N. Glaab, "Historical Perspective on Urban Development Schemes," in Leo F. Schnore, ed., *Social Science and the City: A Survey of Urban Research* (New York, 1967), 211–13.

51. Russell, *Atlanta,* 130–31; Reed, *Atlanta,* 469–71. The law covered cotton, wool, and iron manufacturing and applied for twenty years.

52. Alice E. Reagan, *H. I. Kimball, Entrepreneur* (Atlanta, Ga., 1983), 77.

53. *Atlanta Constitution,* Dec. 30, 1874, Jan. 29, 1878, July 1, 1879, on opening; Reagan, *H. I. Kimball,* 77–90; Russell, *Atlanta,* 138–40; Arthur Reed Taylor, "From the Ashes: Atlanta during Reconstruction, 1865–1876" (Ph.D. diss., Emory University, 1973), 107–8; Royce Shingleton, *Richard Peters: Champion of the New South* (Macon, Ga., 1985), 210–11. Cf. Thomas H. Martin, *Atlanta and Its Builders* (Atlanta, Ga., 1902), 2:381, which identifies the Atlanta Cotton Factory as having begun in 1883.

54. *Atlanta Constitution,* May 6, 1883.

55. These associations sometimes had slightly different names and purposes. See *Atlanta Constitution,* Aug. 21, 1886, Dec. 9, 1888, June 7, 1893, July 28, 1900, Jan. 29, 1902, May 3, 1906, Dec. 9, 1909, July 14, 1913; Nixon, *Henry Grady,* 281–83. See also *Atlanta, the Capital of Georgia and the Coming Metropolis of the South* (Atlanta, Ga., 1884), published by the Atlanta Manufacturers' Association. Wallace P. Reed says the association did not exist between 1875 and 1887, but he may have meant only that it was not a sustained, active institution during this period (*Atlanta,* 471).

56. *Atlanta Constitution,* Aug. 21, 1886. The Manufacturers' Association was formed in cooperation with the Chamber of Commerce (ibid., Aug. 28, 1886).

57. Ibid., Sept. 12, 1886; see also ibid., Oct. 6, 1886, May 11, 1887, for subsequent reports on the association.

58. Ibid., Oct. 22, 1886; *Manufacturers' Record,* Aug. 1, 1885, Jan. 2, 1886; Robert C. McMath et al., *Engineering the New South: Georgia Tech, 1885–1985* (Athens, Ga., 1985), chap. 1.

59. *Atlanta Constitution,* Aug. 21, 1886.

60. Ibid., Sept. 19, Nov. 21, 1886, quoted in McMath, *Engineering the New South,* 14–15.

61. "Asa Griggs Candler," in *Men of Mark in Georgia,* edited by William J. Northen (Atlanta, Ga., 1912), 324–25; Charles Howard Candler, *Asa Griggs Candler* (Atlanta, Ga., 1950); Deaton, "Atlanta," 84–86.

62. Don H. Doyle, *Nashville in the New South, 1880–1930* (Nashville, Tenn., 1985), chap. 1. On the earlier industrial expositions, see *Nashville Banner,* Dec. 20, 1870, Mar. 12, 1872, Mar. 2, 1873, Mar. 18, 19, 1874.

63. Jack Blicksilver, "The International Cotton Exposition of 1881 and Its Impact upon the Economic Development of Georgia," *Cotton History Review* 1 (Oct. 1960): 176.

64. *Atlanta Constitution,* Aug. 29, 1880.

65. Hannibal Ingalls Kimball, *Report on the International Cotton Exposition* (New York, 1882), 93–94. On Kimball's role, see Reagan, *H. I. Kimball,* 91–107.

66. Blicksilver, "International Cotton Exposition," 177–78.

67. *Atlanta Constitution,* Nov. 28, 1880; Mary Roberts Davis, "The Planning of the International Cotton Exposition, Atlanta, 1881," unpublished typescript, 1952, AHS, 14; Kimball, *Report,* 94.

68. Davis, "Planning," 15–16.

69. Ibid., 17.

70. Reagan, *H. I. Kimball,* chaps. 9, 10.

71. Kimball, *Report,* 101; Davis, "Planning," 19.

72. Kimball, *Report,* 101–2.

73. Ibid., 94–96. Eventually Atlantans purchased 363 shares.

74. Atlanta Constitution, Mar. 3, 1881, cited in Davis, "Planning," 20.

75. *New York Times,* Apr. 1, 1881.

76. Davis, "Planning," 20.

77. Kimball, *Report,* 95–100.

78. Davis, "Planning," 20.

79. Kimball, *Report,* 112–15, 129–31.

80. Blicksilver, "International Cotton Exposition," 179.

81. Kimball, Report, 110–11.

82. Ibid., 125; Blicksilver, "International Cotton Exposition," 179.

83. Kimball, *Report,* 178; Augusta Wylie King, "International Cotton Exposition," *Atlanta Historical Bulletin* 4 (July 1939): 191.

84. *New York Times,* Oct. 13, 1881.

85. *Atlanta Constitution,* Oct. 26, 1881.

86. Ibid., Mar. 25, 1881.

87. Ibid., Dec. 3, 1905.

88. Kimball, *Report,* 142.

Chapter 7

1. Albert O. Hirschman, *Exit, Voice, and Loyalty: Responses to Decline in Firms, Organizations, and States* (Cambridge, Mass., 1970).

2. City of Charleston, *Yearbook, 1923,* xxv.

3. *Charleston News and Courier,* Mar. 17, 1898.

4. The chief evidence for Charleston investment patterns comes from the estate inventories of the business elites of 1880, which, it should be noted, usually depict the investments of elderly men. Much capital was also invested in more conservative government bonds as well. On Charleston investments in the South Carolina textile industry, see David L. Carlton, *Mill and Town in South Carolina, 1880–1920* (Baton Rouge, La., 1982), 43–46. On investments in Birmingham, see *Charleston News and Courier,* June 1, 1886; and in Atlanta, ibid., Jan. 25, 1899.

5. Trenholm's address was published in the *Charleston News and Courier,* Feb. 12, 1884, and reprinted as W. L. Trenholm, *The Centennial Address before the Charleston Chamber of Commerce, 11th February, 1884* (Charleston, S.C., 1884). The quotes and ideas that follow all come from Trenholm's address.

6. E. S. Thomas, *Reminiscences of the Last Sixty-five Years* (Hartford, Conn., 1840), cited in Trenholm, *Centennial Address.*

7. *The National Cyclopedia of American Biography* (New York, 1940), 28:376–77; obituary in the *Charleston News and Courier,* Jan. 12, 1901; see also ibid., Jan. 14, 1901, in which the editor quotes from and endorses Trenholm's 1884 address.

8. Charleston Chamber of Commerce, Minutes, Mar. 21, 1868, p. 27, SCHS. The exchange was restored around 1870 and continued as the customs house until 1879, then as the post office until 1896. Later the Daughters of the American Revolution made it a prime example of Charleston's cult of historic preservation (Ruth M. Miller and Ann T. Andrus, *Witness to History: Charleston's Old Exchange and Provost Dungeon* [Orangeburg, S.C., 1986], 42–46). See also the accounts in the *Charleston News and Courier,* Aug. 8, 1868, Feb. 2, 23, 1896.

9. *Roll of Officers of the Charleston Chamber of Commerce during the First Century of its Corporate Life, as Far as Ascertainable, Roll of Members on the CIII Anniversary, Chronologically Arranged, with the Names of the Present Officers, 1887* (Charleston, S.C., 1887), 10–15.

10. William L. Trenholm, *The South: An Address Delivered . . . on the Third Anniversary of the Charleston Board of Trade, April 7, 1869* (Charleston, S.C., 1869).

11. Chamber of Commerce minutes, Oct. 14, 1870, p. 96, Feb. 12, 1872, p. 176.

12. Charleston Chamber of Commerce, *Constitution and Rules of the Corporation of the Charleston Chamber of Commerce, Revised 1886* (Charleston, S.C., 1886), 4–5.

13. *Officers and Members of the Charleston Chamber of Commerce, February 12, 1872* (Charleston, S.C., 1872), 2–8. *Roll of Officers . . . 1887;* Charleston Chamber of Commerce, *Constitution and Rules of the Corporation of the Charleston Chamber of Commerce, Revised 1891* (Charleston, S.C., 1891), 13–15.

14. Chamber of Commerce minutes, Apr. 2, 1868, p. 30; Charleston Board of Trade, Minutes, Apr. 7, 1868, SCA.

15. Board of Trade minutes, May 6, 1868.

16. *Charleston News and Courier,* Apr. 8, 1868.

17. Board of Trade minutes, May 6, July 7, 1868.

18. *Charleston News and Courier,* Apr. 4, 1866.

19. Board of Trade minutes, Jan. 7, 1869.

20. Ibid. See also the board's published proceedings for 1867 and 1871.

21. *Charleston News and Courier,* Apr. 16, 1868.

22. Board of Trade minutes, July 7, 1869, Apr. 6, Mar. 4, June 1, Mar. 2, May 4, 1870, Feb. 7, Mar. 6, 1872, Feb. 2, Apr. 6, May 4, June 1, 1870, Apr. 5, 1871, Jan. 3, 10, Feb. 7, Mar. 6, 1872.

23. *Charleston News and Courier,* Mar. 30, 1872, Mar. 21, 1872.

24. Charleston Cotton Exchange, "Proceedings of the Association, Board of Directors and Committees, 1872–82," 3–6, SCHS.

25. Ibid., 22–23.

26. *Charleston News and Courier,* July 12, 1872.

27. Charleston Cotton Exchange, "Proceedings," 37, 204–6.

28. *Charleston News and Courier,* Dec. 27, 1888, Apr. 12, 1889.

29. When both the Chamber of Commerce and the Cotton Exchange refused to join in a celebration of Cleveland's victory, F. W. Wagener remarked that "it was about time they should learn that the Exchange could get along without them" (ibid., Nov. 27, 1884).

30. On Wagener, see *The Exposition,* Dec. 1901, 501–2.

31. For a biographical sketch of Francis Q. O'Neill, see Yates Snowden, ed., *History of South Carolina* (Chicago, 1920), 5:156–57.

32. *Charleston News and Courier,* Sept. 3, 1885.

33. Ibid.

34. Ibid., May 26, June 1, 2, 3, 25, Aug. 9, 1888; E. Merton Coulter, *George Walton Williams: The Life of a Southern Merchant and Banker, 1820–1903* (Athens, Ga., 1976), 206–18. All quotes relating to the hotel campaign are from the *News and Courier.*

35. Earlier excursions had been tried since at least 1879, but with little publicity and limited success. See *Charleston News and Courier,* Sept. 9, 1879, Mar. 6, May 1, 1880.

36. Ibid., Nov. 15, 1883.

37. Ibid., May 25, 1887, Nov. 30, 1883, Aug. 3, 1887, Oct. 15, 1891, Sept. 23, 1887.

38. Ibid., Sept. 23, Nov. 5, 1887, July 7, Dec. 1, 1888, Nov. 4, 1889, Oct. 3, 1890, Oct. 15, 1891, Oct. 10, Nov. 4, 1892, Oct. 10, 1893.

39. Thomas R. Waring, Jr., ed., *The Way It Was in Charleston, as Recalled by Laura Witte Waring* (Old Greenwich, Conn., 1980), 70.

40. *Charleston News and Courier,* Oct. 27, 1896. See also ibid., Dec. 24, 1897.

41. City of Charleston, *Yearbook, 1893,* 23–25.

42. *Charleston News and Courier,* Oct. 10, 1893. The Young Men's Business League revived the Gala Week in 1896 (see ibid., Sept. 11, Oct. 27, 1896, Dec. 24, 1897).

43. Maury Klein, *History of the Louisville and Nashville Railroad,* Railroads of America (New York, 1972), 293–94; Samuel M. Derrick, *Centennial History of South Carolina Railroad* (Columbia, S.C., 1930), 266–69.

44. *Charleston News and Courier,* Dec. 3, 1896.

45. Robert Goodwyn Rhett, *Charleston: An Epic of Carolina* (Richmond, Va., 1940), 324–25.

46. *Charleston News and Courier,* Dec. 3, 1896. The editor went on to blame Charlestonians for their "commercial supineness in former years," when it might have been possible to build "a great Charleston system." "We had the money with which to have protected our interests, but we lacked the foresight and enterprise and commercial ability to use it for our own protection. While we dug a hole and buried our talent in the earth the Virginians invested theirs in a manner which is now bringing forth sixty and one hundred fold."

47. City of Charleston, *Yearbook, 1894* (the endpiece summarizes the jetty project); Rhett, *Charleston,* 333–35.

48. *Charleston News and Courier,* July 25, 1892.

49. Ibid., Sept. 20, 1883, July 23, Aug. 13, 1884.

50. Rhett, *Charleston,* 326, 344. See *Charleston News and Courier,* Nov. 12, 1890, and Nov. 4, 1891, for early optimistic reports on the East Shore Terminal Company.

51. Thomas W. Shick and Don H. Doyle, "The South Carolina Phosphate Industry and the Still Birth of the New South," *South Carolina Magazine of History* 86 (Jan. 1985): 1–28.

52. John J. Duffy, "Charleston Politics in the Progressive Era" (Ph.D. diss., University of South Carolina, 1963), esp. chap. 4; Doyle W. Boggs, "John Patrick Grace and the Politics of Reform in South Carolina, 1900–1931" (Ph.D. diss., University of South Carolina, 1977), esp. 15–16.

53. *Charleston News and Courier,* June 20, 1894.

54. Ibid., Oct. 14, 30, 1894.

55. Ibid., Oct. 9, 11, Nov. 14, 1894; Rhett, *Charleston,* 325. The seven members of the bureau were to include two from the city council as well (City of Charleston, *Yearbook, 1894,* 238–40).

56. *Charleston News and Courier,* July 7, 1894.

57. Ibid., Nov. 16, 1896.

58. Ibid., Nov. 12, 1896. See also ibid., Nov. 16, 1896, for an account of the league's annual meeting and a list of officers.

59. Ibid., June 8, 1896.

60. See the sketch of Smyth's career contained in a review of Charleston by Atlanta reporters (*Atlanta Constitution,* Mar. 8, 1903).

61. *Charleston News and Courier,* Mar. 27, 1896.

62. Ibid., Apr. 27, June 30, July 23, 1898.

63. Ibid., July 24, Aug. 7, 1898.

64. City of Charleston, *Yearbook, 1899,* xxii–xxviii.

65. *Charleston News and Courier,* Nov. 4, 1898, May 24, 1899; Rhett, *Charleston,* 332.

66. City of Charleston, *Yearbook, 1900,* xix–xx; Rhett, *Charleston,* 332; *Charleston News and Courier,* June 9, Sept. 22, 1899. The last source describes how Charleston beat the "Atlanta spirit" in winning the League of American Municipalities convention.

67. *Charleston News and Courier,* June 1, 4, 9, 12, Aug. 2, Sept. 28, 1898.

68. Ibid., Oct. 11, 1895.

69. City of Charleston, *Yearbook, 1901,* 83–86; Rhett, *Charleston,* 333.

70. The navy's decision is best summarized in Robert G. Rhett's essay in City of Charleston, *Yearbook, 1901,* app., 87–96, and his account in Rhett, *Charleston,* 334–35. See also City of Charleston, *Yearbook, 1900,* app., 83–205; "Official Report of the Naval Board to the U.S. Navy Department," City of Charleston, *Yearbook, 1902.*

71. *Charleston News and Courier,* Feb. 10, May 11, June 16, 1898, Jan. 25, 1899; City of Charleston, *Yearbook, 1901,* 95–96; Rhett, *Charleston,* 331–32.

72. George W. Hopkins, "From Naval Pauper to Naval Power: The Development of Charleston's Metropolitan-Military Complex," in *The Martial Metropolis: U.S. Cities in War and Peace,* edited by Roger W. Lotchin (New York, 1984), 4–5.

73. E. F. B. Conner, *Progressive Charleston* (Charleston, S.C., 1904), n.p. The total federal investment in Charleston harbor was estimated by Conner at $20 to $25 million.

74. *Charleston News and Courier,* Jan. 11, 1906, quoted in Hopkins, "From Naval Pauper," 3. The allusion is to the William Crum affair, which is discussed in chapter 11 below.

75. Rhett, *Charleston,* 336–38 (quote on 336). Before America's entry into World War I, the federal government also built new port terminals, including new ordnance warehouses and corrals for mules and horses on the Charleston Neck.

76. *Charleston News and Courier,* Sept. 19, 1900; this editorial was yet another plea for Charleston to build a modern hotel.

77. J. C. Hemphill, "A Short Story of the South Carolina Inter-state and West Indian Exposition," in City of Charleston, *Yearbook, 1902,* 107, 108.

78. Biographical information on the officers and directors is from *The Exposition,* Dec. 1901, 501–5. See also Hemphill, "Short Story," 109–11, for more information about these and others involved in organizing the exposition.

79. T. J. Neville, *Charleston and Its Prospects, 1899–1900* (Charleston, S.C., 1899), 18, 21–22.

80. Hemphill, "Short Story," 110.

81. Ibid., 111–12, 146, 149, 153 (quote on 146).

82. Ibid., 147.

83. Ibid., 148.

84. South Carolina Inter-State and West Indian Exposition Company, Receivers' Accounts, 1902–4, 1910, SHC.

85. *The Exposition*, Dec. 1901, 495–500.

86. Hemphill, "Short Story," 148–49, 138–39; *The Exposition*, Dec. 1900, 5–6, May 1901, 200–201, Sept. 1901, 369–71, Nov. 1901, 470. For more on this controversy, see chapter 11 below.

87. My thanks to Bruce G. Harvey, who shared early excerpts from his thesis, "An Old City in the New South: Urban Progressivism and Charleston's West Indian Exposition" (M.A. thesis, University of South Carolina, 1988).

88. *Atlanta Constitution*, Mar. 8, 1903.

89. His firm included George M. Trenholm, W. C. Miller, and R. S. Whaley (Snowden, *History of South Carolina*, 3:37).

90. Duffy, "Charleston Politics."

91. *By-Laws, Rules, Officers and Members, Commercial Club, Charleston, S.C.* (Charleston, S.C., 1904), 4; see also Conner, *Progressive Charleston*.

92. *Atlanta Constitution*, Mar. 8, 1903.

93. William C. Miller, "Speech to the Commercial Club," n.d., Miller Papers, SCHS.

Chapter 8

1. E. Digby Baltzell, *Philadelphia Gentlemen: The Making of a National Upper Class* (1958; reprint, Chicago, 1971), esp. chap. 1.

2. David Ward, *Cities and Immigrants: A Geography of Change in Nineteenth-Century America* (New York, 1971), chaps. 4, 5.

3. Baltzell, *Philadelphia Gentlemen*, chaps. 1, 2; Robert H. Wiebe, *The Search for Order, 1877–1920* (New York, 1967).

4. E. Y. Clarke, *Illustrated History of Atlanta* (Atlanta, Ga., 1877), 61.

5. Franklin Garrett, *Atlanta and Environs: A Chronicle of Its People and Events* (Athens, Ga., 1969), 1:811–12, 834–35; Clarke, *Illustrated History*, 65–67.

6. The quote is from Review Publishing Company, *Atlanta of Today* (Atlanta, Ga., 1897), 58.

7. *Atlanta Constitution*, Sept. 2, 1870, quoted in Garrett, *Atlanta and Environs*, 1:845.

8. Garrett, *Atlanta and Environs*, 1:813, 844.

9. Ibid., 1:879–80, 883; Jean Martin, "Mule to MARTA," *Atlanta Historical Bulletin* 19 (1975): 6–10.

10. Garrett, *Atlanta and Environs*, 2:34, 217–19; *Atlanta in 1890: "The Gate City"* (1890; reprint, Macon, Ga., 1986), 7, 10, 11, 14, 19, 22, 39, 68, 79, 80, 87. Timothy Crimmins's introduction to this reprint and the annotations by William A. Richards and Franklin Garrett make this an especially useful source for viewing what Crimmins refers to as the "best face" of Atlanta in 1890.

11. For examples of this use of residential architecture as an indicator of community wealth, see Clarke, *Illustrated History*; *Supplement to the Textile Record of America: International Cotton Exposition and the City of Atlanta* (Philadelphia, 1881), 10–11; *Atlanta of Today*, 57–58; *Atlanta in 1890*; and Edward C. Kirkland, *Dream and Thought in the Business Community, 1860–1900* (Ithaca, N.Y., 1956), 34, 49.

12. Garrett, *Atlanta and Environs*, 1:751.

13. See Martin, "Mule to MARTA," 12, 14, for details on the financial problems of this line.

14. *Atlanta in 1890*, 24, 32, 28. Lots in West End were selling for $40 a front foot, while on the tonier Peachtree Street lots went for three times that amount (*Atlanta Constitution*, Feb. 13, 1887).

15. Quoted in Garrett, *Atlanta and Environs,* 2:222.

16. *Atlanta Constitution,* Nov. 6, 1887; Rick Beard, "From Suburb to Defended Neighborhood: The Evolution of Inman Park," *Atlanta Historical Journal* 26 (1982): 113–40; idem, "Hurt's Deserted Village: Atlanta's Inman Park, 1885–1911," in *Olmsted South: Old South Critic, New South Planner,* edited by Dana F. White and Victor A. Kramer (Westport, Conn., 1979), 195–221.

17. *Atlanta in 1890,* 85, also 11, 15, 31, 84, 90, 91; Garrett, *Atlanta and Environs,* 2:188–89, 191, 367–68, 525; Lamar L. Connell, "Inman Park: Atlanta's First Suburb," typescript, 1950, GDAH. Timothy Crimmins refers to Inman Park as Atlanta's first planned suburb (*Atlanta in 1890,* xxii). In 1884 plans for Peters Park, to be located off of West Peachtree, were formulated in connection with the establishment of Georgia Technological Institute (see *Atlanta Constitution,* Mar. 30, 1884; Garrett, *Atlanta and Environs,* 2:69–70).

18. Garrett, *Atlanta and Environs,* 2:455–57.

19. *Atlanta Constitution,* Apr. 3, 1910.

20. Ibid., Apr. 26, 1892; Garrett, *Atlanta and Environs,* 2:525–26.

21. Garrett, *Atlanta and Environs,* 2:525–27. See *Atlanta Constitution,* May 21, 1911, on the north-ward spread of the city. On the Olmsteds' role in the planning of Druid Hills, see Elizabeth H. Lyon, "Frederick Law Olmsted and Joel Hurt: Planning for Atlanta," in *Olmsted South,* 171–82.

22. Ten of the forty elites analyzed in chapter 4 lived in the country in 1880; twelve occupied Capitol Hill addresses; ten lived out in the West End, and six in the Rutledge Hill area. The remainder lived in other neighborhoods in the city.

23. Nell Fall Handley, interview notes, Waller Collection, Special Collections, Heard Library, Vanderbilt University; William Waller, ed., *Nashville in the 1890s* (Nashville, Tenn., 1970), 187.

24. Waller, *Nashville in the 1890s,* 219.

25. *Nashville American,* Feb. 1, 1886.

26. Ibid.; Handley interview notes.

27. Robert H. Gardner will, Probate Court Records, Nashville and Davidson County Court-house, Nashville, Tenn., vol. 27, pp. 527, 591; vol. 29, p. 117. The estate was estimated at approx-imately $433,500, and Matt received over $164,000.

28. Waller, *Nashville in the 1890s,* 187, 219.

29. Ibid., 202, 294, 300, 309; William Waller, ed., *Nashville, 1900 to 1910* (Nashville, Tenn., 1972), 7, 269; *Nashville Sun,* June 27, 1897.

30. Waller, *Nashville in the 1890s,* 254; *Nashville Banner,* Apr. 1, 1902.

31. Fletch Coke, *Captain Ryman at Home: His Family and Neighbors on Rutledge Hill* (Nashville, Tenn., 1982), 4, 32–35.

32. Waller, *Nashville in the 1890s,* 178–82.

33. *Nashville Banner,* Aug. 24, 1873, July 12, 1866.

34. Mark B. Riley, "Edgefield: A Study of an Early Nashville Suburb," *Tennessee Historical Quar-terly* 37 (1978): 133–54.

35. E. W. Crozier, comp., *The Nashville Blue Book of Selected Names of Nashville and Immediate Suburbs for the Year 1896* (Nashville, Tenn., 1896), 128–32.

36. Waller, *Nashville in the 1890s,* 185–86.

37. Waller, *Nashville, 1900 to 1910,* 18.

38. *Nashville American,* July 30, 1885; Waller, *Nashville in the 1890s,* 9.

39. *Nashville Banner,* Feb. 29, 1872.

40. G. M. Hopkins, *Atlas of the City of Nashville, Tennessee* (Philadelphia, 1889), plates 9, 10; idem, *Atlas of the City of Nashville, Tennessee* (Philadelphia, 1908), plates 9, 10.

41. Paul K. Conkin, *Gone with the Ivy: A Biography of Vanderbilt University* (Nashville, Tenn., 1985), 74.

42. Wilbur F. Creighton, interview notes, Waller Collection.

43. Josephine Farrell, interview notes, Waller Collection.

44. Crozier, *Nashville Blue Book,* 39.

45. *Nashville American,* July 21, 1886; see the *Mirror* (Nashville, Tenn.), June 16, 1892, for details of Acklen's troubled inheritance from his mother, Adelicia Acklen. The *Nashville Banner* reported that a syndicate had acquired the 350-acre tract (July 19, 1906).

46. *Nashville American,* Apr. 14, 21, 1898; Morgan B. Reynolds, *Seventy Years of Belle Meade Country Club, 1901–1907* ([Nashville, Tenn., 1971]), [1–6].

47. Eugene C. Lewis, Samuel J. Keith, Eustace A. Hall, Edgar Jones, and William W. Berry were the incorporators of the company (*Nashville Banner,* Mar. 4, 1905).

48. Annie Somers Gilchrist, *Some Representative Women of Tennessee* (Nashville, Tenn., 1902), 16–24.

49. Waller, *Nashville, 1900 to 1910,* 17–21; John J. Ellis, "Belle Meade: Development of a Southern Upper-Class Suburb, 1905–1938" (M.A. thesis, Vanderbilt University, 1984).

50. Baltzell, *Philadelphia Gentlemen,* chap. 13.

51. Dixon Wecter, *The Saga of American Society* (New York, 1937), 253–55, quoted in Baltzell, *Philadelphia Gentlemen,* 338.

52. Clarke, *Illustrated History,* 107. The Men's Library Association, founded sometime before 1879, may be the closest Atlanta came to a men's club in this period (ibid., 143).

53. *Atlanta Constitution,* June 18, 1893, Apr. 16, Oct. 25, 1882. The first Fulton Club also was short lived (ibid., June 18, 1893).

54. Garrett, *Atlanta and Environs,* 2:60–62; *Atlanta Constitution,* Mar. 25, 1883, Dec. 17, 1911. See *Officers, Members, Constitution and Rules of the Capital City Club of Atlanta, Georgia* ([Atlanta, Ga., 1891]) for a list of members and when they joined. By 1891 there were 278 members, including 87 nonresident members from cities in the North and South.

55. Garrett, *Atlanta and Environs,* 2:62, 151–52, 240, 328, 355, 384.

56. *Atlanta Constitution,* Dec. 17, 1911, June 18, 1893.

57. Garrett, *Atlanta and Environs,* 2:403–5.

58. Ibid., 2:368. An earlier athletic club had been launched without success in 1884 (*Atlanta Constitution,* July 18, 1884).

59. *Atlanta Constitution,* June 23, 1902, June 24, July 7, 1904, June 1, 1913.

60. Garrett, *Atlanta and Environs,* 2:136–38, 143–45, 155–57.

61. *Nashville American,* Apr. 25, 1886, May 13, 1881, Jan. 11, 1882, Feb. 18, 1882. See *Nashville Banner,* June 22, 1907, for a detailed account of the origins of the Hermitage Club.

62. *Nashville Banner,* Apr. 30, 1882, Apr. 25, 1886; Waller, *Nashville in the 1890s,* 138. *Rules of the Hermitage Club, Nashville, Tennessee, 1896* (Nashville, Tenn., 1896).

63. *Nashville Banner,* Feb. 16, 1890.

64. Waller, *Nashville in the 1890s,* 143; *Nashville Banner,* June 25, July 13, Nov. 10, 1898.

65. For the members and rules, see *Constitution and Rules: University Club, Nashville, Tennessee, 1901* [Nashville, Tenn., 1901]. See also *Nashville American,* Mar. 5, 1905, and *Town Topics: The Journal of Society,* Mar. 23, 1905, both quoted in Waller, *Nashville, 1900–1910,* 145–46, 158.

66. *Nashville American,* June 28, 1884, May 9, 1886. Arthur Johnson, "Report on Preliminary Survey of Printed Materials Pertinent to the Waller Collection," typescript, July 1954, p. 12, Waller Collection.

67. *Nashville American,* May 9, 1886; *Nashville Banner,* June 22, 1907, May 28, 1910; Waller, *Nashville, 1900 to 1910,* 144–45, 353.

68. See the files on the Old Oak and Round Table clubs in the Waller Collection.

69. Baltzell, *Philadelphia Gentlemen,* 12, 161.

70. *Nashville American,* Sept. 10, 1888.

71. Quoted in *Chat,* Nov. 17, 1894.

72. Josephine Waller interview notes, Waller Collection; Waller, *Nashville in the 1890s,* 18n; see also the interview notes for Nell Fall Handley, Mary Ewing, Mrs. Joseph Howells (Mannie Lindsay Howells), Waller Collection.

73. *Nashville American,* Nov. 20, 1885.

74. Mary Ewing interview notes, Waller Collection; Waller, *Nashville in the 1890s,* 138.

75. Waller, *Nashville in the 1890s,* 170, 182.

76. *Nashville American,* Dec. 31, 1877, Jan. 3, 1988; a list of those receiving in their homes and the young women assisting them was also printed in the paper.

77. On the summer resort as "an inter-city upper-class neighborhood, see Baltzell, *Philadelphia Gentlemen,* 220–22. Space does not allow more than passing reference to Beersheba and Monteagle and their role in the formation of the upper class in Nashville, but their importance is suggested in Margaret B. Coppinger et al., *Beersheba Springs: 150 Years, 1833–1983* (Beersheba Springs, Tenn., 1983), and Ridley Willis II, "The Monteagle Sunday School Assembly: A Brief Account of Its Origin and History," *Tennessee Historical Quarterly* 44 (Spring 1985): 3–26.

78. Garrett, *Atlanta and Environs,* 2:581. Atlanta had a male Cotillion Club, according to the Dau Publishing Company, *Atlanta Society Blue Book, 1907,* 64, but it is not mentioned in earlier or later accounts.

79. Garrett, *Atlanta and Environs,* 2:581–83.

80. Ibid., 2:689; Wecter, *Saga,* 327–29.

81. Garrett, *Atlanta and Environs,* 2:256, 439, 442.

82. William Raoul, "The Proletarian Aristocrat," 28, 37, typescript, SHC. On Raoul's father, see Maury Klein, *The Great Richmond Terminal: A Study in Businessmen and Business Strategy* (Charlottesville, Va., 1970), 45–47.

83. *Charleston News and Courier,* Feb. 25, 1897.

84. Waller, *Nashville in the 1890s,* 313–15; William Waller lists the weddings of prominent Nashville families and indicates the hometown of outsiders (*Nashville, 1900 to 1910,* 347–52). The Atlanta newspapers included full accounts of society weddings.

85. Waller, *Nashville in the 1890s,* facing p. 237.

86. W. Woodford Clayton, *History of Davidson County, Tennessee* (1880; reprint, Nashville, Tenn., 1971), 430–31.

87. Ibid., 118; *Chat,* Oct. 19, 1895.

88. Dau Publishing Company, *Nashville Society Blue Book* (New York, 1900).

89. Dau Publishing Company, *The Atlanta Society Blue Book: Elite Family Directory, Club Membership, November, 1901* (New York, 1901).

90. Mrs. William W. Geraldton, *Social Directory, Nashville, Tennessee* (Nashville, Tenn., 1911).

91. Social Register Association, *Social Register, Richmond, North Carolina, Charleston, Savannah, Augusta, Atlanta* (New York, 1905); see also the editions for 1910, 1912, 1914, and 1915.

92. On the role of the social register for the northeastern upper class, see Baltzell, *Philadelphia Gentlemen,* 17–24.

93. On Nashville's aspirations as a center for art in the South, see the *Nashville Banner,* Dec. 2, 1905, Apr. 18, 1907, Oct. 12, 1912.

94. Waller, *Nashville, 1900 to 1910,* 141–42.

95. Waller, *Nashville in the 1890s,* 172–73; idem, *Nashville, 1900 to 1910,* 71–72.

96. *Nashville American,* Oct. 24, 1901, Apr. 30, 1905, quoted in Waller, *Nashville, 1900 to 1910,* 61–62, 63.

97. Garrett, *Atlanta and Environs,* 2:480. Dau Publishing Company, *Atlanta Society Blue Book,*

1907, 51–55, shows that the association included male officers and members, but women formed the majority in both categories.

98. Garrett, *Atlanta and Environs,* 2:279.

99. Thomas M. Deaton, "Atlanta during the Progressive Era" (Ph.D. diss., University of Georgia, 1969), 234–35; Garrett, *Atlanta and Environs,* 2:278–80. For a discussion of opera as an important part of American upper-class identity, see Wecter, *Saga,* 459–65.

100. Garrett, *Atlanta and Environs,* 2:547–48.

101. Ibid., 2:567; T. Elden Burton, "The Metropolitan Opera in Atlanta," *Atlanta Historical Bulletin* 20 (Jan. 1940): 37–43.

102. Cf. Wecter, *Saga,* chap. 8, on women in upper-class society.

103. *Nashville Banner,* Oct. 12, 1912.

104. Ann Elizabeth Taylor provides a full account of Nashville women in this movement ("The Woman Suffrage Movement in Tennessee" [Ph.D. diss., Vanderbilt University, 1943]).

105. Walter G. Cooper, *Official History of Fulton County* (Atlanta, Ga., 1934), 816–17.

106. Ibid., 817; Garrett, *Atlanta and Environs,* 2:340; For a list of members and officers, see Dau Publishing Company, *Atlanta Society Blue Book, 1907,* 62–63.

107. John Woolridge, ed., *History of Nashville, Tennessee* (Nashville, Tenn., 1890), 550–51; *Nashville Banner,* Oct. 17, 1868, Mar. 24, 1870.

108. James Douglas Flamming, "The Sam Jones Revivals and Social Reform in Nashville, Tennessee, 1885–1900" (M.A. thesis, Vanderbilt University, 1983), chaps. 3, 4.

109. Herman Justi, ed., *Official History of the Tennessee Centennial Exposition* (Nashville, Tenn., 1898), 145–50, 264–70; Don H. Doyle, *Nashville in the New South, 1880–1930* (Knoxville, Tenn., 1985), 146–49.

110. Matilda Porter, "Centennial Club Reflects Culture and Elevation of Social Standards," *Tennessean,* June 25, 1916, quoted in Charlotte A. Williams, comp., *The Centennial Club of Nashville: A History from 1905–77* (Nashville, Tenn., 1978), 7.

111. *Nashville Banner,* June 29, Oct. 5, 1905.

112. Quoted in Williams, *Centennial Club,* 13; see also *Nashville Banner,* Nov. 4, 1905.

113. Williams, *Centennial Club,* 23–24.

Chapter 9

1. *Charleston News and Courier,* Sept. 16, 1899.

2. The account that follows is from Gabriel Edward Manigault, "Autobiography," 502–6, manuscript, Manigault Family Papers, SHC.

3. Robert Rosen, *A Short History of Charleston* (San Francisco, Calif., 1982), 140–41.

4. *Charleston News and Courier,* Dec. 30, 1898.

5. City of Charleston, *Yearbook, 1910,* 396–97. The Charleston Art Commission was made up of the mayor and representatives of the Carolina Art Association, Charleston Library Society, Charleston Museum, South Carolina Historical Society, and three citizens, whose duty was to review "matters affecting the aesthetic and historic interests of the city" brought before the city council.

6. Mildred Cram, *Old Seaport Towns of the South* (New York: Dodd Mead and Company, 1917), 125.

7. John P. Radford, "Testing the Model of the Pre-industrial City: The Case of Charleston, South Carolina," *Transactions, The Institute of British Geographers,* n.s., 4 (1979): 392–410. This study draws on research from Radford's fuller work ("Culture, Economy, and Urban Structure in Charleston, South Carolina, 1860–1880" [Ph.D. diss., Clark University, 1974]); see also idem,

"Social Structure and Urban Form: Charleston, 1860–1880," in *From the Old South to the New: Essays on the Transitional South,* edited by Walter J. Fraser and Winfred B. Moore (Westport, Conn., 1981), 81–92.

8. Radford, "Culture, Economy, and Urban Structure," 177–92, 266–78.

9. *Charleston News and Courier,* May 7, 1899.

10. This account is reprinted in the *Charleston News and Courier,* July 27, 1897; see also ibid., July 6, 14, 18, 1897, May 7, 1899, for other observations on Charleston's acceptance of the trolley. The streetcar system was consolidated and taken over by a Baltimore syndicate in 1899 (see ibid., Jan. 20, 1899). Suburban development followed the trolley, and local boosters were soon heralding "Greater Charleston" (see ibid., June 3, July 27, 1897). The suburban development of the Neck was stimulated by the exposition of 1901–2, which opened the northwest section of the city to the development of Wagener Terrace and Hampton Park.

11. *Charleston News and Courier,* Apr. 5, 1896; Jack Leland, *Sixty-two Famous Houses of Charleston, South Carolina* (Charleston, S.C., 1988), 28. See also Thomas R. Waring, who notes that the Victorian "era of bad taste in architecture and in furniture passed almost without effect upon Charleston . . . " ("Charleston," in *The Carolina Low Country,* by Augustine Smyth et al. [New York, 1931], 146).

12. "Information for Guides of Historic Charleston, South Carolina," Historic Charleston Foundation, Charleston, S.C., 1985, 147, typescript; Leland, *Sixty-two Famous Houses of Charleston,* 24. Thanks for Jon Poston and Kitty Robinson of the Historic Charleston Foundation for a tour and for information on the Williams and Rodgers properties, and thanks to Wallace Scarborough of the Atlantic Coast Life Insurance Company, who gave me an informative tour of the Rodgers mansion, which his company now occupies.

13. Robert Goodwyn Rhett, *Charleston: An Epic of Carolina* (Richmond, Va., 1940), 336.

14. City of Charleston, *Yearbook, 1882,* 207, quoted in Gene Waddell's introduction to Arthur Mazyck, *Charleston in 1883* (1883; reprint, Easley, S.C., 1983), xii.

15. City of Charleston, *Yearbook, 1882,* 206–7.

16. *Charleston News and Courier,* Feb. 2, Feb. 23, 1896. See also Ruth M. Miller and Ann Taylor Andrus, *Witness to History: Charleston's Old Exchange and Provost Dungeon* (Orangeburg, S.C., 1986), 49–60.

17. See, for example, the account of the Timrod Memorial in City of Charleston, *Yearbook, 1901,* app., 60–61; on City Hall memorials, see *Yearbook, 1882,* 205–21.

18. "Address Presented to the Family of General Beauregard on the Occasion of Receiving his Sword for the City of Charleston," [1893], Miles Papers, file no. 68, SHC; City of Charleston, *Yearbook, 1893,* 273–85.

19. Harriott Horry Rutledge Ravenel, *Charleston: The Place and the People* (1906; reprint, New York, 1922), 507.

20. H. P. Archer, *Local Reminiscences; a Lecture . . . delivered at Charleston, S.C., June 6, 1889* (Charleston, S.C., 1893).

21. *Charleston News and Courier,* Dec. 30, 1986, quoted in E. Culpepper Clark, *Francis Warrington Dawson and the Politics of Restoration: South Carolina, 1874–1889* (University, Ala., 1980), 141–42.

22. *Charleston News and Courier,* May 14, 1890.

23. Clipping from the *Charleston News and Courier,* commenting on a speech by William C. P. Breckinridge in Philadelphia, n.d., in Anthony W. Riecke Scrapbook, 1:61, SCHS.

24. William Heyward to James Gregorie, Charleston, S.C., Apr. 1869, Gregorie Papers, file 11, SHC.

25. G. I. Crafts to William Porcher Miles, Charleston, S.C., Sept. 14, 1878, William Porcher Miles Papers, box 3, file 49, SHC.

26. Julian Street, *American Adventures: A Second Trip "Abroad at Home"* (New York, 1917), 303–4.

27. Harriette Kershaw Leiding, *Charleston: Historic and Romantic* (Philadelphia, 1931), 5; Enid Ewing, "Charleston Contra Mundum," *The Nation,* Nov. 20, 1943, 580.

28. *Charleston News and Courier,* Oct. 7, 1894.

29. Henry J. Middleton to Alicia, Hendersonville, N.C., Aug. 14, 1911, in Middleton Family Papers, box 5, SCL.

30. *Transactions of the Huguenot Society of South Carolina* 8 (Charleston, [1901]), 16.

31. Ibid. 1 (1889): 13–17, 53–54, quoted in Frederic Cople Jaher, *The Urban Establishment: Upper Strata in Boston, New York, Charleston, Chicago, and Los Angeles* (Urbana, Ill., 1982), 417.

32. Wilmot G. DeSaussure to William Porcher Miles, Charleston, S.C., Sept. 21, 1870, in William Porcher Miles Papers, Box 3, file 41, SHC.

33. Wilmot G. DeSaussure will, Probate County Court Records, Charleston County Courthouse, Charleston, S.C., no. 394–15; see also DeSaussure's obituary in City of Charleston, *Yearbook, 1886,* 210–15.

34. George Alfred Trenholm Papers, file 22, SCL.

35. *Charleston News and Courier,* May 8, 1938, reprinted from the *Atlanta Journal,* n.d., and found in the Hinson Collection, card catalog, CLS.

36. Rhett, *Charleston,* 77, 79–80; Ravenel, *Charleston,* 385–86.

37. David Duncan Wallace, *The History of South Carolina* (New York, 1934), 3:428n; *Sholes' Directory of the City of Charleston, January, 1881* ([Charleston, 1881]), 40.

38. *A Sketch of the Charleston Club with Its Constitution and By-Laws and a List of Its Members, 1852–1938* ([Charleston, 1938]), 13.

39. Ibid., 15, 18 (quote on 15).

40. *Mobile Register,* Sept. 20, 1901.

41. *Charleston News and Courier,* Oct. 7, 1894. The article took care not to mention the St. Cecilia Society by name.

42. *Mobile Register,* Sept. 20, 1901.

43. Invitations from 1873 and 1869, in Vanderhorst Papers, SCHS. See also Anne Rittenhouse, "America's Social House of Peers," *Ainslee's Magazine,* Oct. 1905, 76–77.

44. Ravenel, *Charleston,* 426–27.

45. Joseph Barnwell, "Life and Recollections," 364, typescript, SCHS. Barnwell disputed Ravenel's description of the St. Cecilia Society as extremely exclusive. When he joined in 1874 there were 335 members, up from about 100 in the late 1860s when many could not afford the $15 dues, which were reduced temporarily to $10. The late 1860s must have been a low point in membership, and there is no evidence that there were many newcomers entering the society. Barnwell also claimed that only three or four applications were blackballed during his time in the society, from 1874 to 1922. As Ravenel explains, however, questionable applications were usually withdrawn to avoid the embarrassment of a blackball. Barnwell concurred with this statement (Ravenel, *Charleston,* 427; Barnwell, "Life," 383). See also Rittenhouse, "America's Social House of Peers," 76–84.

46. Mrs. T. P. O'Conner, *My Beloved South* (New York, 1913), 150.

47. John Berkeley Grimball Diary, Feb. 8, 1870, SHC.

48. Barnwell, "Life," 378.

49. Ibid., 377–78; Rittenhouse, "America's Social House of Peers," 79.

50. Barnwell, "Life," 379; see also O'Conner, *Beloved South,* 147–50; Street, *American Adventures,* 333–35; and, for a description of a St. Cecilia ball, DuBose Heyward, *Mamba's Daughters: A Novel of Charleston* (New York, 1929), 121–36.

51. Theodore G. Barker memorial to C. R. Miles before the St. Cecilia Society, Nov. 22, 1893, in William Porcher Miles Papers, box 3, file 69, SHC.

52. Rittenhouse, "America's Social House of Peers," 77.

53. Heyward, *Mamba's Daughters,* 115–21.

54. *Mobile Register,* Sept. 20, 1901.

55. *Charleston American,* Jan. 19, 1917, quoted in Street, *American Adventures,* 329–30. See also the reply to Julian Street's criticism of their intrusion on the "effete sanctity of the St. Cecilia" in the *Charleston American,* [Nov. 17?], 1917, pamphlet, SCHS.

56. Ludwig Lewisohn, *Up Stream: An American Chronicle* (New York, 1922), 57–58. Most Germans remained in their own clubs and religious organizations. The German Friendly Society, founded in 1766, was the oldest of some fourteen German societies active in 1890 (George J. Congaware, *The History of the German Friendly Society of Charleston, South Carolina, 1766–1916* [Richmond, Va., 1935]; *History of the Deutsche Zeitung: Sixty Years of Charleston History* [Charleston, 1913]).

57. Henry James, *The American Scene* (1907; reprint, New York, 1967), 414–18.

58. *Guide to Charleston, S.C., with Historical Sketch of the City and Directory of Historic Points* (Charleston, S.C., [1907]) describes the clubhouse, "Belvedere," the former Shubrick home. *Charleston Country Club, 1901–1902* (Charleston, S.C., [1901]), includes listings of rules, officers, members. Cf. *Charleston Country Club, Etiquette of Golf, List of Officers and Members* (Charleston, S.C., 1926).

59. *Mobile Register,* Sept. 21, 1883.

60. *Rules of the Manassas Club, Mobile, Founded November, 1861, Revised and Adopted January, 1862* (Mobile, Ala., 1862) includes a list of members. Correspondence from Mobile historian Caldwell Delaney provided useful information on the Manassas Club (letter to author, May 6, 1987). The *Mobile Register,* Jan. 24, 1880, lists William H. Ketchum, F. S. Parker, R. W. Hallett, D. E. Huger, W. J. Brainard, and C. A. Holt as prominent members.

61. *Mobile Register,* Jan. 24, 1880.

62. Caldwell Delaney to author, May 6, 1987.

63. Bradley Goodyear Smith, *The Athelstan Club: An Enduring Legacy* ([Mobile, Ala.], 1979), 6. By order of the church, the Masonic order was officially forbidden to Catholics, who made up a large segment of the city's population and a portion of its business and professional elite. This ban could have provided another motive for the change, since several Catholics joined Athelstan. The speculation about opening the club to Catholics is my own. Ben H. Harris estimates that eight to ten of the charter members of Athelstan Club were Catholic, but he knew of no religious issue in the conversion from a Masonic lodge to a men's social club (letter to author, Sept. 20, 1978).

64. *Rules of Athelstan Club* (Mobile, Ala., 1873), preface. This is part of a cache of materials on Athelstan found in the cornerstone of the original building at St. Joseph and Dauphin and now in the Museum of the City of Mobile.

65. Ibid., 8–9.

66. Caldwell Delaney to author, May 6, 1987.

67. Smith, *Athelstan Club,* esp. 7–9; *Mobile Register,* July 17, 1977; *Athelstan Centenarian,* Sept. 28, 1973, clippings in MPL vertical files; Palmer Pillans, "Mobile in Two Centuries," 157, 230, typescript, ADAH.

68. A membership list is found in Smith, *Athelstan Club,* 78ff. Religious identifications were provided for many of those in the 1880 economic elite, about thirty-five of whom were Athelstan members. Cf. Alma Esther Berkstresser, "Mobile, Alabama, in the 1880s" (M.A. thesis, University of Alabama, 1951), 194, which states that Jews were excluded from Athelstan; and Joseph M. Proskauer, *A Segment of My Times* (New York, 1950), 12. The quote regarding Jewish separation is

from Mrs. B. H. Beverly, "Jewish People of Mobile," Composition Book, ca. 1938, 60–78, ADAH; Beverly also states that the social dividing line receded radically after World War I, allowing Jews to join gentile clubs and even to intermarry. Alfred G. Moses deals more with individuals and institutions than with the social role of religion (*A History of the Jews of Mobile* [Baltimore, Md., 1904]).

69. Smith, *Athelstan Club.*

70. Harriet E. Amos, *Cotton City: Urban Development in Antebellum Mobile* (University, Ala., 1985), 64–65. Amos describes the early mystic societies as part of a continuing tradition of "pre-Lenten" festivities stemming from the French and Spanish Mardi Gras, but the New Year and Mardi Gras celebrations, and the societies that sponsored each, remained distinct. See also Thomas C. DeLeon, *Our Creole Carnivals: Their Origin, History, Progress, and Results* (Mobile, Ala., 1890), 21; and DeLeon's summary essay, "Mobile's Carnival," *Mobile Register,* Jan. 31, 1895. Bennett Wayne Dean offers a comprehensive history of the local Mardi Gras tradition in *Mardi Gras: Mobile's Illogical Whoop-de-Doo, 1704–1970* (Chicago, 1971), esp. 9–15, 27. The *Mobile Register,* Dec. 31, 1882, includes an account of the early Cowbellions.

71. DeLeon places the Strikers' origins in 1843, whereas Amos places it in 1841 (DeLeon, "Mobile's Carnival"; Amos, *Cotton City,* 65).

72. *Mobile Register,* Jan. 31, 1895.

73. Amos, *Cotton City,* 65; Berkstresser, "Mobile," 196; *Mobile Register,* Jan. 31, 1895; Melton McLaurin and Michael Thomason, *Mobile: The Life and Times of a Great Southern City* (Woodland Hills, Calif., 1981), 74.

74. Clipping, *Mobile Times,* Jan. 1, 1933, in vertical files, MPL; Pillans, "Mobile," 73–75.

75. McLaurin and Thomason, *Mobile,* 74.

76. *Mobile Register,* Jan. 31, 1895.

77. Caldwell Delaney and Cornelia M. Turner, *Infant Mystics: The First Hundred Years* ([Mobile, Ala., 1970]), 2.

78. *Mobile Register,* Jan. 31, 1895.

79. Delaney and Turner, *Infant Mystics,* 2.

80. Ibid., 3–7.

81. Samuel Eichold, *Without Malice: The 100th Anniversary of the Comic Cowboys, 1884–1984* (Mobile, Ala., [1984]). Eichold never discusses the religious issue in the history of Comic Cowboys. The older mystic societies were not exclusively gentile. Joseph M. Proskauer recalls that his father, a prominent Jewish leader of Mobile, was a member of O.O.M. (*Segment of My Times,* 12). The Comic Cowboys and, later, the Continental Mystics, founded sometime in the 1890s, apparently were strictly Jewish (interview with Bob Zeitz, Mobile Public Library, Mobile, Ala., June 1986). The Crewe of Columbus, founded in 1922, originally was made up of Catholics but was opened to other denominations in the 1930s.

82. This same premise seemed to discourage the proliferation of subscribed biographical tributes that flourished in more dynamic towns and cities in the late nineteenth century.

83. *Mobile Register,* Feb. 8, 1877, Dec. 31, 1881.

84. Ibid., Feb. 18, 1890.

85. Mobile Peetryarch Club, *The Mother of Mystics* ([Mobile, Ala.], n.d.).

86. *Mobile Register,* Feb. 28, 1895.

87. Ibid., Feb. 7, 1883, Feb. 15, 1888.

88. In 1894 the first black mystic society, "O.O.D.," formed among "the elite of colored society" and held annual balls until World War I (Dean, *Mardi Gras,* 86–87).

89. *Mobile Register,* Feb. 15, 1888; see also ibid., Feb. 25, 1900, Feb. 25, 1903.

90. Thomas C. DeLeon, the principal organizer, identified the Carnival Association leaders as:

Price Williams, president; Col. D. E. Huger; Charles L. Huger; William H. Barney; James A. McCaa; John L. Rapier; James T. McCaw; Louis Scranton; Hannis Taylor; Thomas P. Brown; James Lyons; A. B. Woodcock; and "a score more" (*Mobile Register,* Jan. 31, 1895).

91. Emily S. Van Antwerp and Kathryn T. de Celle list all the emperors and empresses (kings and queens beginning in 1898) since 1872 (*Queens of Mobile Mardi Gras, 1893–1973* [Mobile, Ala., 1973], 26).

92. *Mobile Register,* Jan. 14, 1877, Jan. 31, 1895, Jan. 20, 1881, Feb. 10, 1891, Feb. 12, Feb. 20, 1880.

93. Ibid., Apr. 19, 1903, Jan. 8, 1882.

94. Ibid., Feb. 7, 1883, Jan. 4, 1893, Jan. 5, Feb. 7, 1894.

95. Ibid., Feb. 10, Mar. 3, Mar. 23, 1897, Jan. 5, Jan. 13, Feb. 24, Nov. 19, 1898, Feb. 15, 1899.

96. Ibid., Apr. 12, 1903, Mar. 2, 1905, Feb. 24, 1903.

97. Rev. J. R. Burgett, *Social Life in Mobile* (Mobile, Ala., 1900).

98. *Mobile Register,* Feb. 11, 1902, Dec. 16, 20, 1903.

99. W. J. E. Cox, *Some of the Immoral and Damnable Effects of Mardi Gras* (Mobile, Ala., 1907).

Chapter 10

1. Joseph Gusfield, *Symbolic Crusade: Status Politics and the American Temperance Movement* (Urbana, Ill., 1963); John Hammond Moore, "The Negro and Prohibition in Atlanta, 1885–1887," *South Atlantic Quarterly* 69 (1970): 38–57.

2. C. Vann Woodward, *The Strange Career of Jim Crow,* 3d edition (New York, 1971). Richard C. Wade (*Slavery in the Cities: The South, 1820–1860,* [New York, 1964]) and Howard N. Rabinowitz (*Race Relations in the Urban South, 1865–1890* [New York, 1978]) both make the case for an earlier emergence of segregation in the cities. See also John W. Cell, *The Highest Stage of White Supremacy: The Origins of Segregation in South Africa and the American South* (New York, 1982), which makes the case for segregation as a product of urbanization.

3. A detailed account of the Grizzard lynching is included in Van A. Cain, "'How Long, Oh Lord, How Long': Race Relations in Nashville, 1885–1900" (M.A. thesis, Vanderbilt University, 1987).

4. Charles Crowe, "Racial Massacre in Atlanta, September 22, 1906," in *The Segregation Era, 1863–1954: A Modern Reader,* edited by Allen Weinstein and Frank Otto Gattell (New York, 1970), 121.

5. For a full exploration of this debate, see George M. Fredrickson, *The Black Image in the White Mind: The Debate on Afro-American Character and Destiny, 1817–1914* (New York, 1971), chaps. 7–10.

6. Rabinowitz, *Race Relations,* 18–23.

7. Stanley J. Folmsbee, Robert E. Corlew, and Enoch L. Mitchell, *Tennessee: A Short History* (Knoxville, Tenn., 1969), 405–9; E. Merton Coulter, *Georgia: A Short History* (Chapel Hill, N.C., 1947), 414–16; Dewey W. Grantham, *Southern Progressivism: The Reconciliation of Progress and Tradition* (Knoxville, Tenn., 1983), 128–32.

8. *Nashville Banner,* Sept. 22, 1874.

9. Commenting on the black exodus to Kansas in 1879, a Nashville editor agreed that "the subtraction of so much muscle" would hurt the South in the short term. But the migration of surplus blacks, he continued, would drain away the worst element of blacks, reduce the political and social problems they presented, improve race relations for those who remained, and create a "vacuum" for white immigrants to take the place of blacks (*Nashville American,* Apr. 1, 1879). For editorial criticisms of the North, see, for example, ibid., Apr. 21, 1876, Nov. 18, 1877, Dec. 26, 1879; *Nashville Banner,* May 28, 1875.

10. *Nashville Union and Dispatch,* Jan. 17, 1868.

11. *Nashville Banner,* Feb. 22, 1870.

12. *Nashville American,* Nov. 8, 1877.

13. W. E. B. Du Bois, *The Negro in Business,* Atlanta University Publications, no. 4 (Atlanta, Ga., 1899).

14. *Atlanta Constitution,* Aug. 5, 7, 9, Dec. 7, 9, 1897. See also Melton A. McLaurin, *Paternalism and Protest: Southern Cotton Mill Workers and Organized Labor, 1875–1905* (Westport, Conn., 1971).

15. *Atlanta Constitution,* June 12, 1896.

16. Ibid., Aug. 31, 1890; see also ibid., Aug. 24, 1880, June 29, 1882.

17. Charles Foster Smith, "The Negro in Nashville," *Century Magazine* 42 (May 1891): 156.

18. *Atlanta Constitution,* Dec. 29, 1877; *Nashville American,* June 10, 1877.

19. See, for example, *Nashville American,* Sept. 27, 1877. See also Fredrickson, *Black Image,* chap. 7.

20. *Nashville American,* Sept. 27, 1877.

21. Fredrickson, *Black Image,* chap. 7.

22. *Atlanta Constitution,* Dec. 29, 1877; Fredrickson, *Black Image,* 206–7.

23. Walter G. Cooper, *The Cotton States and International Exposition and South Illustrated, Including the Official History of the Exposition* (Atlanta, Ga., 1896), 13–14, 27–28, 59.

24. Ibid., 60, 63.

25. *Atlanta Constitution,* Apr. 3, 1895; see also Robert W. Rydell, *All the World's a Fair: Visions of Empire at American International Expositions, 1876–1916* (Chicago, 1984), 85.

26. *Atlanta Constitution,* Sept. 19, 20, 1895.

27. Herman Justi, ed., *Official History of the Tennessee Centennial Exposition* (Nashville, Tenn., 1898), 193.

28. Ibid., 202–3.

29. *Nashville American,* May 1, 1897, quoted in Rydell, *All the World's a Fair,* 89.

30. Michael Katz, *The Irony of Early School Reform: Educational Innovation in Mid-Nineteenth Century Massachusetts* (Cambridge, Mass., 1968).

31. *Annual Report of the Board of Education for the City of Nashville . . . 1872–73* (Nashville, Tenn., 1873), 12. Titles of these annual reports will hereafter be given as *Annual Report, BOE, Nashville, {year}.*

32. Henry Lee Swint, *The Northern Teacher in the South* (Nashville, Tenn., 1941); Andrew D. Holt, *The Struggle for a State System of Public Schools in Tennessee, 1903–1936* (New York, 1938), 16–17, 28–29.

33. Rabinowitz, *Race Relations,* 156–58.

34. *Atlanta Constitution,* Nov. 25, 1879.

35. John Woolridge, ed., *History of Nashville, Tennessee* (Nashville, Tenn., 1890), 443–44.

36. Franklin Garrett, *Atlanta and Environs: A Chronicle of Its People and Events* (Athens, Ga., 1969), 1:820.

37. *Report of the Committee on Public Schools to the City Council of Atlanta, Georgia* (Atlanta, Ga., 1869), 11, quoted in Jerry J. Thornberry, "The Development of Black Atlanta, 1865–1885" (Ph.D. diss., University of Maryland, 1977), 87.

38. Garrett, *Atlanta and Environs,* 1:821–22.

39. Rabinowitz, *Race Relations,* 164–67. See also Rabinowitz, "Half a Loaf: The Shift from White to Black Teachers in the Negro Schools of the Urban South," *Journal of Southern History* 40 (Nov. 1974): 565–94; Thornberry, "Black Atlanta," chap. 3.

40. *Nashville Union and Dispatch,* June 15, 1867.

41. *Nashville Banner,* Mar. 10, 1875. See also the comments on the plans for a private manual training school in ibid., Mar. 13, 1867.

42. Rabinowitz, *Race Relations,* chaps. 6–8.

43. See *Nashville Banner,* Nov. 15, 1867, for a pointed response to the prospect of integrated schools as tantamount to "miscegenation" that would "double the mulattos among us."

44. Ibid., May 28, 1874.

45. Rabinowitz, *Race Relations,* 172–77; Thornberry, "Black Atlanta," 127–35.

46. See Don H. Doyle, *Nashville in the New South, 1880–1930* (Nashville, Tenn., 1985), 135–42, 165–77.

47. U.S. Census Bureau, *Thirteenth Census of the United States . . . 1910,* vol. 3, *Population, 1910* (Washington, D.C., 1913), 762. Other southern cities had comparable figures for black illiteracy: Atlanta, 20.9; Charleston, 27.9; Mobile, 25.9.

48. Average teacher salaries peaked at $710 per year in 1874–75 and fell to $544 within four years, then moved slowly upward to more than $600 after 1900 (see *Annual Report, BOE, Nashville, 1929–30,* 26, for a summary of these and other school statistics).

49. *Annual Report, BOE, Nashville, 1880–81,* and *Annual Report, BOE, Nashville, 1890–91.* By 1896–97 this was standardized in a salary schedule that started white teachers at $35 per month, working up to $50 in the fourth year. Black teachers started at $30 and received $45 in the fourth year. For each additional year whites received an added $5 per month, while blacks received $3 more. In the first year, blacks earned about 86 percent of their white counterparts' salaries; after ten years, 79 percent (*Annual Report, BOE, Nashville, 1896–97,* 86–87).

50. *Annual Report, BOE, Nashville, 1881–82,* 17.

51. *Annual Report, BOE, Nashville, 1894–95,* 55. By 1896–97, following completion of the Napier School for blacks and the move of the Colored High School to Pearl School, the superintendent reported "for the first time" that every black child desiring a seat in school could have one (*Annual Report, BOE, Nashville, 1896–97,* 20–21). The effects of the depression on student enrollments also helped ease the pressure.

52. Thornberry, "Black Atlanta," 131–32.

53. Black enrollment had actually declined since 1872, when 767 students were enrolled (Atlanta Public Schools, *First Annual Report of the Board of Education, for the School Year Ending August 31, 1872* [Atlanta, Ga., 1872], 23; hereafter, *Report, Atlanta BOE, {year}* [year refers to the year in which the report ended, which also varied from the school year to the calendar year]); *Report, Atlanta BOE, 1880,* 6.

54. *Report, Atlanta BOE, 1880,* 6; *Report, Atlanta BOE, 1890,* 10, 15; *Report, Atlanta BOE, 1910,* 5.

55. *Report, Atlanta BOE, 1880,* 6.

56. *Report, Atlanta BOE, 1890,* 10, 15; *Report, Atlanta BOE, 1900,* 32; *Report, Atlanta BOE, 1912,* 5 (includes report for 1910).

57. *Report, Atlanta BOE, 1912,* 24, 25.

58. Ibid., table on endpiece.

59. George Rosen, *A History of Public Health* (New York, 1958), 314, 387–94. James H. Cassedy, *Charles V. Chapin and the Public Health Movement* (Cambridge, Mass., 1962), 126–142; Charles V. Chapin, "History of State and Municipal Control of Disease," in *A Half Century of Public Health,* edited by Mazyck Porcher Ravenel (1921; reprint, New York, 1970), 133–60; Grantham, *Southern Progressivism,* 124–27.

60. Stuart Galishoff, "Germs Know No Color Line: Black Health and Public Policy in Atlanta, 1900–1918," *Journal of the History of Medicine and Allied Sciences* 40 (Jan. 1985): 30–32.

61. John Berrien Lindsley, *Second Report of the Nashville Board of Health for the Year Ending July 4, 1877* (Nashville, Tenn., 1877).

62. U.S. Census Bureau, *Negro Population, 1790–1915* (Washington, D.C., 1918), 320.

63. Ibid., 315. In 1910 death rates for southern blacks in cities of ten thousand or more population were 29.3 per thousand, versus 18.3 per thousand for southern rural blacks.

64. Quoted in Fredrickson, *Black Image*, 249–51. Hoffman's work, Fredrickson asserts, was "the most influential discussion of the race question to appear in the late nineteenth century." Hoffman's findings were initially published in *Arena* in 1892, at which time he predicted that "the negro, like the Indian, will be a vanishing race."

65. Paul B. Barringer, "The Negro and the Social Order," in *Race Problems of the South* (Richmond, Va., 1900), 191–92. Barringer drew from Hoffman's data and praised his "unbiased German mind" (ibid., 189).

66. William Lee Howard, "The Negro as a Distinct Ethnic Factor in Civilization," *Medicine* 60 (May 1903): 424, quoted in Fredrickson, *Black Image*, 268.

67. Charles S. Johnson examined the "justification for segregation in institutions and public places" and found fear of "contamination" a powerful factor in the minds of whites (*Patterns of Negro Segregation* [New York, 1943], 196–201). It is also worth noting that the collapse of Jim Crow's regime came after World War II, when the introduction of new antibiotics and other more effective means of controlling disease lessened the fear of interracial "contamination." Using the index of relative mortality (black death rates divided by white death rates) the national figures show a drop from 1.5 in 1910 to 1.33 in 1940 and then to .99 by 1970. At the same time, black death rates from TB dropped to a little over 1 percent of the 1910 figure. The fear of disease was just one tier in the wall of segregation that collapsed during the 1950s and 1960s, but one that deserves more attention. See U.S. Census Bureau, *The Social and Economic Status of the Black Population in the United States: An Historical View, 1790–1978*, Current Population Reports: Special Studies, Series P-23, no. 80 (Washington, D.C., 1979), tables 88, 89. For a suggestive study of medical theory and segregation in other cultures, see John W. Cell, "Anglo-Indian Medical Theory and the Origins of Segregation in West Africa," *American Historical Review* 91 (Apr. 1986): 307–35.

68. Perhaps the most extreme expression of this came in the Florida law that required separate storage facilities for the textbooks used by blacks (Pauli Murray, *States' Laws on Race and Color* [Cincinnati, Ohio, 1951], 82; see also Doyle, *Nashville in the New South,* chap. 5, esp. 107–20).

69. Stuart Galishoff emphasizes the ways in which the germ theory dictated an attack on disease among blacks, if only to protect whites ("Germs," 22–41). For a discussion of the progress and limitations of the health movement before 1900, see John H. Ellis, "Businessmen and Public Health in the Urban South during the Nineteenth Century: New Orleans, Memphis, and Atlanta," *Bulletin of the History of Medicine* 44 (May–June, July–Aug. 1970): 197–212, 346–71.

70. *Nashville Banner,* Nov. 5, 1910.

71. Galishoff, "Germs," 29.

72. Even with this increase, Board of Health expenditures went from .7 to 1.4 percent of the total city budget between 1892 and 1912. See *Reports of Departments of the City of Nashville . . . 1892* (Nashville, Tenn., 1893) (hereafter City of Nashville, *Reports, {year}*); City of Nashville, *Reports, 1912*.

73. Doyle, *Nashville in the New South,* 156–61, 165–77; Charlotte A. Williams, *The Centennial Club of Nashville: A History from 1905–77* (Nashville, 1978), 9–50.

74. All mortality figures are drawn from the annual reports of the Board of Health.

75. Total deaths for these years equaled 52,405. Combined with pneumonia, which killed 5,194, these diseases accounted for 26 percent of all deaths in Nashville.

76. Marion M. Torchia, "Tuberculosis among American Negroes: Medical Research on a Racial Disease, 1830–1950," *Journal of the History of Medicine and Allied Sciences* 32 (July 1977): 252–68; idem, "The Tuberculosis Movement and the Race Question, 1890–1950," *Bulletin of the History of Medicine* 49 (Summer 1975): 152–68. My thanks to Stuart Galishoff for bringing these articles to my attention.

77. City of Nashville, *Reports, 1899,* 172.

78. John Bessner Huber summarizes much of the contemporary medical literature on black susceptibility to TB (*Consumption: Its Relation to Man and His Civilization, Its Prevention and Cure* [Philadelphia, 1906], 100). George M. Fredrickson covers the biological theories of black degeneracy advanced in the period 1880–1914 (*Black Image,* 228–55, 256–62, 268–71).

79. City of Nashville, *Reports, 1886,* 84; see also *Reports, 1887,* 96.

80. Board of Health, Minutes, July 25, 1904, 198, City Clerk's vault, Nashville and Davidson County Courthouse, Nashville, Tenn.; see also the Board's urging for a slum inspection, ibid., Apr. 17, 1905, 237; Willis D. Weatherford, "Is the Negro Dying Out? Who Cares?" in *The New Chivalry—Health,* edited by James E. McCulloch (Nashville, 1915), 375–84; James Summerville, "The City and the Slum: 'Black Bottom' in the Development of South Nashville," *Tennessee Historical Quarterly* 40 (Summer 1981): 182–92.

81. Board of Health minutes, Feb. 21, 1900, 24–26, 29; Jan. 28, 1907, 287.

82. See, for example, *Nashville Banner,* Nov. 5, 1904; *Nashville American,* Mar. 8, 1904.

83. *Nashville American,* Nov. 11, 1904; see also ibid., Mar. 2, 1904.

84. *Indianapolis Freeman,* Jan. 21, 1905, quoted in August Meier and Elliott Rudwick, "Negro Boycotts of Jim Crow Streetcars in Tennessee," *American Quarterly* 21 (Winter 1969): 757.

85. Board of Health minutes, July 9, 1906, 277.

86. Ibid., Nov. 21, 1904, 217; see also the minutes for June 4, 1906, 275, which reveal earlier efforts to set up dispensaries for examination of sputum samples.

87. City of Nashville, *Reports, 1911,* 190.

88. Board of Health minutes, Jan. 25, 1904, 176; for a similar plea to the mayor and council, see ibid., Oct. 17, 1907, 301.

89. Ibid., Nov. 25, 1912, 76.

90. City of Nashville, *Reports, 1906–1912,* 222, 224, 292, 190, 208, 218, respectively.

91. City of Nashville, *Reports, 1912,* 188.

92. Black deaths from TB accounted for 53 percent of a total 74 deaths in 1912. Blacks comprised 29 percent of dispensary patients (of a total 1,098), 42 percent of admissions to the Tuberculosis Hospital (of 33); and 35 percent of the recipients of milk dispensed to patients (of 40).

93. Black insurance policies significantly reduced benefits for policy holders diagnosed as tubercular, "thereby doing more to propagate [*sic*] the spread of the disease among negroes than anything else" (City of Nashville, *Reports, 1912,* 187). See also Board of Health minutes, Dec. 2, 1912, 78–79.

94. Board of Health minutes, Feb. 14, 1900, 14–21; Dr. Olin West interview, typescript, March 1951, box 3, file 3, Waller Collection, Special Collections, Heard Library, Vanderbilt University.

95. *Nashville American,* June 30, 1905.

96. Ibid., Dec. 21, 1906.

97. Ibid., Jan. 29, 1907.

Chapter 11

1. D. E. Huger Smith, *A Charlestonian's Recollections, 1846–1913* (Charleston, S.C., 1950), 127–28.

2. Thomas Holt, *Black over White: Negro Political Leadership in South Carolina during Reconstruction* (Urbana, Ill., 1977); William C. Hine, "Frustration, Factionalism, and Failure: Black Political Leadership and the Republican Party in Reconstruction Charleston, 1865–1877" (Ph.D. diss., Kent State University, 1979), 251, 266–67. As Hine's careful study illustrates, ethnic politics played an important role in Charleston's Reconstruction-era politics. See also Ira Berlin, *Slaves without Masters: The Free Negro in the Antebellum South* (New York, 1974), 214–16.

3. George M. Fredrickson, *The Black Image in the White Mind: The Debate on Afro-American Character and Destiny, 1817–1914* (New York, 1971), esp. 61. See also Pierre L. Van den Berghe, *Race and Racism: A Comparative Perspective* (New York, 1967); George M. Fredrickson, *White Supremacy: A Comparative Study in American and South African History* (New York, 1981), 130–31, 270; Edward Byron Reuter, *The Mulatto in the United States* (Boston, 1918), chap. 13.

4. Hampton M. Jarrell, *Wade Hampton and the Negro: The Road Not Taken* (Columbia, S.C., 1949). See also Vernon Burton, "Race and Reconstruction: Edgefield County, South Carolina," *Journal of Social History* 12 (Fall 1978): 31–56.

5. Laylon Wayne Jordan provides a searching view of the rise of organized "scientific charity" in Charleston (" 'The Method of Modern Charity': The Associated Charities Society of Charleston, 1888–1920," paper presented at the Fourth Citadel Conference on the South, Charleston, S.C., Apr. 1985). Though sponsored by the city's civic leaders, the Associated Charities Society met a cool reception until the 1890s, when it came under the supervision of Charleston women. Street beggars, said to be legion before the 1890s, were thought to be relatively rare as "rational benevolence" took hold.

6. U.S. Census Bureau, *Negro Population, 1790–1915* (Washington, D.C., 1918), 786.

7. Charles Joyner, *Down by the Riverside: A South Carolina Slave Community* (Urbana, Ill., 1984).

8. Richard C. Wade, *Slavery in the Cities: The South, 1820–1860* (New York, 1964), 326. See also Smith, *Charlestonian's Recollections,* 56–67.

9. U.S. Census Bureau, *Negro Population, 1790–1915,* 786; Hine, "Frustration, Factionalism, and Failure," 243.

10. Smith, *Charlestonian's Recollections,* 58–59. At night servants slept in their own quarters in back of the big house.

11. Harriott Horry Rutledge Ravenel criticizes disloyal servants and adds: "Others, however, remained trusted friends and servants, faithful and affectionate, to the end of life" (*Charleston: The Place and the People* [1906; reprint, New York, 1922], 503–4).

12. David Duncan Wallace, *The History of South Carolina* (New York, 1934), 3:215; Joel Williamson, *After Slavery: The Negro in South Carolina during Reconstruction, 1861–1877* (New York, 1965), 22–23, 47–48.

13. William Heyward to James Gregorie, Charleston, S.C., June 4, Jan. 2, 1868, Elliott-Gregorie Family Papers, file 10, SHC.

14. Henry Hunter Raymond to Mother, Charleston, S.C., July 30, 1865, in Henry Hunter Raymond Papers, SCL.

15. Williamson, *After Slavery,* 51.

16. Augustine T. Smythe to Wife, Charleston, S.C., Aug. 19, 1865, Smythe Letters, SCL.

17. John Berkeley Grimball Diary, Apr. 8, Nov. 12, 1877, SHC.

18. *Charleston News and Courier,* Feb. 12, 1882.

19. Francis Butler Simkins and Robert Hilliard Woody, *South Carolina during Reconstruction* (Chapel Hill, N.C., 1932), 359; Belton O'Neall Townsend, "South Carolina Society," *Atlantic Monthly* 39 (June 1877): 675; Williamson, *After Slavery,* 311.

20. U.S. Census Bureau, *Report of the Population of the United States at the Eleventh Census: 1890,* pt. 2 (Washington, D.C., 1897), 648.

21. Smith, *Charlestonian's Recollections,* 127–28.

22. DuBose Heyward, *Mamba's Daughters: A Novel of Charleston* (New York, 1929), 3, 35–36, 38–39, 61, 71–72, 155.

23. George B. Tindall, *South Carolina Negroes, 1877–1900* (Columbia, S.C., 1952), 284–85; E. Horace Fitchett, "The Status of the Free Negro in Charleston, South Carolina, and His Descendants in Modern Society," *Journal of Negro History* 32 (Oct. 1947): 441; Simkins and Woody, *South*

Carolina, 368; Michael P. Johnson and James L. Roark, eds., *No Chariot Let Down: Charleston's Free People of Color on the Eve of the Civil War* (Chapel Hill, N.C., 1984).

24. Holt, *Black over White,* 20.

25. Townsend, "South Carolina Society," 677; Holt, *Black over White,* 43–71, 126, 162.

26. *Columbia Daily Register,* June 24, 1888, quoted in Tindall, *South Carolina Negroes,* 200; on St. Mark's separation, see also ibid., 194–200. There were other observations of continued snobbery and conflict separating blacks and mulattos in Charleston during Reconstruction and after (see Williamson, *After Slavery,* 314–15, 316–17; Mamie Garvin Fields, *Lemon Swamp and Other Places: A Carolina Memoir* [New York, 1983], 63–64; E. Franklin Frazier, *Black Bourgeoisie: The Rise of a New Middle Class in the United States* [New York, 1957], 98, 117, 165).

27. A. Toomer Porter, *Led On! Step by Step: Scenes from Clerical, Military, Educational, and Plantation Life in the South, 1828–1898* (New York, 1898), 186–98, 332–33.

28. Hine, "Frustration, Factionalism, and Failure," 148.

29. Vernon Burton describes the same volatility in race relations in the upcountry ("Race and Reconstruction," 31–56).

30. *Charleston News and Courier,* Dec. 5, 1884.

31. J. Morgan Kousser, *The Shaping of Southern Politics: Suffrage Restriction and the Establishment of the One-Party South, 1880–1910* (New Haven, Conn., 1974), 84–91, 145–52.

32. Edward Hogan, "South Carolina To-Day," *International Review* 8 (1880): 105–19, quoted in John P. Radford, "Culture, Economy, and Urban Structure in Charleston, South Carolina, 1860–1880" (Ph.D. diss., Clark University, 1974), 308.

33. Radford, "Culture, Economy, and Urban Structure," 244–53, 301–9; see also idem, "Social Structure and Urban Form: Charleston, 1860–1880," in *From the Old South to the New: Essays on the Transitional South,* edited by Walter J. Fraser, Jr., and Winfred B. Moore, Jr. (Westport, Conn., 1981), 81–92.

34. U.S. Census Bureau, *Negro Population, 1790–1915,* 107. For further data on Charleston's unusual lack of racial segregation, a pattern that held true until after World War II, see Karl E. Taeuber and Alma F. Taeuber, *Negroes in Cities: Residential Segregation and Neighborhood Change* (Chicago, 1965).

35. T. J. Woofter, *Negro Problems in Cities* (Garden City, N.Y., 1928), 52–53; similar maps of Chicago, New York, or Winston-Salem show striking contrast with the Charleston pattern. Mamie Garvin Fields, in *Lemon Swamp,* gives a vivid description of residential integration that persisted even as Jim Crow became firmly entrenched in many areas of public life in Charleston.

36. Quoted in Tindall, *South Carolina Negroes,* 304–5.

37. *Charleston News and Courier,* Apr. 3, 1885, quoted in Tindall, *South Carolina Negroes,* 294–95.

38. *Charleston News and Courier,* Feb. 25, 1897.

39. City of Charleston, *Yearbook, 1912,* 405.

40. Mamie Garvin Fields provides a telling account of the newness of segregation in early twentieth-century Charleston from the perspective of a young black woman (*Lemon Swamp,* chap. 4).

41. *New York Times,* Feb. 13, 1893.

42. Ibid., Jan. 21, 1892; *Charleston News and Courier,* Apr. 20, July 6, 15, 1892; Tindall, *South Carolina Negroes,* 49–50.

43. Owen Wister, *Lady Baltimore* (New York, 1906), 167, 54.

44. Fredrickson, *Black Image,* 216–21.

45. E. Culpepper Clark, *Francis Warrington Dawson and the Politics of Restoration: South Carolina, 1874–1889* (University, Ala., 1980), 192, 199–200; Williamson, *After Slavery,* 110; Tindall, *South Carolina Negroes,* 153–68. Dawson was not consistent in his support of black exodus. He criticized

proposals for black deportation in 1886, complaining that "it would knock the base from under the fabric of the New South" (*Charleston News and Courier,* May 13, 1886); see also ibid., Dec. 19, 1888.

46. Carlyle McKinley, *An Appeal to Pharaoh: The Negro Problem and Its Radical Solution,* edited by Gustavus M. Pinckney, 3d ed. (1889; reprint, Columbia, S.C., 1907), 34, 48, 49–50, 51, 128, 183.

47. Isaac DuBose Seabrook, *Before and After, or the Relations of the Races at the South* (Baton Rouge, La., 1967), 143, 146–48, et passim.

48. *Charleston News and Courier,* Sept. 17, Nov. 14, Dec. 23, 1889. See also the introduction by John Hammond Moore to Seabrook, *Before and After,* 16–17.

49. *Charleston News and Courier,* May 2, 1892, Jan. 7, 1899.

50. Ibid., Oct. 13, 1896; see also ibid., Sept. 1, Nov. 19, 1896, Apr. 29, June 28, 1897. George B. Tindall describes an earlier experiment in 1890 that led to a white assault that drove black workers from a cotton mill. He also explains that the Charleston Shoe Factory brought in blacks to replace striking white workers (*South Carolina Negroes,* 131–32). See also David L. Carlton, *Mill and Town in South Carolina, 1880–1920* (Baton Rouge, La., 1982), 158–60.

51. *Charleston News and Courier,* Oct. 13, 1897, quoted in Tindall, *South Carolina Negroes,* 132.

52. Tindall, *South Carolina Negroes,* 133–34.

53. *The Exposition,* Sept. 1901, 369; see also ibid., Dec. 1900, 5, May 1901, 200–201, July 1901, 272.

54. Ibid., Nov. 1901, 470; Louis R. Harlan and Raymond W. Smock, eds., *The Booker T. Washington Papers* (Urbana, Ill., 1977), 6:145–48, 202–5, 238, 387. My thanks to Bruce G. Harvey, who graciously brought the latter source to my attention; see his "An Old City in the New South: Urban Progressivism and Charleston's West Indian Exposition" (M.A. thesis, University of South Carolina, 1988).

55. J. C. Hemphill, "A Short Story of the South Carolina Inter-State and West Indian Exposition," in City of Charleston, *Yearbook, 1902,* 139.

56. DuBose Heyward, "The Negro in the Low Country," in *The Carolina Low-Country,* by Augustine T. Smythe et al. (New York, 1931), 185.

57. Ibid., 185–87.

Epilogue

1. Paul M. Gaston, *The New South Creed: A Study in Southern Mythmaking* (Baton Rouge, La., 1970).

2. Jonathan M. Wiener, *Social Origins of the New South: Alabama, 1860–1885* (Baton Rouge, La., 1978), 218–19. Cf. C. Vann Woodward, *Origins of the New South, 1877–1913* (Baton Rouge, La., 1951), chap. 6.

3. Gaines M. Foster interprets this movement as a "forward looking" partner of the New South (*Ghosts of the Confederacy: Defeat, the Lost Cause, and the Emergence of the New South, 1865 to 1913* [New York, 1987], 6).

4. Dewey W. Grantham, in *Southern Progressivism: The Reconciliation of Progress and Tradition* (Knoxville, Tenn., 1983), offers a comprehensive interpretation of southern progressivism as the product of the urban middle class.

5. Steven Hahn, *The Roots of Southern Populism: Yeomen Farmers and the Transformation of the Georgia Upcountry, 1850–1890* (New York, 1983).

6. David L. Carlton, *Mill and Town in South Carolina, 1880–1920* (Baton Rouge, La., 1982); Jacquelyn Dowd Hall, James Leloudis, Robert Korstad, Mary Murphy, Lu Ann Jones, and Christopher B. Daly, *Like a Family: The Making of a Southern Cotton Mill World* (Chapel Hill, N.C.,

1987); James Douglas Flamming, "The Making of an Industrial Community: The Crown Cotton Mills of Dalton, Georgia, 1880–1940" (Ph.D. diss., Vanderbilt University, 1987).

7. See James C. Cobb, "Beyond Planters and Industrialists: A New Perspective on the New South," *Journal of Southern History* 54 (Feb. 1988): 45–68; and Michael Wayne, *The Reshaping of Plantation Society: The Natchez District, 1860–1880* (Baton Rouge, La., 1983).

8. V. O. Key, *Southern Politics in State and Nation* (New York, 1949).

Index